THE CASTLES OF

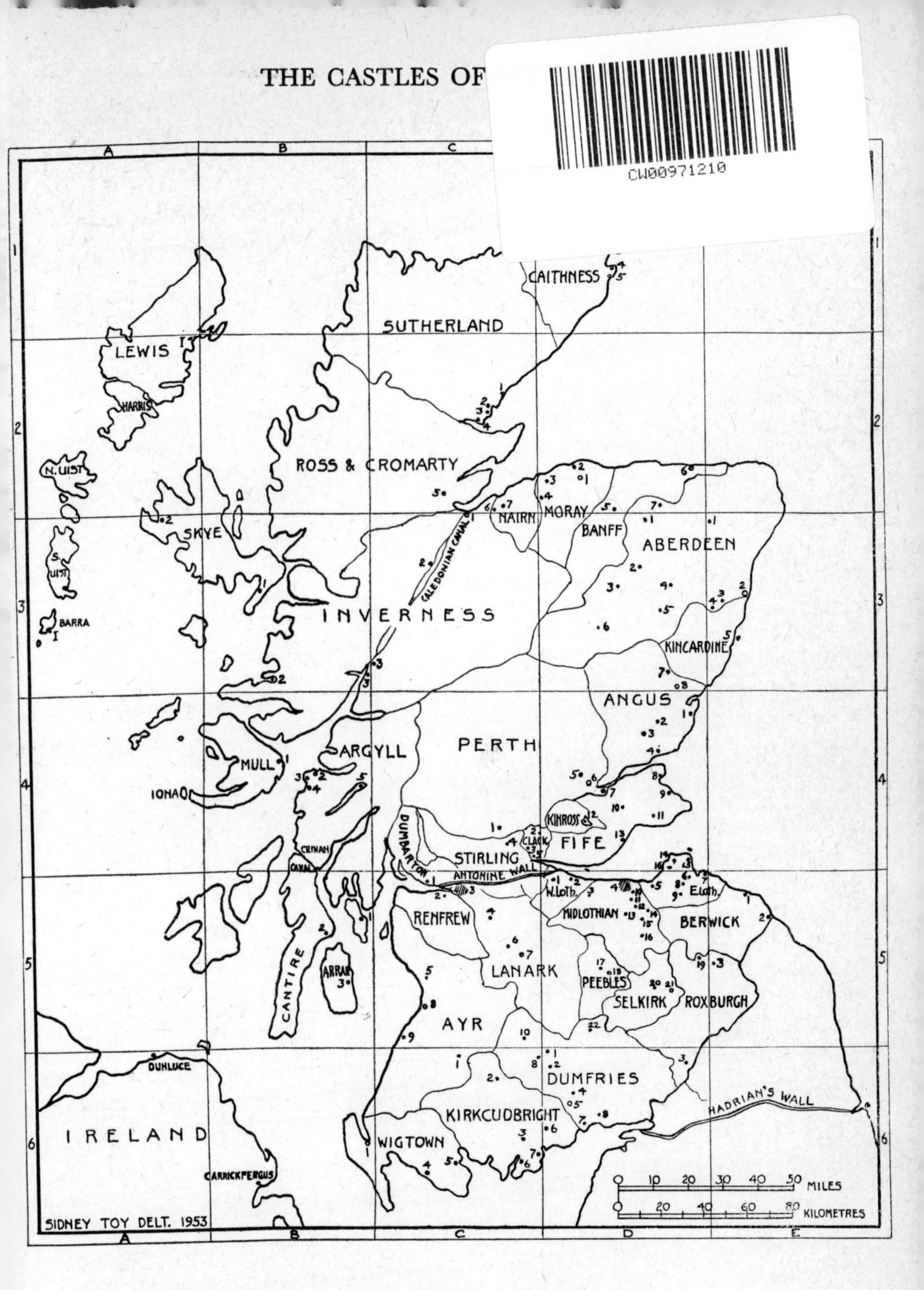

For ENGLAND AND WALES see back end-papers

By the same author:

A HISTORY OF FORTIFICATION

THE STRONGHOLDS OF INDIA

THE FORTIFIED CITIES OF INDIA

Sidney Toy

THE CASTLES OF GREAT BRITAIN

by

SIDNEY TOY, F.S.A., F.R.I.B.A.

Illustrated with plans and photographs by the author

FOURTH EDITION

HEINEMANN
LONDON

FIRST PUBLISHED 1953
SECOND EDITION 1954
THIRD EDITION 1963
FOURTH EDITION 1966
REPRINTED 1970

Heinemann Educational Books Ltd
LONDON EDINBURGH MELBOURNE TORONTO
SINGAPORE JOHANNESBURG AUCKLAND
HONG KONG IBADAN NAIROBI NEW DELHI

ISBN 0 435 32995 2

PUBLISHED BY
HEINEMANN EDUCATIONAL BOOKS LTD
48 CHARLES STREET, LONDON W1X 8AH
Printed in Great Britain at the St Ann's Press,
Park Road, Altrincham

This Book is Dedicated

to

THE EARL OF CAWDOR

and

WILMA MAIRI COUNTESS OF CAWDOR

In recognition of the care and wise attention bestowed on their invaluable heritage and home

CONTENTS

LIST OF ILLUSTRATIONS

PREFACE

THE history of the development of the art of fortification during the Middle Ages forms not only a fascinating study but, in that there is always something to learn from successes and failures of the past, a highly instructive line of research. An earlier work by the author on the subject dealt with the fortifications of Europe and the Levant generally, and it was not possible within the limited space to treat in particular with the development in any one country. From that general background one can now examine the history of the forts and castles of Great Britain with some measure of detail.

In reviewing the Anglo-Saxon and Norman periods, while well aware of the disputed points and of the arguments adduced on both sides by Round, Freeman, Oman, Armitage and others, the author has considered it best to confine himself to independent investigations, both of the buildings themselves and of the documents relative to them. And here it should be noted that documentary evidence is not always reliable; many contemporary statements of total destruction, for example, are grossly inaccurate, as in the case of Barnwell Castle. That extravagant statement in this respect is not confined to old documents was amply demonstrated during the recent war. Again and again "totally destroyed" was found on examination to mean simply damaged. Moreover, much new evidence, resulting from excavation, has come to light within recent years, solving many earlier problems.

Though it is not possible to include within the confines of a single volume mention of all the forts and castles of Great Britain, most of the outstanding examples are noted; and in the selection for particular and detailed description choice has been made of those having the best preserved original features of the period reviewed. The author has examined personally the castles he describes, measuring and plotting the plans, elevations and sections, and taking photographs. He has often returned many times to the same building to verify some point which has arisen in drawing out the plans or consulting old documents. A technical knowledge of building construction, the main principles of which are constant through all ages, has enabled him to understand many points otherwise obscure.

In the main the castle is considered in its military aspect, as a fortress, and its domestic arrangements in so far as they influence or are ancillary to its military functions. In the use of terms the author, avoiding pedantic and discursive arguments, has chosen those terms most generally understood; as, for example, for the citadels of the early Norman period the name *shell keep* is used as being at once descriptive and simple. Except in cases where special treatment is indicated, as where deep basements occur, the word *storey* is used throughout to mean one of all the stages into which a building is divided, the first storey being the lowest.

The author tenders his thanks to all those from whom he has received help in the production of this work and in particular to Professor Ian A. Richmond, C.B.E., M.A., LL.D., F.B.A., F.S.A., who kindly read and annotated the second chapter, and to Alan Hill, M.A. He also gratefully acknowledges information obtained from many published works on the subject, especially the following: *The Inventories of the Royal Commission on Historical Monuments,* London and Edinburgh; *The Mediæval Castle in Scotland,* by W. M. Mackenzie; and the excellent monographs on Scottish castles by Dr. W. D. Simpson, C.B.E., M.A., F.S.A. To the numerous governing bodies and private owners throughout the country who kindly granted him permission to examine the buildings in their charge, he offers special thanks. All the drawings have been prepared and all the photographs, except where otherwise stated, were taken by the author.

PREFACE TO THE SECOND EDITION

As a second edition of this book has now been called for, the opportunity has been taken to add a description of St. Michael's Mount (p. 264), and new plans of Sherborne Castle and Fincastle. At the same time a few minor corrections have been made in the text.

On the end-papers two maps have been introduced—one of Scotland at the front of the book, and one of England and Wales at the back. It is hoped that these, with the keys attached, will enable the reader to identify readily the position of the various castles described.

PREFACE TO THE THIRD EDITION

In this edition minor revision and addition to some existing accounts have been made and the work now includes descriptions of the castles of Carisbrooke, Isle of Wight; Berkeley, Gloucester; Castle Rushen, Isle of Man; Maxstoke Castle, Warwick; Caister Castle, Norfolk; Haddon Hall, Derbyshire; Farleigh Castle, Somerset; Berwick-upon-Tweed; and the fortifications thrown round London in 1643 during the Civil War. There are also a number of new plans to illustrate the additional text.

S.T.
November 1962

PREFACE TO THE FOURTH EDITION

In preparing this new edition, the author has taken the opportunity to make further minor revisions and add descriptions of Hedingham Castle and Knaresborough Castle. These are accompanied by full plans and illustrations.

*London, W.*1.
14 *North Audley Street,*

CHAPTER ONE

FORTIFICATIONS FROM PREHISTORIC TIMES TO THE ROMAN INVASION OF A.D. 43

It has been far too generally assumed that the peoples inhabiting Great Britain before the Roman Invasion were primitive races of uncultured manners and customs. This traditional conception of their character and habits is deduced largely from Caesar's account of them; an account resulting from a cursory visit to the coast and restricted to islanders who were at war with him and had been at war with the Belgae for many years previously. When, before his invasion, Caesar summoned some merchants to his camp and enquired concerning Britain and its people, he could learn nothing from them.[1] Their attitude was obviously obstructive, for they must have known something of the country and the people with whom they traded habitually; and there can be little doubt that much of the information Caesar obtained from the Britons themselves was misleading and was deliberately intended to mislead.

Fortunately, thanks to modern investigation and archaeological research, much has been learned of the cultural status of the Early Britons. The museums of London and the Provinces now include among their collections works of outstanding artistic merit, such as the Early British bronze shields, richly decorated with embossed designs and enamel, now in the British Museum, which were wrought by the inhabitants of this country at periods long anterior to the Roman settlement. Descriptions of the British given by Tacitus and other contemporary historians of the invasion and settlement under Claudius, A.D. 43, are far more reliable than those of Caesar. Tacitus, speaking of the inhabitants of Britain, describes a race of prowess and strategic ability in the conduct of war as well as of conspicuous intelligence in carrying out the constructive works of peace. He further states that their association with Rome tended rather to their detriment than improvement.[2] Isolation from

[1] Caesar, *De Bello Gallico,* IV, 20.
[2] Tacitus, *Life of Agricola,* C, 21.

the general trend of activities on the continent was doubtless an unfavourable factor in their development, but that the inhabitants of Britain included races of considerable culture is now amply proved.

Judging from the substructures, as revealed by excavation, the military works of the Early Britons were of both formidable character and scientific design. Generally the sites chosen for their fortifications were defended naturally and required but simple artificial works to convert them into powerful strongholds. Promontories, or peninsulas jutting out into the sea and joined to the mainland by a narrow neck only, were the obvious sites for those dwelling near the coast. Here the only works required were a series of ditches and ramparts thrown across the entrance to the promontory, or across both ends of the causeway of the peninsula. St. David's Head, Pembrokeshire, and Trevelgue Head and Dinas Treryn, both in Cornwall, are examples of such sites.

The fortifications of St. David's Head consisted of three lines of walls and ditches thrown across the approach to the headland. The outer wall was a formidable structure of dry-built stone and appears originally to have been about 15 ft. high and 12 ft. thick at the base. The other two walls are breastworks of loose stone and each of them, like the outer wall, is defended by a ditch. The entrance was by way of a causeway thrown across the ditches and a single passage, 7 ft. wide, through each wall. Dinas Treryn is on a headland which juts out into the sea five miles south-east of the Land's End and rises 250 ft. above the water; among its masses of piled-up boulders is the great Logan Rock of Treryn. The fort was defended by three lines of ditches and ramparts which are thrown across the approach to the mainland; the ramparts being still 15 ft. high in places. Both St. David's Head and Dinas Treryn forts relate to prehistoric times.

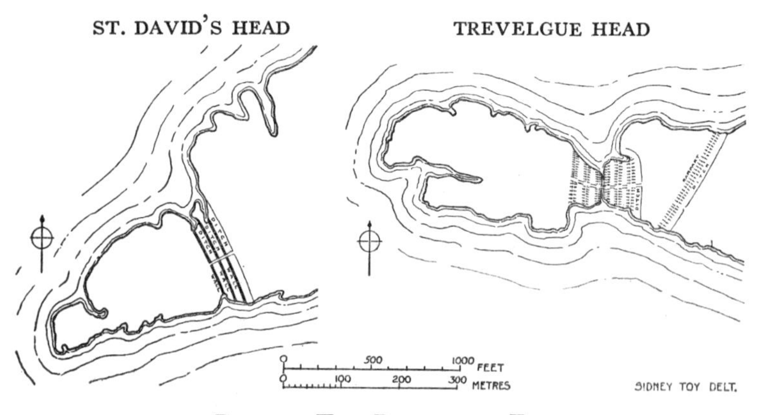

PLANS OF TWO PREHISTORIC FORTS

Trevelgue Head, two miles east of Newquay, is actually an island with precipitous sides, cut off from the mainland by a narrow and deep chasm which was doubtless spanned by a movable bridge. The approach to the fort on the land side was defended by four lines of ramparts and ditches, carried across the mainland from one side of the cliff to the other. The three inner lines are parallel with and close to the chasm and even now, after long years of exposure to disintegrating elements, the ramparts are from 10 ft. to 20 ft. high and the ditches about 20 ft. across. The outer line is thrown diagonally across the headland so as to enclose a sort of bailey between it and the other three. On the island side of the chasm are three further lines of ditches and ramparts. This fort is undoubtedly prehistoric and belongs probably to a period about 1000 B.C.

Tintagel, a lofty headland standing out into the sea on the rugged coast of north Cornwall, possesses natural defences of so conspicuous and formidable a character that, though no definite statement to that effect can be made, it was probably a prehistoric fort. The headland is precipitous on all sides except where it joins the mainland by a narrow neck of rocky soil. Again and again, from mediaeval to modern times, large portions of the causeway have fallen down, carrying with them whatever defences they contained.

Dwellers in inland districts generally selected sites on the summits of hills or land promontories. Outstanding examples of the former are Maiden castle, Dorset; Old Sarum, Wilts.; Herefordshire Beacon and Midsummer Hill, Herefordshire; Corsehope Rings and Kaimes Hill, Midlothian; and Traprain Law, East Lothian. Land promontories or spurs, as those of the Clifton Camps on either side of the Avon, were defended on the sloping line of approach by ditches and ramparts and are precipitous on all other sides. The hill forts were defended all round by one or more lines of ditches and ramparts; often there were four concentric lines and these, towering up as they do tier above tier, present a most formidable appearance to this day.

The strength of the gateways consisted largely in the difficulty and danger of approach to them; as at Maiden castle and Hod Hill, where the gateways are defended by a series of cross ramparts involving sinuous passages of approach, or at Mount Caburn, Sussex, where the approach to the gate is by a path on the edge of a precipice. At Blackbury castle, Devon, the gateway is covered by an outwork through which runs a passage defended by a rampart on either side. At Winklebury, Wilts., and Bury castle, Somerset, the approach was defended by two outworks which had to be passed in succession before the inner gate was reached.

Maiden castle covers an extensive oval area on the crown of a hill 432 ft. above sea level and is defended all round by several lines of ramparts and ditches. The site was occupied as early as 2000 B.C., the eastern portion was fortified about 300 B.C., and the defences of the western portion, about two-thirds of the whole, were constructed about 100 B.C. Recent excavations have shown that the ramparts consist of earth, chalk, clay, and rubble, faced with stone and buttressed at intervals by upright timber posts. A series of post holes on the top, spaced at from 4 ft. to 2 ft. 6 in. apart, belong to defences of a later period; the original wall, of which a portion still remains, was of stone.[3]

Old Sarum, on the top of a conical hill one and a quarter miles north of Salisbury, is one of the most imposing of our ancient forts; it is defended by two concentric lines of fortifications with a

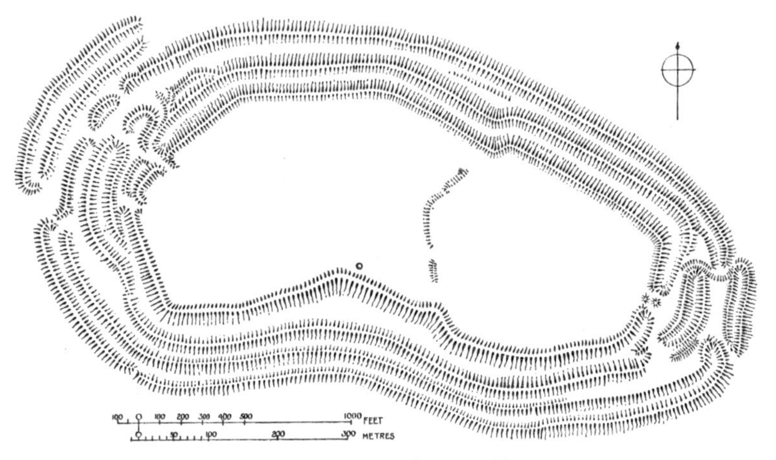

PLAN OF MAIDEN CASTLE, DORSET

wide level space between them. The outer ring is referable to an ancient but unknown period; it has a ditch of great depth and width and a rampart about 60 ft. high. The inner defences were built principally in the twelfth century.

Hereford Beacon Camp rises in two tiers to an oval space, 1,114 ft. above sea level, which is defended by a deep ditch and high rampart. The foot of the mount on which this citadel of the camp stands is defended on the north by a ditch and rampart and on the south by a series of terraces. Spurs run out north and south from the foot of the mount and the whole area is enclosed by another ditch and rampart. Midsummer Hill Camp is on the summit of a hill 937 ft. above sea level; it is defended by a ditch and two lines of ramparts, one on either side of the ditch. Both of these camps date from 300 B.C. to 400 B.C.

[3] Maiden Castle, Dorset. *Report of Research Comm. Soc. of Antiqs.*, No. 12.

Worlebury Camp, Somerset, is a hill fort divided into two parts by a ditch which is partly natural and partly dug out; it dates from about 400 B.C. The eastern part was the citadel and was protected on one side by the dividing ditch and on the other three sides by a huge wall of dry-built stone. This wall was constructed by first building a nucleus and then adding to its thickness by building other walls against it on either side; it is 38 ft. thick and, even now, is 16 ft. high from the ditch outside and 8 ft. from the ground inside. On the east, the more vulnerable side of the citadel, the wall is defended by a ditch which is cut out of the natural limestone rock, and beyond the ditch a second wall and four other ditches. Ancient dwellings have been found within this camp.

Corsehope Rings Fort stands on the summit of a high hill 1,300 ft. above sea level; it is surrounded by four lines of ramparts and is an imposing sight. Kaimes Hill Fort is 800 ft. above sea level; its defences consist principally of walls about 12 ft. thick. Traprain Law occupies a commanding position with a prospect extending for many miles around. Its summit, 700 ft. above sea level, is defended naturally on all sides either by sheer cliffs or precipitous crags and the fortification, following the edge of the cliff, consists of a rampart 6 ft. thick, revetted with stone.

Cow castle, on Exmoor, and Grimspound, on Dartmoor, are among prehistoric forts; built of dry-stone walls, many of the stones of which on the outer faces are boulders set up on end. These fortifications consist sometimes of a single enclosing wall and sometimes of two concentric walls built close together. At Whit Tor Fort, on Dartmoor, also prehistoric, there are two walls, running concentrically, about 10 ft. apart and each about 10 ft. thick. Brent Tor Fort is of a similar character. Chun castle and a number of similar forts in Cornwall are circular and are each defended by a massive stone wall which has a rubble core faced on both sides with well-built stonework.

A method of defence developed in the rocky parts of Wales and Scotland was to build a terrace round the hill top, supported by a wall of stone or of stone and timber; a breastwork on the terrace would complete the defence.

In the North of Scotland, the Outer Hebrides, Orkney and Shetland, a remarkable type of defensive structure, called a broch, was developed about the first century B.C. Brochs were circular in plan with walls from 12 ft. to 16 ft. thick, pierced by a low and narrow tunnel-like door; the internal diameter is about 25 ft. In some cases the wall is carried up so high that the structure becomes a round tower consisting of two concentric shells, tied together at intervals by long stones. The outer shell is steeply battered, while the inner one is practically vertical. The most perfect example of a tower broch is at Mousa, in Shetland, which still stands to the height of about 45 ft. Its outer wall is unbroken by any aperture save for the doorway on the ground floor, but four series of slits run up the inner wall. Chambers, stairways, and galleries are formed in the space between the shells.

Walls built of timber and masonry somewhat similar to those surrounding the Gallic towns occur in Scotland and North Wales. The wall consists of two built masonry faces, spaced widely apart and tied together at intervals by timber beams; the interspace being filled in with rubble and timber bonders. As the beam ends were exposed on both faces the wall could be ignited and, fanned by a strong wind, would become a huge kiln capable of generating sufficient heat to fuse the rubble core. Most stones, with the exception of pure sandstones, associated with timber in this manner can be fused in intense heat, the alkali in the timber acting as a flux. Many of the Scottish forts constructed in this manner have been burned and the most conspicuous part of the wall is the fused core, the faces having collapsed when the tie beams were burned through. Such are the fortifications known as Vitrified Forts. The vitrification was clearly not a deliberate process adopted by the builders but the result of incendiary attack by the enemy.

Now timber has been employed as a bonding material with masonry from ancient times to the end of the mediaeval period. Buried well within the walls, without air it will not burn; even the Gallic walls were described by Caesar as fire resisting.[4] But walls of this character when built in haste or without regard to the disposition and conservative use of the timber and the proper ramming of the infilling material can be destroyed and the stones fused by kindling large fires against them. Experiments made in recent years in Scotland on test walls, built with a fairly liberal use of wood, through bonding timbers exposed on both faces of the wall, the infilling unrammed with earth, and fires kindled in a high wind, proved this to be the case.[5]

In districts where timber was plentiful and stones scarce, large stakes, densely intertwined with branches of trees and thorns, were sometimes employed as fortifications in lieu of walls.

WEAPONS AND MILITARY OPERATIONS OF THE ANCIENT BRITONS

Though there is considerable evidence of the siege and defence of their cities, as at Maiden castle, Dorset, the Britons fought principally in the open field. Even when attacked near their strongholds they preferred to fight in front of their fortifications and not

[4] Caesar, *op. cit.*, VII, 23.
[5] *Proceedings Soc. of Antiqs. of Scotland*, Vol. LXXII, 1938, 44–55.

behind them.[6] Their strength lay in their infantry, who took the field with long swords and shields and were provided with immense quantities of missile weapons, which they cast at the enemy in volley after volley.[7] They also had a particularly strong arm in highly skilled bodies of charioteers. Caesar records that in order to create confusion during an engagement the charioteers drove about in all directions, hurling missiles as they went. Each chariot contained a driver and one or more combatants. In the course of a battle, and as the chariot was dashing on, the latter would leap down and fight on foot while the driver retired to a position where he could be ready to receive the combatants again if hard pressed. This arm possessed at once the mobile qualities of cavalry and the stability of infantry. Its units could gallop their teams down the steepest hills without loss of control and could check and turn them in an instant. The men could get out and run along the pole, stand on the yoke, and then with lightning speed dart back into the chariot again.[8] A third arm consisted of strong forces of cavalry. From about 100 B.C. hand-slings were among the principal weapons of the Britons. At Maiden castle, Dorset, vast numbers of sling stones, mainly beach pebbles, were found in the huts and assembled ready for use at strategic points.[9]

[6] Caesar, *op. cit.*, V, 9.
[7] Tacitus, *op. cit.*, 36.
[8] Caesar, *op. cit.*, IV, 33.
[9] Maiden Castle, Dorset, *op. cit.*, 48–49.

CHAPTER TWO

ROMAN FORTIFICATIONS IN BRITAIN

WHATEVER were the motives which induced Caesar to invade Britain in 55 and 54 B.C., the invasions were not followed by an attempt at conquest; the Roman forces were immediately withdrawn and the island was left severely alone for nearly a hundred years. The expedition of A.D. 43 was undertaken with the definite purpose of subjugating Britain to the Roman power, an object found to be of no easy achievement. Fifty years of unremitting struggle, of defeats as well as victories, were absorbed before Roman rule was established throughout the country; while continuous internal risings and incursions from the north down into the heart of the country were of so serious a character as to require virtual reconquest again and again during the next hundred and twenty years. It was not until the early part of the third century, after a lapse of nearly a hundred and seventy years and following the campaigns undertaken by the Emperor Severus in person, that the authority of Rome was definitely established.

Meanwhile, however, the Romans had constructed their usual system of military roads, traversing the land in all directions, had built camps and fortresses at strategic points in all parts of the country, had constructed frontier lines and had founded several cities, including London and Colchester. By A.D. 46, three years after the invasion, they had built a line of forts along the Fosse Way, which from the coast of Devonshire ran north-east through Bath, Cirencester, and Leicester to Lincoln; and by A.D. 74 they had established legionary fortresses at York, Chester and Caerleon-on-Usk. Agricola probably constructed the military road called the Stanegate, between the Solway and the Tyne, and by A.D. 81 his troops had reached the fringe of the Highlands.

Early in the second century, finding the Lowlands of Scotland difficult to subdue, the Romans strengthened the Stanegate by a series of forts and a few years later brought the frontier back to this line and built the fortification known as Hadrian's Wall.

Again, under Antoninus Pius, the Antonine Wall was constructed between the Forth and the Clyde. But, following the serious risings of the latter part of the second century, this advance line was finally abandoned and under the Emperor Severus, who spent the last three years of his life in this country and died at York in 211, Hadrian's Wall, greatly strengthened and to some extent remodelled, was re-established as the northern frontier.

The camps constructed by the Romans in their earlier campaigns in Italy and elsewhere had developed into a general plan which was pursued, with some variations, in their permanent fortresses; often a temporary camp, strengthened and remodelled in stone, became a permanent fortress. This process of development often occurred in Britain, as at York and Chester. The camps were normally rectangular, though there were exceptions, dictated by the character of the site, as at Whitley Castle, Northumberland; they were defended all round by a rampart, rounded at the corners, and by one or more ditches. There were usually four gateways, one near the middle of each side; the principal gateway, normally in one of the shorter sides, being the *porta praetoria.* From the porta praetoria a road, called the *via praetoria,* led directly towards the middle of the camp to the *principia,* or headquarters of the commander. On one side of the principia was the commanding officer's residence, the *praetorium,* on the other side the *horrea,* or strong storehouses; and running along in front of the whole three was the *via principalis,* terminating at one end in the *porta principalis* and at the other in the *porta sinistra.* A street called the *via decumana,* in line with the via praetoria, ran from behind the principia to the fourth gate, the *porta decumana*; and another road, the *via quintana,* ran parallel with the via principalis and often terminated in a gate at either end, making six gates in all. A road ran all round the camp inside the rampart. The main portion of the enclosure was occupied by long narrow blocks of barracks.

The ramparts of the camps built by the Romans during their campaigns of penetration and subjugation of Britain were normally constructed of clay, or of turf, or partly clay and partly turf, sometimes on a foundation of gravel or stone; the gates and the internal buildings were of timber. In a fort of about A.D. 80, near Ambleside, Westmorland, the rampart was defended by timber towers and the main gateway, probably also of timber, had guardrooms.[1] The camps were defended by one or more ditches, normally one, but in some examples in Northumberland and Scotland there are many lines of ditches. At High Rochester, Northumberland, four lines of ditches are carried all round the camp. The gateways, in

[1] *Transact. Cumbld. and Westmorld. Antiq. and Archæol. Soc.,* 2nd Ser., XVI, XXI.

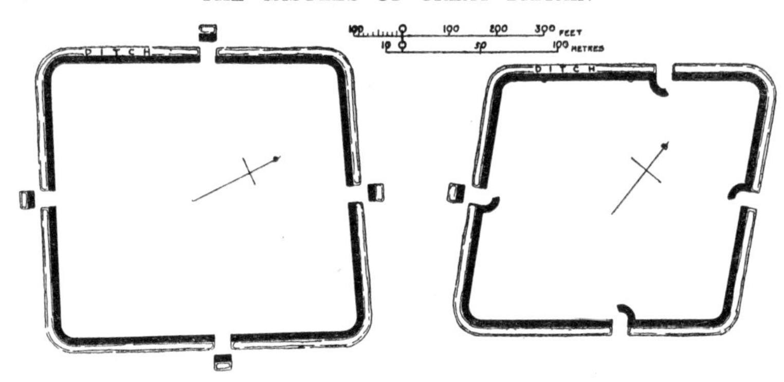

PLANS OF ROMAN CAMPS AT RIDESDALE, NORTHUMBERLAND

lieu of doors, were often defended by traverses or *clavicidae*, as in the camps at Ridesdale, Northumberland. In the camp known as Birdhope II, the gateways are defended by traverses, or detached pieces of rampart and ditch placed parallel with and in front of the entrance. In that known as Camp IV at Chew Green, they are defended by *clavicidae,* here quadrant-shaped pieces of rampart, deflected inwards or, less often, outwards. Sometimes the gateway is defended by both traverses and *clavicidae*, as at Camp IV, Chew Green.

The defences of the permanent fortresses constructed by the Romans, and of the towns they founded, were of a stronger character than those of the temporary camps, many of which, as remodelled, became permanent.

Colchester, as rebuilt about A.D 70–80, was surrounded by a stone wall, 8 ft. thick, a large portion of which is still standing up to a considerable height. The city has a rectangular plan with rounded corners and appears to have had six gates, two on the north, two on the south, one on the east and one on the west; the lower parts of the west, or Balkerne, gate still remain. There were also two posterns, one at the east end of the north wall and the

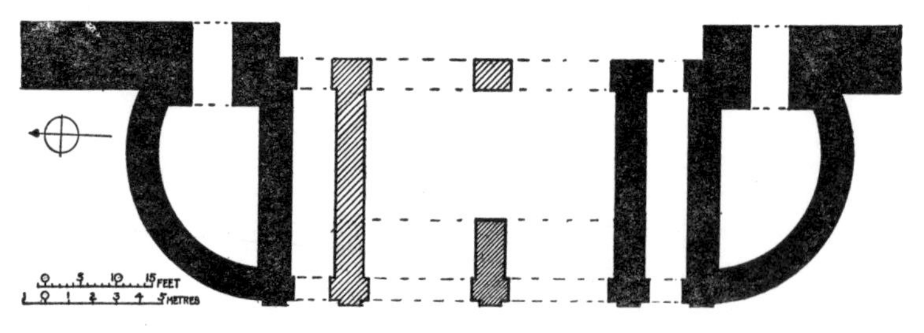

COLCHESTER. PLAN OF THE BALKERNE GATE

other at the south end of the west wall. The wall is bonded by brick lacing courses, four bricks thick, and strengthened by internal towers; it was backed by a rampart of earth 20 ft. thick. Round towers, of which six remain, projecting externally and spaced at intervals in the line of the wall, belong to defences added subsequent to the Roman occupation. The Balkerne Gate had two carriage ways and two footways; it projected out 30 ft. from the face of the wall, flanked by quadrant-shaped towers, and must have presented a most singular and striking appearance.

In London, recent excavations have disclosed that the city walls, which were built about the middle of the second century, incorporated at the north-west corner a rectangular Roman fort, also

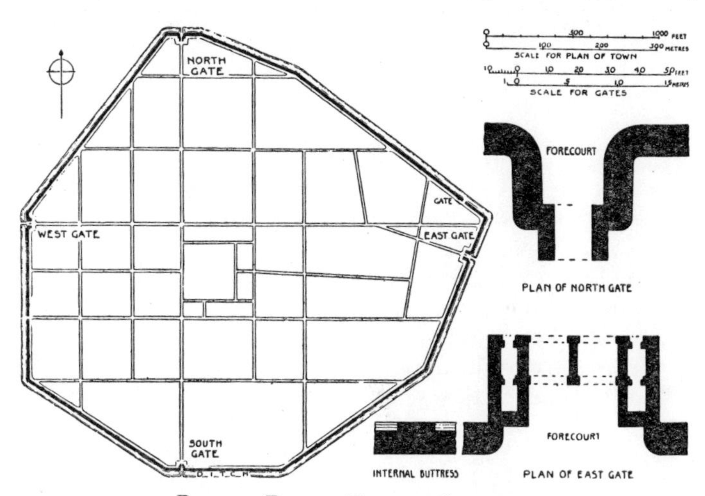

PLAN OF ROMAN FORT AT SILCHESTER

of stone, established some fifty years previously. The city walls, of which portions still remain, varied in thickness from 7 ft. to 9 ft., were constructed of a concrete core with cut stone facing, bonded at intervals with brick lacing courses, and had a plinth on the outer face. They were originally backed by an earthen rampart. All the gates have been destroyed. Newgate, the foundations of which were discovered some years ago, had two passageways, each 12 ft. wide and was flanked by a square tower on either side. As originally built the curtain had no wall towers. The towers, some of which appear to have been solid up to the level of the wall walk, and the whole length of the wall along the north bank of the Thames, were later Roman additions. The area of Roman London was 330 acres, about three times that of Colchester.

Silchester, Hants, was fortified in stone about A.D. 200. It is polygonal in plan and was defended all round by a ditch. The wall is 9 ft. 6 in. thick at the base, diminishing by internal offsets to 7 ft. 6 in. at the top; it has a concrete core faced with flints and is bonded at intervals with courses of flat stones. There are no wall towers, but the wall is strengthened at intervals of about 200 ft. by internal buttresses, 12 ft. wide, which are of the thickness of the wall at the base and, rising without offsets, maintain that thickness to the top. The wall is backed by a rampart of earth 20 ft. wide. Here the rampart belongs to an earlier fort, of about A.D. 145, on the outer face of which the stone wall was added; the main gateways are built in line with the inner side of the rampart, thus leaving a space in front commanded on three sides by the defence. There are four main gateways, those on the north and south being single and those on the east and west double gates; a subsidiary gate on the east led to the amphitheatre (p. 11).

York was established as a legionary fortress in A.D. 71–74 and as first built was defended by a rampart of clay and its internal structures were of timber. But in 107–108 the rampart was replaced by a stone wall and the gateways, towers and internal buildings were all reconstructed in stone. Caerleon-on-Usk, another example, appears to have been of clay and timber when first established, but in 99–100 it was rebuilt in stone.

Agricola's frontier line across the isthmus between the Forth and Clyde appears to have consisted of a chain of forts defended by stockades and ditches and connected by a military road; it was clearly a temporary fortification. Stanegate, a military road between the Solway and the Tyne, was strengthened by forts about A.D. 117.

Hadrian's Wall, built A.D. 122–125, between the Solway and the Tyne, was a formidable and permanent frontier occupying a site of great natural defences. It lies to the north of the Stanegate, at distances from it varying from about one to three miles. The wall is constructed of stone with a concrete core and is 73 miles long. For the greater part of its length it is about 7 ft. 6 in. thick; but a portion running for twenty-three Roman miles, between the North Tyne and Newcastle, is about 9 ft. 6 in. thick. For the main part it stands on a very broad foundation and it would appear that as originally designed the whole was to be ten Roman feet, or about 9 ft. 6 in. thick. But it is evident that the design was modified early in the course of the work. The height to the wall walk was probably about 15 ft. For long stretches the wall runs on the top of high ridges with precipitous falls on the north side, but on lower ground it is defended by a deep ditch with a level terrace, or berm, between the ditch and the wall (p. 30a).

The forces defending this frontier were quartered in sixteen forts, spaced along the line at intervals of about four miles; some of them being entirely on the south side of the wall, as Borcovicium, while others projected part-way through it, as Chesters and Rudchester. These forts are constructed on the usual Roman model, described above, and Borcovicium, about midway in the length of the wall, may be taken as a typical example.

Borcovicium, or Housesteads, has a rectangular plan, rounded at the angles, and is enclosed by a stone wall, 5 ft. thick, backed by a clay rampart 15 ft. thick at the base. The wall is faced with coursed rubble and bonded at vertical intervals by a single course of stone slabs; on the north, where the frontier wall is on the cliff face, the wall of the fort is continuous with it. Square towers project internally from the angles and sides of the fort. There are four gates, each having a double carriage way and a tower on either side with a guardroom in the lower storey. In all the gates one of the carriage ways was found to have been walled up. This blocking was probably done in A.D. 142, when the frontier was advanced to the Forth and Clyde line and only a small garrison left at Hadrian's Wall. Each carriage way was closed by a two-leaved door working on pivots, and stones with socket holes for the pivots still remain in position, as do the stones in the centre against which the doors closed. The buildings within the fort were all of stone and were divided by the *via principalis* and the *via quintana* into three main sections; the middle section containing the *principia,* the *praetorium,* and the *horrea.* On the north of the via praetoria there was a long storehouse, but otherwise the other two sections were occupied by blocks of barracks.

The *principia* is a rectangular structure having an open entrance court at the east with a colonnaded portico, and an inner court with a row of chambers on its west side. The *praetorium,* now in

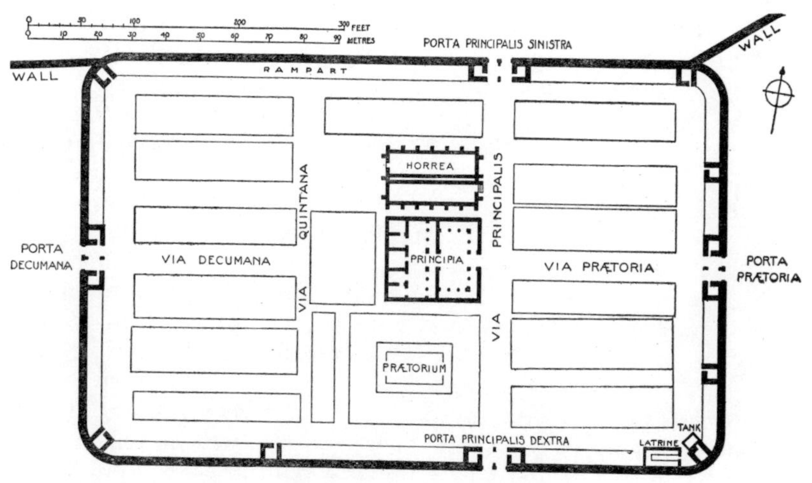

PLAN OF BORCOVICIUM OR HOUSESTEADS

a very fragmentary condition, appears to have consisted of halls and chambers ranged round a central courtyard. The *horrea,* or granaries, were long stone structures, strongly built and buttressed, which stood immediately to the north of the principia. The floors were raised to keep the stores from damp and the doors at either end opened on to platforms against which the carts for loading and unloading could be brought. Directly inside the north gate there is a large water trough, built of stone blocks, and nearby is a circular tile hearth indicating the site of a smithy. At the south-east corner of the fort there was a latrine for common use; it was a rectangular structure having a central passage with a long row of seats on either side, built over a deep drain. Nearby is a large tank which supplied the water for flushing the drains; it is constructed of stone slabs, grooved, and jointed with lead. The sewer from the latrine passes out below the wall and discharges at a point down the hillside away from the fort.

At every Roman mile between the forts there was a mile-castle, a rectangular building measuring about 60 ft. by 70 ft. internally, projecting inwards from the wall; and between the mile-castles the wall was again divided into three equal sections by two turrets, or signal stations, about 13 ft. square internally.

Hadrian's Wall, in itself, could have been of no great value against massed attack. For there were no stairways to the wall walks other than those at the forts, mile-castles, and signal stations, and therefore no means of ready access to the battlements for troops rushed along the road to repel an attack at an intervening point. But it was a serious obstacle to raiding parties and might even hold in check for a short time large bodies while they were being outflanked by troops issuing from the north gates of the forts. It was also a continuous elevated sentry walk.

Between the Stanegate and the Wall there is a third frontier line, the Vallum, a flat-bottomed ditch, 27 ft. wide, with a berm and a rampart on either side. This line runs along in straight stretches for the full length of the wall; it long remained a puzzle as to its purpose and date. As the result of investigations carried out in 1935–36, it now appears to be definitely established that the Vallum was formed at a period shortly after the building of the wall, and that its purpose was to protect the frontier garrisons from marauding raids from the south. In its original condition this deep, steep-sided ditch and double rampart presented a formidable obstacle to surprise attacks from the rear.

Towards the middle of the second century the Roman campaigns carried out to the north of Hadrian's Wall resulted in the conquest of the Lowlands, and the frontier was moved northwards to the line of Agricola's forts between the Forth and Clyde. In 142–43 a continuous rampart, called the wall of Antoninus

Pius, was thrown across the country from Bo'ness on the Forth to Old Kilpatrick on the Clyde, and nineteen new forts, some of them on the sites established by Agricola, were built at intervals of about two miles along the line. The rampart is thirty-six miles long and for the first nine miles from the east it is constructed of clay; in the other three-quarters of its length it is built of sods, laid grass to grass and in regular courses like brickwork. Throughout the whole of its length the rampart stands upon a heavy stone foundation, 14 ft. wide, with a curb of large stones on either side. The rampart was about 10 ft. high, had sloping sides and there was a walk about 6 ft. wide on the top. It was defended by a ditch 40 ft. wide for the greatest part of its length, though much narrower in places where it has been cut through solid rock; it is 12 ft. deep. There is a berm between the rampart and the ditch, varying in width from 20 ft. to over 60 ft.

The forts vary in respect of the materials of their defences; some have ramparts of clay, others ramparts of turf, while others again are defended by stone walls; they have two or three, most of them three, lines of ditches. Within the forts the central administrative blocks were of stone while the barracks were of timber. There are no mile-castles or turrets on the Antonine wall, but the forts are less than two miles apart and therefore much closer together than those on Hadrian's Wall.

The wall of Antoninus proved to be no lasting barrier to the tribes beyond it, for frequently during the next sixty years these northern peoples broke through the frontier and spread themselves out in the country to the south of it. Eventually, finding the Lowlands quite untenable, the Romans transferred their frontier back again to the line of Hadrian's Wall, which, in the early part of the third century, they greatly strengthened and fortified.

During the greater part of the third century the activities of the Romans in Britain appear to have been devoted rather to the arts of peace than of war, but towards the end of the century a serious menace arose from without. From about A.D. 285 raids by Saxon and other Low German tribes on the south and east coasts of England began to assume serious proportions and to be pursued with ever-increasing violence and frequency. From 286 to 293 these forces were held at bay by the Britons under Carausius, a Roman admiral, who, having been condemned to death by Diocletian, landed in Britain, set up his standard there and ruled in his own name. Carausius was slain by one of his own officers, Allectus, who immediately assumed his position and pretentions. These events had, perforce, to be connived at by Rome for the time because the imperial armies were then fully engaged elsewhere. But in 296 the Emperor Constantius, determined to put an end to the insurrection, came in person to Britain, met and routed Allectus, whom he slew, and advanced to York, making that city his headquarters for the subjugation and administration of the country.

As soon as order was restored throughout the country the Romans set themselves to meet the menace from abroad and to put an effective check on the raids from across the North Sea. For military purposes Britain was then divided into two parts; the northern part, with its headquarters at York, under a commander named the Duke of Britain, and the southern part under one called the Count of the Saxon Shore. The latter officer had charge of an entirely new series of forts, known as Forts of the Saxon Shore, which were now being built along the east and south coasts of England between the Wash and the Solent.

These new forts, together with similar forts erected on the west coast, as at Cardiff and Caernarvon, were built during the latter part of the third and the first part of the fourth century. They were generally larger and of much greater strength than the older cohort-forts and were defended by massive and lofty walls and by ditches. They were normally rectangular, though irregular plans occur, as at Pevensey and Lympne. Some have rounded while others have square corners, and most of them have towers at the sides as well as at the corners. The wall towers now project on the outside of the curtain instead of on the inside as in the older forts. This disposition gave greater range to the *ballistae* mounted on the towers and insured the defence of the whole outside faces of the walls from one tower to the other. The gates were few and generally narrow. There are still very substantial remains of a large number of these forts and their character can best be appreciated by the examination of such outstanding examples as Burgh Castle, Suffolk; Bradwell-juxta-Mare, Essex; Reculver, Richborough, and Lympne, in Kent; Pevensey, Sussex; and Portchester, Hampshire.

Burgh castle was rectangular, or nearly so, and enclosed an area of about six acres. Three of its walls are still standing, in places up to the height of the wall walk, 16 ft. above the ground. The fourth wall, a long side, on the river bank, and pieces of the adjoining walls at either end, have been destroyed. The walls are 8 ft. thick and are built of flint rubble, bonded at vertical intervals with brick lacing courses. The corners are rounded and protected by external round towers; round towers also project at intervals from the curtain. At the top of the wall of one of the towers there is a hole for the turntable of a military engine. There is a gateway in the middle of the remaining long side and a postern in each of the end walls.

Bradwell-juxta-Mare was a rectangular fort with rounded corners; it is not possible to state its precise extent since the sea wall, on the east, and portions of the walls adjoining it have been entirely destroyed. The remaining walls are in a very fragmentary condition, the highest portion being only about 4 ft. above the level of the ground outside. The walls are 12 ft. thick and built of rubble faced with a hardened clay-stone called *septaria*; they are bonded with brick lacing courses. There are cylindrical towers of considerable projection at the corners, which are slightly rounded, and along the sides. The fort was defended by a ditch.

Of Reculver all that now remains are the east and south walls and the corner connecting them, but these stand to a considerable height; the corner is rounded. The walls are 10 ft. thick at the base, diminishing by offsets to 8 ft. at the top; there are no lacing courses and there are no wall towers. The fort was defended by a ditch.

Richborough stands on the site of an earlier defensive work and within its walls are the foundations of a rectangular structure, of about A.D. 90, which is probably all that remains of a triumphal monument. Broken pieces of marble slabs forming the casing and fragments of gilded bronze statues belonging to this monument have been found in large quantities in the soil near by. The fort as built in the latter part of the third century was rectangular, but the east wall with the portions of the north and south walls immediately adjoining it have disappeared owing to the falling away of the ground on this side. The three remaining walls stand, in places, to the height of about 25 ft. above the ground and preserve many of their original features. The walls are 11 ft. thick and are faced with squared stone and bonded with brick lacing courses.

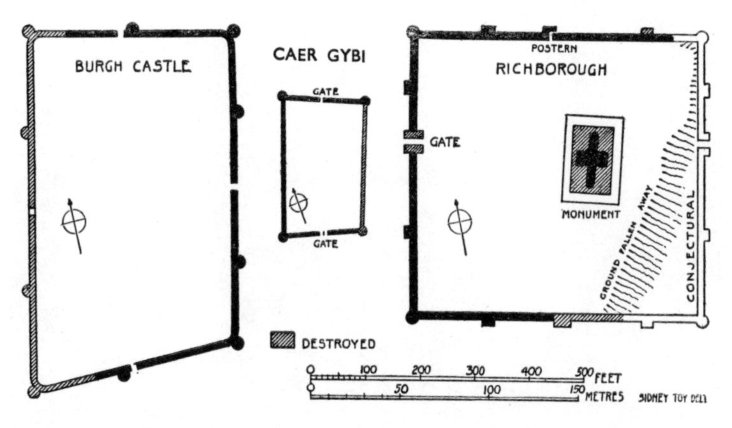

PLANS OF TWO FORTS OF THE SAXON SHORE, AND OF CAER GYBI

The corners are square but round towers project from them and there are square towers at intervals along the sides. There was a gateway, 11 ft. wide, near the centre of the west wall; it was flanked by rectangular towers which projected both outside and inside the wall. A postern is formed in a buttress near the middle of the north wall and so contrived as to provide a right-angled turn through the wall, the door being on the side of the buttress and thus under full command of the defenders on the wall. There was probably a similar postern on the south, but the corresponding buttress here has been destroyed.

Lympne appears to have been pentagonal in plan. Owing to the existence of numerous springs in the clay soil on which the fort was built landslips have occurred and now while large portions of the wall are distorted and thrown much out of their original positions other parts have fallen down. The south wall has disappeared entirely, but traces of it were found by excavation in 1894. Though the fort is now in a fragmentary condition huge masses of walling remain, standing in places to the height of 23 ft. The walls are from 12 ft. to 14 ft. thick and are built of stone bonded at vertical intervals with brick lacing courses. There are round wall towers at the angles and along the sides of the fort, some of them solid up to the wall walk but others containing small chambers at ground level. There is a gateway in

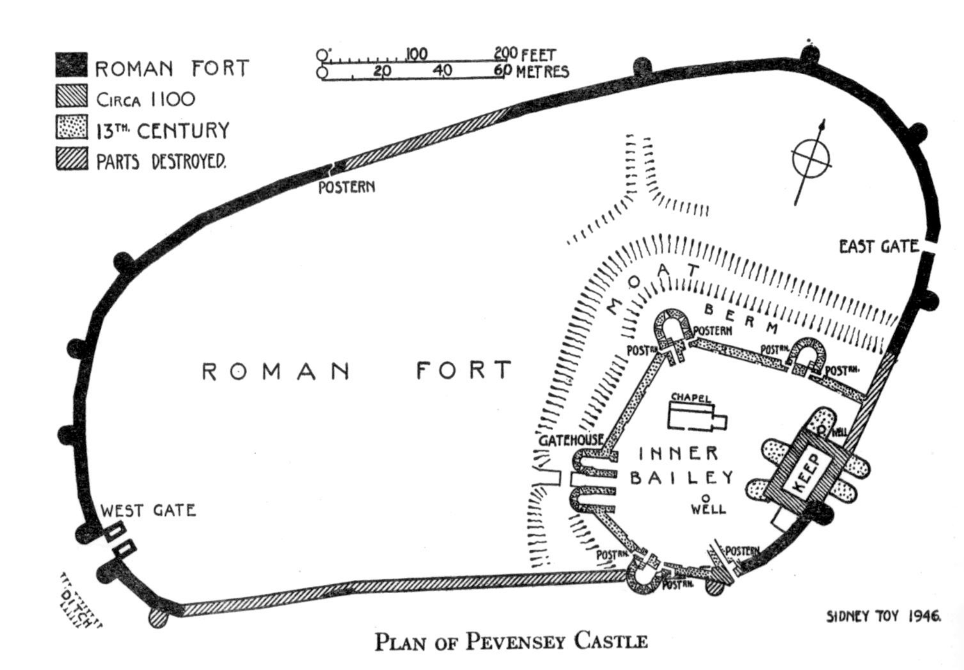

PLAN OF PEVENSEY CASTLE

the east wall which is 11 ft. wide and is flanked by solid towers, projecting on the outside; there are several posterns.

Pevensey has an unusual ovoid plan and an area of over eight acres. Except on the south, where a large portion of the curtain has fallen down, and a wide gap on the north, the walls stand to a considerable height, reaching in places up to the level of the wall walk 25 ft. above the ground. On the north-west the base of the parapet also remains. The walls were originally backed by a rampart, long since removed. They are 12 ft. thick and are built of flint and sandstone rubble, faced with coursed sandstone and ironstone and bonded with brick lacing courses; they stand on a foundation of flint and chalk, held together by a timber framework. Round towers, built solid up to the level of the wall walk, project at intervals from the curtain. The curtain appears to have been built in sections for there are straight vertical joints at intervals in its length all round.

The main gateway is at the west end of the fort; it is 9 ft. wide and has a guardroom on either side. This gateway is set so far back from the faces of the towers by which it is flanked as to leave a considerable space in front, commanded by the defence on three sides like those at Silchester noted above. There is another gate, 11 ft. wide, at the east end of the fort; this gate has no towers. When first built the fort stood beside the sea, which has now receded a mile away towards the south-east, and the east gate probably admitted to the harbour. On the north there is a postern which runs sinuously through the wall. The curtain was defended by a ditch fed by the sea. Pevensey was taken by the Saxons in 491 and probably lay derelict from that time until about 1100, when the Normans built a castle within it.

Portchester castle is the most complete of the series. It owes its good condition to the repairs carried out during the Middle Ages and to the fact that it escaped being slighted in the seventeenth century. It is a rectangular fort and the walls are complete all round, still standing in places up to the height of 20 ft. above the ground. A long piece of the east wall was rebuilt in the mediaeval period. The corners are square and the area of the fort is about nine acres. The walls are 10 ft. thick and are built of flint, bonded with lacing courses of brick and stone slate. The fort was strongly defended by round wall towers, one projecting from each corner and four, at intervals, from each side; of the twenty originally built fourteen still remain. These towers are all hollow from the ground up (p. 20).

The existing gateways, one in the middle of each of the east and west walls, date from the mediaeval period but they doubtless occupy the sites of original Roman gates, that on the east opening towards the sea. The fort was defended by single ditches on the

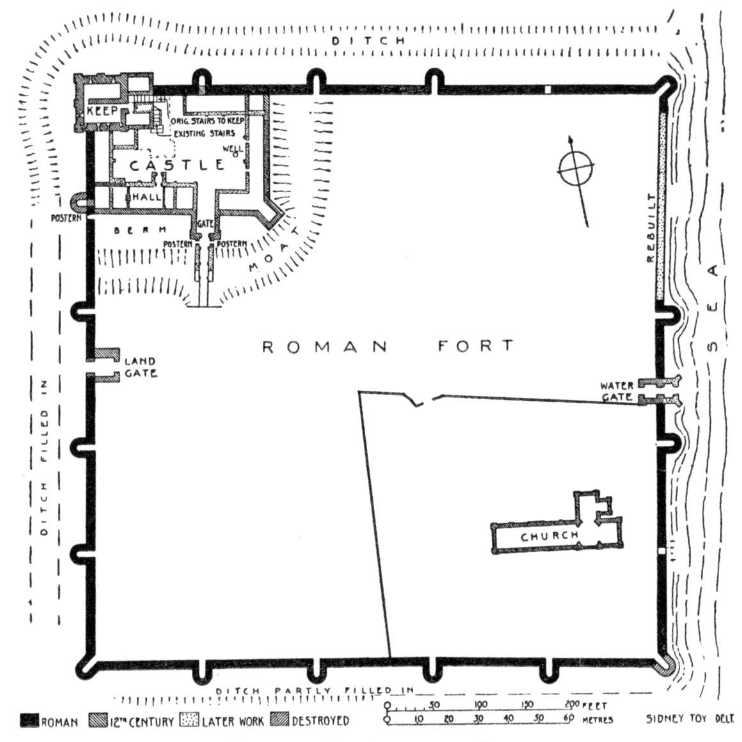

PLAN OF PORTCHESTER CASTLE

north and south, and probably on the east, and by double ditches at the land side on the west. Portchester also was occupied at a later period by the Normans, who built a castle at the north-west corner and used the rest of the fort as the outer bailey.

Good examples of forts built at this period on the west coast are at Cardiff, Caernarvon, and Caer Gybi near Holyhead.

Cardiff is a rectangular fort one side of which is slightly deflected; it encloses nearly eight acres. The lower parts of the Roman walls, which have been built upon in modern times, still exist practically all round, rising at the south-east to the height of 17 ft. above the ground. The walls are 10 ft. thick and have a concrete core faced with dressed limestone, bonded at irregular intervals with a course of flat stones; they are backed by an earthen rampart. The corners are rounded and as originally built, during the latter part of the third century, the fort had no wall towers; but the corner at the south-east has a considerable rounded bulge outwards. The towers were added in the first part of the fourth century; they are semi-octagonal and are placed at the corners and at intervals along the sides. The central tower on the east side is hollow, but all the others are solid up to the level of the wall walk.

There was one gateway in the middle of the north wall and probably a corresponding one on the south, but the latter was rebuilt in the Middle Ages. The north gateway is 9 ft. 10 in. wide and still retains the stone sockets in which the pivots of the great doors worked. The gateway is flanked by semi-octagonal towers which were added at the same time as the wall towers. The curtain was defended by a broad ditch. The fort was later occupied by the Normans, who threw up a mound at the north-west corner.

Caernarvon and Caer Gybi, both rectangular, are among the smaller forts of this period. Caernarvon stands 150 yards west of a Flavian fort of about A.D. 75; it encloses an area of a little over an acre and its walls are 5 ft. 6 in. thick and still stand in places to the height of 12 ft. Caer Gybi is a little less than an acre. Three of its sides stand to the height of the wall walk, 12 ft. above the ground, and include the base of the parapet. The wall is 5 ft. 6 in. thick and is faced with roughly dressed stone and bonded with courses of flat stones. At each corner a cylindrical tower, built solid up to the wall walk, projects out to the extent of three-quarters of its circumference, thereby thoroughly commanding the walls between them. There is a gateway in the middle of each of the north and south walls, but both have been rebuilt and that on the north is quite modern (p. 17).

While these coastal defences were being perfected, Hadrian's Wall was repaired and the walls of the Roman fortresses, where they had been broken down, were rebuilt and strongly fortified. The fortress at York, having been greatly damaged, received especial attention; the north-west and south-west walls were rebuilt entirely and were strengthened by wall towers and an earthen rampart. Two powerful corner towers were also projected out from either end of the north-west wall; that at the west, called the Multangular tower, still remains. The Multangular tower is a ten-sided structure which projects so far out from the rounded corner of the fort as to permit of a sweep of three-quarters of a circle outside the walls for an engine mounted upon it. It thus fully commanded the outer faces of both of the walls running up to the corner. Internally the tower was divided by a cross wall, built to support the upper floor and the engine mounted on it; and projecting inwards from the corner was a rectangular building which probably contained rooms for the guard. The existing upper part of the tower was added in the thirteenth century (p. 30a).

These precautions and defensive measures secured a certain amount of tranquillity for about fifty years, but meanwhile serious trouble was again brewing in the north. The Scots from Ireland had invaded and settled on the west and south-west coasts of Scotland and in 367 they joined forces with the Picts and the Saxon rovers in a combined attack on England. These hordes swept across the Wall, overcame and put to rout all the forces opposed to them, slew in combat both the Duke of Britain and the Count of the Saxon Shore and, carrying death and destruction before them, spread themselves over the country. Again a leader, this time Theodosius, one of the greatest soldiers of his day, was sent out from Rome to restore order. Theodosius drove the enemy north of the Wall and across the seas and immediately repaired the defences they had damaged.

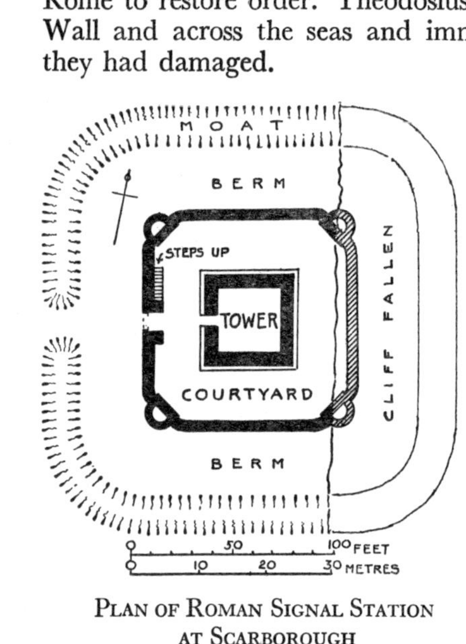

PLAN OF ROMAN SIGNAL STATION AT SCARBOROUGH

As an additional protection against raids from across the North Sea, the Saxon Shore defences were now extended northwards by the construction of a line of signal-stations on the headlands of the Yorkshire coast from the Humber to the Tees. Each station consisted of a tall stone tower, about 43 ft. square externally and probably 100 ft. high, and a battlemented wall enclosing a courtyard at the foot of the tower; the whole defended by a ditch and a wide berm between the ditch and the wall. The enclosing wall had a tower at each of its rounded corners, an entrance gateway, looking landwards, and a stair to its battlements near the gateway. The floors of the central tower were of timber, supported on posts built up from the ground, and they were reached by wooden stairs or ladders. The purpose of these stations, which formed a normal part of both the Greek and Roman systems of defence, was that from their summits the approach of Saxon raiders might be seen from a great distance far out to sea, so that by means of fire, smoke, semaphore, or other signal, warning could be sent at once to headquarters.

All these towers were thrown down and for many centuries their ruins lay buried beneath the soil, but thanks to modern excavation some of them, as at Filey, Scarborough, Goldsborough, and Huntcliffe, have been brought to light. The station at Scarborough is incomplete owing to the falling away of the cliff, but the foundations of others, including that at Filey, have been found complete. Though these stations vary slightly in detail, they are all of the same general design and as described above. They represent the last phase of Roman fortification in this country, and their complete destruction may be some indication of the power and violence of the invasion which followed, and perhaps helped to stimulate, the Roman departure.

ROMAN SIEGE OPERATIONS

The siege engines and siege operations of the Romans are considered at some length in a previous work by the author.[2] In Great Britain the Roman military operations appear to have been confined largely to open campaigns and there is little record of their use of engines or of resort to siege operations in this country. At Birrenswark, Dumfries, there is a Roman camp, associated with lines of circumvallation, which appears to have been set up during the siege of a defended position standing on the top of the hill. The camp is of the usual rectangular form and is enclosed by a rampart and a V-shaped ditch. There are three gates on the north, facing the hill-top, and one on each of the other three sides, all six being covered by oval-shaped traverses. A paved walk is carried all round the camp inside the rampart. In an attack on a British stronghold near the Great Stour during Caesar's invasion the Romans threw up a rampart in front of the fort and assailed the position by forming a *testudo,* or tortoise.[3] A *testudo* was formed by a body of men, generally a maniple, who, holding their shields above their heads, closed up together until the shields overlapped and formed a roof over the whole unit. Protected by this shell-like covering the formation, resembling a huge tortoise, advanced to the walls as a single body.

[2] Toy, *Castles,* pp. 27, 40.
[3] Caesar, *op. cit.,* V, 9.

CHAPTER THREE

ROMANO-BRITISH AND ANGLO-SAXON FORTRESSES
A.D. 400 TO 1066

THE period between the departure of the Romans in the fifth century and the settlement of the Normans in the eleventh century is one of very considerable obscurity in the history of fortifications in Great Britain; and it is a period about which, failing reliable evidence, theory and conjecture, often based on weak hypothesis, have been allowed to play all too prominent a role.

The withdrawal of Roman troops from Britain in the early part of the fifth century was probably a much more gradual process than is often supposed. A document, known as the *Notitia Dignitatum* and compiled about 428, gives lists of officers and men at that time holding various Roman stations in the north of England.[1] This document, though not beyond criticism in some of its details, does indicate a coherent and orderly disposition of troops in Britain long after the fall of Rome in 410. Certain it is that the Roman fortifications were held, probably by forces composed of an ever-increasing proportion of British personnel, against the swarms of invaders which now fell upon the east and south coasts of England. Pevensey, then called Anderida or Andredecester, was occupied by the Britons until 491, when it was laid siege to and taken by the Saxons. The *Anglo-Saxon Chronicle* records under that date " this year Aella and Cissa besieged Andredecester and slew all that dwelt therein so that not a single Briton was there left ". In reference to the same place and event, Henry of Huntingdon writes that Andredecester was a strongly fortified city and that it was taken by strategy. Old Sarum was occupied by the Britons until 552, when it also was overwhelmed.[2]

Though it is clear that the country had been deprived of the flower of its fighting forces, both Roman and British, for service in Gaul and Italy, those that remained were still capable of offer-

1 A manuscript of this document is in the Bodleian Library at Oxford.
2 *Anglo-Saxon Chronicle,* sub. 552.

ing effective resistance under skilful leadership. In 450, led by Ambrosius Aurelianus, they engaged and overcame the invaders in pitched battle.[3] But as wave after wave of invaders descended on the country, from overseas and from the north of the Wall, Britain was kept in a state of turmoil for many centuries. Still during that time there were many relatively peaceful and brilliant periods.

By the middle of the sixth century the Angles had established themselves in the north of England, had founded the kingdom of Northumbria, and had fortified its chief seat, Bamburgh, with a stone wall.[4] Other parts of the country were subsequently occupied, and by the close of the sixth century the Saxons, Angles, and Jutes had spread themselves over the land and had parcelled it out in the provinces of the Heptarchy. The reference to Bamborough in the *Anglo-Saxon Chronicle*, under date 547, is said to be an insertion by a later scribe, but the statement is supported by Nennius and there is no reason to doubt its accuracy. Nor is it reasonable to question the fortifications being of stone because Penda, King of Mercia, made an attempt in 633 to set fire to the houses within the town by means of sparks blown by the wind from huge fires he kindled outside the walls[5]; especially since the attempt was unsuccessful.[6]

Bede paints a glowing picture of the prosperity and elegance of Northumbria under Edwin and his immediate successor in the first part of the seventh century. He writes of towns, villages, castles and country seats, widespread throughout the province; and of drinking fountains, with cups attached, placed at intervals along the highways for the use of travellers.[7] Emulation is a quality innate in mankind and there is no reason to suppose that this high state of civilization was confined to Northumbria, nor that Bede had overstated the case in regard to that province. The exquisitely beautiful works in gold, bronze, and glass found in the Taplow Barrow, dating 620 to 640, and those even more elegant examples of goldsmiths' work of the same period, inlaid with coloured enamel, of silver plate and beaten bronze, found in the Sutton Hoo Anglo-Saxon ship burial are among the finest artistic productions of any age or people. Though the collections contain some foreign pieces much is purely native work.

Though now after the lapse of many centuries remains of the defensive works of the Anglo-Saxons are scarce, it is impossible to assume that races so dexterous in the field of art were ignorant of the current principles of fortification. That they were highly skilled in the design and construction of stone churches is evident

[3] Bede, *Eccles. Hist.*, Bk. I, C, XVI.
[4] *A.S.C.*, 547.
[5] E. A. Armitage, *Early Norman Castles*, 12.
[6] Bede, *op. cit.*, III, 16.
[7] Ibid., II, 16.

from examples which remain, as at Brixworth, Monkwearmouth, and Jarrow, all built in the seventh century, and at numerous other places, built at various periods up to the time of the Norman Conquest. The fact that the churches have remained while the defences have to a large extent disappeared is because the uses to which churches are put are practically constant throughout the centuries, whereas the design of a fortification must advance *pari passu* with the invention of new weapons and the introduction of new methods of attack. It is probable that the rubble cores of many mediaeval walls, refaced at later periods, are of Anglo-Saxon construction.

That the Anglo-Saxons knew well how to construct a stone building, even on infirm soil, and took pains to do so, is illustrated by their work at Crowland in 948 preparatory to the laying of the foundations of their stone church. Hard earth was brought on to the site from elsewhere and mixed with the loose soil of the marsh, the whole being consolidated by an immense number of oak piles driven into the ground.[8]

Fragments of stone walling which might well have formed part of post-Roman defensive works are found here and there throughout the country, but perhaps the most complete example of the earlier period is at Tintagel, Cornwall. Much of the rubble walling of Tintagel castle, which is largely deprived of its facing, probably dates from the fifth century of our era. In a county like Cornwall where stone has been the traditional building material from prehistoric times to the present day it is often practically impossible to assign a precise date to walling on the sole evidence of its facing, much less of its core. The author has examined and taken photographs of a wall of a hut at Chysauster, near Penzance, said to date from about 100 B.C., of a wall built of a similar granite ragstone at Carbis Bay about a hundred and fifty years ago, and of a third wall built in the same district quite recently. The three photographs show a remarkable similarity both in construction and facing.

The wealth of absurd legend, embellished with anachronistic detail, which has grown up about Tintagel has aroused so much prejudice in favour of the ascription of later dates to its buildings and has tended so much to obscure the essential facts of its history that it will be necessary to dwell shortly on this subject. Now that the accumulation of debris and vegetable growth has been removed from the walls it is possible to examine them to greater advantage, and it is quite clear that the dating given in the "official guide" is inaccurate. It is evident, for example, that the inner gateway on the mainland is of much more ancient date than its outward extension, and that the Great Hall on the island was not the earliest

[8] *Ordericus*, Ed. Bouquet, Bk. XI, 243.

building there but was an insertion in a much older curtain wall, a part of which was cut away for its reception (pp. 30b, 31, 32).

Tintagel comes into prominence in connection with the ravishing of Ingerna, the beautiful wife of Gorlois, Duke of Cornwall, by Uther Pendragon, and with the birth of Arthur. Uther Pendragon was the brother and successor of Ambrosius Aurelianus, mentioned above, and the events occurred about A.D. 500. Geoffrey of Monmouth, whose *History* was first published in 1139, and Wace, whose *Roman de Brut* was completed in 1155, both describe the castle of Tintagel, obviously from material not now available. Geoffrey's is the more detailed narrative.[9]

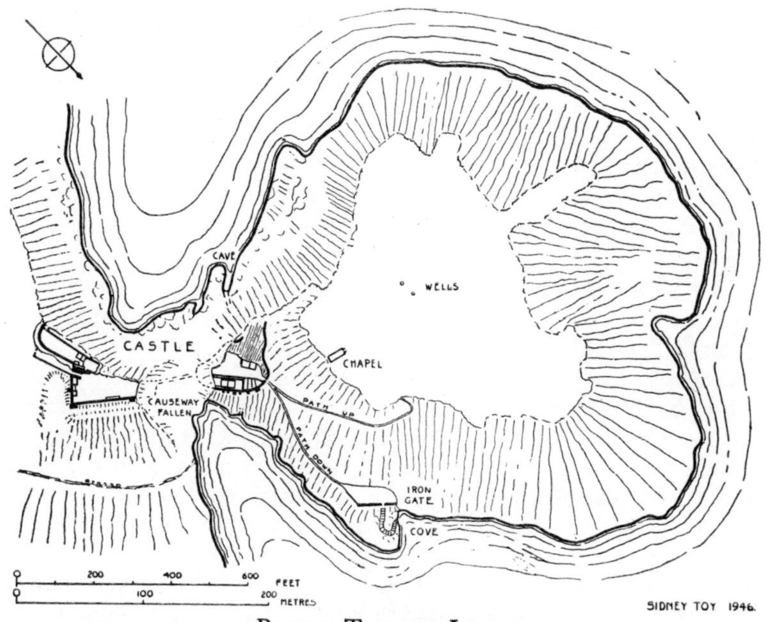

PLAN OF TINTAGEL ISLAND

Gorlois, aware of the king's designs on his wife, placed her in the strong fortress of Tintagel while he himself entered and prepared to defend his other castle of Dimilioc, which is probably to be identified with Dunhevet, the ancient name of Launceston. The king, having spent a week in fruitless attempts to take Dimilioc, repaired to Tintagel and, failing to take that castle also, made a disconsolate appeal to one of his followers for advice. He received the reply " who can advise you in this matter when no force will enable us to have access to her in the fortress of Tintagel. For it is situated on the sea and on every side surrounded by it and there is but one

[9] *Hist. Reg. Brit.*, Geoffrey de Monmouth, Ed. Griscon & Jones, 424.

entrance into it, and that through a straight rock, which three armed soldiers shall be able to defend against the whole power of the kingdom." Wace writes that Tintagel belonged to Gorlois' father and his ancestors before him, and that the fortress standing on a tall cliff near the sea is inaccessible from all sides save that on which the gate is placed. Failing to obtain entrance to the castle by force of arms the king had resort to a despicable stratagem, and by that means entered the castle and attained his ends.

We are not concerned here with the question of the Arthurian stories, either in regard to the person of Arthur or to his numerous exploits. There is, however, no reason to doubt the existence of a powerful British chieftain in the west of England at the period assigned to Arthur, nor to regard the embellishments of his exploits by later writers as conclusive evidence of the purely legendary character of the hero. No reasonable person suggests that Charlemagne and Roger Bacon were mythical characters because of the impossible powers and activities attributed to them. In respect to the venue of the activities of the British hero, Monsieur J. Loth, after an exhaustive study of the subject, arrived at the conclusion that the centre of the Arthurian stories was unquestionably Cornwall.[10]

But it is relevant to our subject that the story of Geoffrey de Monmouth, in so far as it relates to the siege and defences of Tintagel, would be archaic in character in Geoffrey's day and therefore, if not pure invention—which is inadmissible in view of the work as a whole—must have been copied from ancient manuscript. The story is further relevant in that the description it gives of the site on which the castle stood agrees with the site of Tintagel Castle of the present day. Three men holding a narrow causeway against an army recalls a similar situation in the defence of ancient Rome against the Etruscans.[11] But the defence is in no manner applicable to the military operations of Geoffrey's day, when King Stephen was conducting his campaigns throughout England with formidable long-range siege engines. With an engine of Geoffrey's time, mounted on the cliff opposite the castle, Tintagel would have been reduced to submission in a few hours. Geoffrey's description of the site as a bold and lofty promontory with precipitous sides, standing out into the sea and joined by a narrow causeway agrees precisely with that of Tintagel in Cornwall, except that owing to extensive falls of earth and stone what was a causeway is now a ravine (pp. 27, 30b, 31 and 32).

It is reasonable to infer, therefore, from the available documentary evidence that Tintagel existed as a fortified stronghold long before the twelfth century. If there was no such place at that

10 *Romans de la Table Ronde*, J. Loth, 1912, Ch. VI.
11 Livy, *History of Rome*, II, 10.

time then Geoffrey's early critics would certainly have said so. William de Newburgh, a chronicler of the late twelfth century, whose work, by common consent, is of far inferior quality to that of Geoffrey, while pouring contempt on the latter's account of Arthur's exploits, does not question the existence of Tintagel. Even Newburgh's trenchant remarks come ill from one whose own work is packed with extravagant and impossible tales, recorded as historical events.

The castle has been in utter ruins for many centuries and there is no record of its being the subject of attack, or reliable note of its occupation by any of its owners during the whole mediaeval period. The principal works of addition to which one can assign any definite date are a rectangular building on the island, containing the Great Hall and its offices, and the formation of a bailey on the mainland. Both of these works are referable to the twelfth century and were probably carried out by Reginald, Earl of Cornwall, 1140–1175. The castle was acquired by Richard, Earl of Cornwall, and titular King of the Romans, in 1236, but there is no record of his ever having lived there. The charge of harbouring his nephew David at his castle of Tintagel was a piece of malevolent gossip furbished up by Richard's enemies and characterised as false by the only chronicler who records it.[12]

In any case it is clear that the castle has been in ruins since the thirteenth century. The roof of the Great Hall was taken down about 1330 "because the hall was ruinous and the stones thereof were of no value"[13]; and about the same time a smaller building was erected within the ruined walls of the hall. Any subsequent repairs to Tintagel, except perhaps to the chapel which stands on the top of the cliff high above the castle, must have been of a very minor character. The castle was in an advanced state of decay in 1337, as shown by the *Caption of Seisin* then drawn up; and although the Black Prince issued general orders for the repair of this as well as his other castles in Cornwall there are no indications of any serious defensive works actually carried out at Tintagel at this time.

In 1359 the castle was reported to be "utterly without garrison"[14]; and an order issued to the non-resident constable in 1364, offering inducement to the chaplain at Tintagel to remain there, contains the candid admission that "the castle, as the constable well knows, is now deserted."[15] By the sixteenth century the causeway had fallen away, as shown in a drawing by John Norden, made about 1584, leaving a wide gap between the two

[12] Matthew Paris, Vol. IV, 487.
[13] *Caption of Seisin,* XI, Edw. III, E.120, (5) (29).
[14] *Register of Edward the Black Prince,* Pt. II, 166.
[15] Ibid., 207.

portions of the castle; and the gap was further widened in 1846 when another fall brought away not only large quantities of earth and rock but the portions of the walls they supported. A cave, flooded at high tide, passes underneath the castle from one side of the island to the other.

Tintagel is divided into two parts, one on the mainland and the other on a peninsula which, though called an island, is joined to the mainland by a narrow ridge of rock. When first selected as the site of a castle the causeway connecting the two parts must have been so much higher than it is at present that the pathway of approach it carried down from the entrance gateway on the mainland to the platform on which the fortifications on the island were built must have been an easy slope.

The portion of the castle on the mainland consists of two wards, a lower ward, or bailey, and an upper ward, the latter running along beside the bailey and projecting far out beyond the entrance gateway. It is clear that in the early period the curtain wall of the lower ward did not exist and that the approach to the causeway was by a narrow path cut out of the side of the rock; the path having the precipitous face of the upper ward on the west and a steep fall to the valley on the east. The path was spanned by a formidable gateway, of which the east pier still stands up to the height of 15 ft. The remains of this old entrance rise immediately within and in line with the twelfth-century gateway to the bailey; they belong to an ancient structure and may well be referable to the fifth century of our era.

The upper ward is long and relatively narrow. It runs north and south, commanding from a great height a long stretch of the approach road and the whole transit of the bailey from the entrance gate to the causeway. A strong wall, 7 ft. thick, runs round the top edge of the rock on the east side of the ward, curving to the west at the south end of the ward and ending in a precipice. Though it is not possible to assign a precise date to this wall, the thickest in the castle, it is older, possibly much older, than the lower ward and its curtain. For there are clear indications that this thick wall originally extended northward to the line of the ancient gate and, turning east, passed over that gate, and that when the lower ward was built in the twelfth century this old wall was cut back to line with the later and thinner curtain. The wall on the west side of the upper ward is of later mediaeval date; it stands on the edge of the cliff with a sheer drop down to the rocks at sea level; part of a chamber at the south-west corner has fallen away. Heavy falls of rock have involved the disappearance of the whole north end of the ward together with the wall it supported, but a fragment of masonry down in the lower ward probably indicates the line of the north wall and its termination at the east, which was carried

[Photochrom

HADRIAN'S WALL NEAR BORCOVICIUM, SHOWING PRECIPITOUS FALLS ON THE NORTH SIDE.

YORK. THE MULTANGULAR TOWER, EXTERIOR FROM THE SOUTH-WEST.

Tintagel Castle. Portion on the Island, looking seaward.

Tintagel Castle. Portion on the Mainland from the Island.

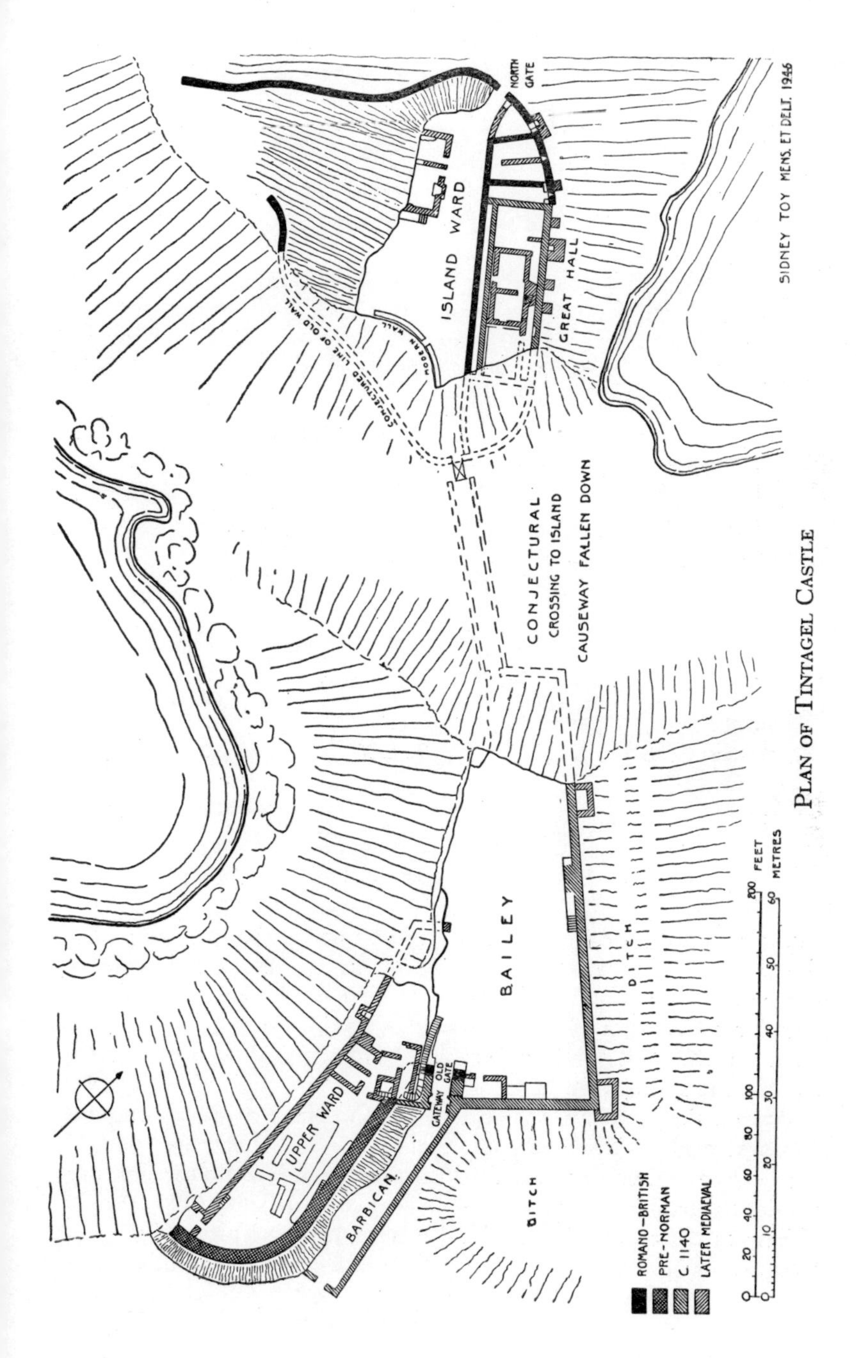

PLAN OF TINTAGEL CASTLE

down the rock at this point. Within the ward are foundations of building of indeterminable date.

When the lower ward was constructed its south and east curtain walls were built up from the virgin soil and the ground within levelled up by filling in on the east side. This is clear on examination of the exposed section occasioned by the falling away of the ground at the north end of the bailey. Ditches were then formed on the outside of the walls. The gateway into the bailey formed an extension outwards of the ancient gate; it is 18 ft. long and its ashlar facing still remains 3 ft. high on either side of the passage. The door, 8 ft. 7 in. wide, is placed midway in the passage and when closed was secured by a heavy timber bar, which was drawn across the gateway from out of a hole on the east side and fitted

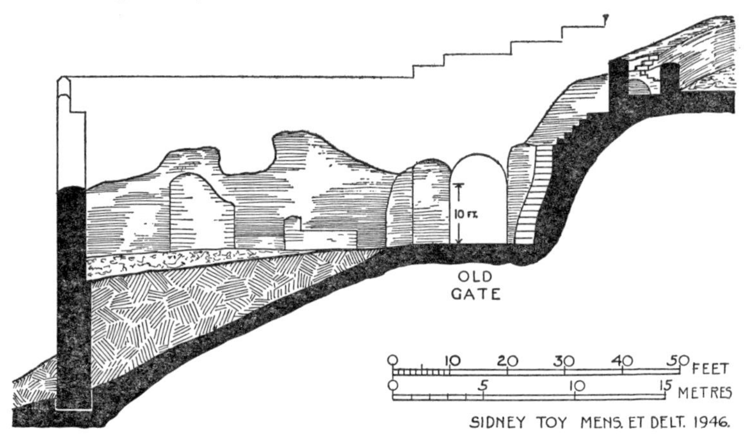

TINTAGEL CASTLE. SECTION THROUGH BAILEY AND UPPER WARD, LOOKING SOUTH

into a socket on the west side. There was no portcullis. A long and narrow barbican runs out in front of the gateway. The walls of the bailey are straight and were defended on the east by two rectangular towers not bonded to them. There are steps to the wall walk on the east wall and remains of internal structures built against the south wall. The whole work of this bailey, both in the design of the gateway, which is similar to those at Sherborne and Newark, and of the walls, relates to the twelfth century, while it bears no resemblance to the fortifications being built in the first part of the thirteenth century, as at Pembroke and Beeston.

The fortifications of the island stand on a level piece of ground scooped out naturally halfway up the face of the cliff and bounded on one side by the sheer face of the rock, which rises up from that level to the top of the cliff, and on the other side by a ledge with a rapid fall down to the sea. The only defence of this site considered requisite was a lofty curtain wall, still 25 ft. high at one place, which was carried round the edge towards the sea and up the face of the rock at both ends. Domestic and other structures were then built against the curtain. The approach from the causeway was at the south end of the ward and at the north end a gateway in the curtain opens on to two paths, one leading down to a small cove where a boat could land at the foot of a flight of steps cut in the rock, and the other leading up to the chapel on the top of the cliff. At a later period the approach from the cove was defended near the landing by a wall with an entrance called the Iron Gate.

At the approach from the causeway the whole of the curtain wall, except for a piece high up on the rock, and the south end of the Great Hall, have all been precipitated down the face of the cliff. But at the northern portion of the ward the original curtain remains, from the north end of the Great Hall on the east to the termination of the wall on the top of the cliff on the west. Two buttresses and a latrine tower were added to the wall in mediaeval times and stepped coping has been built on its summit in recent years, but the curtain itself and the north gateway piercing it are original and are of early character.

If the story of the early history of this castle is archaic in character, its design and structure are no less so; and in visualizing Tintagel as it appeared when first built account must be taken of the qualifying effects of heavy falls of rock as well as of natural erosion. The structure of both the curtain on the island and the old gateway on the mainland indicates an early, probably Romano-British, date, while in design the evidence of ancient character is still more clear. A fortress backed against the face of a cliff on a precipitous peninsula and defended by a wall in front, a narrow causeway of approach, and a gateway across the path leading to the causeway bears no sort of resemblance in design to the fortifications being built in this country from the eleventh century onwards. But it is just the kind of isolated fastness as might be chosen and occupied by a powerful prince in the centuries immediately following the Roman withdrawal.

Launceston castle appears to have been one of the strongholds of the post-Roman lords of Cornwall. At the time of the Norman Conquest it was held by the Bishop of Exeter, who then gave it to Robert de Mortain in exchange for two manors in Devonshire.[16] The castle is mentioned twice in the Domesday and in neither case is there any suggestion that Robert built it. On the contrary, the record makes the definite statement that the exchange was *pro castelli Cornualia*, and it is a pure quibble to contend that because a statement disagrees with a preconceived theory it must be

[16] D. B. Devonshire, *Terra Episcopi de Exonia.*

incorrect, or must mean something other than what it says. The point that Domesday does mean what it says is strongly stressed in a paper by Mr. Horace Round in a case where such insistence favoured his own argument.[17] Though it is not possible now to identify any portion of the ruins of Launceston castle as belonging to a time previous to the eleventh century, the wall of the shell keep, having the unusually massive thickness of 12 ft., might well incorporate a core of masonry of a much earlier period. The high mound on which the keep stands is a natural hillock, as was proved by recent excavation, and is such as has been selected as a site for fortification from prehistoric times. There is every reason to credit the documentary evidence that the position was fortified in days long before the Norman invasion.

It is evident from constant references in the early chronicles that the Anglo-Saxons, following their occupation of the country, defended themselves behind the existing Roman walls of London, York, Colchester and other towns. But constant strife among themselves and continuous warfare with bands of rovers from across the seas were factors inimical to the establishment of fixed defences. The conflict was almost ceaseless and it was a war rather of pitched battles than of sieges. Both the Anglo-Saxons and the Danes, however, threw up fortifications in the course of their campaigns and, during the short periods of respite, the former constructed formidable frontier lines across the country to protect their territories from invasion.

The finest of these frontier lines is Offa's Dyke, which runs for a hundred and twenty miles from the Wye on the south to the estuary of the Dee on the north, following roughly the modern border line between England and Wales. For the most part this great barrier consists of a high rampart and a deep ditch, the ditch being on the west side of the rampart and the rampart consisting of the material dug out of the ditch. Slight variations, due to the nature of the ground covered, occur here and there; as when passing through marshy soil there is a ditch on both sides; and on steep slopes facing west the material for the rampart is taken from the east side. Asser, writing in the ninth century, attributes the construction of this dyke to Offa, King of Mercia 757–796,[18] and recent investigations have resulted in the support of his statement.[19] Towards the north the defence is doubled by another barrier, known as Watt's Dyke, which runs along about thirty-six miles parallel with it.

Many other dykes and systems of dykes exist here and there

[17] J. H. Round, *The Castles of the Conquest*, Archaeologia, 1902, 13.

[18] *Asser*. Ed. Stevenson, 1904, par. 14.

[19] Vide *Dykes*, by Sir Cyril Fox, Antiquity, 1929, 13, and later papers in Archaeol. Cambrensis.

throughout the country, thrown up either between the territories of the Anglo-Saxon kings, as Wansdyke, with its subsidiary Bokerly Dyke, between Wessex and Mercia, and the Cambridge dykes between Essex and East Anglia; or at strategic points, as across ridges from one ravine to another. Wansdyke runs through Somerset and Wiltshire from a point near Portishead on the Bristol Channel to Inkpen near the borders of Hampshire, a distance of sixty miles; its subsidiary, Bokerly Dyke, is at its eastern end and is four miles long. The Cambridge dykes are a system of four parallel barriers which extend eastwards from points near Cambridge. Though each barrier consists of both a rampart and a ditch they are known locally as ditches and are called respectively, north to south, Devil's Ditch, Fleam Ditch, Brent Ditch, and Bran Ditch. Devil's Ditch, about eight miles in length, is the finest and longest of the system. Recent investigations carried out on both the Wansdyke and Cambridge systems have resulted in the definite conclusion that they are post-Roman and belong to the Anglo-Saxon period.

In addition to these frontier lines there were, during the ninth century, many fortified strongholds of Anglo-Saxon and Danish construction. Such of these forts as can be definitely attributed to the Danes are obviously temporary camps; but others, of more permanent character, must have been built by the Anglo-Saxons.

In 868 the Danes, arriving at Nottingham, defended themselves within the citadel—*arcis muniti*. The Saxons on their approach attacked this position, but their attempts to break through the wall —*murum*—having failed a peace ensued.[20] Now it is quite clear that the *arx* must be that strong and elevated spur, conspicuous for miles around, now occupied by Nottingham Castle; for the site corresponds in every respect to the common use of the term. It is also clear that this stronghold was defended by a stone wall. The fact that the Danes seized and occupied the citadel is no proof that they built its defences; they also seized and occupied the old fortifications at York and elsewhere. It is much more probable that the defences were already in existence when the Danes arrived at Nottingham, for they would have had no time for the building of such permanent works.

The distinction between such strongly fortified positions as Nottingham and those depending entirely, or almost entirely, on their natural strength was well appreciated by both the Saxons and their foes. In 878 a fleet of enemy ships arrived off the coast of Devon and a large force landed and pursued their course of devastation inland. A company of Alfred's men assembled for protection in the fastness of Cynuit—which has been identified with Kinnet Castle on the River Taw. Here the site was defended on all

[20] *Asser*, par. 30.

sides but the east and the Saxons had to content themselves with such protection on this vulnerable side as the exigencies of the occasion allowed. The invaders, on their advance, easily recognized the improvised character of the defences and, assuming that the Saxons were likewise ill provisioned, decided to lay siege to the position. The Saxons, knowing that they were in a desperate case, saved themselves by a determined dash out upon the besiegers at a time when they were least expected. In the event the Saxons slew twelve hundred of the enemy and drove the rest back to their ships.[21]

Meanwhile not only Britain but the whole of Western Europe was in a state of turmoil at this period. The peoples of Italy, France and Germany were all engaged in a continuous and desperate struggle for existence, either between the sections of which they were composed or against wave after wave of invaders. From the fifth to the tenth century the military architecture of those countries consisted largely of the repair of existing Roman fortifications or the building of others on the same model. But following the extensive raids by the Normans in the north of France, Charles the Bald in 862 ordered the construction of fortresses at all points to resist the invaders. The response to this order was immediate; bishops began to repair and rebuild the walls of their cities and powerful lords to build castles. The latter were now being raised in such numbers as to become a menace to the authority of the crown and an edict was issued ordering the destruction of all those that had been built without royal licence; but in 869 orders were given for the fortification of all towns between the Loire and the Seine.

In Britain, where these activities across the channel cannot have been unknown to such sagacious and provident rulers as Alfred the Great and his immediate successors, similar influences were at work. But it was not until after the Peace of Chippingham in 879 that the Anglo-Saxons were able to turn their attention to systematic fortification. It was essential for the progress of the nation that its people should be provided with adequate defence and be at least secure from sudden attack. Therefore, in addition to the walled cities already existing, other burghs, or fortified towns, were built in suitable positions in various parts of the country. During the reign of Alfred the Great existing cities and towns were restored and new ones were built where required. Houses for the king's use, admirably constructed of stone and wood, were raised and some royal seats were pulled down and rebuilt in stone in more suitable places.[22]

Florence of Worcester, a late eleventh-century chronicler, who is accredited with having used a superior copy of the *Anglo-Saxon Chronicle*, says that Alfred took a personal interest in building

[21] Ibid., 54. [22] Ibid., 91.

technique, himself designing some of the machinery used in building construction, and that in his day vast numbers of skilled workmen of all trades flocked to this country from abroad.[23] Some of the castles the king had ordered to be built were never completely finished, owing either to enemy action or to the obstructive jealousy of Alfred's own lords.[24] Others were garrisoned as occasion required. In 894 when Alfred marched into Kent with part of his army to meet his enemies there, he was careful to leave adequate forces in his castles and cities nearer home.[25]

From 910 to 921 Edward the Elder and his sister Ethelfleda, Lady of the Mercians, repaired the walls of existing cities, built citadels, and fortified about twenty towns, including Tamworth, Hertford, and Towcester.[26] Recent writers have made great point of the use of the word *burh* in the *Anglo-Saxon Chronicle* in respect to these activities; contending that the word applied to a town only. But it is unwise to stress the use of the word to such a degree. *Burh* or *burg* in its various forms was widely used in Western and Northern Europe and whether applied to a town or, more frequently, to a chieftain's fastness invariably implied a fortified place.

Mediaeval writers often used such words as *oppidum*, *municipitum*, *castrum*, and *castellum* quite indifferently. Describing an attack on Alençon, about 1030, the chronicler uses first the word *castrum*, then *munitionem*, and thirdly *oppidum*, all in reference to the same place and to the same attack upon it, and this is one instance among many.[27]

The fortifications being built in France in the tenth century often included a high mound which had its own ditch and was surmounted by the leader's particular stronghold, as at Blois and Samur.[28] These known cases are not necessarily the first; nor is it equitable or just to deny to our own people initiative we are prepared without question to attribute to others. The citadel at Bridgnorth was built upon a high natural rock, following ancient usage. At Tamworth there was no such eminence. The statement in the *Anglo-Saxon Chronicle* that Ethelfleda built, or wrought, a burh there implies something new; for Tamworth was the capital of the kingdom of Mercia and was probably fortified at least from the time of Offa. Florence of Worcester says that the town was restored in 914. It is therefore not unreasonable to infer that the high mound at Tamworth, which is probably for the most part artificial, was raised at this period.

Before the Norman Conquest the English were in the forefront

[23] *Florence of Worcester*, Ed. Thorpe, 1848, 886, 887.
[24] *Asser*, 91. [25] *Florence of Worcester*, 894.
[26] Ibid., 913, 914, and *A.S.C.*, 910–924.
[27] *William of Jumièges, Historiae Normannorum*, 259a.
[28] *Gesta Ambasiensium Dominorum*, Spicilegium, 273.

of the nations of Europe in the fields of art and industry. This fact is evident from such illuminated MSS. and other artistic productions as are still preserved and is strongly emphasised in the writings of the chroniclers. So Ordericus: "They—the Normans—had subjugated a nation greater, and richer and more ancient than their own; illustrious for its saints and wise men, and powerful kings, who had earned a noble reputation by their deeds, both in war and peace."[29] William of Poitiers, a Norman who was chaplain to the Conqueror and who would have no desire to overstate the case in their favour, writes of the English that they are "A nation indeed by nature always disposed to fight, descending from the ancient Saxons, the most ferocious of men. They could not be overcome except by very great force; they had recently conquered with great facility the king of Norway, supported by a great and valiant army." Again, "The women of England are very skilful in needlework and the working of gold lace, and the men are distinguished in all the arts. It is for this reason that the Germans, who are very dexterous in these arts, are accustomed to dwell among them. They have merchants who go by sea to far-off lands taking their skilfully wrought wares."[30] William the First, having drained the country of its treasures, sent part of the loot to the Pope and distributed a portion among the churches and monasteries of France. "He sends to Pope Alexander for the church of St. Peter at Rome incredible sums of gold and silver and ornaments which would appear precious even at Byzantium."[31]

It is quite evident, therefore, that the Anglo-Saxons so far from being backward were among the most highly cultured people of their day, and it is not reasonable to assume that such a people neglected the arts of fortification, prevalent in their time, in the pursuit of which their very lives depended.

We know, however, very little of the precise form of the fortifications built in this country during the ninth and tenth centuries. The *Anglo-Saxon Chronicle* states tersely that the towns and fortresses referred to were built or repaired, though in the case of Towcester it says that it was surrounded by a stone wall. Other chroniclers often mention stone in their descriptions of works of construction. So that while timber was probably employed as the main defensive material where it was plentiful, stone scarce, and haste an important factor, there can be no doubt that the principal fortifications were of stone.

The illustrations in the Anglo-Saxon MSS. which depict towns surrounded by stone walls and towers are only helpful in that they probably indicate the general character of the work, for the illus-

[29] *Ordericus*, Bk. XI.
[30] *William of Poitiers*, Ed. Duchesne, 203c, 210c.
[31] Ibid., 206c.

trations have been closely copied from more ancient types. The Psalter Harl. MS. 603, now in the British Museum, for example, dating about A.D. 1000, contains drawings which have often been reproduced as illustrative of Anglo-Saxon life and buildings. But these drawings were meticulously copied from those of a manuscript of the ninth century, now in the library at Utrecht and known as the Utrecht Psalter, and they again from still earlier classical types. One can, however, discern from these drawings that the Anglo-Saxon conception of a fortification was of a large dwelling area, defended by a wall, and of a strong point, or citadel, on higher ground at one end of it; a plan common to all periods from the earliest times. One of the most conspicuous buildings shown within the defences is a chapel, evidently adapted, by the addition of Christian symbols, from a temple in the original drawings.

Dover castle in the latter part of the Anglo-Saxon period must have been a fortress of this kind; the citadel being the oval space on the highest point above the cliff, occupied by the pharos and the church, and the dwelling area on the lower ground, now called the middle bailey, running inland from the citadel; the whole being defended by stone walls. The first clear reference to the castle occurs in the *Anglo-Saxon Chronicle*, which states that in 1048 Eustace, Earl of Boulogne, made an attack upon it and was driven off with great loss.[32] It is probable that there was a Roman fort here, protecting the pharos, but there can be no doubt the site was defended about the latter part of the tenth century when the relatively large church of St. Mary in Castro was built. The church was not monastic and must have been built to serve the garrison of the castle and not the inhabitants of the harbour town below.

After another long period of desperate struggle and open warfare the building of fortifications received a fresh impulse in 1042 on the accession to the throne of England of Edward the Confessor. Edward had spent the greater part of his life in Normandy and was strongly influenced by its people and their activities; he soon introduced many of his Norman friends into this country and installed them in important offices. At this period the Normans were building private strongholds of a type which have become known as "motte and bailey", consisting of a fort elevated on a motte, or mound, and an enclosed bailey, or ward, at the foot of the mound. This type constitutes no new idea or plan, except in so far as it is produced on a relatively small scale, but corresponds in all essential points to the citadels and lower towns of antiquity and later times.

Castles of this period which have been identified with those referred to in the chronicles include Hereford castle, Ewyas Harold, Robert's castle, and Richard's castle.

[32] *A.S.C.* and *Florence of Worcester*, 1051.

Hereford castle was built about 1048.[33] It consisted of a mound and bailey and stood within the city walls on the south-east side of the city. The mound, which was frequently referred to in early documents, has been levelled to the ground, but the bailey is still outlined by high banks. The castle suffered serious damage from an attack in 1055 but was again in occupation in 1067. Though its original materials of construction are unknown, it was clearly defended by stone walls in 1181.[34] Ewyas Harold, Herefordshire, identified with "Penticost's" castle, and Clavering castle, Essex, identified with "Robert's" castle, were both in occupation in 1052.[35] Ewyas Harold consists of a mound about 70 ft. high and a

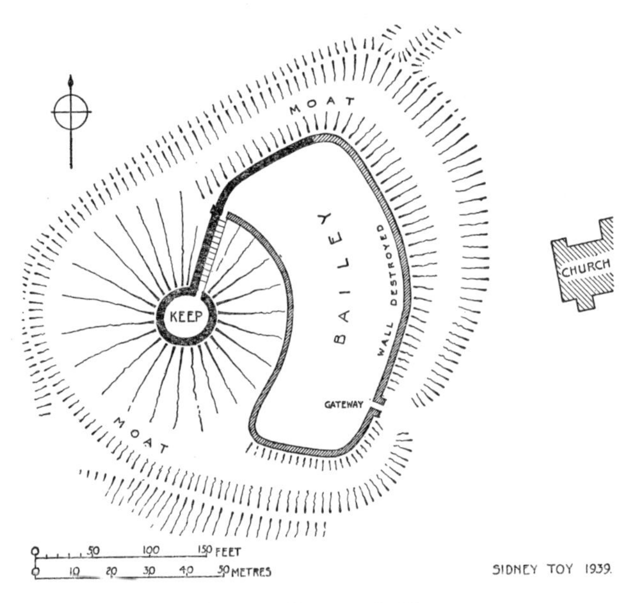

Plan of Richard's Castle

bailey running south-east from it; the mound was surrounded by a shell keep which has been destroyed and the foundations grubbed up. Clavering was a formidable castle consisting of one ward, which is surrounded by a deep moat 75 ft. wide and has a long rampart on the north side.

Richard's castle, five miles south of Ludlow, is doubtless the *castella Avreton* of Domesday; it was held about the year 1052 by Richard Fitz-Scrob, one of the Normans to whom Edward had granted large estates in this country. Richard probably built the castle, which at the time of Domesday was held by his son

[33] *A.S.C.* [35] *A.S.C.*, 1052. [34] *Pipe Roll*, 8 Henry II, 1181.

Osbern.[36] The castle consists of a high mound, defended originally on the top by a circular wall, and a single bailey on the east side of the mound. The mound, now thickly covered with trees and undergrowth, is probably composed principally of the natural bed of slaty stone, of which outcrops are seen on the road of ascent to the castle; the walls of the castle are built of this material.

The flat top of the mound was enclosed by a shell keep, part of the foundations of which are still visible, and the bailey was defended by a high curtain wall which, on the north side, was extended up the mound to join the keep. There is no indication of an ascending wall on the south side of the keep and it is highly probable that the wall at the south-west corner of the bailey was returned northwards along the base of the mound to the north-west corner. The keep, otherwise completely isolated from the bailey, had a single way of approach; and that way was protected on the right flank by a high wall running up the mound. There was one gate to this approach at the foot of the mound from the bailey and another at the top of the mound into the keep. The wall running up the mound and a considerable length of its continuation northward along the side of the bailey remains in places up to the height of from ten to twelve feet; it is 5 ft. 9 in. thick and still retains its faces on both sides. A buttress-like projection at the foot of the mound was probably associated with the lower gateway to the keep. There was an outer gateway at the south-east of the bailey and the whole castle was surrounded by a deep ditch.

Richard's castle, abandoned for centuries and now fallen into a great state of decay, still remains a most valuable example of a pre-Conquest castle, built of stone, mostly taken out of the ditch, set in thick mortar.

[36] D. B. Hereford, *Terra Osberni filii Ricardi.*

CHAPTER FOUR

NORMAN CASTLES WITH SHELL KEEPS

On the arrival and settlement of the Normans in 1066 castles in unprecedented number were raised here and there throughout the land. Ordericus remarks that one of the reasons why the invasion succeeded was that in England there were but few of those fortresses which the Normans call castles.[1] The value of these widely dispersed and well placed strongholds to subdue and hold in subjection whole districts had been amply demonstrated in France. William, following the Roman example, brought his full military equipment across the Channel with him. The Romans when on the march carried their siege engines in sections on muleback and reassembled them on the scene of action.[2] William brought over a pre-fabricated fort in his invading ships. The timbers for this fort had all been cut, shaped, framed and pinned together in France, then dismantled and the pieces packed in huge barrels and taken on board the ships. On disembarking at Pevensey, a suitable site having been chosen, the fort was re-erected complete by the evening of the day on which the fleet arrived.[3]

After the battle of Senlac Hill and his subsequent penetration through England William ordered a thorough survey of the country to be made and castles to be built in suitable places, especially in those districts then unfortified.[4] That there were castles and fortified towns in England at that time is clear from the fact that in the course of his campaign and before he returned to Normandy in 1067 William placed his followers in charge of them. Ordericus' statement, noted above, that there were but few of those structures which the Normans call castles, no doubt had especial reference to those of the motte and bailey type. Whatever lack there was in this respect was now soon rectified. During the thirty years follow-

1 *Ordericus*, XI, 242.
2 Josephus, *The Jewish War*, III, VI, 11.
3 Maistre Wace, Roman de Rou, Ed. Andresen, 6533–6550.
4 Florence of Worcs. 1067; *Ordericus*, XI, 242; Will. of Jumièges, 290d.

ing the Conquest castles of this type were raised in great profusion throughout Britain.

The mound in these castles varies from 10 ft. to 100 ft. in height and from 100 ft. to 300 ft. diameter at the base. It was of three kinds, according to thc nature of the soil occupied. Natural hillocks, as those at Belvoir, and Pontefract; the lower part natural and the upper artificial, as at Tickhill and Tutbury; and entirely artificial, as the two at York. Mounds have often been described as artificial before any investigation as to their composition has been made. The mounds at Windsor castle and Launceston castle, frequently referred to as artificial, have both been found on investigation to be composed of virgin soil.

Occasionally the mound stood alone surrounded by its ditch, but normally it was protected by one, two, or more outworks or baileys; the baileys being arranged in such order, dictated by the character of the site, as would best defend the keep standing on the mound. If there were two baileys they were arranged in line in front of the mound, or on either side of it, or again side by side in front of the mound. A ditch was carried all round the castle and also between the mound and the bailey and between the baileys. Often when the castle was first formed the keep was connected with the bailey by one wall and stairs only up the mound, as at Launceston and Berkhamsted. Windsor and Arundel

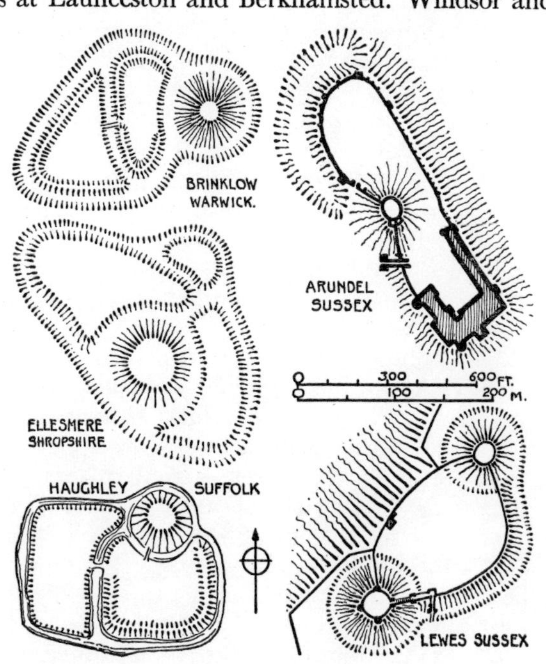

PLANS OF EARLY NORMAN CASTLES IN ENGLAND

were doubtless of this form when first constructed. Many of the castles built at this period do not belong to any particular type and have no mounds, as the Tower of London, Colchester castle, and Old Basing. The castles at Pevensey and Portchester were each built within the walls of a Roman fort.

Many of these castles have been destroyed utterly, while others have been so radically transformed that the materials of their original construction must be a matter of conjecture. With such buildings as the White Tower, Tower of London, and the keep at Colchester there is no question; they are and were originally of stone. But it has been too often assumed by recent writers that the mounds and baileys of this period were fortified by timber defences only; and this wooden theory is made to apply even to such counties as Cornwall, where timber is scarce and stone plentiful and where stone has been the general building material from prehistoric times to the present day. There can be no doubt that the castles at Launceston and Trematon in Cornwall, and that at Totnes in Devon, were all of stone from the first. The difficulty of assigning stonework to a definite period in districts where traditional methods of building are constant through many centuries has already been remarked.

The paucity of remains of stone castles of the early Norman period is due in some measure to the pillage of stone for building purposes. At Topcliffe, Yorks, every stone has vanished from the site of what was the principal castle of the Percies for six centuries, and the same fate has befallen the stone keep of Barnstaple castle, Devon. In some cases only foundations remain while in others masonry may still lie buried beneath the soil. On a hill site at Lydney, Glos., hitherto considered to be an earthwork, the foundations of a stone-built castle of the twelfth century were brought to light in 1929, and it is not improbable that still earlier masonry lies hidden at other sites.

Timber was of great value for temporary camps and forts which had to be constructed in haste. The Norman castles in England were founded to overawe and govern the districts in which they were built; many, serving only a temporary purpose, were subsequently abandoned. A large number must have been constructed hastily and with such materials as were available and, having regard to the facility with which they were destroyed, were doubtless built of wood. Many of the unlicensed or "adulterine" castles raised in haste in England during Stephen's reign and destroyed after the treaty of 1153 were probably also of this material.

Where the mound was entirely artificial the defences built at once on its summit must have been of timber and such a fortification is depicted on the Bayeux Tapestry and is described by Jean de Colmieu, writing about 1130. Speaking of the flat country in the north of France south-east of Calais he says: "It is the custom of the nobles of that neighbourhood to make a mound of earth as high as they can and then dig about it as wide and deep as possible. The space on top of the mound is enclosed by a palisade of very strong hewn logs, strengthened at intervals by as many towers as their means can provide. Inside the enclosure is a citadel, or keep, which commands the whole circuit of the defences. The entrance to the fortress is by means of a bridge, which, arising from the outer side of the moat and supported on posts as it ascends, reaches to the top of the mound."[5]

Excavation carried out in 1949–50 on a mound at Abinger, Surrey, revealed a small castle of this character. The mound at Abinger is about 35 ft. diameter at the flat summit and 20 ft. high from the bottom of the surrounding moat to the summit. Investigations at the top disclosed a close row of post holes round the edge and other post holes outlining a rectangular space in the middle; the former being obviously for palisading and the latter for a small but strong timber keep. The moat is relatively wide and deep. In line across the moat at one point are two plinths of soil, left standing when the moat was first dug out for the support of the posts, or piers, carrying a timber bridge; the bridge ascending from the outer side of the moat to the top of the mound. All is as described by Jean de Colmieu and, allowing for licence of art and limitations of material, as depicted on the Bayeux Tapestry for the castles of Dol and Dinan. The history of this little fortification appears to be that it was raised about 1100, remodelled about 1140 and finally destroyed following the treaty of 1153.

Lambert d'Ardres, writing clearly of what was considered a wonder, mentions a timber keep built in the eleventh century in the flat country of northern France. He describes a structure of three storeys containing halls, chambers, a guardroom, and a chapel on the upper floors, and storerooms on the ground floor.[6] There is no evidence of the existence at any time of such an elaborate timber keep in this country.

The perishable character of timber and its liability to destruction by fire renders it an unsuitable material for permanent fortification. From the earliest times fire has been one of the principal weapons of offence, and although stone buildings, since they incorporate much wood in floors, roofs and internal fittings, are not proof against its attacks, the damage done to them is partial and often reparable. With timber the destruction is total. The Normans were well aware of these facts and there can be no doubt that where local conditions were suitable, the mound a natural hillock, and haste not a particularly urgent factor, the keep on the summit

[5] Jean de Colmieu, *Vie de Jean de Warneton.*
[6] Lambert d'Ardres, CXXVIII.

of the mound was built of stone from the beginning. It is probable also that some of the shell keeps which stand upon partly natural and partly artificial mounds were built of stone from the first, the foundations going down to the virgin soil. At Skenfrith, Mon., where there is a round keep of the late twelfth century rising from an entirely artificial mound, the foundations of the keep are carried down through the mound to the natural soil. With the forced local labour the Normans employed,[7] working the men sometimes day and night,[8] stone walling could be raised with great rapidity. Of the Norman castles represented on the Bayeux Tapestry one is clearly built of stone while two others are depicted much in the same manner as is Edward the Confessor's church at Westminster Abbey, known to have been built of stone.

There still exists in England and Wales a large number of castles which were either founded or acquired by William the First or his companions; many of them are mentioned in Domesday and contemporary chronicles. Some of them, including Windsor, Durham, Tamworth, and the Tower of London, have been occupied ever since they were first built. The White Tower, Tower of London, and all other rectangular keeps of the period are of stone, and there can be no doubt that shell keeps standing on natural soil, such as those at Windsor, Launceston, and Totnes, were also built of stone from the first.

The keep is that focal point in a castle to which, in time of siege, the whole garrison retired when the outer works had fallen and was therefore the strongest and most carefully fortified part of the defences. It generally had a well and contained all the offices, living and service rooms, kitchen, storerooms, and latrines, necessary to sustain a long siege. As originally built it generally stood in line with the outer defences, so that while one side of it looked towards and commanded the operations in the bailey, the other side commanded the field and the approaches to the castle; the latter side also presented a line of escape should the keep itself be captured from the bailey.

In many of the castles built during the latter part of the eleventh and first part of the twelfth century the keep consisted of a high ring wall, circular, ovoid, or polygonal in shape, with the living rooms ranged against the inside face of the wall round a central courtyard. Such a building has become to be known as a shell keep, a name which is both descriptive and convenient. Many of these structures are of considerable size and strength.

Windsor castle was built by William the First soon after the Conquest and at the time of Domesday was held of him by a tenant-in-chief.[9] When first formed it consisted of a mound, with

[7] Henry of Huntingdon, 2073. [8] Flor. of Worcs., A.D. 1100.
[9] D. B. Berks., *Terra Regis*.

its defences, and a bailey stretching eastward from the mound; the approach to the keep from the bailey running up the mound at the curtain on the south. The mound is mainly a natural chalk bed, as proved by recent excavation, and not artificial as described in Sir William Hope's monumental work on the castle[10]; it is scarped all round and protected by a ditch. The keep on the summit of the mound, called the round tower, is roughly round on plan though considerably flattened in places, particularly on the south side. It is composed of two shells; the wall walk of the outer shell forming a terrace 10 ft. wide round the base of the inner shell. The outer shell, like most of the masonry of the castle, is built of local sandstone, called heath-stone, and its wall walk rises 15 ft. above the mound. It stands on the virgin chalk and though repaired at successive periods and largely refaced in modern times doubtless is substantially the shell keep built by William about 1075.

What internal buildings existed in the keep or within the bailey at this period is now impossible to determine. But by the early part of the twelfth century the domestic amenities must have been of a developed character, for in 1114 Henry the First held his court at Windsor and in 1121 celebrated there his marriage with Adela of Louvain (pp. 48, 48a).

About 1175 extensive building works were carried out by Henry the Second, who rebuilt the curtain wall, raised halls and offices on the north side of the bailey, fortified the lower ward, and remodelled the keep. At the keep Henry constructed a large tower immediately within the old shell, retaining the latter as a base round his new work. The wall of the tower is 4 ft. 9 in. thick above a battered plinth, is strengthened at intervals by wide buttresses, and originally rose, with one external offset, to the height of about 34 ft. above the terrace. The approach to the keep was by way of flights of steps on top of the wall running up the mound on the south; the steps, protected by a parapet on either side, leading to the terrace at the foot of the tower. The original entrance into the tower from the terrace has been obliterated by many alterations, but it was probably near the top of the steps of approach.

The buildings erected by Henry the Second within the tower were doubtless of timber and ranged round a central court as at present; for incorporated in the existing timberwork, which dates from the fourteenth century, are beams and posts reused from a much older period. There can be no doubt that the keep at this time contained all the rooms and offices necessary to sustain a siege. The main windows would open on the court. Within and on the north side of the tower there is a well, 6 ft. 4 in. diameter and 165 ft. deep; it is lined with dressed stonework to the depth of 60 ft. 6 in. below the surface of the ground.

[10] *Windsor Castle,* W. H. St. John Hope, Pt. II, 544.

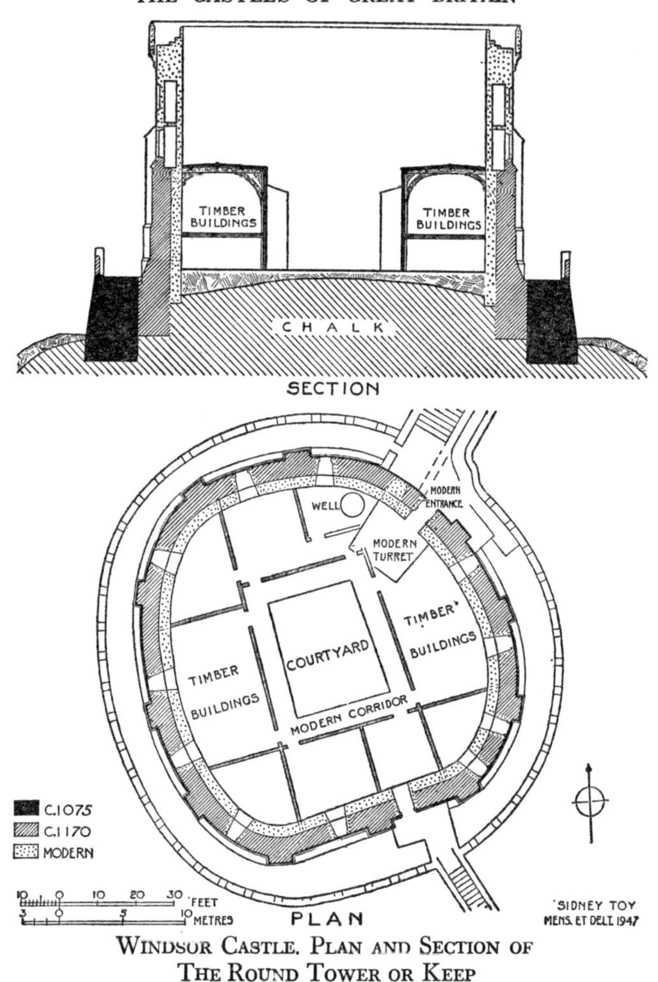

WINDSOR CASTLE. PLAN AND SECTION OF THE ROUND TOWER OR KEEP

About the middle of the fourteenth century Edward the Third remodelled the interior buildings of the keep and constructed a new approach to it up the mound on the north-east side. These internal buildings still exist; they are of oak, are of two storeys, and are ranged round a rectangular courtyard. The upper storey contains lofty halls and chambers and is covered by low-pitched timber roofs.

This keep was subjected to much alteration in 1826, considerable refacing was done and new windows were inserted. The tower was raised by 30 ft. to its present height of 64 ft. above the terrace and, in order to support the additional weight thus imposed, 3 ft. of brickwork was added on the inside of the tower all round, bringing the wall to its present thickness of 7 ft. 9 in. A brick

Windsor Castle. The Round Tower.

Launceston Castle. The Keep from the East.

Tamworth Castle from the South-East.

Colchester Castle. Partition Wall in Keep.

Durham Castle. The Keep from the South.

stair-turret was also built, rising from the ground to a height well above the parapet. The internal timber structures, however, were not heightened and, but for the insertion of partitions, stairways and plaster ceilings, were allowed to remain much as left in the fourteenth century. Despite these modern works and the repairs necessary from time to time the Round Tower of Windsor castle is still one of the most perfect shell keeps in existence.

Launceston castle was acquired soon after the Conquest by Robert de Mortain and in whatever condition he received it there can be little doubt that the castle was remodelled in his time. Robert held his court at Launceston and must have had an establishment of considerable strength there. The castle consists of a mound, surmounted by a powerful shell keep, and a bailey running southward from the mound. The approach to the keep is by a long flight of steps up the mound against the wall forming a continuation of the north wall of the bailey; the keep was joined to the curtain of the bailey on one side only. In the thirteenth century the steps up the mound were protected by a wall on either side and roofed in, a tower was built at the foot of the flight and the entrance into the keep at the head was defended by a portcullis. The bailey curtain and the south gateway were built in the twelfth century and the north gateway in the fourteenth century.

The mound is a natural knoll composed of a slaty stratum and rises to a great height above the bailey. The keep on its summit is composed of two shells of which the outer alone dates from the eleventh century. The outer shell is of ovoid shape, is 12 ft. thick and 30 ft. high to the wall walk, and has a battered plinth crowned by a bold torus moulding. It is entered by the doorway at the head of the flight of steps and has two mural stairways to the wall walk. On the west side of the shell there is a small mural chamber which had a ventilating shaft 8 in. square but apparently no other opening save its doorway; it was probably a prison.

Such internal structures as existed within the keep at this early period were destroyed when the inner shell, actually a round tower, was built about 1240. The tower rose some 35 ft. above the wall walk of the outer shell and the space between the shell and the tower was roofed over to form a wide terrace. There was a battlemented walk at the base of the outer shell; so that when put in a state of defence the keep had three tiers of fighting lines. The first consisted of the battlements at the base of its shell, the second the wide terrace midway in its height, and the third the battlements of its central tower; a most formidable structure, especially in view of the commanding position it occupies.[11]

Totnes castle is mentioned in a charter of about 1080 as being then in possession of Judhel, one of the companions of William

[11] Vide *The Round Castles of Cornwall,* Archaeologia, Vol. LXXXIII, 1933.

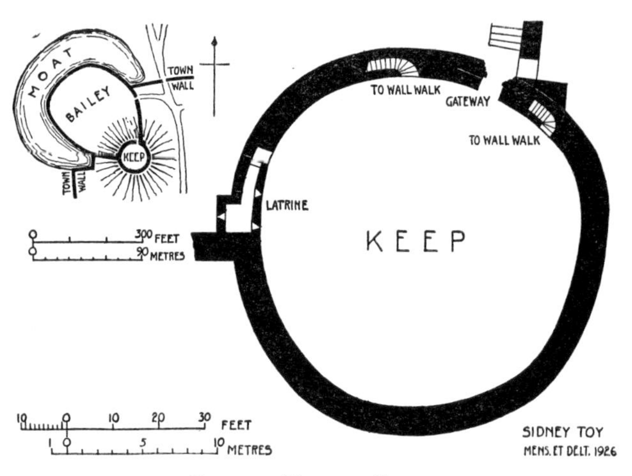

PLAN OF TOTNES CASTLE

the First. It consists of a high mound which, considering the geological formation of the district is most probably virgin soil, and a bailey extending northward from it; the mound is surmounted by a shell keep and there is a curtain wall round the bailey. The castle dominates the town of Totnes, the mound jutting into the town and its bailey extending outside the town walls. Formerly

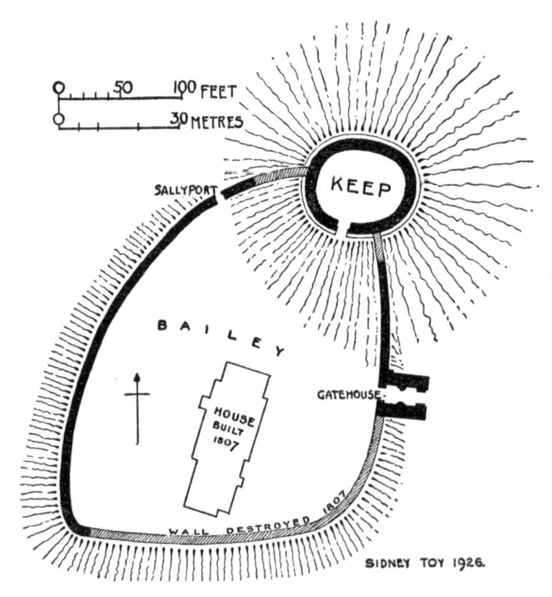

PLAN OF TREMATON CASTLE

the whole castle was surrounded by the wet ditch which still exists at that part of the bailey outside the town, but the portion at the foot of the mound inside the town has been filled in.

The keep is an irregular round shell with an average internal diameter of 70 ft.; the wall is 6 ft. 6 in. thick and 15 ft. high externally to the level of the wall walk. The present entrance doorway near the east curtain relates to the restoration carried out in the latter part of the thirteenth century. All the internal buildings of the keep have been destroyed. Two mural stairways rise to the wall walk and there is a latrine on the west side. The curtain from the bailey now runs up the mound to join the keep on two sides, but there are indications that the piece climbing the mound on the east is of later date than that on the west. The thin walls of the latrine projecting out from the keep near the west wall form a conspicuously vulnerable point, indicative of later work, and although its traces have been obliterated this may be the site of the original entrance. When the present entrance, near the east curtain, was built the mural stairway near it was partially blocked and a triangular projection was built on the outer face of the keep to receive the end of the east curtain, which would otherwise abut at an acute angle.

Trematon castle is mentioned in Domesday.[12] It consists of a mound crowned by an ovoid shell keep, and a bailey surrounded by a curtain wall. Here the curtain on both sides runs up the mound to join the keep. The buildings which were ranged round the internal face of the shell have been destroyed, though traces of them are still to be seen.

Tamworth castle was held after the Norman Conquest by Robert le Despenser and in whatever condition he received it there is no doubt he was largely responsible for its present form. The lower part of the wall of the keep and the causeway thrown across the ditch and leading up to it doubtless date from the eleventh century; the upper part of the keep was either rebuilt or refaced later. The keep is a polygonal shell, 7 ft. thick above a battered plinth, 25 ft. high to the wall walk, and 106 ft. internal diameter. A square tower near the entrance gateway projects slightly outside but mainly inside the shell. As at Launceston and Totnes, there are two mural stairways to the wall walk; but here, owing to later alterations, both are partially blocked. There is a deep well within the keep and latrines are formed near the stairways (pp. 48b, 52).

At present there is very little trace of the original buildings within the shell. Tamworth Castle has enjoyed almost continuous occupation from the time it was built to the present day, and the living quarters have been kept in line with advancing customs. The present structures include a fine hall, living rooms, and offices, of

[12] D. B. Cornwall, *Terra Comitis Moritonensis.*

two and three storeys; they date principally from the fifteenth to the seventeenth century. The causeway which carries the approach road across the ditch is 8 ft. thick and is built of herringbone masonry.

In herringbone masonry the material composing each course, flat stones or brick, is not laid horizontally but tilted up about 45 degrees. Bond is obtained by tilting the stones in each succeeding course in the reverse direction to that below it; two courses of such work present much the appearance of a herring bone. Sometimes the bond is strengthened by the introduction of a horizontal course between the herringbone work, as in the causeway at Tam-

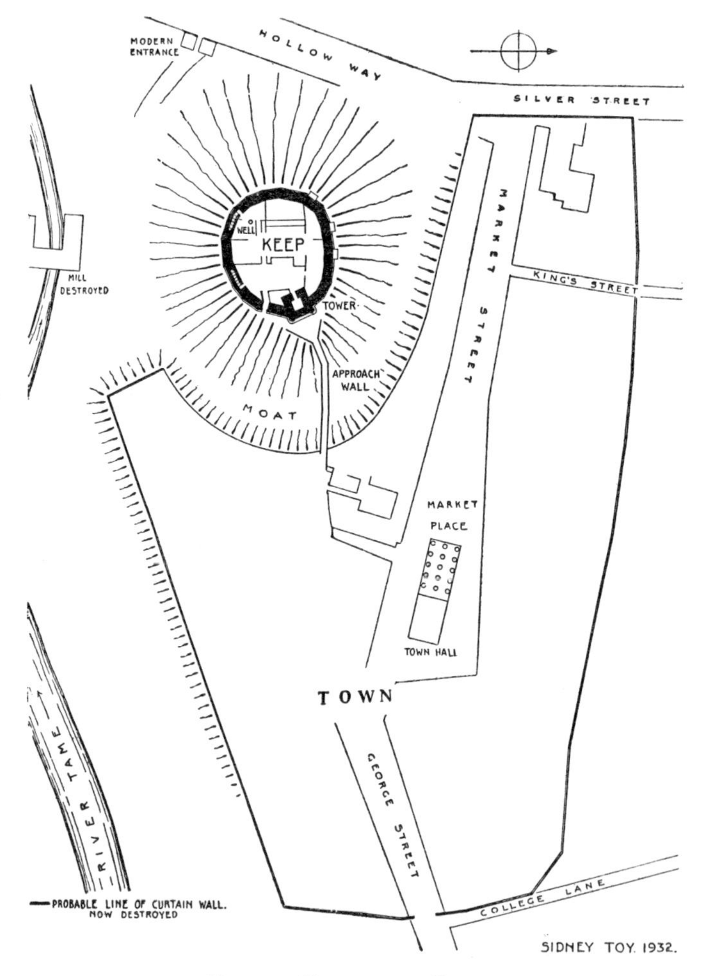

PLAN OF TAMWORTH CASTLE

worth. This method of construction does not belong to any particular period. It was used by the Romans, the Saxons, and the Normans; it was used in Switzerland in thirteenth-century work. Even during the last hundred years it has been employed by local workmen and with suitable material in places so far remote from each other as the coasts of Cornwall and the shores of the Bosporus. It is sometimes associated with ordinary masonry. In the cross wall of the keep at Colchester while the lower part of the wall is built of courses of stones laid flat the upper part is entirely of herringbone work (p. 48b). There is therefore no reason to suppose that the causeway at Tamworth is of any earlier date than the keep to which it leads.

Berkhamsted castle, Herts., was held in the eleventh century by Robert de Mortain and was possibly built by him. It consists of a mound with shell keep and a bailey stretching southward from the mound; a wet ditch passing round the whole castle and between the mound and the bailey. Here there is a second ditch carried round the castle outside the first and having bastion-like projections on the outer bank. The outer ditch is doubtless a later defence and the projections, which appear to be of one work with the outer bank and not additions to it, were made for attack on the enemy's

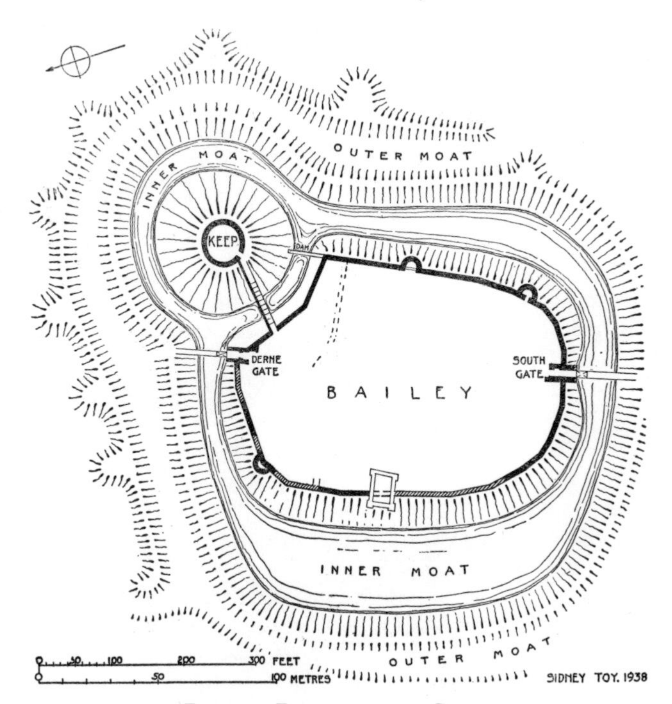

Plan of Berkhamsted Castle

flank in the event of an assault. The walls and buildings of the bailey are in a very ruinous condition and the curtain is stripped of its facing on both sides. But even in this bare condition the wall still stands up starkly in places to the height of the wall walk, some 15 ft. above the ground.

The keep, of which the base of the wall only remains, is slightly ovoid; its foundations are doubtless carried down to the chalk bed of the hill-side on which the castle is built. A stone causeway carrying the flight of steps of approach from the bailey runs across the ditch and up the mound to the keep. There was no other wall as suggested in the " official " guide. The east curtain of the bailey is turned back along the counterscarp opposite the mound and the short wall in line with the east curtain is simply a dam across the ditch with no continuation up the mound to the keep. Within the keep there is a well and there are traces of a fireplace and a stairway.

It is interesting to observe that at Windsor, Launceston, Tamworth, and Berkhamsted, among other examples, there was only one wall up the mound from the bailey to the keep, the passageway being either upon the wall or against its inside face. This appears to have been the earlier plan. The second wall, as at Trematon, Tickhill, and Totnes, indicates either a slightly later date for the whole work or an addition to an already existing castle.

Warwick castle was fortified by William the First, as stated by Ordericus,[13] but there is no proof that the mound did not exist before that time; the four houses destroyed by William when laying out the castle probably stood in the area which was now to be the bailey. Nor is there any evidence, as claimed by E. A. Armitage, in the expenditure of a small sum in 1173 for a *breteschie* that the keep of that date was of wood. The more general application of the word *bretesch* is to hoarding and most probably this is the meaning here. Hoarding, a most ancient form of defence, was in use in England in the latter part of the twelfth century, as at Norwich in 1187 and Winchester in 1193.

The castle consists of a high mound, which carries the fragmentary remains of a shell keep, and an oblong bailey extending eastward from the mound. It is defended on the south by the River Avon and on all the other sides by a wide and deep moat. The keep projected largely outside the bailey and the remaining portion is made up of the three sides facing the bailey between the curtain walls.

Unfortunately, this fragment was so drastically remodelled in the latter part of the seventeenth century, when £20,000 were spent on works on the castle, that, perched on the summit of the mound, it assumes the aspect of a feature in " landscape garden-

[13] *Ordericus*, XI, 242.

ing" rather than that of a fortification. The walls were refaced, turrets built on the top of them, and a parapet built round the inside face of the keep instead of at the outer face. The entrance doorway was rebuilt, without defences and with a wide chamfer on the side against which the leaves of the door should rest when closed. But these remaining walls, clearly thought to be in too good a condition to be pulled down, were preserved and strengthened by building five buttresses against their outer faces. They indicate a shell keep of some eight or nine sides with an average internal width of 55 ft. As can be seen from a piece at one end the original thickness of the wall was 6 ft. 1 in., but at the time of the remodelling the three panels were thickened to 7 ft. In form and character, therefore, this keep is probably referable to the latter years of the eleventh century.

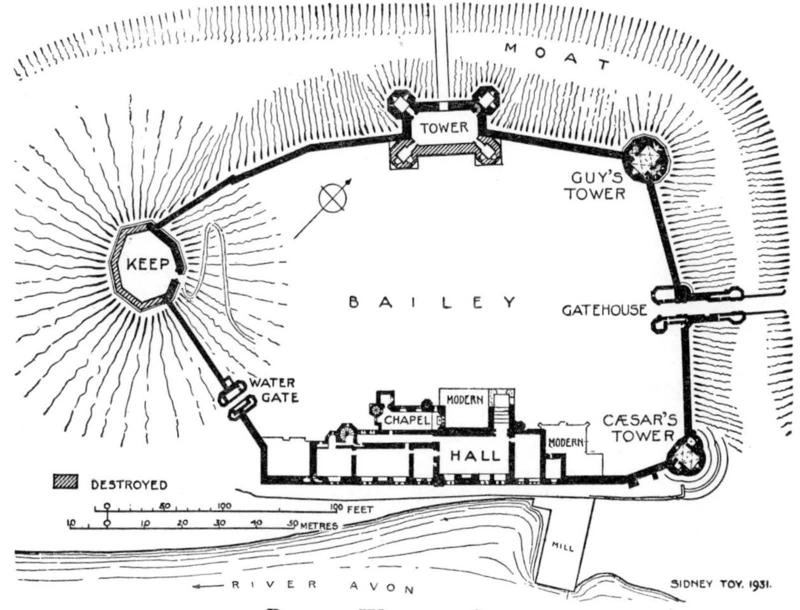

PLAN OF WARWICK CASTLE

The castle suffered considerably during the civil wars of the thirteenth century; but in the fourteenth century it was refortified, a strong wall, with a gatehouse in the centre and a powerful tower at either end, was built on the east side of the bailey and extensive living and service quarters were erected against the curtain overlooking the river. In the fifteenth century a large tower with corner turrets was added near the middle of the north curtain and in the sixteenth century a water gate to the river was built between the living quarters and the keep.

Durham castle was begun in 1072 as a strongly fortified residence for the Bishop of Durham and has been in episcopal occupation ever since. It stands beside the cathedral on an outcrop of sandstone rock overlooking and high above the River Wear. As seen from the opposite hill on the west these two magnificent structures form one of the finest architectural groups in Europe.

The castle has a triangular plan; the buildings of the bailey that are ranged along the edge of the cliff above the river forming the base and the mound the apex. Portions of the original buildings, dating from the latter part of the eleventh century, still remain. These parts include a chapel, built against the curtain at the north-east of the bailey; the part of the curtain running up the mound from the chapel to the keep; portions of the walling of the keep; and parts of the entrance gateway to the bailey. In the second half of the twelfth century Hugh Pudsey, Bishop of Durham, 1153 to 1195, erected palatial buildings on the north side of the bailey, and towards the end of the thirteenth that valiant and potent prelate, Antony Bek, rebuilt the Great Hall on the west. Many bishops of later periods contributed to the production of the existing group of remarkably fine buildings (pp. 48b, 57).

The keep forms an irregular octagon, supported by buttresses at seven of its angles and by the north curtain on the eighth. The mound is probably composed mainly of sandstone rock on which the castle stands and of which it is built; the foundations of the keep going down to the natural bed. From an entry in a fourteenth-century chronicle that Bishop Hatfield constructed a stronger tower within the castle for the greater protection of the city, the inference has been that he rebuilt the keep.[14] But in the same entry occurs the definite statement that Hatfield also rebuilt, *de novo construxit*, the bishop's hall and the constable's hall, which we know was not the case. What was done to the keep in the fourteenth century probably included the gutting and remodelling of the interior, and perhaps the repair of the battlements. The outer wall of the keep was clearly not rebuilt in the fourteenth century. As shown on the drawing by the Bros. Buck, 1728, the building had the same form as at present. It is a shell keep similar to that at Lincoln, unquestionably of Norman construction, and bearing no sort of resemblance to the powerful keeps being raised in the fourteenth century, as at Dudley and Warkworth.

In a rhapsody, written about 1145, Laurence of Durham describes the keep of that period as having an outer wall and internal timber buildings rising high above the wall.[15] Owing to a mistranslation *Intus enim cubitis tribus altius area surgit* has been held to refer to the three terraces of the mound and the wall to have

[14] Dunelm, Script. Tres., Surtees Soc., Vol. 9.
[15] Surtees Soc., Vol LXX.

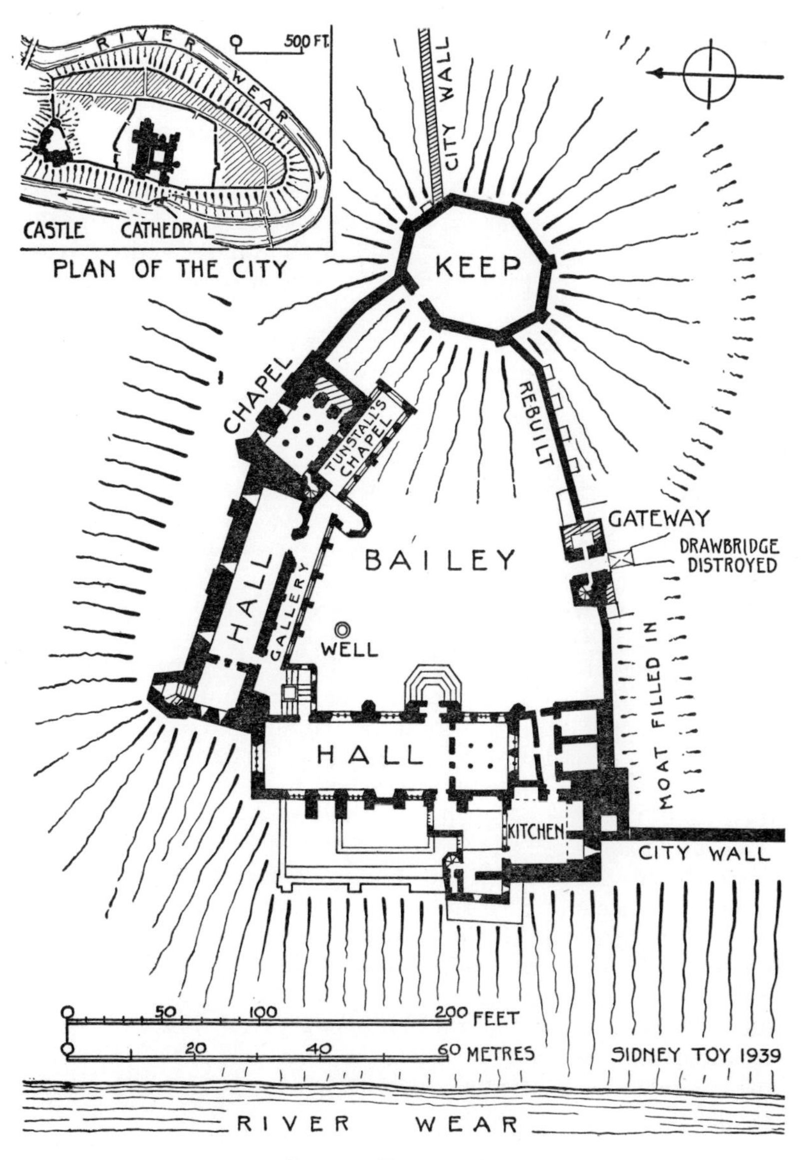

PLAN OF DURHAM CASTLE

been at the foot of the mound and not on its summit. But, apart from the fact that the three terraces on the mound were laid out by Bishop Cosin in 1670, what Laurence does say is that the ground level inside the keep was three cubits higher than that outside. He says of the wall of the keep that it was embellished by noble projections, each projection dying into the grim wall; an effusive but fairly accurate description of the buttresses with their off-sets and weathering gradually, as they rise, falling back to the general face of the wall.

On its conversion to the purposes of Durham University in 1838–40 the keep was again gutted, its interior remodelled on a new design and the outer wall with its buttresses subjected to drastic repair and reconstruction. So extensive were these operations that the keep is now often referred to as having been rebuilt completely in 1840. But on a close examination of the outer wall of the keep, made recently, the author found that while the upper part of the wall had been rebuilt entirely, the lower part, though extensively repaired, had not been rebuilt. It is not possible to say how much of the old core exists, but here and there are large patches of the original facing, having stones deeply pitted with weatherworn holes and others, probably bonders, set upright against the quarry bed. The facing of the north curtain wall of Barnard castle, by common consent Norman work, is built in precisely the same manner, with the same kind of stone, and shows the same weatherworn effects as the old facing of this keep.

On some sides of the keep are straight joints, where new masonry, differently coursed, abuts against the old work; a fact which in itself is clear evidence of repair as distinct from rebuilding. Throughout all its vicissitudes, and despite its present pseudo-gothic appearance, this structure still retains the form and much of the substance of the Norman shell keep, built about 1100.

Tickhill, Castle Acre, and Tonbridge, are among other examples of mound-and-bailey castles built in the eleventh century and still retaining fragments of their shell keeps. Tickhill has a magnificent mound, 75 ft. high, and Castle Acre an unusually large keep, 160 ft. diameter, and most formidable ramparts.

Tonbridge castle was held in 1088 by Bishop Odo and his confederates against the forces of William Rufus.[16] The ovoid shell keep on the mound is now very ruinous, standing only about 8 ft. above the mound outside; the ground inside the keep is 4 ft. above that outside. The wall is so ruinous that it is now difficult to determine its exact original thickness; but it was unusually thin, being only from 4 ft. to 5 ft. thick above the plinth; two substantial buttresses were built against its south-east face at a much later period. The keep appears to have been built in the eleventh century,

16 *A.S.C.* and *Florence of Worcester*, 1088.

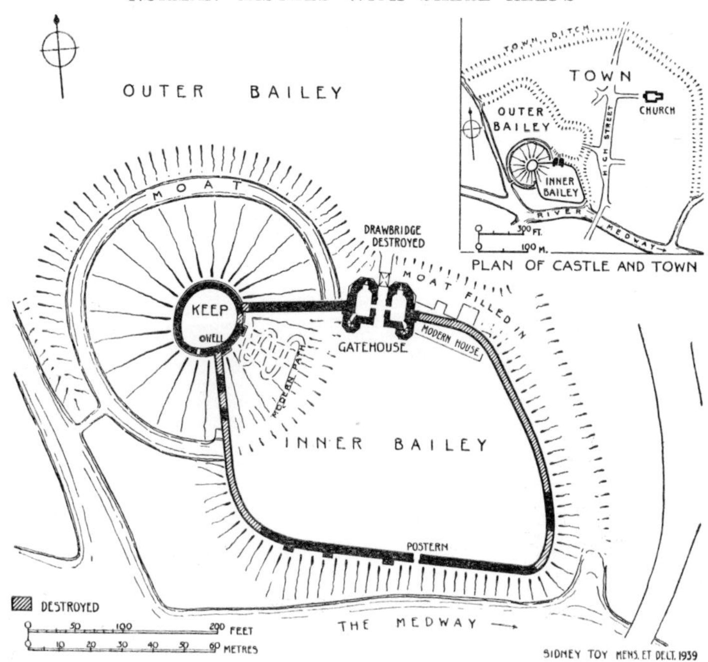

TONBRIDGE CASTLE

but refaced and the plinth added in the latter part of the twelfth century. Within the keep, on the south side there is a well and in the centre a deep excavation exposing the foundation, on the natural soil, of what was probably the central support of the internal buildings (pp. 222b, 243).

The curtain wall of the bailey has a deep battered plinth, is 9 ft. thick immediately above the plinth and rises in off-sets both within and without. It was built about 1180, probably in place of a less substantial structure. Two walls were then carried up the mound to the keep but there are indications that originally there was only one such wall, that in line with the gatehouse. The fine gatehouse, built about 1300, will be referred to later.

At York William the First built two mound-and-bailey castles, which stood facing each other across the Ouse on the south side of the city. That on the right bank can still be traced; that on the left bank survives to the present day, with Clifford's Tower occupying the site of the original keep on the mound. Each of the castles at Lincoln, Lewes, and Deganwy has two mounds.

Lincoln castle stands within and on the west side of the Roman city, the Roman wall forming the west enclosure of its large rectangular bailey. It was built in the latter part of the eleventh century and has one gateway on the east, another on the west and a postern at the south-east. On the south of the bailey there are two mounds. The larger mound interrupts the line of the south curtain wall, and the polygonal shell keep by which it is surmounted stands half within and half without the bailey. The other mound supports a square tower, called the observatory tower, which is vaulted in two storeys, was probably built about 1100 and enlarged in the fourteenth century. A drum tower was added at the north-east corner of the bailey in the thirteenth century.

The keep is a large multangular shell, 8 ft. thick and 20 ft. high to the wall walk; it was built about 1080. It has a plinth and a shallow buttress rising from the plinth at each angle. The entrance gateway is at a point well away from the curtain wall and is approached from the bailey by a straight flight of steps up the mound. A postern on the outer face, outside the bailey, leads directly to the city.

At Lewes the mounds are at each end of a long oval bailey. The castle was in existence at the time of William the First and probably in its original state the keep was on the north mound, though all buildings on that mound have disappeared long since. But the powerful shell keep on the south mound, a large portion of which still remains, must have been begun soon after the foundation of the castle, for it dates from about 1080, and the curtain wall of the bailey, the original part of the outer gateway and the wall tower between the gateway and the keep are all of the same period. The tall barbican extending in front of the old gateway was added in the fourteenth century (p. 43).

The keep had an ovoid shell, 7 ft. thick above a deeply battered plinth, and 19 ft. high from the courtyard to the wall walk; it rises with one external offset. The entrance gateway was defended by a square tower of which only fragments of foundations remain; the gateway has been destroyed. In the thirteenth century two towers, rising from the ground outside to a point high above the parapet, were built against the outer face.

Deganwy castle is situated on high ground overlooking the mouth of the River Conway; its two mounds are natural hillocks. The castle was fortified and held for William Rufus in 1088 by Robert de Rhuddlan.[17] It was rebuilt by the Earl of Chester in 1211 and repaired by Henry the Third in 1245. In 1263 it was destroyed by Llewelyn ap Griffith and was never restored. To-day, after centuries of use as a quarry for building material, but few and scattered fragments remain of what was for many years one of the most powerful castles in North Wales.

Arundel, Cardiff, Restormel, Rothesay, Farnham, and Berkeley are all examples of shell keeps built in the first part of or about the middle of the twelfth century. Some castles, as Alnwick and

[17] *Ordericus,* Bk. XI.

Wigmore, have citadels so extensive as to become rather inner wards than keeps.

Arundel castle has a plan similar to that of Windsor, a high mound with a shell keep in the middle of the castle and two long and relatively narrow baileys extending in opposite directions from the mound. Here it is probable that both baileys, called the upper and lower wards, were fortified at the same time. For, apart from the fact that there is no difference in character between the curtains, the south ward, which contains the remains of the most ancient buildings of the castle, is on lower ground than the other. The entrance to the keep, like that at Lincoln, is placed well away from the curtain. During the latter end of the eleventh century Arundel was held by Robert de Belesme. Robert probably began the keep, which bears considerable resemblance to his keep at Gisors in Normandy, and Henry the First completed it (p. 43).

The mound is 70 ft. high and was defended all round by a ditch. The keep is an ovoid shell, 9 ft. thick and complete up to and including the parapet; it has a battered plinth and is strengthened at intervals by wide pilaster buttresses. Internally it measures 60 ft. by 54 ft. Projecting from the south side, at the junction of the keep with the curtain, there is a small square tower which, though slightly later in date than the keep, appears to have been included in the original design. This building, called the Well tower, contains a chapel and a well and, like those in similar positions at Tamworth and Lewes, defended the entrance to the keep. The original entrance to the keep was by a wide round-headed doorway of three orders, enriched with chevron and other mouldings. It is placed facing down the lower ward at a point considerably east of the curtain wall. In the thirteenth century this gateway was blocked and a new entry to the keep was formed, which was protected by a forebuilding and approached by a flight of steps up from the wall walk on the curtain.

Internally the keep is gutted but corbels on the wall indicate the positions of the beams and trusses of the internal buildings. These structures were of timber; they were of two storeys and must have been lighted from windows in an open courtyard for there are no windows in the shell wall. Access to the wall walk was probably by internal stairways, now removed; the existing spiral stairway formed in the thickness of the wall is not original. The keep has been extensively repaired.

Incorporated in the palatial modern buildings of the lower ward are remains of twelfth-century work, including two windows and a doorway. The principal gateway into the castle enters the south, or lower, ward; it was built in the early part of the twelfth century, is defended by a portcullis and a two-leaved door, and surmounted by a tower. In the thirteenth century a strong barbican was added, flanked at the outer end by a tower on either side and defended by a drawbridge, a portcullis, and a two-leaved door. A gateway leading from the town to the upper ward was also built at this latter period.

Cardiff castle was built within and on the west side of the Roman fort, the mound occupying the north-west corner of the fort and the bailey stretching southward from it. On the mound there is a polygonal shell keep which was built during the first part of the twelfth century. It is twelve-sided; its wall is 9 ft. thick and 30 ft. high and has no buttresses. The entrance is on the south, towards the bailey, and is now approached through the lower storey of a semi-octagonal tower which was built against the keep in the fifteenth century; the passage being protected by a portcullis. Within the keep are the remains of a large fireplace and a sink. Palatial modern buildings on the west side of the bailey incorporate mediaeval domestic quarters.

At Restormel, Cornwall, the defences and buildings of the bailey, which stood to the west of the keep, have disappeared but the shell keep remains up to and including the parapet. The keep stands on a hill and is founded on natural soil, but there is no mound other than that formed by the soil thrown up against its wall from the wide and deep ditch by which it is surrounded. It is circular with an internal diameter of 109 ft.; its wall is 8 ft. 6 in. thick, above the plinth, and 26 ft. high from the courtyard to the wall walk. It

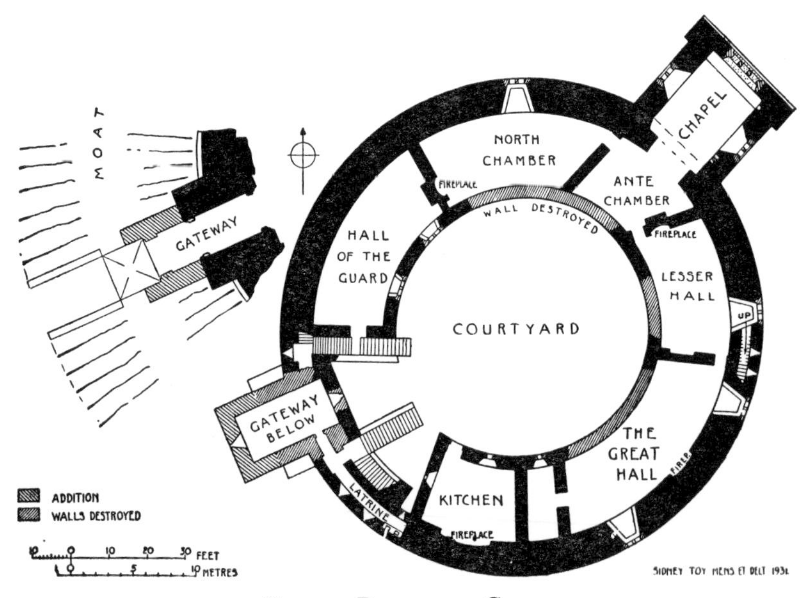

PLAN OF RESTORMEL CASTLE

was probably built early in the twelfth century and as first constructed consisted of the shell wall, with an entrance gateway on the south-west, and a square tower projecting out from the wall at the north-east. The tower defended the approach up the hill from the River Fowey. There is a well on the east side of the courtyard.

Considerable alterations were made in the thirteenth century. The internal buildings were remodelled with living, domestic, and military quarters, two storeys high, disposed round a circular courtyard. A chapel was formed in the upper storey of the tower, the east and west walls of the tower being thinned down on the inside for this purpose, and a gatehouse was built at the entrance to the castle. The gateway was defended by a portcullis. The Black Prince held his court twice at Restormel, once in 1354 and again in 1362, spending Christmas there at the latter period. Great preparations were made for these visits and repairs and alterations effected.[18] This was probably the most brilliant period in the history of the castle but from that time it was allowed to fall into gradual decay.

Rothesay castle on the Isle of Bute consists essentially of a shell keep similar in all respects to those described above, but here there is no other bailey than that enclosed within the shell itself; the towers built against the keep, and the gatehouse are later additions. In its original state, without the wall towers, this castle was probably built about 1150. One could only accept the later dates often assigned to it on the assumption, for which there is no evidence, that its builder was unfamiliar with the developments of his day and erected a shell keep when his neighbours were building the castles of Bothwell and Dirleton on far more advanced lines. The castle is surrounded by a wide and deep moat with a berm between the moat and the wall (pp. 64, 66a).

The shell is ovoid, is 9 ft. thick above a battered plinth, and was originally 20 ft. high to the level of the wall walk; it measures internally 160 ft. by 134 ft. The original entrance, though restricted in width, is still preserved and there is a postern, now blocked, on the west. Shortly after the siege of 1230, during which the wall was breached and considerable damage done to the castle generally, the defences were strengthened by the erection of four towers, placed at equal distances apart, against the outer face of the shell. That these towers were additions, not included in the structure of the original design of the castle, is clear from the fact that behind them the shell wall is continuous, both in character and contour, with its faces between the towers. As seen from the points in the shell which were occupied by the destroyed towers and are now exposed, two long grooves were dug out of the face of the shell at each point to form toothing for the tower to be built against it.

[18] Register of Edward the Black Prince, Pt. II, 9, 60, 128, 168, 185, 198.

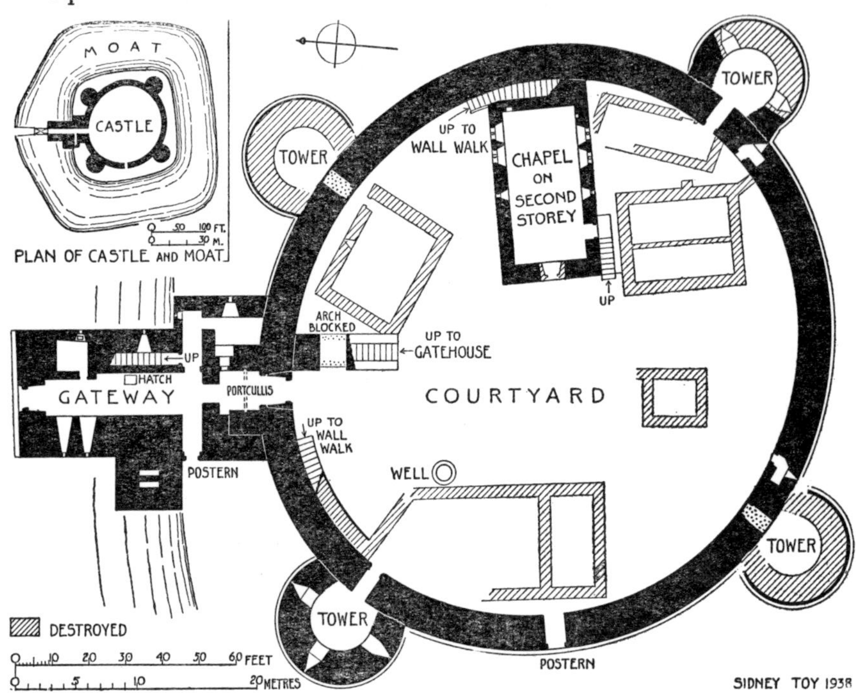

PLAN OF ROTHESAY CASTLE

Considerable alterations were made in the latter years of the fifteenth century. The walls of the castle were then raised 10 ft. all round and a gatehouse, providing all residential amenities, was built out in front of the entrance. In raising the castle wall the old wall walk between the northern towers was retained and roofed over as a mural passage, to provide access to the upper floors of those towers and the gatehouse and to some structure it was proposed to erect within the castle. Between the gatehouse and the north-west tower the old, and lower, parapet, with its embrasures filled in, and the hoarding beam-holes below can be seen on the outer face of the shell. Both the old postern in the shell and another on the west side of the gatehouse open on to the berm between the castle and the moat.

Within the castle are the remains of stone buildings arranged in a somewhat haphazard manner; the principal of those standing above the bases of the walls being a two-storey structure with a chapel on the upper storey. Two stairways, built against and running concentric with the inner face of the wall, led to the old wall walk, while a later stairway rises straight up to the rooms of the gatehouse. When the gatehouse was built a dovecot was formed in the upper part of the north-west tower.

Farnham castle was built in 1140 by Henry de Blois, Bishop of Winchester, brother of King Stephen. As first constructed the castle consisted of the present shell keep and the triangular bailey stretching southward from it; the outer bailey with its towers and gatehouse was added in the fourteenth century. The mound is a natural hillock, deeply scarped all round to form high vertical faces against which the walls of the keep are built. Therefore the outer face of the keep rises up from the courtyard of the bailey but the ground level inside is that of the summit of the mound. Constructed in this manner, while the battlements are easily accessible from within, the keep presents to the exterior a formidable wall of great height and strength, the breach of which would lead to but small advantage. A wide and deep moat, cutting through the hill at the back, is carried all round the keep (p. 66a).

The keep is a large polygonal shell with buttresses at each angle, every third buttress being particularly wide and massive; it is 175 ft. diameter internally. The gateway is on the south-east and is approached by a narrow causeway, which now rises up by flights of steps from the courtyard but formerly led across from upper rooms in the east range of the bailey buildings. The gateway was defended by a drawbridge over the moat, a machicolation, a portcullis, and a two-leaved door, and there is a guardroom on the left side of the passage within. About 1520 Bishop Fox rebuilt the upper part of the gatehouse in brickwork and some details of this period remain, including a window and two fireplaces. The battlements of the keep have been destroyed and only fragments remain of its internal stone buildings; there is a series of latrines on the north-east side.

The buildings of the bailey are complete on all sides and, although much remodelling has been done from time to time, still retain a considerable amount of original work. The Great hall on the south was originally divided into a nave and two aisles, the arcades on either side being of oak; the high-pitched roof was probably continuous over both nave and aisles. On the south are four original round-headed windows, now blocked flush with the wall. About 1670 the hall was remodelled; the north wall was heightened and large windows opened in it, the arcade on the north was removed and that on the south partly destroyed and partly buried in a new wall built in line with it. One post, complete with its scalloped capital, can still be seen, and in 1880 two others were found buried in the wall.

The kitchen, west of the hall, was remodelled in the thirteenth century and wide fireplaces were inserted in the fourteenth century. The chapel at the south-west corner of the courtyard was built about 1140. About 1540 Bishop Fox built a large and tall entrance tower on the south side of the castle; it is of red brick, decorated with diaper work of black brick and flanked by turrets on either side. The residential quarters on the east side of the bailey were remodelled in the seventeenth century.

Carisbrooke Castle, Isle of Wight, stands on the site of a Roman Camp vestiges of which still remain. The castle consists of a shell-keep, standing on a high mound, and a large rectangular bailey. The keep and the curtain wall round the bailey were built about the middle of the twelfth century. The keep, roughly rectangular, measures internally 58 ft. by 45 ft.; its wall was originally much higher than at present, the upper parts having been destroyed; it is approached by long flights of steps which ascend the mound against the curtain wall of the bailey, and is entered through a gateway on the west which was rebuilt in the fourteenth century. The existing internal buildings of the keep, which include a well 160 ft. deep, date principally from the sixteenth century though the latrine projecting out from east wall was built in the thirteenth century.

The bailey is entered from the west through an imposing gateway of two periods; the inner half dating from the thirteenth century and the outer half, with its flanking towers, from the fourteenth century. The buildings of the bailey are of various periods from the twelfth to the sixteenth centuries and include the great hall which juts out into the bailey from the north, with the domestic offices built against the wall on the north and the residential quarters at the far end, well into the bailey, on the south. A square well-house, just south of these quarters, contains a large wooden wheel which was perhaps originally a "tread wheel"; the bucket and rope passing over the wheel is now drawn up by a donkey. The chapel of St. Nicholas on the west of the bailey was built in 1905 on the site of a mediaeval chapel.

In the latter part of the reign of Elizabeth, 1587–1601, the whole castle including what appears to have been an eastern bailey was enclosed by a fortification built for defence by artillery, with bulwarks at strategic points.

Berkeley Castle is described in Appendix A, page 279.

Restormel Castle. The Keep from the West.

Farnham Castle. The Keep from the South.

Rothesay Castle from the South-West

or three floors, with a drawing place at each floor. Latrines, approached through mural passages with one or two turnings, were formed in the outer walls.

Roofs constructed of timber and covered, as they often were, with shingles, were always vulnerable points of attack by torches and other incendiary missiles. As a protection against such attacks the walls of the keeps were carried up on all sides high above the roof line so as to form a screen behind which the roofs were effectively masked and shielded.

The Tower of London was built about 1080 within the city and at the south-east corner of the Roman walls. As first constructed the castle consisted of the White Tower and a bailey, later called the inner bailey, between the tower and the Thames. The walls of this bailey were built about 1097 when William Rufus made a levy in many parts of the country for that purpose. The middle bailey appears to have been formed about 1190 when its south wall and the belltower were built, but it was largely rebuilt in the thirteenth century. The outer bailey, forming a wide terrace round the castle, the outer moat, the three outer gates, in line one behind the other, and the semi-circular barbican were all works carried out by Edward the First about 1300 (pp. 66b, 69).

The White Tower was one of the earliest rectangular keeps to be built in this country, as it is now one of the finest and best preserved structures of its kind in Europe. It rises to the height of 90 ft. to the top of the parapet and has a turret at each corner extending high above that level. There is an apsidal projection at the south-east corner and a large circular turret at the north-east corner. The first forms the east end of the chapel and its crypt and subcrypt, and the turret contains a spiral stairway running from the base to the battlements. The walls are built of ragstone rubble with ashlar dressings; they vary from 12 ft. to 15 ft. thick at the base and are supported by pilaster buttresses at the corners and at intervals along the sides. A cross wall running north and south and carried up the full height of the tower divides the interior into two unequal parts at each storey. The western part is the greater and is the same size in all storeys. The eastern part is subdivided in all storeys; the southern section being occupied by the chapel of St. John and its undercrofts. Originally the keep was of three storeys only, but the two large halls of the third storey, corresponding with the chapel and its triforium, were, at a later period, subdivided into two storeys by the insertion of a floor at the level of the mural gallery.

The entrance was at the west end of the south wall at second storey level; it was reached through a forebuilding, long since destroyed, and admitted directly into a hall 92 ft. long by 37 ft. wide; it is now blocked. The hall was lighted by many windows, now

Restormel Castle. The Keep from the West.

Farnham Castle. The Keep from the South.

Rothesay Castle from the South-West

Tower of London from the Thames.

CHAPTER FIVE

NORMAN CASTLES WITH RECTANGULAR KEEPS

DURING the same period that castles having keeps of shell type were being built, others with rectangular keeps were raised in various places throughout the country; the first of them being built within the Roman walls of London, Colchester, Canterbury, and Pevensey. There was nothing new either in design or purpose in rectangular keeps; such structures were built by the Romans, by the Byzantines in the sixth century, and by the French at the end of the tenth century.

These keeps are strong tower-like structures with thick walls and wide buttresses of low projection. Normally they were built on the firm ground of the bailey, but at Lydford the keep stands on a mound and at Clun it is built on the slope of a mound, the outer wall rising up from the ditch. They are of from two to four storeys and are generally divided internally by a partition wall. The entrance doorway is usually on the second storey and is reached by a stairway built against the side of the keep, the stairway often being contained in and protected by a forebuilding. At Newcastle and Dover the entrance was on the third storey. From the entrance floor access to the lower and upper storeys and the battlements is obtained by straight or spiral stairways.

The principal, or great, hall was generally on the second or third storey and often had a mural gallery running round its walls at a level high above the floor. Mural chambers open off the hall and other large apartments. Fireplaces were formed in one of the outer walls. There was generally one and, in later keeps, sometimes two chapels, formed either in the main or in the forebuilding. In many keeps, as at Castle Rising, Newcastle, and Dover there is a postern, providing means both of making a surprise attack on the enemy and of effecting escape in the event of the main entrance being carried. The well was often of great depth and lined with stone throughout its upper portion; at Newcastle this steining is continued to the bottom. The well pipe was often carried up through two or three floors, with a drawing place at each floor. Latrines, approached through mural passages with one or two turnings, were formed in the outer walls.

Roofs constructed of timber and covered, as they often were, with shingles, were always vulnerable points of attack by torches and other incendiary missiles. As a protection against such attacks the walls of the keeps were carried up on all sides high above the roof line so as to form a screen behind which the roofs were effectively masked and shielded.

The Tower of London was built about 1080 within the city and at the south-east corner of the Roman walls. As first constructed the castle consisted of the White Tower and a bailey, later called the inner bailey, between the tower and the Thames. The walls of this bailey were built about 1097 when William Rufus made a levy in many parts of the country for that purpose. The middle bailey appears to have been formed about 1190 when its south wall and the belltower were built, but it was largely rebuilt in the thirteenth century. The outer bailey, forming a wide terrace round the castle, the outer moat, the three outer gates, in line one behind the other, and the semi-circular barbican were all works carried out by Edward the First about 1300 (pp. 66b, 69).

The White Tower was one of the earliest rectangular keeps to be built in this country, as it is now one of the finest and best preserved structures of its kind in Europe. It rises to the height of 90 ft. to the top of the parapet and has a turret at each corner extending high above that level. There is an apsidal projection at the south-east corner and a large circular turret at the north-east corner. The first forms the east end of the chapel and its crypt and subcrypt, and the turret contains a spiral stairway running from the base to the battlements. The walls are built of ragstone rubble with ashlar dressings; they vary from 12 ft. to 15 ft. thick at the base and are supported by pilaster buttresses at the corners and at intervals along the sides. A cross wall running north and south and carried up the full height of the tower divides the interior into two unequal parts at each storey. The western part is the greater and is the same size in all storeys. The eastern part is subdivided in all storeys; the southern section being occupied by the chapel of St. John and its undercrofts. Originally the keep was of three storeys only, but the two large halls of the third storey, corresponding with the chapel and its triforium, were, at a later period, subdivided into two storeys by the insertion of a floor at the level of the mural gallery.

The entrance was at the west end of the south wall at second storey level; it was reached through a forebuilding, long since destroyed, and admitted directly into a hall 92 ft. long by 37 ft. wide; it is now blocked. The hall was lighted by many windows, now

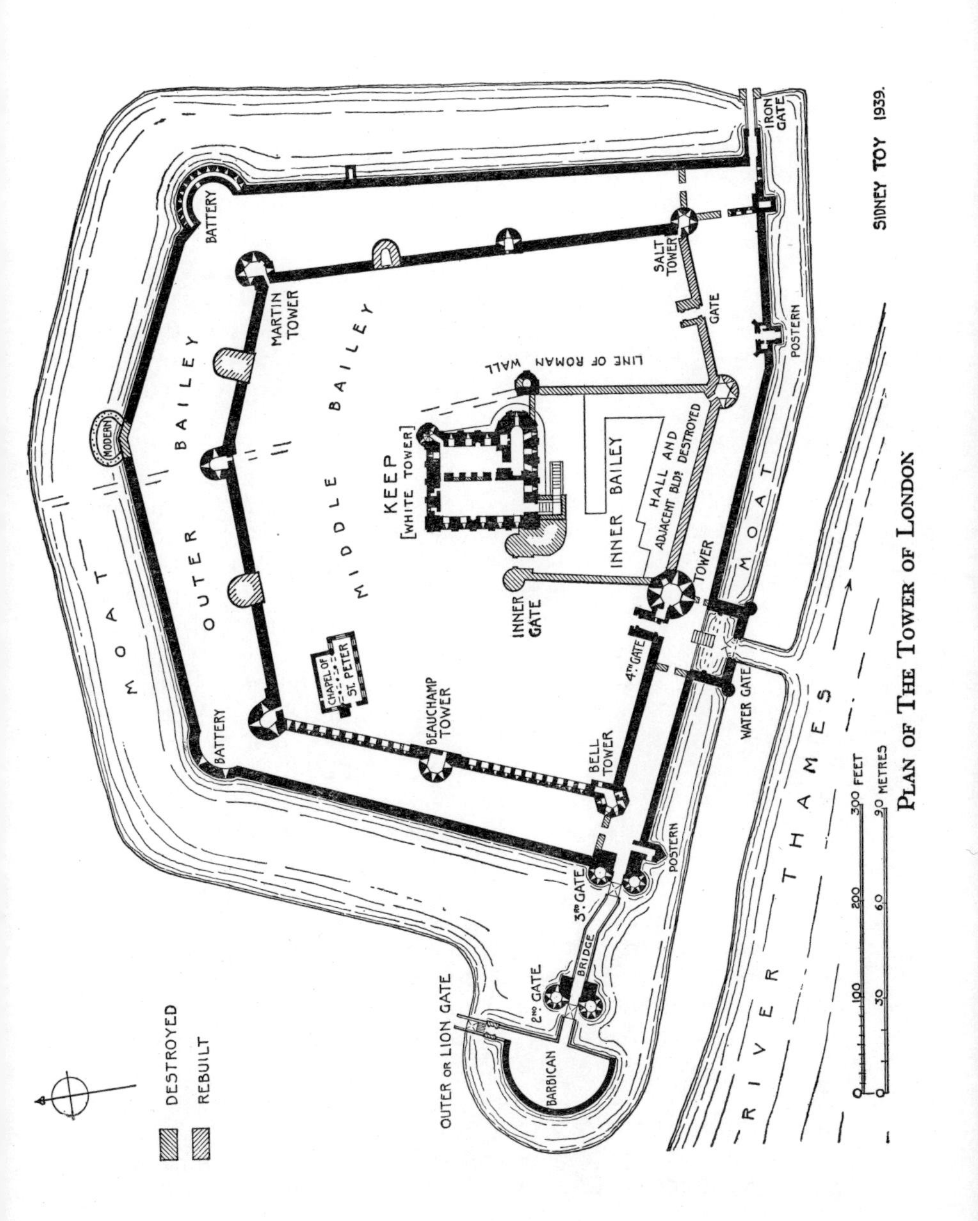

PLAN OF THE TOWER OF LONDON

considerably widened; there is a fireplace near the middle of the west wall and there were two latrines in the north wall. A doorway through the partition wall leads to a smaller but still spacious hall, with a fireplace, and, through the hall, to the crypt of the chapel. A wide spiral stairway at the north-east corner leads to the basement and to the upper floors and the battlements. The basement is lighted by small windows, placed high on the outside face of the walls and having their internal openings deflected downwards to a level near the ceiling; there is a well in the largest room.

On the third storey are the great hall, the great chamber, and the chapel. A mural gallery, 16 ft. above the floor, runs all round the outer walls and opens on to the triforium of the chapel. The great hall occupies the western portion of the storey; there is a latrine at the north-west corner but there is no fireplace. Two spiral stairways, one in each of the turrets flanking the west wall, lead up to the battlements, thus providing ample and direct access to the fighting lines from the great hall. In the great chamber there are two latrines in the north wall and a fireplace in the east wall. The flues from all the fireplaces in the tower after passing up a short distance within the wall terminate in loopholes at the re-entering angles of the buttresses on the outside face. The chapel is a well designed structure with nave, aisles, apsidal chancel and ambulatory. The arcades are continuous round the apse and consist of circular pillars, with capitals of varied designs, and round arches. There are two tiers of windows, one opening to the south aisle and the ambulatory and the other to the triforium; the chapel is covered by a stone barrel vault.

Colchester castle was built near the centre of the town and had an inner bailey around the keep and an outer bailey extending to the town wall on the north; the defences of both baileys have been destroyed. The keep was built about 1080 upon Roman substructures and bears marked resemblance to the White Tower. It covers a much larger area and was designed on a more elaborate scale than the latter, but the principles of design and the disposition of parts are the same in both buildings. At present the keep stands to the height of the two lower storeys only; the third storey was never completed or has been destroyed (pp. 48b, 71, 80a).

There is no record of the existence of a third storey to this keep and there are strong indications that the original design was never fully carried out and that the design was altered when the building had reached its present height; it was probably found to have been conceived on too grandiose a scale. When little more than the existing height was attained the building appears to have been roofed over and its defences and internal apartments adapted to the limitations of a two-storey keep. The original entrance was by a doorway at the west end of the north wall at second storey level; it was approached by a flight of steps built against the north wall and defended from an arrow-loop, looking down the steps. But early in the twelfth century a new and relatively wide entrance doorway was opened out on the south side at first storey level, and it would appear that the upper floor was then replanned to contain the great hall, the great chamber and, what was to be the crypt, the chapel itself. All that exists of the third storey is the low base of its walls.

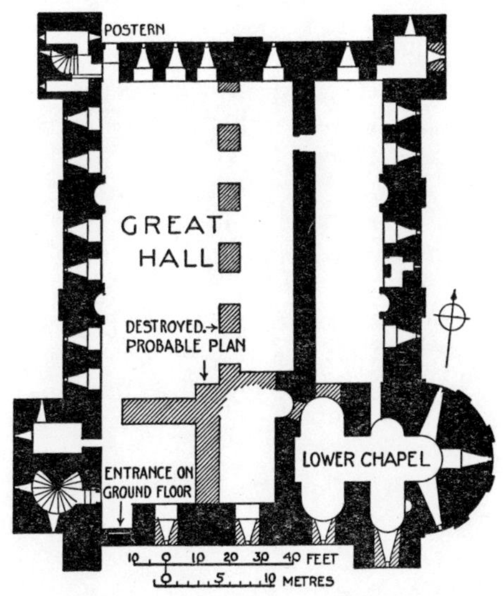

Colchester. Plan of The Keep, Second Storey

Towards the end of the seventeenth century and after standing roofless and derelict for a long period the keep was sold for its building materials. But the attempt to pull down such sturdy walls for such small-sized materials must have proved an unprofitable enterprise and was abandoned. There is no evidence of such extensive demolition as the destruction of the principal storey of so large a building would involve, and the damage wrought at this time was probably confined for the most part to the pulling down of the western cross wall and the internal rooms near the south doorway. The walls are built of rubble with lacing courses of Roman brick; they have freestone dressings to the height of the first storey and are strengthened at the corners by square turrets and at the sides by pilaster buttresses. The upper part of the remaining cross wall is of herringbone work.

The south doorway was formerly entered through a forebuilding, now destroyed; it is of two moulded orders, was defended by a portcullis, and gave entry to the lower storey. Near the entrance there is a well and the main stairway of the keep. The southern third of the building was occupied by the chapel and its substructure and rooms stretching westward from the chapel to the west wall; the remaining two-thirds was divided by two cross walls, running north and south, into three long apartments. Owing to the destruction of the western cross wall and the rooms at the south-west it is now somewhat difficult to determine the original disposition of the interior. But the great hall must have been the large apartment on the west side of the keep and the middle section was probably an aisle opening on to the hall by an arcade. The hall has two fireplaces, is lighted by many windows, here retaining their original size, and has a latrine and an additional stair to the battlements at the north-west corner. The great chamber on the east side of the keep has two fireplaces and a latrine; at the north end there is a doorway to a chamber in the corner turret and at the south end a doorway to the chapel.

The main stairway, formed in a rectangular turret at the south-west corner of the keep, is one of the largest and finest spiral stairways of its period. It has a large newel, is 16 ft. diameter internally and, like most of the spiral stairways of the time, the steps are composed of relatively small material, built upon a spiral vault.

Canterbury castle was built by William the First;[1] it is mentioned in Domesday and there is no doubt that the site referred to in that document is the one on which the existing keep stands. Dane John, at one time thought a possible site, was one of four mounds standing within a Roman cemetery in one of which a Roman cremation interment was found. The castle was built within and on the south side of the ancient city, the Roman wall forming one side of its rectangular bailey. In 1166 the bailey was extended eastward and as then completed had a gateway to the city on the north and one to the field, the Roman Worth Gate, on the south. All the defences of the bailey have been swept away and now the keep, which was at its south-west corner, stands isolated and in ruins (p. 73).

Since the first references to expenses for works on the castle occur in 1173–74, when the sum of £24. 6. 0. was spent on the keep and castle, and in the following year when £5. 11. 7. was spent on the keep, it has been suggested that the keep is referable to that period. But it has been assumed far too often that entries in the Chancery rolls of small sums for building works indicate major operations. Reference to such expenses before 1160 are rare and when at the time of Henry the Second they become more frequent and when, as here, the sums are small, they refer obviously to repairs or minor alterations and relate rather to old than to

[1] William of Poitiers, 208d.

new castles. The design and details of the keep at Canterbury show clearly that this structure is one of the earliest of its kind in England and was built about 1080.

The keep, measuring externally 88 ft. by 76 ft., covers less than half the area of the keep at Colchester; it was originally of three storeys but the third storey was pulled down early in the nineteenth century, when the structure was sold for its building materials. The cross walls were also taken down at this time and the work of demolition was only abandoned when it was found too costly an undertaking. The walls are built of rubble with Caen stone dressing, they are 9 ft. 2 in. thick, have deep battered plinths and are strengthened by buttresses at the corners and sides.

Internally each storey was divided into three main sections by two walls, running east and west, and the two lateral sections were subdivided by short walls running north and south. The entrance doorway has been destroyed but there are indications that it was at the west end of the central hall at second storey level and was

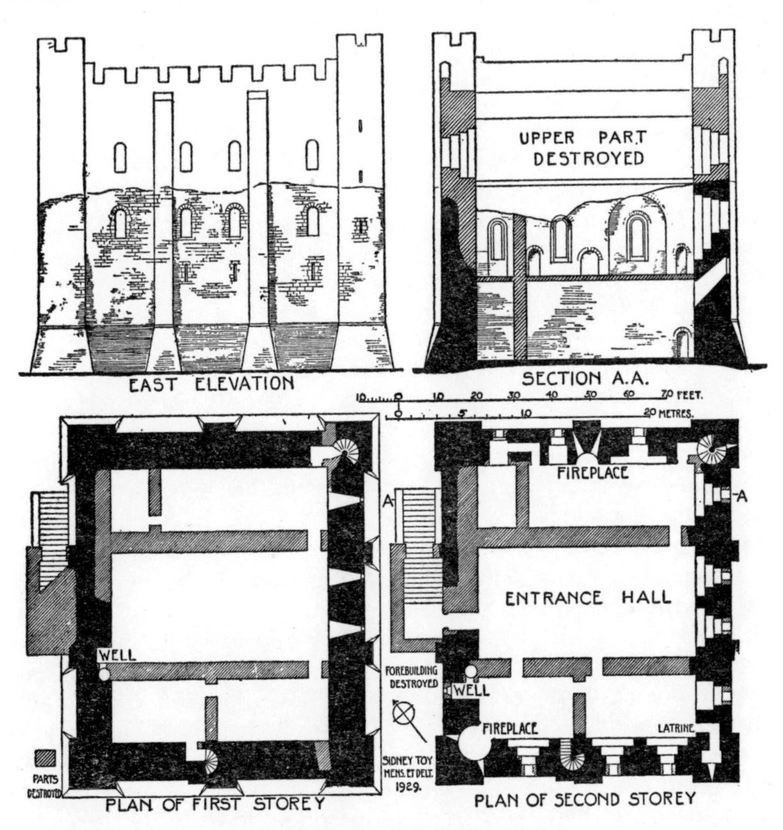

CANTERBURY CASTLE. THE KEEP

approached by a flight of steps, built against the west wall and protected by a forebuilding. Since the partition walls no longer exist the doorways and other features they contained can only be recovered from drawings made before their destruction. The large central hall of the second storey was lighted by two windows at the east end but apparently had no fireplaces. On the north of the hall there was a long room lighted by three windows and having a round backed fireplace with flues passing through the wall to the outside face. A small chamber at the west end of the room was reached by a mural passage running round the end of the short partition wall.

On the south side of the hall were two rooms, that on the west being the kitchen and the other probably a sleeping room with a latrine in the south-east corner. The kitchen has a large circular fireplace of unusual design in its south-west corner. It is 8 ft. 10 in. diameter, rises 20 ft. up the wall without diminution in size, and at that height is finished with a domed vault with flues issuing through loopholes at the re-entering angles of the buttresses outside. The lower part of the fireplace, where combustion occurs, is faced with herringbone masonry. A deep recess on the north-east corner of the kitchen gave access to the well, which had another drawing place in the basement. All the rooms of this upper storey were well lighted by windows having internal jambs which are not splayed in the more usual manner but are stepped back in three orders, the innermost order of that at the east end of the north wall forming a recess 15 ft. wide and 20 ft. high; the windows in some of the early keeps in France are formed in this manner.

A spiral stairway at the north-east corner of the keep led up to the third storey and the battlements and down to the basement, and a short stairs in the south wall led from the kitchen to the basement, where were the storerooms. Three of these storerooms had no windows of any kind while the other two received only such light and ventilation as could be admitted through loopholes; the loops being set high up in the outer face of the east wall, above the floor level of the second storey, and having their inner openings deflected rapidly downwards to the basement.

Pevensey castle was built in the latter part of the eleventh century at the east end of the Roman fort. It consisted of a rectangular keep, of which the Roman wall formed one side, and a bailey extending eastward from the keep into the fort, then an inhabited town. The castle of that period must have been of considerable strength for when attacked by William Rufus in 1088 the king pounded away at its walls with his siege engines for six weeks without effect and it was only the want of supplies and the knowledge that Robert's cause had failed that induced the garrison to surrender. The defences of the bailey were rebuilt in the thirteenth century, the gatehouse and wall towers belonging to that period. The wide berm which passes round the walls between the curtain and the ditch and the provision of six sally-ports, reached by steps down from the courtyard and opening on to the berm, are noticeable features in the defensive system (p. 18).

The keep as first built about 1080 was a plain rectangular structure, measuring internally 57 ft. by 32 ft., and having an apsidal chapel which projected eastward beyond the line of the fort. In the thirteenth century it was strengthened by the addition of five heavy turrets, built against its corners and sides; the turrets on the west side being deflected in order to point towards the entrance gateway into the bailey. A forebuilding was also raised against its south side. The remains of the keep, consisting of the lower part of the walls only, were for a long period buried beneath debris and accumulated soil, now removed.

In some castles of the latter part of the eleventh century the strong point of the fortification is a gatehouse, or a rectangular structure built close beside the main gateway. Exeter, Ludlow, and Chepstow are examples.

Exeter is described by Ordericus as a rich and ancient city, fortified with much care. He writes that in preparation for William's attack in 1068 the citizens built or repaired walls and towers and strengthened the defences all round. On William's arrival he found the gates closed against him and crowds of defenders posted on the walls and outworks. After eighteen days of violent attack the walls were undermined and the city fell. William then ordered a castle to be built within and at the north corner of the city; the city wall forming two sides of a rectangular bailey. The gatehouse is of this period. There are remains of two wall towers, of late date, on the east and of a square tower, the lower part of which was originally solid, on the west. The curtain walls still stand almost to their full height on the west but are broken down elsewhere; all the mediaeval buildings of the bailey have been swept away.

The gatehouse, which appears to have been virtually the keep, stands on the line of the curtain between the bailey and the city; there are still two storeys of single rooms above the gateway but the upper parts of the walls and the battlements have been destroyed. All the rooms of the gatehouse must have been reached from the wall walk on the curtain, for there are no indications of approach from below. The room above the gateway was lighted from the side towards the city by a twin window, each of the two lights of which has a wide opening and a triangular head, a design pointing to the use of Saxon methods and labour. The room above has a window to the bailey of a single light with a triangular head. Whatever other amenities the building contained may have been in an upper floor, now non-existent (pp. 80a, 145).

Ludlow castle is one of the most powerful and complete examples of mediaeval military architecture in Great Britain. Its walls and towers are in good condition and its ranges of internal buildings of all periods from the eleventh to the sixteenth century, though roofless and somewhat weatherworn, are still in excellent state of preservation.

The castle stands on elevated ground on the left bank of the River Teme and is defended on the north and west by steep slopes down from the walls and on the east and south by two ditches, one between the two baileys and one between the outer bailey and the town. The inner bailey was built about 1090, and the keep, the curtain, and the wall towers, are all of that period. The original gateway to the bailey was through the keep. The outer bailey was added in the latter part of the twelfth century and its curtain wall

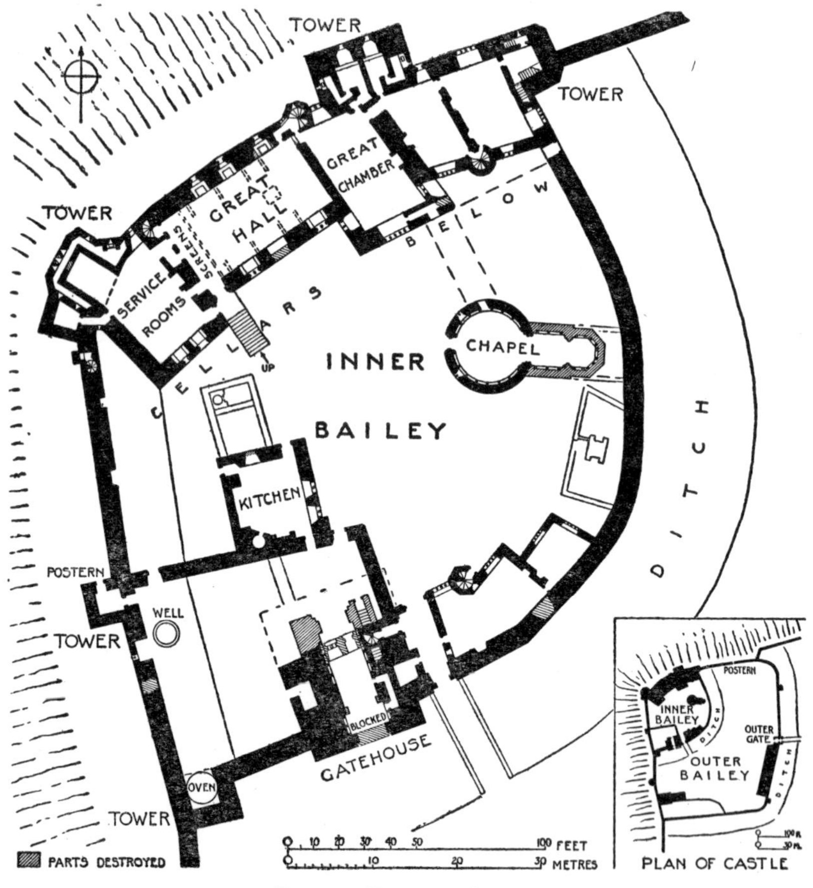

PLAN OF LUDLOW CASTLE

and the outer gate, now in ruins, are of that period; the buildings within the outer bailey, all of later date, are ruinous. A postern in the north wall of the bailey is built of old moulded stones and its door is plated with stone slabs.

Standing against the north wall of the inner bailey is an exceptionally fine range of domestic buildings, dating from the latter years of the thirteenth and early years of the fourteenth centuries. They include the great hall, the great chamber, and a tower which projects outside the curtain and contains many tiers of chambers. The living rooms to the east of the great chamber were rebuilt in the sixteenth century. In the thirteenth century a special court for the keep was formed by walling in a space within the bailey north of the keep. There is a well in this court, and built in a wall tower at the south-west is a large oven, 12 ft. 6 in. diameter, with a domed roof.

The keep, called the great tower, though begun about 1090 was not finished until early in the twelfth century. At first it was of two storeys only, the gateway and a lofty storey over the gateway, the walls rising up to considerable height all round to screen and protect the roof of the hall, which was the principal apartment of the upper storey. The hall was originally reached by a stairway which, from a doorway in the courtyard, passed up in the thickness of the east wall of the gateway. On the east side of the hall there are two deep recesses and on the west side is a doorway leading to a sleeping chamber, 16 ft. long by 8 ft. wide. There is a latrine at the south end of the chamber. At the south end of the hall are doors, one on either side, leading out to the wall walk on the curtain. It is interesting to note that the doorway opening to the wall walk on the west side of the keep and that to the latrine, both dating from early years of the twelfth century, have heads composed of a flat lintel with a corbel projecting out on either side to diminish the span. The original stairway to the battlements is now blocked; it was in the east wall (pp. 76, 80a).

In the latter part of the twelfth century a new gateway to the bailey was made through the curtain immediately to the east of the keep. The old gateway was blocked at both ends, covered with a vault and converted into a prison. The hall was then divided into two storeys and a further storey was formed in the roof space. In the fifteenth century the north end of the keep either fell or was taken down and the north wall was rebuilt 11 ft. farther back, the size of the keep being diminished to that extent. The lower stairway from the courtyard was blocked at the bottom and the present spiral stairway built.

The chapel of St. Mary Magdalene within the bailey is one of the few round churches remaining in this country. It dates mainly from the early years of the twelfth century and consisted originally of a round nave and a chancel with eastern apse; the chancel has been destroyed but the nave remains. The nave is a remarkably beautiful building, richly embellished with chevron and other Norman ornament, and having a wall arcade all round the interior.

Chepstow castle was begun by William Fitz-Osbern about 1070; it stands on a narrow and high tongue of rock which runs out eastward between the River Wye and a deep ravine, with a fall from west to east. On the north are high precipices down to the river and on the south steep descents to the ravine. The middle part of the tongue is gathered in to the form of a narrow ridge and on this ridge the keep was built; there were two baileys, one at either end of the ridge, and they were connected by a narrow passage running along beside the keep. The keep with its strongly guarded passage occupies the full width of the ridge. The west bailey was defended by a deep ditch, dug through the tongue from side to side, and it is probable that the east bailey had a similar defence, but its original disposition is obscured by later work.

In the thirteenth century the castle was considerably enlarged and strengthened; the west bailey, now called the middle bailey, was rebuilt and a new and powerful ward, called the lower bailey, was thrown out at the east, and a barbican, with an additional ditch, was built on the west.

The keep, built about 1070, was so drastically altered in the thirteenth century and its interior is now so completely gutted that it is difficult to determine its original disposition. It now forms one large hall of three storeys, measuring internally 89 ft. 4 in. by 28 ft. 9 in. at the west end and 30 ft. 6 in. at the east end. The east end wall and the south wall, the sides most open to attack, are 8 ft. 6 in. thick; the other two walls are thinner; all the walls are strengthened by pilaster buttresses. The original entrance was at second storey level and was reached by a mural stairway which passes up the east wall from a doorway, itself 7 ft. above the ground outside; the doorway was protected by a forebuilding, since destroyed. At a later period the lobby inside the doorway, from which the mural stairway ascends, was continued straight through the wall.

The second storey, entered by a door at the south-east corner from the mural stairs, was the principal floor of the building; it was lighted by windows in the north wall, opening out over the roof of the passage between the baileys, and has in its south and west walls continuous series of deep recesses, which were perhaps sleeping cubicles; some of them have been blocked. There can be no doubt that the floors of this and the third storey received intermediate support from posts running down the axial line of the building; for although the clear span is not too great for the timber floors and roofs of the period there is no indication of the use of the heavy beams that would be required for such a span.

When the keep was remodelled in the thirteenth century a cross wall was built from side to side dividing the structure into two unequal sections; the greatest, that on the east, was the great hall and the other probably the great chamber. The cross wall, on the evidence of its design and the angle of the springing of its arches, must have been a richly moulded arcade of two arches having a central pier in line with the posts supporting the floors. The suggestion that after these alterations were made the third storey had no floor but that a timber gallery passed along the north and east walls is untenable. For, not only would such a barrack-like structure be utterly incongruous to a hall so richly decorated, but the walls show no indications of the beams and brackets necessary for the support of a gallery.

The basement, containing the storerooms, was probably reached from the floor above by steps, since removed; the existing doorway, broken through from the passage on the north, is relatively modern. The storerooms received light and ventilation through three small windows opening on to the passage. From the great hall a spiral stairway at the south-east corner, in continuation of the mural stair of entrance, leads up to the third storey, and from this level another stairway opening out from a window jamb at the north-west corner of the keep leads to the battlements. The passage between the baileys on the north side of the keep rises above the sheer face of the cliff; it was defended by a gate at either end and lighted from windows in its outer wall (p. 160).

Castles with rectangular keeps built during the first half of the twelfth century followed on much the same lines as those noted above. The portcullis is now introduced in the gateways and there is evidence of machicolations in the entrance passages. Meutrières, or arrow-loops, commanding the field and the gateway passages, also come into prominence. As in the earlier work the fireplaces have round backs and their flues pass to the outside face of the wall. In the later works of the latter half of the century there is an ample provision of mural chambers, the fireplace is straight backed and its flue passes straight up the wall to a chimney, and the entrance is often on the third instead of the second storey. Sherborne, Rochester, Hedingham, Castle Rising, and Kenilworth are examples of castles built during the first half of the twelfth century; Norwich, Scarborough, Clun, and Portchester of those built during the middle part; and Bamborough, Richmond, Newcastle and Dover of those built in the latter half of the century.

Sherborne castle was built about 1120 by Roger, Bishop of Salisbury. Though there appear to have been some outworks, now destroyed, the castle consists essentially of a bailey with straight sides and splayed corners. A feature of this castle is that the main internal buildings are grouped together about a square courtyard, near the middle of the bailey and well away from the walls. The rectangular keep occupies a commanding position at the south-west corner of the group, jutting out south and west beyond the other buildings. There is a gatehouse of the early period at the south-west of the bailey; and modern investigations have brought to light the foundations of a second gate, with outward extensions, on the north; a third gate, on the north-east; and a tower at the north-west. There was probably another tower, not yet investigated, at the south-east. The castle is surrounded by a wide and deep moat.

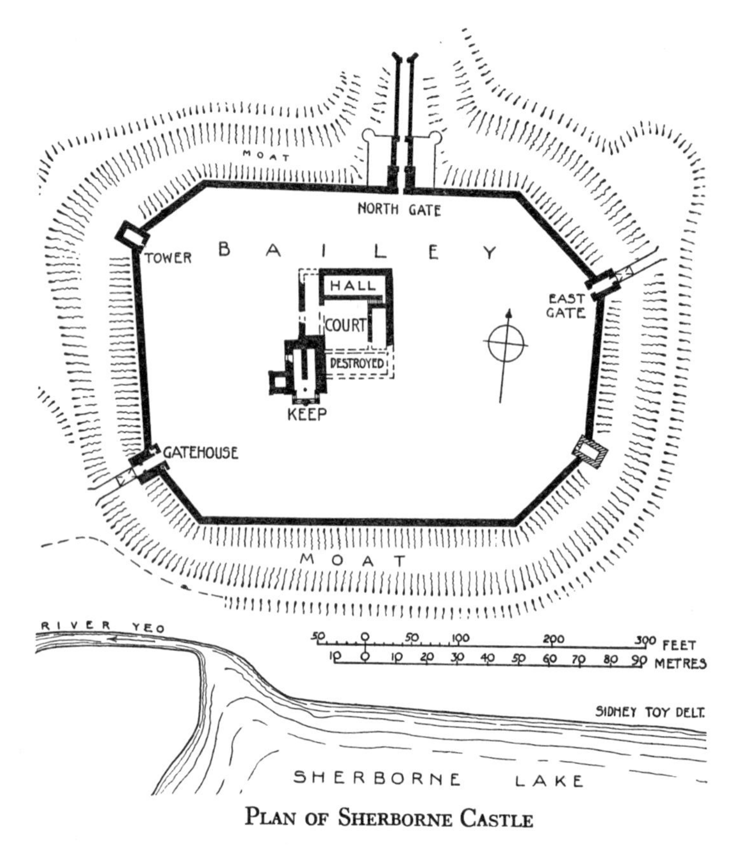

PLAN OF SHERBORNE CASTLE

The keep, built at the time of the foundation of the castle, is in a very ruinous condition though its walls still stand in places to the height of about 50 ft. above the ground. The walls are 9 ft. thick and when first built the keep measured internally 37 ft. by 23 ft., but soon after its completion the south end wall was taken down and 15 ft. added to its length; the walls of the extension being less than half the thickness of the original work. The basement is divided into two barrel-vaulted cellars by a thick wall

Colchester Castle. The Keep from the South-East.

Exeter Castle. The Gate-house.

Ludlow Castle. The Great Tower from the Outer Bailey.

Rochester Castle. The Keep from the North-West.

running axially. At the south end, where the extension occurs, the partition wall gives place to two arches, divided by a circular pillar with scalloped capital. The second storey has no partitions but forms a single hall 52 ft. long. There was a forebuilding, now very ruinous, which contained the steps of approach to the keep.

The castles of Devizes and Old Sarum, now reduced to foundations and bases of walls, were also built about 1120. In both castles the keep is in line with the curtain on the opposite side of the bailey from the gatehouse, while the hall, the principal chambers and the domestic offices are grouped in ranges nearby but distinct from the keep.

Newark castle, built about 1130 by Alexander, Bishop of Lincoln, now consists of the western half of what appears to have been a rectangular bailey; the eastern half of the bailey has been destroyed. The remains are extensive and of imposing character. They include the original gatehouse and adjoining portion of the curtain west of it, the whole of the west curtain on the right bank of the Trent, with a tower near the middle and one at either end, and the vaulted undercroft of the great hall. Much rebuilding and alteration took place in the thirteenth century when the north-west tower, which has a bottle-necked prison in the basement, was built. There is a watergate through the west wall.

The gatehouse, like those at Exeter and Ludlow, combined the functions of gateway and keep. Its setting in the curtain is unusual. The curtain on the west is in line with the gatehouse but that on the east runs obliquely, forward, thus commanding the entrance and providing a point of attack from its battlements on the flank of an approaching enemy. There was a drawbridge over the moat, working between two walls which project out from the gatehouse. There were probably machicolations in the fore part of the passage but the only other defence was a two-leaved door, placed midway in the passage and secured by a heavy timber bar; there was no portcullis. The upper floors have been much altered at later periods; they were reached by a spiral stairway which is entered from the courtyard.

Rochester castle was built within and at the south-west corner of the Roman city, two walls of which formed part of its curtain. It stands on the right bank of the Medway, has a lozenge-shaped plan, with the long axis running north and south, and was formerly divided into two baileys by a cross wall. The inner bailey, with the keep built against the Roman wall, is at the south end of the castle and the whole work was surrounded by a moat. The castle was begun in 1087 and was held against William Rufus in the following year. The gatehouse and large portions of the curtain have disappeared entirely and those parts of the curtain and of the wall towers which remain are most fragmentary and ruinous.

The keep, built about 1130, is one of the most imposing and best preserved structures of its type. It is of four tall storeys, with a turret at each corner and a forebuilding, containing the entrance porch with chapel above, at the north-east corner. The walls are 12 ft. thick at the base and rise, with a considerable batter, to the height of 113 ft.; the turrets projecting up another 12 ft. A cross wall, rising through the full height of the keep, divides each storey into two almost equal sections. The entrance is at second storey level and is by way of flights of steps which begin at the outer face of the west wall, turn round the north-west corner and rise to the porch. The steps were defended from the porch and by a gate, now destroyed, thrown across them at the corner; there was a drawbridge immediately in front of the porch. Passing through the entrance to the porch, another doorway, defended by a portcullis, admitted to the main body of the keep (pp. 80b, 86a).

The two large rooms of the second storey were lighted by small windows, have each a round-backed fireplace with a flue passing to the outer face of the keep, and have mural latrines. A well shaft in the cross wall has a drawing place here, another in the floor below, and a third in the great hall above. From the second storey two spiral stairways in opposite corners of the keep rise to the upper floors and the battlements, that at the north-east corner also descending to the first storey. The great hall is on the third storey. Here, the cross wall being pierced by an arcade, the room extends across the whole floor. There are two tiers of windows, the upper tier opening on to a mural gallery, 14 ft. above the floor. There is a fireplace in each of the north and south walls and there are four latrines. The fireplaces are similar in form to those below; their arches, as well as those of the arcade and the internal openings of the windows are all enriched with mouldings and chevron ornament. After the siege of 1215, when a breech was made in the keep, the south-east turret was rebuilt in its present round form, and the curtain wall was rebuilt farther out, clear of the keep, at the same time.

Hedingham castle now consists of the keep, which stands on a natural mound surrounded by a moat, and a bailey; the defences of the bailey have been destroyed. The moat is now crossed by a bridge built in the early part of the sixteenth century.

The keep is a noble and well-preserved structure, built about 1130. It is of four storeys without partitions, each storey having one large central room. There is a turret at each corner, two of them still rising 20 ft. above the battlements, and there is a pilaster buttress midway between the turrets on each side. The floor of the second storey is supported by heavy beams, but the floors of the third and fourth storeys received intermediate support from arches of a single span, thrown from side to side across the middle of the keep; the lower arch is broken down.

The entrance is at second storey level and is reached by a flight of steps, built against the west wall and formerly enclosed in a forebuilding, now destroyed. The doorway into the keep was defended by a portcullis, operated from a window recess above, and a heavy timber bar. Both the second and third storeys are lighted by windows set in wide and lofty internal recesses, have mural chambers opening out of the main room, and each has a fireplace similar to those at Rochester. The great hall is on the third storey; it is a lofty room with two tiers of windows; the upper tier opening on to a mural gallery, 12 ft. 6 in. above the floor. A spiral stairway at the north-west corner rises from the basement to the battlements. *See Appendix B.*

At Castle Rising the keep stands in the middle of the bailey, which is surrounded by a wide and deep ditch, and there are two outworks, one on either side of the bailey. Except for the fragmentary ruins of the gateway all the defences of the bailey have disappeared, and apart from the keep the sole remnants of the bailey buildings are the foundations of an apsidal chapel of the Norman period.

The keep was built about 1140 and its walls are still complete up to and including the base of the parapet; it is of two lofty storeys. There are turrets at the corners and pilaster buttresses at intervals along the sides; the turrets and buttresses being faced with ashlar and the panels of walling between them with coursed rubble. That elegance as well as strength was a factor in the design is shown by the unusual external embellishments; the turrets and buttresses having vertical roll mouldings and the forebuilding being decorated with arcading.

The entrance is at the second storey and the stairway of approach in the forebuilding was defended by three doors, one at the foot, one midway and the third into the porch at the head. The middle doorway is defended by a machicolation opening out from the floor of a passage in its vault and by an arrow-loop commanding the first flight of steps from the same passage. The entrance into the keep from the porch, a richly moulded doorway of three orders, is blocked and the present entrance is by a narrow doorway broken through at the side.

Internally the keep is divided into two unequal parts by a wall running lengthwise. In the lower storey there is no further division but in the upper storey both sections are subdivided, the larger to form the great hall and the kitchen, and the other the great chamber, the chapel and ante-chapel. The chapel and the porch, both on the east side of the keep, being lower than the other apartments have an additional storey formed over them. Originally the great hall had an arcade of three arches running axially through it; but this, together with the supporting arcade below, has been destroyed. A mural gallery runs along the north wall of the hall at floor level, having windows on the outside and opening to the hall by wide arches. The kitchen and its offices are at the west end of the hall and in the north-west turret of this section there is a fireplace with a large circular flue, 5 ft. 6 in. diameter, which rises at that size a considerable height up the wall with loopholes to the outside and then, gathering over, ascends as an ordinary flue to the top of the wall; the flue is doubtless a later extension.

A passage at the south-east of the great hall leads to the chapel and, farther on, crossing above the middle gate of the forebuilding, to a postern which opens out in the east wall high above the ground. The chapel and ante-chapel both have remains of rich decoration. Two wide spiral stairways in corner turrets descend to the basement, where there is a well, and rise to the battlements. An interesting development in the sanitary arrangements of this keep is the concentration of the latrines on one side of the building, here on the west.

Kenilworth castle as first completed during the first half of the twelfth century stood within the limits of the present inner bailey, a natural knoll of sandstone and gravel; the castle was defended all round by a wide and deep moat. The keep and the curtain walls on the north and south sides of the bailey are of the early period, as are the foundations of a rectangular structure at the south-east of the bailey brought to light in 1931; but the other original buildings have given place to elaborate structures of later periods. The outer bailey and extensive outworks were added in the thirteenth century (pp. 137, 139, 153).

The keep, called Caesar's tower, is an exceptionally powerful building; its walls are 14 ft. thick above a deep battered plinth and are strengthened at the corners by massive turrets of deep projection and at the sides by wide buttresses. It is of two tall storeys, the lower 20 ft. and the upper 25 ft. high. The walls rise high above the upper storey to protect and mask the roof, and the floor of the lower storey inside is 19 ft. above that of the ground outside on the north, the side exposed to the field. So that the total height on this side to the crest of the parapet must have been about 80 ft.; and the height of the turrets 100 ft. When the castle was "slighted" in 1648 the north wall of the keep was blown down entirely and the parapet and upper parts of the turrets destroyed.

The entrance was at the upper storey by a doorway at the south-west corner of the keep, which was reached by a flight of steps built against the west wall. The steps were removed in 1392 when an annex was added at the west end of the building. Internally there is no cross wall, each of the two storeys consisting of one spacious hall, augmented by large and lofty window recesses. The heavy floor and roof beams were supported on wide offsets in the walls. In the upper storey there are two windows in the west wall, with round heads and tall sills, which retain their original form except that they have been enlarged by the removal of the outer order; all the other windows were altered in the sixteenth century when large mullioned windows were inserted in the recesses. The head of an original window can be seen above the lintel of the westernmost window on the south. The original fireplace, if any, must have been in the north wall; the small fireplace in the west wall was inserted about 1570. At the south-east corner of the hall there is a well which has a drawing place both here and in the storey below, and at the north-east corner there is a spiral stairway leading down to the lower storey and up to the battlements.

In the lower storey one original window remains intact in the east wall; it is of unusual design. It has a tall and narrow opening, 7 ft. 3 in. high by 4 in. wide, placed midway in the thickness of the wall, with widely splayed jambs and trumpet shaped heads opening out to the exterior as well as the interior. Both turrets on the east side of the keep are built solid up to the floor level of the upper storey, except that part of the north-east turret is occupied by the stairway. The south-west turret was also solid up to the same level before 1570 when the lower part was hollowed out to form additional chambers. The north-west turret is occupied by three tiers of latrines, one opening out from each of the two storeys and the third reached from the battlements; so that here all the latrines are assembled in one corner turret. The battlements of the keep are in two tiers.

The keep at Lydford is a small rectangular building of two storeys, standing on the top of a low mound; it dates about 1150, is built of rubble, and has neither turrets nor buttresses. The entrance is at ground floor level, on the north side of the keep facing towards the bailey. The door was secured by a stout timber bar but there was no portcullis. Straight mural stairways lead to the upper levels. Internally the keep is divided by partition walls into three sections in the lower storey and two in the upper storey. The basement windows are splayed both outwards and inwards from small openings midway in the thickness of the wall. There are traces of a bailey but all its defences have been destroyed (p. 86a).

Portchester castle is built at the south-west corner of the Roman fort; it has a rectangular bailey of which two sides are formed by the Roman walls. The curtain walls within the fort, the keep, the square tower at the south-east corner, and the main part of the gatehouse, all date from the twelfth century. The keep stands at the north-west corner of the bailey with its north and west sides projecting beyond the line of the Roman walls. A moat, fed through a sluice in the north wall, passes in front of the two sides of the castle within the fort, leaving a wide berm on either flank of the gatehouse on the south. In the fourteenth century the gateway was extended outwards and defended by two portcullises. The great hall and its offices which were built against the curtain within the bailey were rebuilt in the fourteenth century and later periods but fragments of the original work including internal wall arcading still remain (p. 20).

The keep was originally of two tall storeys with its walls rising high above the roof. In the latter part of the twelfth century the walls were raised, a third storey was formed in the space occupied by the old roof, and a fourth storey above. The existing gable-like parapets are of much later date. The walls, up to the original height, are strengthened by buttresses on the exposed sides, north and west.

The entrance was at the second storey, through a forebuilding which is now very ruinous; the forebuilding having a chapel on one side of the entrance and a guardroom on the other. A cross wall, running east and west, divides the interior into two sections. The north room of the entrance floor has a fireplace with wide flue rising vertically up to a dome and there issuing to the outside face by loopholes, like that at Castle Rising, without the later extension, and reminiscent of the large one at Canterbury. There is a well in the south room and both rooms are provided with mural latrines. A spiral stairway on the south rises from the ground floor to the upper parts of the keep. The windows of the ground floor are splayed both inside and out like those of Lydford.

Corfe castle presents a most formidable aspect as seen when approached from the north, the hill-top on which it stands crowned by the imposing ruins of its keep. The castle stands on an isolated hill in the middle of a range which stretches across the centre of the Isle of Purbeck; the hill is almost entirely surrounded at its foot by a natural moat formed by two streams. The site was occupied in the first part of the eleventh century by a hall, the remains of which are still standing, but the earliest part of the castle is the curtain wall surrounding the inner bailey at the summit of the hill. This wall is from ten to twelve feet thick and was built during the latter part of the eleventh century. The keep was built about 1140 and the middle and outer baileys were added during the thirteenth century[2] (pp. 86a, 86b, 87, 151).

The keep stands against the inner face of the south wall of the curtain, looking towards the approach to the castle. It was of three storeys, the first a low basement and each of the others 24 ft. high.

[2] Corfe Castle, *Archaeologia*, LXXIV, 1929.

LYDFORD CASTLE. THE KEEP FROM THE SOUTH.

ROCHESTER CASTLE. INTERIOR OF KEEP.

CORFE CASTLE. WALL WALK THROUGH THE KEEP.

of steps built against the west side, the lower part of the flight being exposed and the upper part enclosed in a forebuilding. The stairs of descent from here to the two lower floors have been destroyed, but a spiral stairway at the south-east corner rose to the battlements. In the sixteenth century the old roof was removed and a fourth storey formed in the roof space. Shortly after the keep was finished an addition was made on the south side, the new work rising up from the low ground outside the curtain. In making this addition the wall walk on the curtain was not obstructed but carried straight through the new building as a lofty barrel-vaulted passage.

A remarkable feature of Corfe castle is the excellent quality of its masonry. The walls are composed of a core of chalk and rubble faced with a very durable limestone, quarried locally, and the mortar used is so powerful that when the castle was blown up by gunpowder in 1646 whole masses of masonry having fallen down, in places as much as 40 ft., have held together so tenaciously as to remain on the ground unbroken to the present day.

Of Norwich castle the only surviving portion is the keep, which was built about the middle of the twelfth century; all other parts of the castle having either been absorbed in later structures or pulled down and built over. During the early part of the eighteenth century the keep itself was completely gutted and its battlements taken down. In 1790 its walls were refaced externally and the forebuilding reconstructed, and in 1894 it was reroofed and fitted up as a museum. The keep is of three storeys and was divided internally by a cross wall, now destroyed. The entrance was at the third storey and was reached by flights of steps in a forebuilding at the east side of the keep; the great hall was on this floor. Two spiral stairways at opposite corners rose from ground level to the battlements. There was a well in the cross wall.

Guildford castle, Surrey, and Clun castle, Salop, both have a rectangular keep standing on the edge of a mound, the outer end rising up vertically from the ditch and the inner end based on the top of the mound. So placed, while less excavation was necessary in order that the whole building should stand on natural soil, as it doubtless does, the defenders on its battlements commanded and could enfilade the outer face of the curtain on either side. Both keeps were built about 1150. Guildford castle consists of the keep on the mound, and two baileys stretching in line from the keep towards the river; the mound is surrounded by a wide ditch. On the top of the mound there still remains a piece of the wall of a polygonal shell keep which existed long before the present keep was built. Only fragments now remain of the defences and buildings of the baileys. They include walls of a group of domestic buildings in the inner bailey, dating from the twelfth century; parts of the inner gateway, of about 1300; and walls incorporated in a seventeenth-century house adjacent to the gateway.

The keep stands on the east slope of the mound, projecting outward from the old shell wall, which was broken through for its reception. The east wall, rising up from the ditch and facing towards the field, is 14 ft. thick above a battered plinth and stands upon virgin chalk. The other walls are 10 ft. thick and no doubt rest on the same natural bed; deep excavations made in 1887 led to that conclusion. It is of three storeys, the floor of the first storey being on a level with the top of the mound. The walls are buttressed at the corners and midway in their sides and are built mainly of chalk marle, the buttresses being principally of ashlar and the panels of walling between of rubble with some herringbone courses.

The entrance was at the second storey by a door in the south wall, 14 ft. above the ground, and appears to have been reached from the wall walk on the old shell. It is a relatively small keep, measuring internally at the base 26 ft. 3 in. by 23 ft.; there are no partitions, and the floors were of timber, supported on offsets in the walls. The second storey was lighted by two windows, one in each of the east and west walls; there is a mural chamber at the north-west and a latrine at the north-east. A doorway at the south end of the west wall leads first to a vestibule and then, turning the corner within the wall, to a mural chapel running eastward from this point; both the chapel and vestibule are embellished with wall arcades. This little oratory was for many years used as a prison and there are numerous graffiti on its walls.

Access down to the ground storey must have been by a trap-door in the entrance floor. The third storey and the battlements were reached by a spiral stairway, the steps of which have been taken out, at the north-west corner of the keep. In the third storey a window, looking towards the bailey, has a spacious level sill which is placed so high above the floor as to require a stair of access, formed within the wall. At the south-east corner there is a double latrine. There are no original fireplaces in the keep. The fireplaces in the second and third storeys are insertions of a much later date.

Clun castle has a high mound at the point of a sharp bend of the River Clun and inner and outer baileys stretching from the mound away from the river. A deep moat encircles the mound and the baileys. The site was probably fortified by Robert de Say, who owned the land at the time of Domesday; a small rising on the mound and fragments of a curtain wall may belong to this period; the wall towers were added later.

The keep is of four storeys, two of them below the level of the top of the mound, and, although still standing to nearly its full height, is in a very ruinous condition. It is a rectangular building rising on the north side of the mound with the long sides running north and south, its north end wall rising up directly from the ditch; there was a turret at each corner. The south wall, rising from near the top of the mound, has been destroyed together with the turrets on either flank; there was no cross wall. The original entrance was probably at the third storey, through a doorway in the destroyed wall, and the main stairway, now non-existent, in one of the south turrets. A straight mural stairway leads from the second storey down to the basement and to a narrow postern; the postern was probably broken through the relatively thin wall at the foot of the stairway at a later date. The existing turrets on the north are solid in the two lower storeys but contain chambers at third and fourth storey levels. In each of the second, third, and fourth storeys there is a fireplace with flue passing up to the top of the wall.

Scarborough castle stands on a wide flat-topped peninsula which juts out into the North Sea 300 ft. above sea level and is connected to the mainland by a narrow isthmus; the isthmus being cut across by a natural gorge midway in its length. On the eastern edge of the promontory are the remains of the Roman signal station noted in Chapter Four. The whole promontory, of which the castle occupies but a relatively small portion, is defended on the south-west by a powerful wall, a steep declivity, and a wide and deep moat, called Castle Dyke. On all other sides of the flat table top there are precipitous falls down to the sea. The castle is built at the head of the isthmus, on the land side of the promontory, and consists of a rectangular keep, a bailey to the south of the keep, a funnel-shaped outwork, a bridge across the gorge and a barbican at the far end of the bridge. The bridge has a tower in the middle and a drawbridge on either side of the tower (pp. 86b, 91, 92a).

The site was first fortified about 1140 by William le Gros, Earl of Albermarle, who built a tower on or near the position occupied by the existing keep. In 1155 the castle was ceded to Henry the Second, who rebuilt the keep and strengthened the other fortifications. The curtain walls probably belong to this period though strengthened by towers at a later date. The bridge and barbican were built in the thirteenth century. It was a powerful castle on a formidable site. Though many times besieged it was never taken by force of arms, but only by means of stratagem or on account of the exhaustion of the defenders' supplies. Even the artillery of the Roundheads when brought against it in 1645 was powerless to effect its fall. It was only after entry into the castle had been obtained by other means than force, and there was no opposition, that the parliamentary army was able to carry out the works of destruction it then effected.

The keep is of four storeys with wide buttresses at the corners and midway in the sides, the corner buttresses having a bold round vertical moulding at the angle. The west wall, which was the vulnerable side and was blown down in 1645, was 15 ft. thick; the other walls are 12 ft. thick. There was a forebuilding, containing the steps of approach and now in ruins, on the south side of the keep. The entrance was at the second storey through a wide doorway from the forebuilding and opened on to a large room covering the whole internal space. This room was lighted by windows with wide and tall internal recesses, has a round-backed fireplace with flue carried vertically up the wall, and a mural chamber. A narrow stairway on the left of the entrance led up to the battlements of the forebuilding and a spiral stairway in the west wall led down to the basement. Two arches, one above the other and both now broken down, thrown across the middle of the keep gave central support to the floors of the third and fourth storeys.

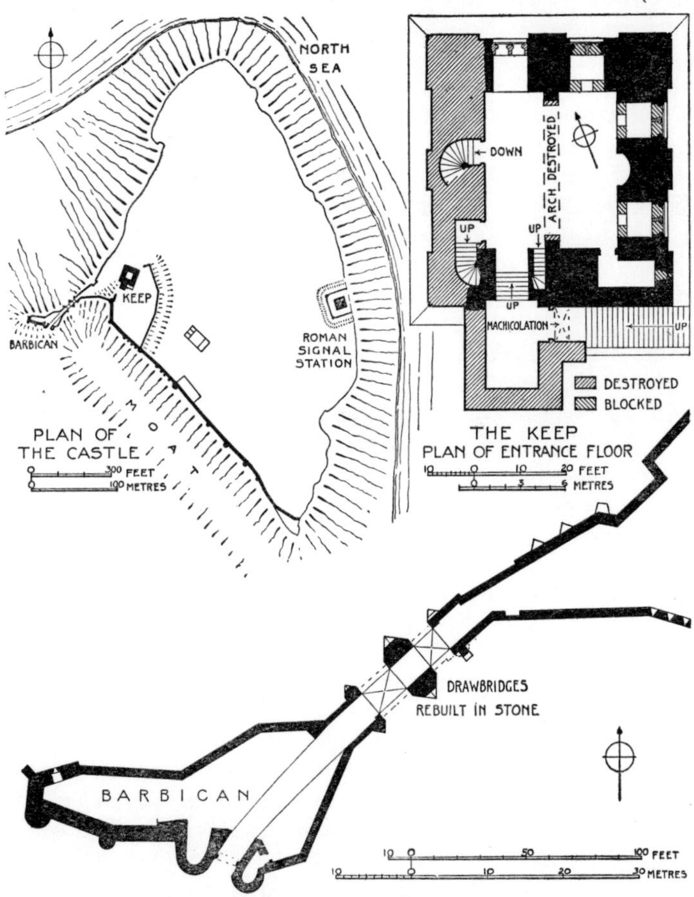

PLAN OF SCARBOROUGH CASTLE

The stairway from the second storey to the upper levels was probably in one of the two west corners; there is no indication of the continuation upwards of the stairs to the basement, as has been suggested. The third storey was the great hall; it was well lighted, has a fireplace similar to that below, and there are mural chambers in the existing corners. A small doorway, formed in a window, opens out to the battlements of the forebuilding side by side with that at the top of the stairs from the second storey. The fourth storey was well lighted but appears to have had no fireplace or mural chambers.

The castles of Middleham, Bamburgh, Carlisle, Appleby, Brougham, and Norham, in the north of England, and of Goodrich, Herefordshire, all have rectangular keeps of about 1170–75. Their entrances are at the second storey and all except that at Middleham, which is of two storeys, were originally of three storeys with their walls rising high above the roof. The keep at Middleham stands in the centre and largely fills a rectangular bailey with ranges of domestic and service quarters, built during the fourteenth century, on all sides. Within the keep are two wells, one at each end of its vaulted basement.

The keeps of Bamburgh and Carlisle have been subjected from time to time to considerable works of alteration and reconstruction. In both, at a later mediaeval period, a new entrance was opened at ground floor level near a straight mural stairway leading from this entrance up to the floor above. At Bamburgh the great hall, which is on the third storey, has a mural gallery high above floor level.

Bamburgh castle stands by the sea on a long and relatively narrow rock of basalt which runs roughly north and south and rises with precipitous sides 130 ft. above sea level. The inner bailey, itself long and narrow, is at the south end of the rock; it is exposed on the west side but covered on the east by the long road of approach to the outer bailey. The outer bailey extends over the middle third of the rock and the northern third is occupied by a fortified outwork. The keep, from a point between the inner and outer baileys, commands the whole castle in all directions. The domestic and service quarters of the castle are ranged along the west side of the inner bailey; they date largely from the latter part of the thirteenth century and include the fine King's hall, the Captain's hall, and a spacious kitchen. The whole castle has been extensively restored.

Carlisle castle stands on the north side of the city, from which it is separated by a wide moat; it consists of two baileys with the keep, standing clear of the walls, at the south-west of the inner bailey. The site was fortified in 1092 but the earliest part of the existing defences to which a definite period can be assigned is the keep, dating about 1170. The keep has been remodelled since first

Scarborough Castle. The Keep from the South-East.

Scarborough Castle. Interior of the Keep.

Richmond Castle. The Keep from the South.

Newcastle. The Keep from the South.

built; it is now divided into four in place of three storeys and the cross walls are later mediaeval insertions. The outer gatehouse, which has its gateway passing through one side instead of through the middle of the structure, was built in the latter part of the thirteenth century. The inner gatehouse was rebuilt in the fourteenth century.

At Appleby, Westmorland, the keep, 31 ft. 6 in. square internally, was originally of three storeys and had no cross walls. The cross wall was built in the seventeenth century and the fourth storey appears to have been added at the same time. Brougham Castle, in the same county, has a square keep of about 1175. It is of four storeys, was entered through a forebuilding at the second storey, and has a spiral stairway ascending from base to summit at one corner and tiers of latrines at another. The fourth storey was remodelled about 1300. A mural gallery at its floor level is of this period as is the fine little octagonal oratory, with vestry adjoining, at its south-east corner. The oratory has a trefoil-headed east window, an aumbry and a piscina.

Norham castle belonged to the princely bishops of Durham and was built by Bishop Flambard in 1121. It consists of an inner and outer bailey, with the keep projecting beyond the curtain at the south junction of the baileys, and standing on the right bank of the Tweed. The eastern part of the outer gateway is of the early period; it is of two bays divided by flat pilasters and is covered by a barrel vault. Originally the wall of the inner bailey formed a large shell keep; the present rectangular keep was built about 1170. Situated on the border country between England and Scotland, Norham Castle has been attacked, seriously damaged, and subsequently repaired on many occasions; since the sixteenth century it has fallen into decay and is now in a very ruinous condition.

The keep is the most complete part of the castle and except for the east side, which has been destroyed above the basement, stands up to the height of the wall walk, 90 ft. above the ground. It measures internally 58 ft. by 40 ft., has a cross wall running lengthwise and was originally divided into three storeys. In the sixteenth century the old roof was removed and two additional storeys formed within the roof space.

At Goodrich the keep is all that remains of the castle of about 1170 which was otherwise rebuilt at the end of the thirteenth century. It is a relatively small keep of three tall storeys and was entered at the second storey. A spiral stairway at one corner rises from the second storey to the higher levels, but there is no structural stairs to the basement, which must have been reached by way of a trap-door and timber stairs (p. 176, 216a).

The keeps at Richmond, Yorks., built about 1175, Newcastle,

1172–77, and Dover, 1181–87, are among the most imposing and best preserved structures of their kind in the country.

Richmond castle has a triangular bailey with its base on the edge of the cliff overlooking the River Swale and the other two sides running up the hill to meet the keep at the apex. An outwork, called the Cock Pit, extends eastwards from the south-east corner of the bailey, and there was a barbican, now destroyed, covering the gateway at the north of the bailey. There were two posterns in the east wall and apparently one in the west wall. The north, east, and west walls of the curtain, the north gateway, three square towers projecting out from the east wall of the curtain, and a large two-storey building called Scolland's hall at the south-west corner of the bailey, were all built by Alan of Brittany about 1075. The keep was built over the original gateway a hundred years later.

Robin Hood tower, the northernmost wall tower on the east curtain, is of three storeys, the two lowest, each covered with a barrel vault, dating from the eleventh and the third from the fourteenth century; the first storey is the chapel of St. Nicolas. The middle tower has fallen and only the lower parts of its walls remain. The south, or Gold Hole, tower is of two storeys of which only the first, containing latrines and their pits, is of the eleventh century. The upper floor was rebuilt in the fourteenth century as a private chamber with a fireplace and a latrine. The gateway on which the keep now stands must have projected outside the curtain. When the keep was built the outer arch was either removed or absorbed in the new wall but the inner arch was retained and blocked; the arch has now been opened out. It is a tall opening 11 ft. 6 in. wide, enriched on both the inner and outer sides with shafted jambs of two orders; when it was blocked a new gateway was opened in the curtain to the east of it. Scolland's hall and St. Nicolas's chapel are described in Chapter Seven (pp. 92b, 95, 142b).

The keep is of three storeys, the first being the old gate blocked at both ends; it has shallow buttresses at the corners and sides and rises with external offsets to the height of 100 ft. 6 in. The entrance is at the second storey and is reached from the wall walk of the curtain adjoining the keep on the east. There is no cross wall but a large octagonal pier built in the centre of the old gateway formerly supported the floor of the second storey and probably, rising higher, also of the third storey. The pier is now the central pillar on which the ribs of the fourteenth-century vaulting of the first storey converge; it stands over a well and had a drawing place on one side, now blocked. The original stairs from the second storey down to the first has been replaced by a spiral stairway of much later date; the upper levels are reached by straight flights of steps formed in the thickness of the south wall. By this arrangement ascent to the battlements is checked midway by the necessity

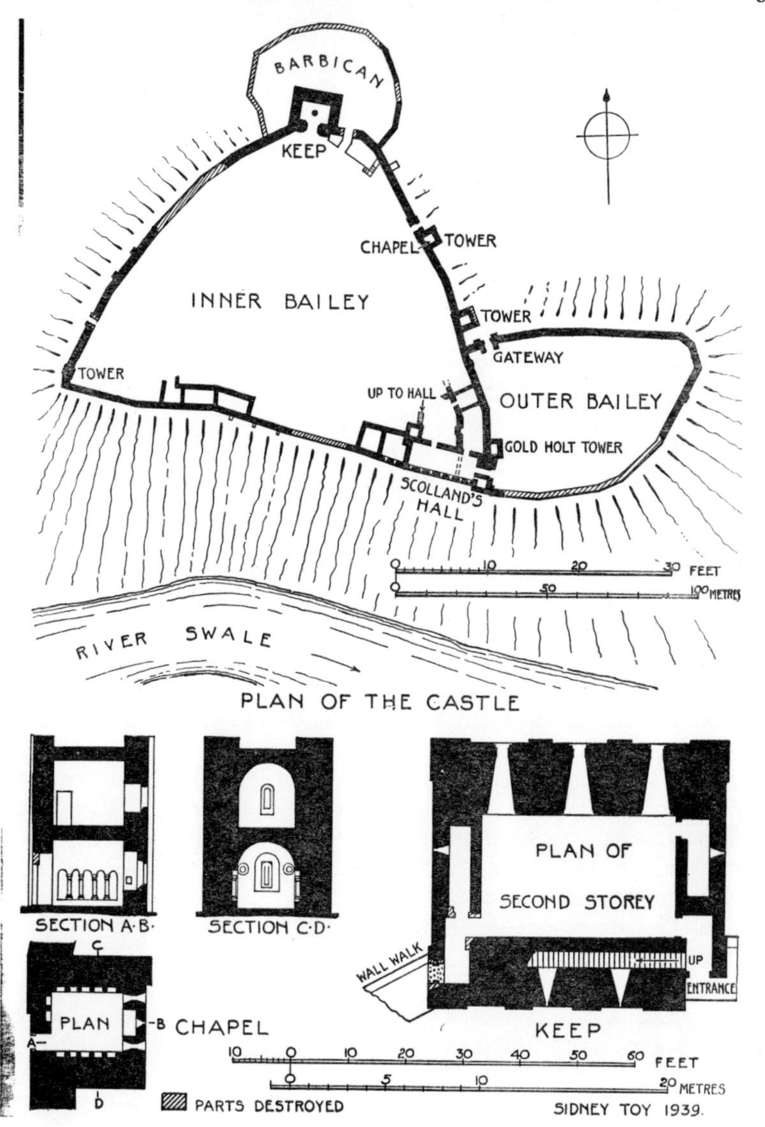

PLANS OF RICHMOND CASTLE

of passing through the whole length of the upper room from the top doorway of the first flight to the bottom doorway of the second. The second and third storeys each consist of a large room with a mural chamber at either end.

The keeps of Newcastle and Dover have many points of resemblance. Both have their entrance doorways at the third storey and in each case the long stairway of approach is enclosed, and strongly defended by a forebuilding. In each also there are many mural chambers and there is a mural gallery, high above floor level, running round the walls of the great hall. The keep at Newcastle, being much the smaller building, has no cross wall while that at Dover is divided by a cross wall running from base to summit.

The castle of Newcastle-upon-Tyne, now surrounded by the city, was first built in 1080 by Robert Curthose, eldest son of William the First. It stands on the left bank of the Tyne 100 ft. above the river and has a triangular shaped bailey which was protected along its base by the river, on the east by a ravine and on the west by a moat. There was a gateway in the west wall and a postern in each of the south and east walls. Most of the defences of the bailey have been destroyed but parts of the east and south curtains, dating probably from 1168, of the south postern and of a wall tower in the south curtain are still standing. There are also remains of the great hall and its offices against the east curtain. The Blackgate at the north-west is described in Chapter Seven.

The keep is built of sandstone at the recorded cost of £911. 10. 9. It is of three storeys with buttresses at the corners and sides; the north-west buttress taking the form of a multangular turret. The forebuilding is on the east side of the keep, its ground floor being entirely occupied by a richly decorated chapel of three vaulted bays. This chapel was obviously for the use of the garrison in general and not especially for those occupying the keep, for the only original entry was from the outside; the existing opening to the basement of the keep was broken through in later times. The stairway up to the entrance into the keep passes over the roof of the chapel, turns left in face of a guardroom, and by another flight reaches the entrance at third storey level (pp. 92b, 97).

The entrance doorway admits directly to the great hall, a lofty room, 30 ft. by 23 ft. 9 in., well lighted by windows placed high in the wall. A mural gallery runs round on all sides 30 ft. above the floor. Originally there was no fireplace in the hall but a large mural room opening out from its south side called the King's chamber, has a fireplace and a latrine, the latter being well lighted and ventilated and reached by a long passage with a right-angle turn. Another latrine similarly designed and ventilated opens off the hall. A doorway at the north-east of the hall leads to a well chamber which has a recess on either side of the well for a bucket. The well is 99 ft. deep and is lined with stone all the way down. There is no other drawing place from the well than this chamber but water was conveyed from here by means of pipes, to drawing places in other parts of the keep. Two of these drawing places have been identified, one at the central pier in the basement and the

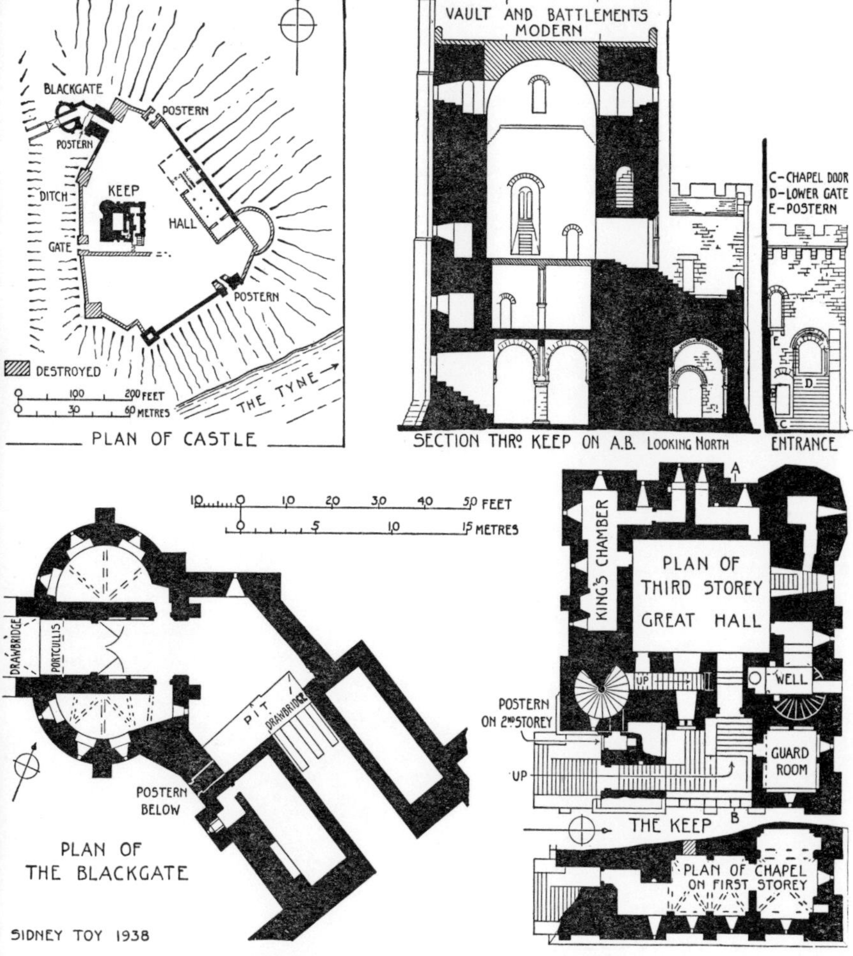

NEWCASTLE. PLANS OF THE CASTLE

other in the passage leading to the east postern. The old roof over the hall has been replaced by a vault.

From the hall a spiral stairway at the south-east corner of the keep descends to the lower storeys and also rises to the battlements. At second storey level a passage from the stairway leads to a postern, 20 ft. above the ground. Originally there was a wall which ran along near and parallel with the south side of the keep towards the west curtain and, when required, a bridge was thrown between the postern and the walk on this wall. The second storey has a large mural chamber, called the Queen's chamber, at the north end of the main room; it has a fireplace and a latrine and from it flights of steps descend to another room below the chamber. The first storey is covered with a stone vault the ribs of which converge on a central pillar. A postern, of later date, opens from a mural chamber on the west side of the keep at this level.

Another stairway from the great hall, leading out from that at the south-east corner, passes up through the thickness of the east wall to the foot of a spiral stairway at the north-east corner, rising to the gallery and the battlements. So that in the event of the hall being carried by storm the defenders on the battlements by using

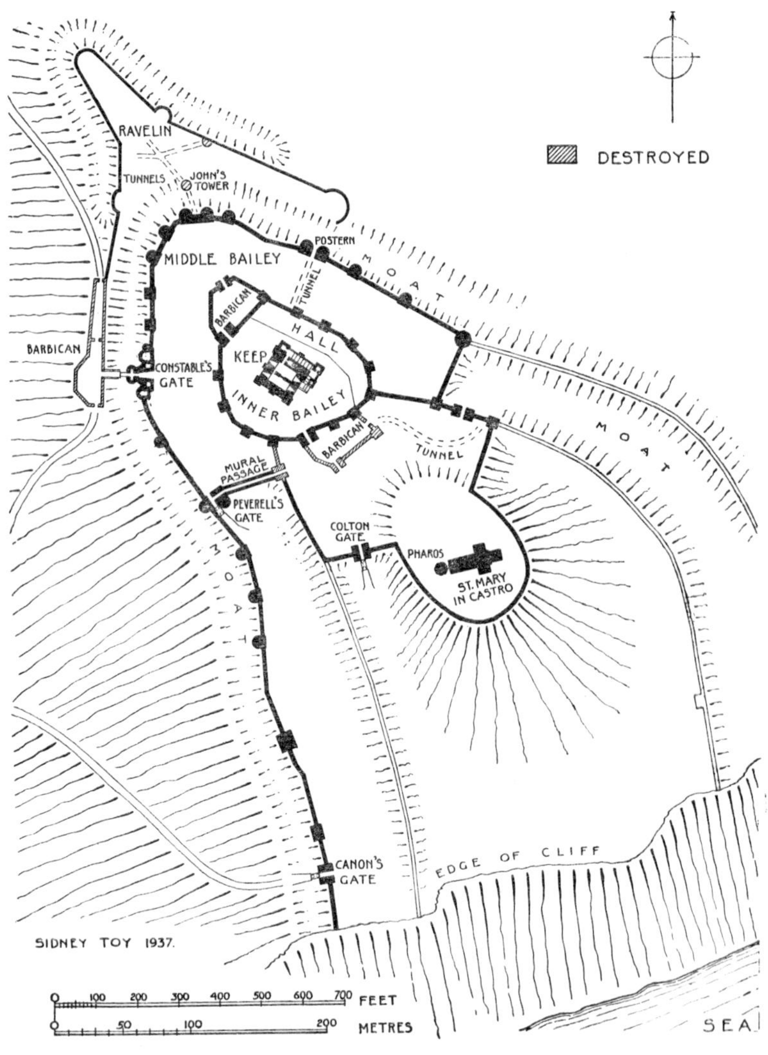

PLAN OF DOVER CASTLE

the north-east stairway could descend to the east postern without having recourse to the upper part of the south-east stairway or passing through the hall. They were also in position to attack from the rear those of the enemy who were rushing up the south-east stairway from the hall. The original fireplaces of this keep have straight backs, splayed sides and segmental heads, and their flues, when first formed, after a short ascent within issued on the outer face of the wall. The tiers of latrines for the three storeys are all formed in the middle of the west wall.

Dover castle, as noted in Chapter Three, existed in Anglo-Saxon times. Harold is said to have strengthened its defences before leaving for Normandy in 1064 and the castle of that period is described by William of Poitiers as a fortress of great strength. After his victory at Senlac, the Conqueror marched directly on Dover castle as being a position of first importance. It must have been then a formidable stronghold for its main defences were considered adequate for more than a hundred years afterwards, covering a period of great progress in military architecture when Dover castle was governed by some of the first soldiers of the age. The defences were not neglected for wall towers were added to the curtain and isolated towers were built as advanced posts; the lower part of Colton tower is of this period and, of the isolated towers, one stood until 1775 and the foundations of two others have been brought to light (pp. 98, 101).

Between 1168 and 1188 the castle was completely remodelled by Henry the Second, who spent some £5,000 on the works. Henry built a new inner bailey at the north-west of the old lower ward, with a barbican in front of each of its north and south gateways, and raised a great rectangular keep in the centre of the courtyard. The existing curtain, the wall towers, and the gateways of the inner bailey, though refaced and in some cases altered in detail, are all substantially of this period. The curtain rising up to about the same level as the wall towers, is unusually high; all the towers are square and project outwards. There is a gateway, called King's gate, on the north side of the bailey and another, Palace gate, on the south; both have vaulted passages and were originally defended by portcullises and two-leaved doors. The gateway into the north barbican is out of alignment with the King's gate, thus involving a sharp turn and the exposure of the flank of any enemy advancing through the barbican. The south barbican has been destroyed. The outer line of defence with its towers and gateways, enclosing the inner bailey and extending southwards on either side to the edge of the cliff, was built in the thirteenth century and the underground passages are of the same period.

The keep is of three storeys and rises with two offsets to the height of 83 ft.; square turrets at the corners rise 12 ft. higher.

The walls are well buttressed and of great strength, they vary in thickness from 17 ft. to 21 ft. and contain many mural chambers in each storey. The forebuilding is at the east and south-east of the keep; it is strengthened by towers and encloses three long flights of steps, the lowest on the south side and the others rising against the east side of the keep. At the head of the first flight there is a chapel, richly decorated with clustered pillars and chevron moulded arches. A doorway at the corner opens to the second flight which has, midway in its height, a postern leading out from the second storey of the keep. The postern has been altered but was doubtless in the original design, to be used either for escape or for a rear attack on an enemy rushing up the stairway. At the head of the second flight there was a drawbridge and a doorway, and at the top of the third flight a guardroom and the entrance into the keep, at third storey level. The guardroom looks directly down on and commands the flights of steps of approach.

On the left of the entrance passage into the keep there is a chamber containing a well, called Harold's well. The well is about 350 ft. deep and is lined with stone to a depth of 172 ft. below the mouth. As at Newcastle there was no other direct drawing place, but a recess beside the well contained a tank from which supplies of water were conveyed through lead pipes to other parts of the keep. Another stone-lined shaft formed in the central tower of the forebuilding on the same level as this well has never been completely investigated and much speculation has arisen as to its purpose. The statement in the "official guide" that the shaft contained a hoist for getting stores up from the cellars is untenable. For there is no opening from the cellars to this shaft, which is 32 ft. back in the thickness of the wall from the inner face, and it is unreasonable to suppose that the stores were taken out into the courtyard to be hoisted up through a shaft opening on to it, probably in the face and under the fire of the enemy. The shaft is most probably another well, partly filled in, of which the straight stairway running in its direction in the second storey of the keep, and now blocked, was a drawing place. As noted above there are two wells in the keep at Middleham.

Internally the keep is divided by a cross wall into two large halls in each storey; the halls of the second and third storeys being well lighted from windows at either end, and having commodious mural chambers opening out of them. Originally there were no fireplaces in the central halls, the existing ones being inserted in Tudor times; but, as at Newcastle, there were fireplaces in the mural chambers, here principally altered at later dates. The latrines are arranged in tiers over a pit in the middle of the north side of the keep, the entrances to them passing beneath the high sills of the windows.

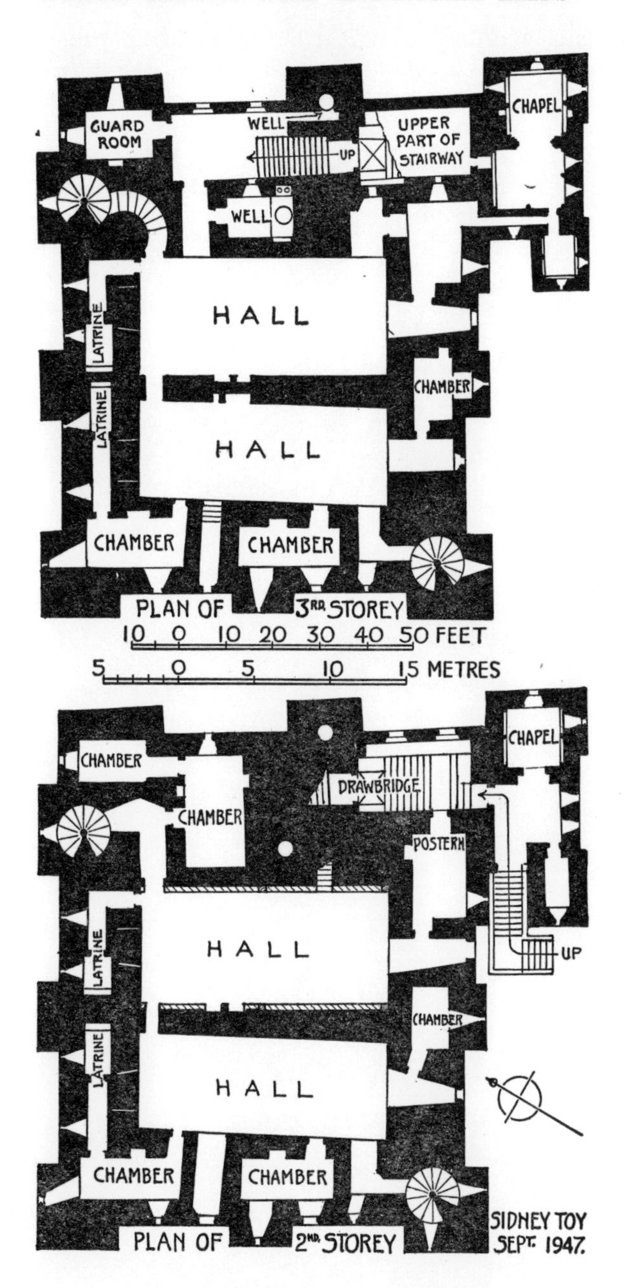

Dover Castle. Plans of The Keep

The entrance floor contains the principal apartments; there is a gallery running all round the walls, high above floor level, and a passage at the south-east corner leads to a second chapel, built over the other in the forebuilding. The second chapel was evidently for the special use of those occupying the keep. The old roof of the keep was taken down in 1800 and the existing brick-vaulted roof with flat upper surface for the support of artillery constructed in its place. Two wide spiral stairways at opposite corners of the keep descend from the third storey to the basement and rise to the battlements, with doorways at each level. In the second storey the large hall on the east side of the keep retains the old oak posts and struts, now partly embedded in the brickwork, which supported the old floor above.

The keep at Dover is one of the largest and most elaborate of these great structures as it was one of the last to be built.

Castle Rushen is described in Appendix C, page 282.

CHAPTER SIX

DEVELOPMENT OF CASTLES FROM 1160 TO 1270

DURING the whole of the twelfth century there was a constant stream of military forces passing to and fro between Europe and the Levant. The wars between the Crusaders and Saracens far from being confined to the main crusades were incessant and the expeditions to Palestine continuous. Pilgrimages to the holy shrines in Italy, Spain and other continental countries were also of frequent occurence. On their return from these expeditions the leaders of the crusades and the pilgrims were not slow in applying to their own fortifications the principles of defence they had proved to be effective, or had observed, abroad.

The rectangular keeps and towers built at that time in Western Europe had the great disadvantage of presenting vulnerable corners to the sapper and miner, since the enemy could be attacked from one side only and was sheltered by the corners from attacks on the other side. In the Levant the towers were frequently circular or polygonal, thus giving the enemy no corner screen. But a rectangular is much more convenient than a circular plan for the disposition of the interior rooms, and the development of the latter was very gradual in Western Europe; it was not until the end of the twelfth and the beginning of the thirteenth century that the round replaced the square form in this country.

Meanwhile many keeps of a transitional character were built, combining some of the advantages of both forms. Normally they were either polygonal or had a polygonal or circular body with turrets projecting from it. The keeps of Odiham castle, Hants., and Chilham castle, Kent, both built about 1160, are octagonal; Chilham having two projections from its sides.

Odiham castle, standing on an inner bend of the river Whitewater, has two baileys, divided and defended all round by a moat. The keep, the only remaining stone structure, is in a very ruinous condition but still stands to the height of about 40 ft.; it is of three storeys, rises with two external offsets and measures internally

40 ft. across from side to side. There is a buttress at each angle. The entrance has been destroyed but it appears to have been at the second storey; both the second and third storeys have fireplaces and were well lighted.

The keep at Chilham, just half the size of that at Odiham, has been kept in repair and although considerably modernized is of great interest. It consists of an octagonal tower and two projections from its sides, one a forebuilding and the other a stair turret. Flat pilaster buttresses which projected from the middle of each side

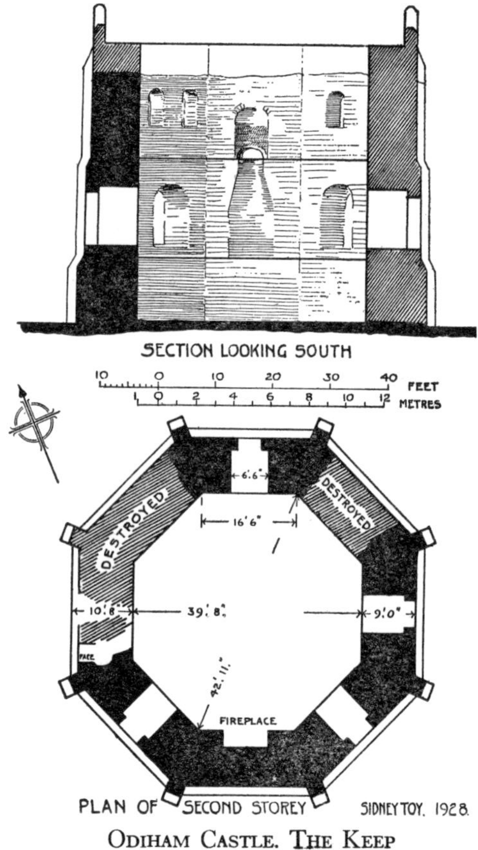

ODIHAM CASTLE. THE KEEP

of the tower have been cut away. The keep stands in a rectangular courtyard the enclosing curtain of which, though itself of later mediaeval date, probably rests on the foundations of a wall contemporary with the keep. The forebuilding stands on a stone structure which appears to have been a dwelling house of the latter part of the eleventh century.[1]

[1] Vide *The Antiquaries Journal,* Vol. VIII, 350.

Orford castle, Suffolk, built by Henry the Second between 1166 and 1170, and Conisborough castle, Yorks., built about 1180, both have transitional keeps with projections round a central nucleus.

The keep at Orford, the sole structural relic of the castle, is polygonal on the outside and circular internally. Three square turrets, spaced at equal intervals round the keep, and a forebuilding in the angle between the south turret and the main structure, project out from its face. The forebuilding contains the entrance porch with a basement below and a chapel above. The keep is of three storeys and its walls are carried up high above the third storey to protect the roof; the turrets rise 20 ft. above the main parapet.

The entrance is at the second storey and is reached by a straight flight of steps up to the porch of the forebuilding; the passage between the porch and the keep was barred by two doors. In the interior each of the second and third storeys consists of one large circular room and chambers in the turrets opening out from the room; each of the large rooms has a fireplace and is well lighted. A room opening out of the second storey in one of the turrets was the kitchen; it has two large fireplaces and a sink. One of the turrets contains a spiral stairway running from the first storey to the battlements. The others contain chambers, and since the chambers if made the same height as the halls would be disproportionately high they are subdivided into two stages for each storey; the lower chambers being reached by passages opening from the window recesses of the halls and the upper ones by passages leading round from the stair turret. There are two chambers in the turrets above the roof level, one of them having a double oven. In the basement there is a deep well, lined with dressed stone all the way down, and cut in the stonework are hand and foot holes for descent to the bottom.

Conisborough castle consists essentially of a single bailey on a high natural mound, the mound being scarped all round and surrounded by a ditch. There was an outwork on the south side of the castle but there are now no traces of its defences. The bailey is defended by a curtain 7 ft. thick and 35 ft. high, with wall towers at important angles built solid up to the wall walk. The gateway is in a very ruinous condition; it has a long and narrow barbican with a turn midway in its length, thus involving the maximum exposure of the enemy's flank. At the north-east, on the opposite side of the bailey from the gateway, the curtain is interrupted by the keep, which has one side exposed to the field. Domestic and service quarters were built against the curtain on three sides of the bailey (pp. 106, 116a, 159, 161).

The keep is a tall cylindrical tower of four storeys supported by six massive buttresses; the wall is 15 ft. thick above a very high batter which is carried round all the buttresses. The buttresses are

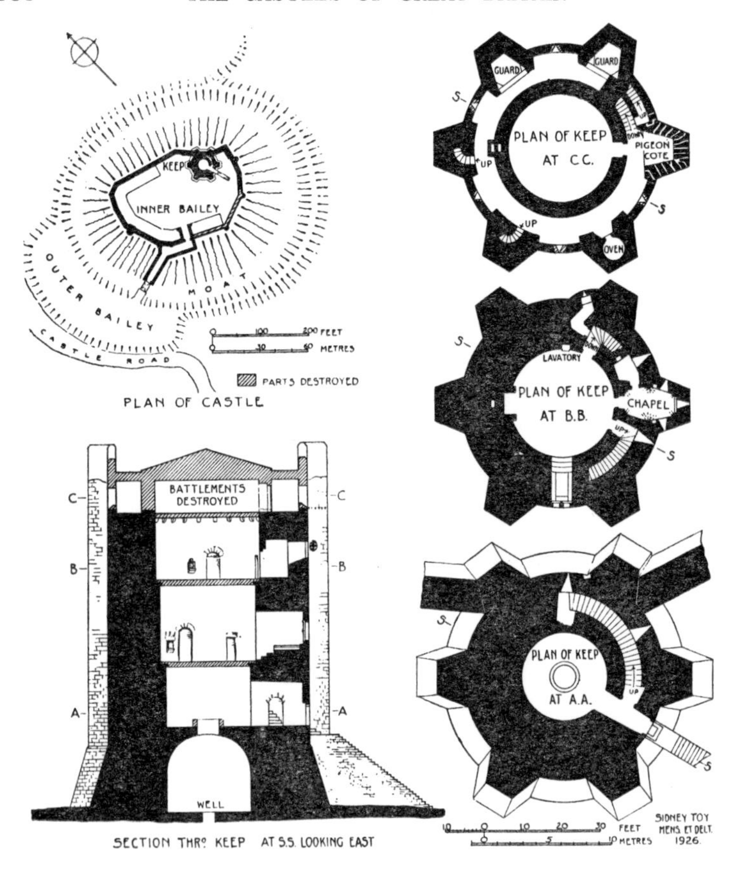

CONISBOROUGH CASTLE

spaced at equal intervals round the tower and rise to its full height; except for the chapel in one of them at the fourth storey they are built solid up to the battlements. The entrance is at the second storey and is now reached by a modern flight of steps up from the bailey; it was probably defended by a gap and drawbridge in front of the door. The basement has a stone domed vault and the entrance floor is paved with stone; the upper floors were of timber, resting on offsets in the wall. There is no window or fireplace either in the entrance floor or the basement and the only access to the latter, where there is a well, is through a hole in the centre of its vault.

From the entrance floor a mural stairway, running concentrically with the wall, leads up to the third storey and similar stairs rise from the third to the fourth storey and from that level to the battlements. Each of the third and fourth storeys has a two-light window, a fireplace, a stone lavabo basin, and a latrine; the last reached at the end of a zig-zag passage. On the fourth floor there is a richly decorated chapel, formed partly in the wall and partly in the south-east buttress; a small sacristy opening out of the chapel on the north.

The battlements are in a very ruinous condition but it is clear from the parts that remain that both the wall and the buttresses were carried up to form a screen round the roof and that there were two fighting lines, one above the other. The lower line was from a covered gallery running round the roof at gutter level, and the upper from the wall walk 12 ft. above the gallery. Three small vaulted chambers, all formed in the buttresses, open on to the gallery. One of them was a dovecot and is pierced by numerous holes about 6 in. square. In a fourth buttress at the same level there is an oven; it is 5 ft. 8 in. diameter, 3 ft. 7 in. high to the crown of its domed vault, and has a rectangular sinking in the middle of its flat floor 1 ft. 7 in. by 1 ft. 4 in. by 6 in. deep. The interior wall of the gallery running round the keep at this level was 3 ft. 8 in. thick and was originally carried up round the roof to the height of the upper wall walk; the upper walk was reached from the gallery by two stairways the lower parts of which still exist.

The keeps of Longtown castle, Herefordshire, and of Skenfrith and Caldicot castles, Mon., are cylindrical towers with semi-circular projections on the outside. They were all built about the end of the twelfth century.

Longtown castle consists of a keep on a high mound and two baileys stretching in line southward from the keep. It stands on the western half of a rectangular camp of much earlier but unknown date. The curtain walls and the inner gateway are very ruinous but are contemporary with the keep; the outer gateway has been destroyed. The inner gateway is flanked by solid round towers and was defended by a portcullis midway in its length (pp. 108, 116a).

The keep is of two storeys and consists of a circular tower 45 ft. diameter externally, with three round buttress-like projections spaced at equal intervals round the tower; it has a battered plinth 10 ft. high and the wall rises with two internal offsets to a level high above the roof. One of the buttresses provides the necessary thickness for a spiral stairway which rises from base to summit, another encloses a latrine at second storey level, while the third strengthens the wall at the point where the fireplace and its flue occur. The entrance, now destroyed, appears to have been at the first storey, the floor of which was level with the top of the plinth, and was reached by a flight of steps up the mound. The first storey contains the principal room. It has a fireplace and three two-light windows; a large cupboard is formed in one jamb of each of the

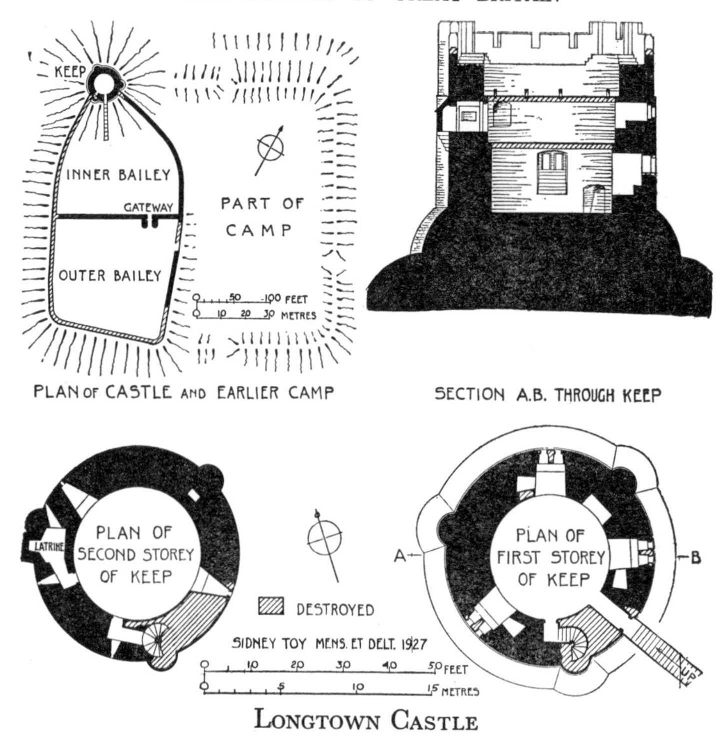

LONGTOWN CASTLE

windows. The upper floor contains the latrine; this storey is relatively low, has no fireplace and no other windows than two narrow loopholes.

Skenfrith castle consists of a keep on an artificial mound and a quadrilateral bailey; the keep standing isolated within the bailey. The bailey was defended by a moat on three sides and the river Monnow on the fourth. The gateway now destroyed was in the middle of the north wall; there was a tower at each corner of the curtain and one near the middle of the west wall, the last a slightly later addition. In the east wall there is a postern to the river. One of the corner towers has been destroyed. It is worthy of note that the upper floors of the three remaining towers are all on exactly the same level as though set out by a precise instrument (p. 109).

The keep is of three storeys and has a tall battered plinth with a large roll moulding at the head; a semi-circular turret containing a spiral stairway which projected at one side has been destroyed above the plinth. Excavations made in 1925 proved that the mound is artificial, composed of rubble and sand, and that the foundations of the keep, with rough faces on both sides, are carried down through this material to the natural soil beneath. The entrance to the keep was at the second storey and the foot of the stairs was at this level, rising from here to the summit. The basement, which must have been entered from a trap-door in the room above, received only such light and ventilation as came from two loopholes which, rising from a level near the ceiling, opened on the outer face above the plinth (p. 160). The keep is very ruinous and its upper part has disappeared.

Caldicot castle has a large rectangular bailey defended by a high curtain wall, with round towers at the salient angles, and by a moat which runs all round the walls. There are three gateways, one in each of the north, south, and west walls. The west gateway with the tower that surmounts it was built in the early part of the thirteenth century; the passage has a right-angle turn midway in its length. The entrance is on one side of the tower, under direct fire from the curtain and a wall tower facing it. The first part of the passage is defended by a two-leaved door, machicolations consisting of two circular holes in the vault, and a portcullis; within, the passage takes a turn right before continuing to the courtyard. Both the gateways on the south and north of the bailey are fine structures of about 1310.

The keep, built about 1190, stands at the north-west corner of

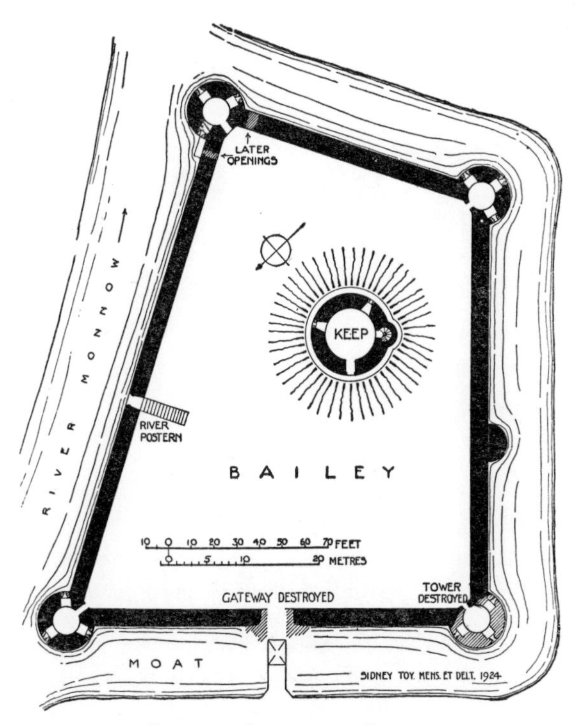

PLAN OF SKENFRITH CASTLE

the bailey, protruding largely beyond the walls and having its one round turret facing the field. The mound on which it stands was formerly surrounded by a moat, and it appears that the keep was the first part of the castle to be built, for the curtain on the south covers one of its loopholes. But there is no doubt that the curtain was in the original design and was raised soon after the keep was finished. The keep is of four storeys and contains fireplaces,

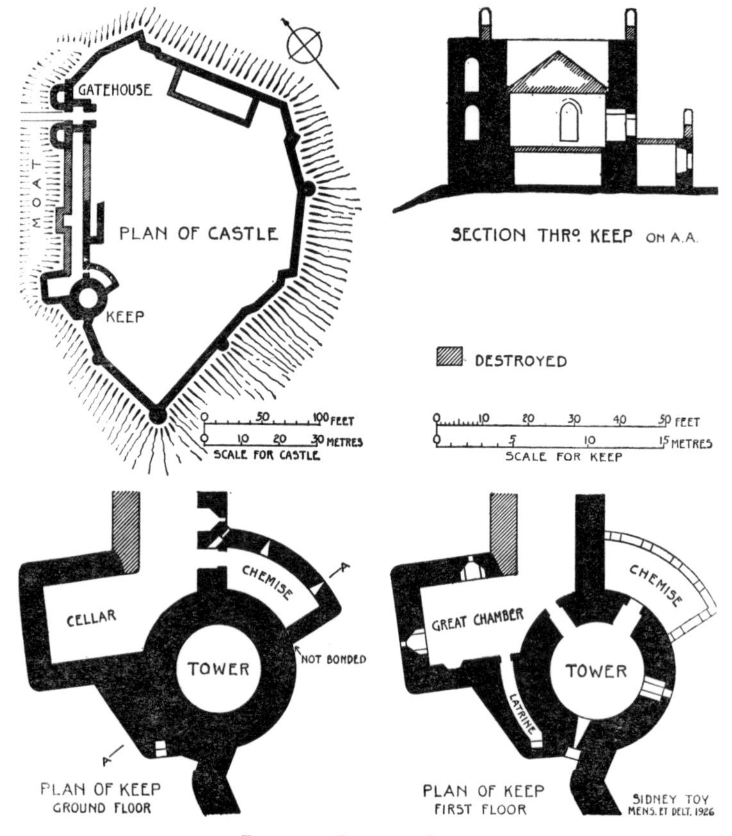

PENRICE CASTLE, GOWER

latrines and a well. The entrance is at the second storey and from here a stairway, concentric with the keep, descends to the basement and a spiral stairway rises to the summit. The projection from this keep, occupying as it does a vulnerable point outside the walls, assumes the character of an additional defence and is solid from the basement up to the fourth storey. Its value as a spur, however, must depend on the enemy's ignorance, or knowledge, of its structure. For there is a spacious chamber hollowed out in its base, below the upper surface of the mound, which would make sapping a simple operation. The spurs of the donjons in Normandy are solid from foundation to summit.[2]

Penrice, in Gower, South Wales, and Helmsley, Yorks., have transitional keeps of other designs.

Penrice castle stands at an isolated position on the western side of Gower. It consists of a single rectangular bailey, defended by a moat on the north side, where the gateway, the residential quarters, and the keep are built in line; the keep being at the south-west corner. The curtain wall has solid round towers at three of its salient angles. The castle was built about 1190 and although now in a considerable state of ruin retains original features of great interest. The gateway is flanked by round towers with flattened outer surfaces, the towers containing guardrooms. One wing of the residential quarters, adjoining the keep and projecting northward beyond the curtain wall, contained the great chamber at the second storey. This room is lighted by two windows with stone seats, has a fireplace and a latrine, and a doorway out of it, or what may have been its ante-chamber, admits directly to the keep (p. 110).

The keep is of two storeys and rises high above its roof line; it has a circular body with a chemise covering that quarter of its face which looks towards the bailey. This keep is so closely associated with the great chamber it adjoins, and from which it is entered at second storey level, that their conveniences and defences are complementary. There is no stairway in the keep and while its basement must have been entered through a trap-door in the floor above, its battlements were reached from the adjoining building. The chemise appears to have been of one storey only with a flat roof and battlements. It was entered from the ground floor of the residential quarters and has three arrow-loops directed towards the bailey; its flat roof and battlements were entered from the second storey of the keep.

Helmsley castle has a rectangular bailey and a barbican and outwork at the east end of the bailey. It was defended by two lines of ditches; the inner ditch passing round the curtain and through the barbican, and the other passing round outside the first, running between the barbican and the outwork, and on either side of the outwork to the river Rye. Both ditches were fed by the river. The curtain round the bailey was built about 1170 and the keep, which stands in the middle of its north wall, about 1190. At the north-west corner of the bailey there is a round tower with a bulbous projection. The east gateway and the barbican were built in the thirteenth century. The castle is in a very ruinous condition. The exposed outer half of the keep was destroyed in 1649 but

[2] Vide *Castles*, 116–119.

the inner half still remains to its full height of 100 ft. above the level of the bailey.

The keep, projecting half without and half within the bailey, is an excellent example of transitional design. On the outside, exposed to the sapper, it is rounded while within the curtain, where the form most suitable to the occupants could be permitted, it is square. It is of four storeys, the first and second only dating from the twelfth century; the two upper storeys with the turrets were added about 1290. The entrance was at the second storey and was approached from the wall walk of the curtain on either side. From this level stairs descended to the basement; the stairs to the upper levels, probably in the destroyed part, no longer exist. From the basement a postern opened on to a berm outside the curtain.

The arduous campaigns of the Third Crusade resulted in further developments in military architecture, as well in Western Europe as in Palestine. Weak spots in some of the existing fortifications had been clearly demonstrated. The Crusaders had seen the great execution wrought by the powerful siege engines then in use and the dire effects of sapping and mining. They had also been brought into direct contact with the highly developed fortifications of the Byzantine Empire, evolved during the period when Western Europe was wrapped in the throes of open warfare.

The site now chosen for a castle, where such choice was possible, was on the summit of a precipitous hill; the citadel, or inner bailey, being backed against the cliff. The main defence was concentrated on the less precipitous and more vulnerable side, where there were often two or even three lines of defences. Both Pembroke castle, built about 1200, and Beeston castle, Cheshire, about 1225, are of this order. To existing castles one or two outer baileys were added on the lines of approach, as at Corfe and Chepstow. Where the old castle stood on relatively level ground it was often surrounded by a new bailey, as at Kenilworth. The living quarters with the hall, domestic offices, and chapel, were now built in the court of the inner bailey. The keep, often no longer the ordinary residence of the lord but essentially the last line of defence, is smaller than those built previously but of more powerful and scientific design.

Pembroke castle stands on a promontory at the junction of the Pembroke river with the Monkton Pill. As seen from the other side of the river and looking towards the point of the promontory the castle presen` a most imposing sight with its walls and towers soaring up on the summit of precipitous cliffs. There are two baileys, the inner bailey on the point of the promontory, built about 1190–1200, and the outer bailey, added during the first half of the thirteenth century. The inner bailey is triangular with its apex at the point of the promontory. Its buildings, with the keep in the middle, are ranged against the south curtain and were formerly defended by a ditch which ran along between the baileys from one face of the cliff to the other. The gateway and a considerable portion of the curtain have been destroyed. The buildings to the east of the keep include two large halls which run side by side, with the wall between common to both. Beneath the outer hall, which projects out from the curtain, there is a large cavern, called Wogan, cut out of the rock. It was reached from the hall by a winding stair and probably had a gate to the river, to be used either for the reception of supplies or for escape. A wing from the inner hall extended to the keep, with a doorway into the keep at third storey level (pp. 113, 114, 151, 154, 159).

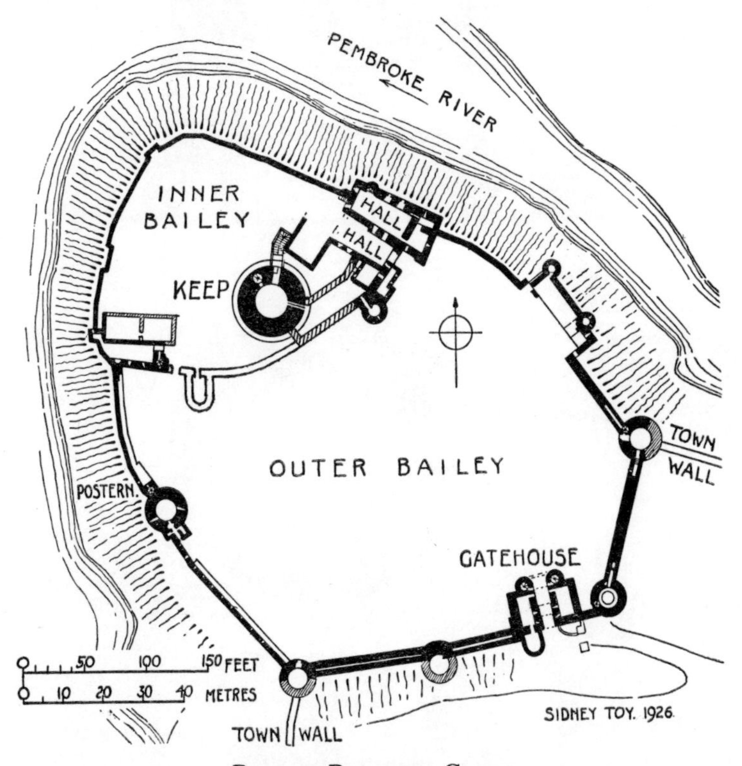

PLAN OF PEMBROKE CASTLE

The outer bailey is defended by a curtain with strong towers at the angles; the tower next east from the gatehouse is crowned with a stone dome. A long section of the south curtain wall, the most vulnerable side of the castle, is doubled; the extra 8 ft., bringing the total thickness to 15 ft., being added on the inside. The gatehouse is described in Chapter Seven.

The keep is a fully developed cylindrical tower without any adjuncts and is the finest mediaeval round tower in the country.

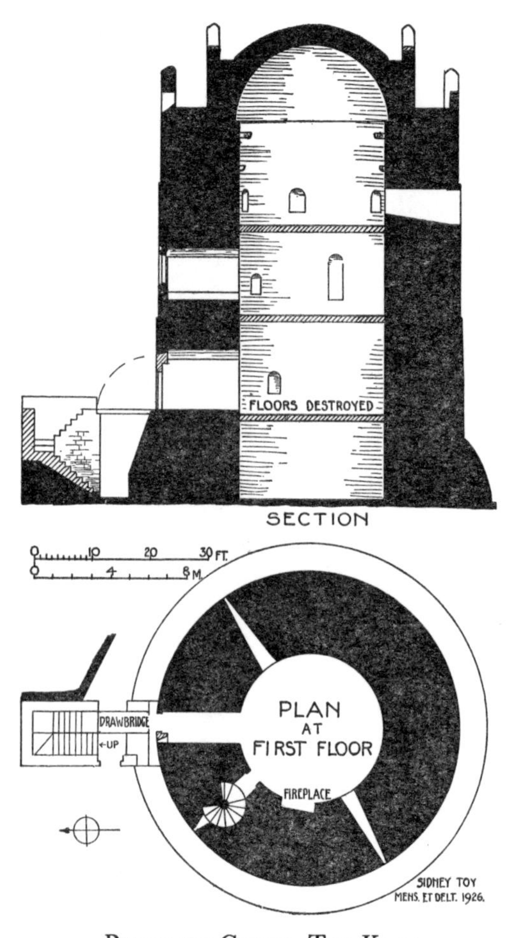

PEMBROKE CASTLE. THE KEEP

It is of four storeys, is 53 ft. external diameter, and rises with two offsets from a widely spread plinth to the height of 80 ft. The wall, averaging 15 ft. in thickness, is 1 ft. 7 in. thicker at the point where the stairway occurs than on the opposite side. The entrance was at the second storey and was reached by a flight of steps up to a drawbridge which spanned a gap in front of the doorway. All the interior rooms are circular and there are no wall chambers. The entrance floor has a fireplace but no windows other than two narrow loopholes. A spiral stairway leads from here down to the basement and up to all the higher levels. The basement had no other openings than two loopholes, now blocked. The rough opening, now the entrance to the keep, which has been driven in through the plinth to the foot of the stairway clearly relates to post-military times and the horizontal hole in the opening was made for the timber bar securing the door then placed there.

The third storey was the principal room of the keep; it has a two-light window, a fireplace, and two loopholes, and although there is no latrine in the keep a doorway from this room leads out

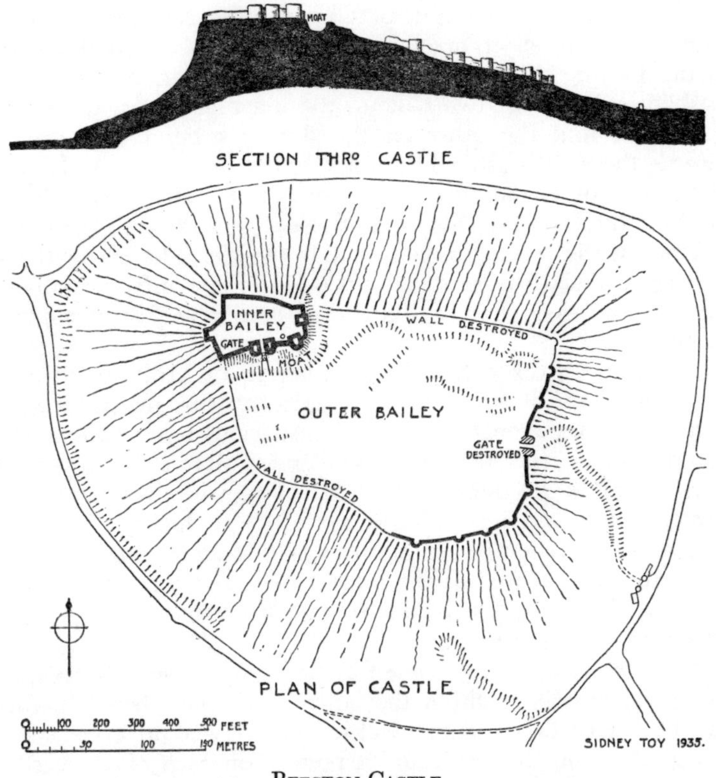

BEESTON CASTLE

to the adjacent domestic buildings, as noted above. The window is richly decorated on the outside with dog-tooth ornament and a carved head. The fourth storey has a two-light window of similar character to that below and four loopholes, but no fireplace. This storey is covered by a stone dome, rising at its crown 30 ft. above the floor of the room; the dome is 7 ft. thick at the haunches and 4 ft. at the crown and is strongly built. A ledge 9 in. wide for the support of the timber centre on which it was built runs round at the level of its springing line and corbels for the main truss of the centre still remain in the wall. At the battlements there were two fighting terraces, one round the base of the dome and the second, behind and above the first, round its haunches. At the time of siege hoarding was built out in front of the lower parapet and holes for the brackets of this temporary structure are to be seen all round the keep immediately below the arrow-loops.

Beeston castle, now a shattered ruin, appears to have had no special keep, unless the large wall tower to the east of the gate-house served that purpose. It was built by the redoubtable Randolph de Blondevill, Earl of Chester. The castle is perched on a high hill with sheer precipices on three sides and a steep slope on the fourth. The strength of Beeston lies largely in its inaccessibility. There are two baileys; the inner bailey on the summit of the hill and the other on the sloping ground that stretches towards the south-east. The inner bailey was strongly defended on the side of the approach by a gatehouse and two wall towers, and by a ditch 35 ft. wide by 30 ft. deep, cut through the natural rock across the promontory from side to side. The excavation of such an artificial ravine some two hundred and fifty years before blasting operations were known was a remarkable feat of engineering (p. 115).

Framlingham castle, Suffolk, founded about 1100 but rebuilt in the early years of the thirteenth century, has many distinctive features of exceptional interest. The spacious inner bailey, standing on a hillock with steep sides, is defended all round by a powerful curtain wall 8 ft. thick and 44 ft. high, with rectangular wall towers at frequent intervals rising still 20 ft. higher. There was a large outer bailey on the south and east and a smaller one on the west, both, as well as the inner bailey, surrounded by ditches. The inner bailey with adjoining fragments of that on the west constitute the principal remains.

With the exception of some fragments of walling the ranges of mediaeval buildings within the inner bailey have been destroyed, but the fine curtain and the wall towers are well preserved. There is a gateway on the south and a postern on each of the east and west sides; the gateway was somewhat altered in the sixteenth century when the barbican was added. The west postern opened on to a fortified bridge which is built out into the ditch and leads to a tower at the far end. From this tower, standing well out from the curtain, it was possible to command and sweep the whole outer face of the wall on the west side of the bailey and obstruct all enemy activities there.

There is a tower over the gateway and there are twelve wall towers. Three of the towers are solid in the lower part but the

Conisborough Castle from the South.

Conisborough Castle. The Keep from the West.

Longtown Castle. The Keep from the West.

Barnard Castle. The Keep from the North-West.

Pembroke Castle. The Keep from the South.

Bothwell Castle. The Keep from the Bailey.

others have open gorges towards the bailey; circulation of the wall walk through the towers being maintained by timber bridges thrown across the gorge with a door on either side. The battlements of the towers must have been reached from the wall walk by means of ladders. The open gorges below the wall walk were originally covered by the buildings of the bailey, while above it they were enclosed by timber framework and boarding.

At Laugharne castle, Carms., there is a strong circular keep of three storeys, all vaulted. The vault of the third storey, which is a very lofty room, is a pointed stone dome that rises high above the battlements.

Barnard castle, County Durham, was founded towards the end of the eleventh century. It stands on high precipitous ground on the east bank of the Tees and consisted of four baileys, or wards, of which the inner and town wards still retain large portions of their defences. The north wall of the town ward, standing in places to the height of the wall walk, dates from about 1100 and is built of the same kind of red sandstone as are the oldest portions of the keep at Durham. The walls in both cases are constructed in the same manner and the stones of which they are composed show precisely the same effects of weathering. The round, arched gateway in this wall is original. The inner ward is at the north-west corner of the castle, with a residential range built against the curtain overlooking the river. The keep is at the north end of the range and, as at Penrice, was so closely associated with the living quarters that their functions were complementary. The inner walls of the range have been destroyed, but that part of the curtain against which it is built stands to the height of the wall walk. The great hall is in the middle of the range (pp. 116b, 118).

The keep is a circular structure of three storeys with a deep battered plinth at its base; it projects half without and half within the curtain. On the side towards the courtyard it has an angular projection which encloses a vaulted chamber. Above the chamber the projection rises in pyramidal form and dies back into the circular face of the keep. This projection is in no sense a defensive spur, like those in Normandy, which are solid and rise to the full height of the tower; it is simply an adjunct with vulnerable thin walls and was built in this form to give a straight end to the hall range it adjoined. Having regard to its general design and its original details, there can be no doubt that this keep was built in the early part of the thirteenth century and not at the later period often suggested.

The entrance was from the hall range at the second storey, opening on to the passage, now partly blocked, on the south side of the keep. The passage admits to a circular room, 21 ft. diameter, which has a fireplace and was originally lighted only by two arrow-loops;

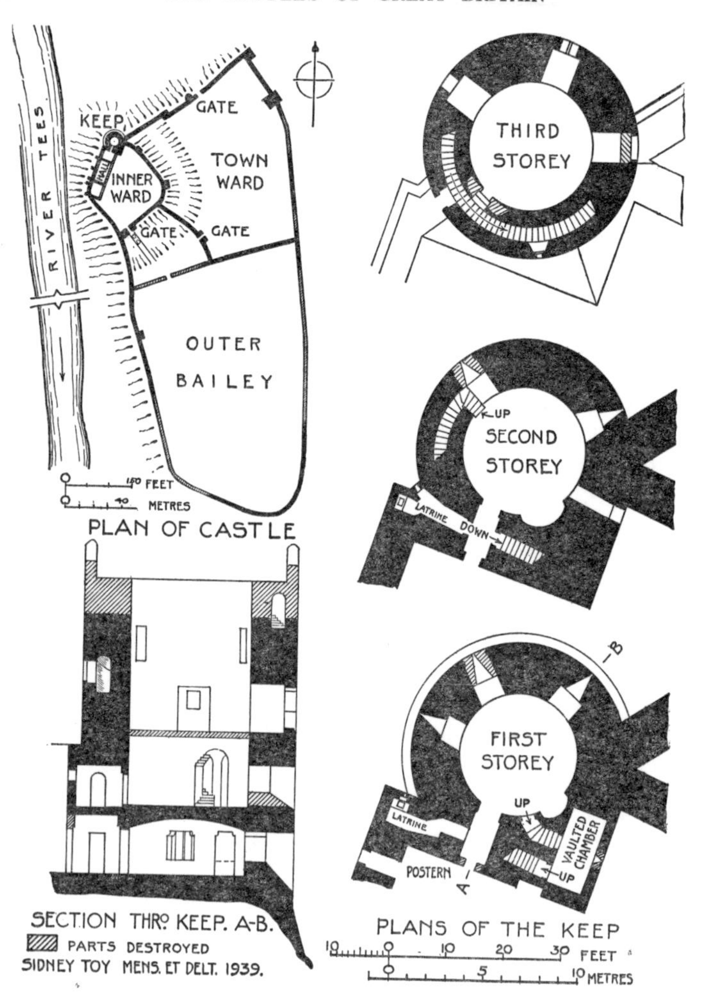

BARNARD CASTLE

a latrine opens out from the entrance passage. The stairway down to the basement also opens out from the entrance passage, while another mural stairway, concentric with the keep, rises to the upper levels from a jamb of one of the arrow-loops. At a later period this loophole was converted into a wide window with a round head. The stairway to the basement descends first to the rectangular chamber in the projection and then to the basement room. The chamber is covered with a barrel vault and had a loophole to the courtyard, now broken away. The basement has three arrow-loops a fireplace and a latrine; it is covered with a low saucer-shaped vault. A passage on the south leads to the hall range and although the opening into the range is now much broken away and altered there was doubtless a small doorway here leading to the postern in the curtain close at hand.

The stairway ascending the keep from the second storey reached first a door on the right opening on to the wall walk of the east curtain and then a door on the left opening to the floor of the third storey. This storey has two long arrow-loops, looking towards the field, and a doorway, now blocked, opening on to the wall walk on the north curtain. The upper parts of both the loopholes have been opened as windows at a later period. The winding stairway continues up to the battlements, which have been destroyed.

Dirleton castle, East Lothian, Kildrummy castle, Aberdeenshire, and Bothwell castle, Lanarkshire, all built or begun in the early part of the thirteenth century, have each a circular keep at a salient angle in the curtain. There is a close resemblance between the plans of the last two.

Dirleton castle stands on a rocky promontory, following round its contour and enclosing a rectangular courtyard with ranges of buildings on the east and south sides. At the south-west angle there is a group of three towers, the middle one square and the others circular; the largest circular tower is the keep. There were towers at the north-east and south-east corners of the castle, but these have been destroyed down to the plinth, together with the original curtain between them. The whole of the east side of the castle is now occupied by a long heavy range built about the middle of the fifteenth century. At the north-west corner of the castle where the rock falls away precipitously there is no tower.

The keep is so closely connected with the adjoining towers and with the structure built across the corner behind it that the whole group must be considered as forming one unit. At present the group is of two storeys and contains fireplaces, latrines, and a well; the upper parts of the walls have been destroyed. The keep is 40 ft. external diameter with walls 10 ft. thick, and although round externally the lower storey is six-sided and the upper storey seven-sided internally, the sides being very irregular in both cases. Each of the storeys is covered with a ribbed vault. The gateway into the castle, rebuilt in the fourteenth century, is an imposing structure which was strongly defended by a wide and deep ditch, a draw-bridge, portcullis, machicolations and two-leaved doors.

Kildrummy castle is built on a roughly pentagonal plan with the gatehouse at the most salient angle and a tower at each of the other angles. It stands on a promontory having its north side, which is much longer than the others, overlooking a ravine with a circular tower of bold projection at either end. The tower at the west end, occupying the highest point in the promontory, is the keep, that at the east end, the most complete in the castle, which is otherwise very ruinous, is known as Warden's tower; both are circular externally and internally. The other two towers, projecting half without and half within the bailey, present semi-circular faces to the field and square ends to the bailey. There is a postern, defended by a portcullis, in the curtain beside the Warden's tower and outside the postern a tunnel, the vault of which has fallen in, led down to the stream at the bottom of the ravine.

There are strong reasons to believe that Kildrummy was built by Gilbert de Moravia, Bishop of Caithness 1223–45, a powerful churchman who was treasurer under Alexander the Second. The hall and residential quarters, of which the chapel was a prominent feature, are on the north and east sides of the bailey. In order to secure more correct orientation for the chapel and to give it greater length it was built obliquely across the courtyard and thrust through the east curtain, where it protrudes much farther out from the face of the wall on the north than on the south. Though there is evidence that the curtain was broken through for the chapel, the building of the latter with its beautiful group of three lancet windows in the east wall must have followed closely on the earlier work.

The gatehouse has been destroyed down to within a few feet of the ground. Its remains show distinct traces of alteration subsequent to its first construction, particularly in the fifteenth century when the defences of the passage were rebuilt and the barbican added, but there is no reason to suppose that it is of later date than the rest of the castle. Kildrummy was clearly designed by an expert well acquainted with the latest developments in military architecture, and there is nothing in its plan suggesting a later period for this gateway than those of the middle bailey at Corfe or the outer bailey at Chepstow, both built in the first part of the thirteenth century.

Unfortunately the keep, which is 50 ft. in external diameter, has been destroyed down to the basement and its loss is all the more poignant in that descriptions of it, as it existed down to the eighteenth century, depict a structure of great strength and elegance. It was of many storeys, all vaulted, the vaults having round eyes in their crowns, like those of the Tour de Constance at Aigues Mortes; a mural gallery ran all round the wall of the second storey. The existing basement has a dressed stone vault and in the centre of its floor there is a square well, cut roughly out of the rock.

Bothwell castle stands on a promontory formed by a sharp loop-shaped turn in the Clyde, and is defended by precipitous banks on the sides towards the river, where the rock is scarped to its contour, and by a ditch on the land side. It was begun in 1242 and the keep as well as the base of the walls all round belong to the castle as first finished. Here the defences were centred round a great circular keep, placed at one corner of a pentagonal bailey. The outer half of the keep was thrown down in 1314 when the whole castle was laid in ruins. In 1336 Bothwell was again put in a state of defence but was reduced to about half its original size. A new wall was built from east to west across the bailey and while the southern half was re-fortified the northern half was levelled with the ground. The gap in the keep was closed by a straight wall built across the middle of the tower. Though considerable damage was done to other parts of the castle in a siege of 1337 the keep appears to have remained uninjured at that time (pp. 116b, 121).

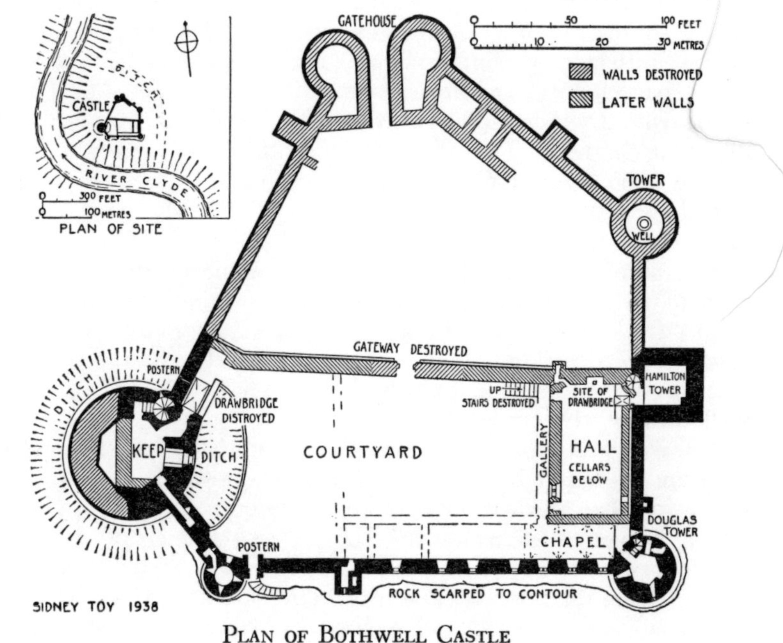

PLAN OF BOTHWELL CASTLE

The keep was circular on the outside, 65 ft. external diameter, and octagonal within; it is of four storeys, the first storey being below the level of the bailey, and the remaining portion still rises to the height of the wall walk. A deep moat on the bailey side isolated the keep from the other buildings of the castle. The entrance is at the second storey and is skilfully placed near the curtain at the north end of the moat. Here a pointed projection stands out from the keep, and the doorway is set on that side of the projection next to the curtain. Thus the approach is in line with and close against the curtain, and is commanded from the wall walk above. The doorway was defended by a drawbridge, across the moat, a portcullis and a door; the drawbridge and portcullis being operated from a small vaulted chamber above the entrance passage. Above the chamber the projection, like that at Barnard castle, dies into the keep in pyramidal form.

The entrance passage leads into a fine hall having a two-light window, enriched with jamb shafts, to the courtyard. On the walls, rising from corbels at the angles and forming an arch on each side of the octagon, are labels which at first sight suggest wall ribs of vaulting but are actually wall arcades. The floors were of timber, the first and probably the second being supported by an octagonal pier which still remains in the basement. The first floor was also supported on stone arches thrown diagonally across the keep from the pier to the walls on either side. A doorway on the south side of the entrance hall leads to a latrine and one on the north side to a spiral stairway which rises from the basement to the battlements. In the basement there is a well. The fourth storey, with a window of two trefoiled lights to the courtyard, was the great chamber. The timber floor of the fourth storey and the roof of the keep were both supported on wall posts with wide spreading struts and the long vertical chases for the posts are still to be seen in the sides and angles of the walls.

The parapet has been destroyed but on the north side of the keep at parapet level are four boldly projecting corbels, spaced from 2 ft. 2 in. to 2 ft. 11 in. apart. They belong to a triple machicolation, two sections of which commanded the entrance to the keep, and the third the exit from the spiral stairway on to the wall walk of the curtain.

The wall walks on the curtains leading north and south from the keep are protected by parapets on the side towards the bailey as well as on that towards the field and were covered by high pitched roofs, the verges of which still remain on the walls of the keep. The doorway to the south walk leads directly out from the keep while that on the north leads out from the stairway. The latter was closed against the keep and secured by a strong timber bar; so that in the event of the entrance to the keep being forced by the enemy the defenders could escape on to the wall and bar the door against him. There are two posterns in the walls near the keep, one to the moat outside the keep and the other in the south curtain. When complete this great tower at Bothwell was one of the finest circular keeps in Britain; it had its own water supply and other domestic requirements, was powerfully fortified, and could be held as well against an enemy within the bailey as one outside the walls of the castle.

The upper parts of the south and east curtains of the bailey, the ranges of buildings, including the hall and chapel, now standing against these curtains, and Douglas tower at the south-east corner, were all built in the latter part of the fourteenth century but it will be convenient to describe them here.

The hall stands on a range of three barrel-vaulted cellars and runs north and south along the east curtain, of which it stands clear by but a few inches. The doorways and windows are all in the west wall, facing the courtyard. There is a doorway at either end of this wall, and in addition to a large traceried window at the dais end on the south there is a continuous row of ten clerestory windows. The chapel at the south end of the hall, now largely destroyed, was an elegant structure of three vaulted bays; it is level with the hall and with the second storey of the Douglas tower and all three were in communication. There is now no stairway down to the basement of any of them; but while the basements opened from doors at the ground floor, this level was probably reached by a stairway from the courtyard up to a gallery, which ran along in front of the hall to the south range.

Douglas tower is a powerful structure of four storeys and is complete up to the boldly projecting corbels of its machicolated parapet. It is entered at the second storey and from here a spiral stairway rises to the upper levels; all storeys above the basement are well lighted rooms, each containing a hooded fireplace and a latrine. The top room has a wall arcade. A square tower at the north-east corner of the bailey, called Hamilton tower and now destroyed down to the basement, was a part of the original castle which appeared to have been fitted up as a strong point for use while the restoration of 1336 was in progress. For on the side towards the courtyard there was a drawbridge, designed on the counterbalance principle, which must have been taken away when the hall was built. The chases for the beams of the bridge when raised are still to be seen in the walls.

Clifford castle, Herefordshire, built on the river Wye early in the thirteenth century, has an irregular polygonal plan with boldly projecting round towers at strategic points of the curtain and a powerful gateway facing the line of approach.

At Pontefract and York the keeps are built on a quatrefoil plan, like the donjon at Étamps, forty miles south of Paris. The keep at Pontefract, by far the larger and more powerfully constructed of the two, dates about 1230 while Clifford's tower, as the keep at York is called, was built between 1245 and 1259.

Pontefract castle is mentioned in Domesday under the name of the castle of Ilbert, and from that time its defences were kept so closely in touch with the requirements of each succeeding period that before its destruction in the seventeenth century it was one of the most powerful strongholds in Britain. Cromwell's report to Parliament on the occasion of the siege of Pontefract in 1648 is illuminating on this point, especially since it was written by one of the greatest soldiers of the day. "The place is very well known to be one of the strongest inland Garrisons of the Kingdom; well watered; situated upon a rock in every part of it, and therefore difficult to mine. The walls very thick and high, with strong towers; and, if battered, very difficult of access, by reason of the depth and steepness of the graft."[3] Though great quantities of powder and other ammunition were sent to the investing army following this report the castle held firm and it was not until the Royalists' cause was lost by the execution of the King and when its supplies were utterly exhausted that the garrison surrendered. That the castle remained impregnable after a continuous siege of twelve months, during which the commander had twice received and

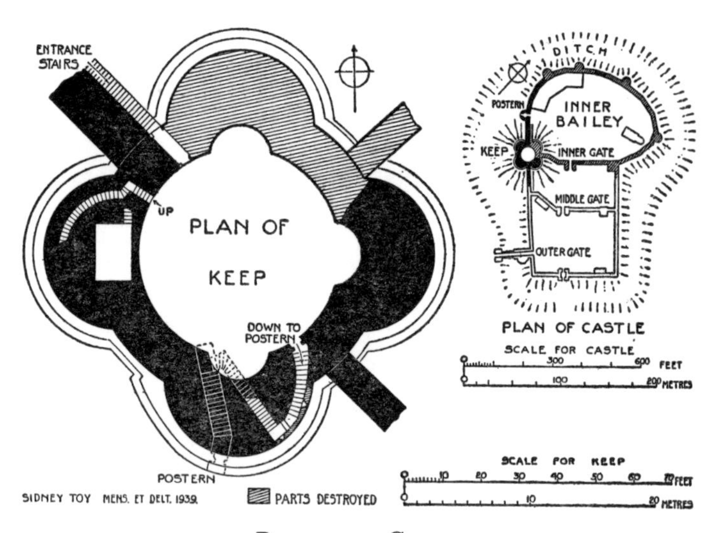

PONTEFRACT CASTLE

twice refused an offer by Parliament of £2,000 for its surrender is of itself eloquent proof of its enormous strength.[4]

Having obtained possession, the order then issued by Parliament for its destruction was carried out so thoroughly that the whole castle was practically levelled with the ground, and nothing now remains but the base of the keep, the lower part of Piper's tower, portions of the west curtain on either side of the keep, and a few scattered fragments of masonry here and there along the foundations of the walls. From these remains, however, and from old drawings and descriptions it is possible to recover with fair accuracy the general disposition of the defences of the castle. A thorough survey made recently by the author of this volume has disclosed the true plan of the keep.

[3] Diary of Nathan Drake, Sieges of Pontefract Castle, R. Holmes, 192.
[4] *Calendar of State Papers*, 1648–1649, pp. 118, 160.

The castle consisted of an oval shaped bailey, built on a rocky hill of sandstone, and two outer wards running in line south from the bailey; the whole surrounded by the deep "graft", or ditch, that Cromwell found so formidable. The main entrance was at the south-west of the outer ward. The bailey was surrounded by a strong curtain, with towers at frequent intervals, and had a gateway on the south and two posterns on the west; one of the posterns passing through Piper's tower and the other opening out into the ditch from the base of the keep. The remains of the curtain date from the latter part of the twelfth century; the keep, which is not bonded to the curtain, was built in the first part of the thirteenth century.

The keep stands on the highest point of the rock, where the rock projects well out into the ditch at the south-west of the bailey. In plan it has a circular nucleus, 77 ft. external diameter and 12 ft. thick, from which four large lobes project at the cardinal points. The lobe that stood within the bailey has been destroyed entirely. The other three are outside the bailey and rise from the bottom of the ditch, where there is a tall and widely spread plinth. In preparation for the construction of the keep the rock on which it stands was first scarped round to its contour. The rough faces were then thickly revetted, the massive plinth built, and the revetment carried up to the top of the rock; the inner portions of the walls of the keep standing on the natural rock at the top of the mound and the outer portions on that at its foot. On this foundation the tower rose up to a great height.

The entrance to the keep was by way of a flight of steps ascending against the curtain on the north side; the entrance doorway has been destroyed. Internally the south and east lobes have semicircular apses. The west lobe encloses a rectangular chamber. A mural stairway opening out of the main hall rises concentrically with the west lobe and has in its course a passage to the chamber. Another stairway leading out from the east side of the south lobe descends by zig-zag flights down to the postern opening on to the ditch. In the course of the descent there is a small chamber of the same width as the stairs and 7 ft. long. The lower half of the first flight down is now an open gallery, the outer wall having been broken through. It is probable that the relatively thin wall at this point was pierced by arrow-loops, commanding the outer face of the west curtain.

York castle stands on the right bank of the Ouse on the south side of the city. It consists of a keep called Clifford's tower, standing on a high mound, and a large bailey stretching southward from the mound; a ditch formerly ran all round the castle and between the mound and the bailey. The bailey is now occupied by modern official buildings and its mediaeval defences have been

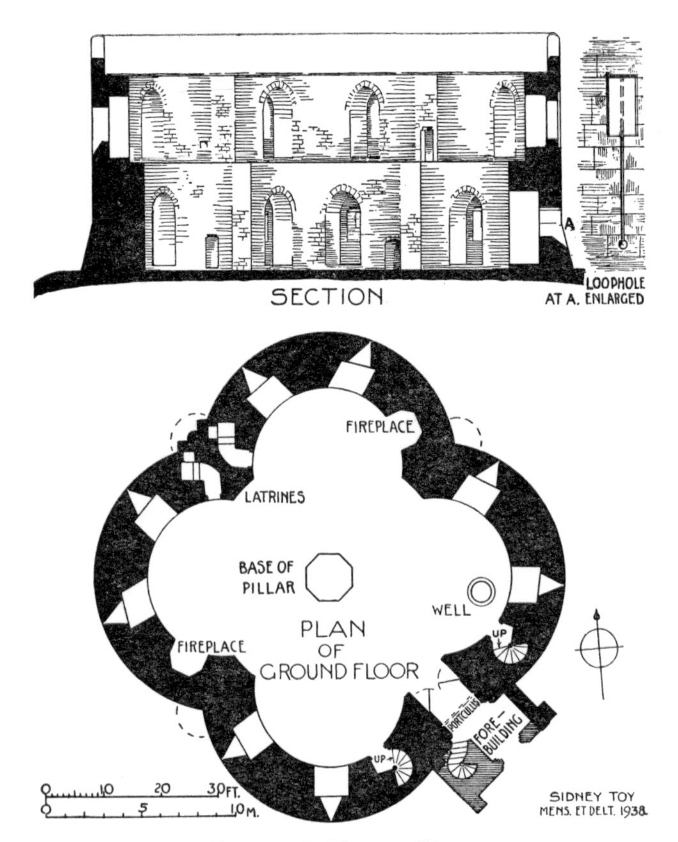

CLIFFORD'S TOWER, YORK

destroyed but the keep, standing on the site of an earlier structure, is almost complete save for its floors and roof (pp. 126, 128a).

Clifford's tower has a purely quatrefoil plan and is of two storeys only. Though its walls are 9 ft. thick at the head of a battered plinth, it is more shell-like in form, less substantial, and not nearly so high as was the keep at Pontefract. There can be no doubt that the building belongs to the thirteenth and not the fourteenth century, as suggested in the "official guide", largely on account of its shouldered arches. Since it is quite clear that the chapel within the tower was built in the thirteenth century the writer of the guide suggests that the chapel has been removed from some other site and rebuilt here. But shoulder arches often occur in much earlier work, as in the Great tower at Ludlow, about 1120, and the Carrickfergus tower at Warkworth, about 1200. The chapel, obviously of about 1250, has suffered from violence and distortion and two of its walls were rebuilt in the seventeenth century. The arcade against the inner wall was probably set in position after the wall behind it was built, and both it and the arch at the west have been altered. But the east arcade, now partly built over at the south end, is clearly contemporary with the wall in which it occurs and the chapel itself is a part of the original design (pp. 126, 128a).

The keep was built during the third quarter of the thirteenth century, when a large sum of money was spent on the castle. The details not only of the chapel but of other parts of the tower are unquestionably of this period, as the large corbels at the bases of the turrets and the arrow-loops in the great lobes. At a later period turrets projecting out from walls were supported on corbel courses, forming conical brackets, as in the outer gate at Harlech and the water gate at Beaumaris. The arrow-loops, before mutilation, were long narrow slits with circular enlargements at the foot. The square openings at the head of the loopholes are not original but were cut out at a later period to give light to the interior, which must have been very dark hitherto. The only original windows are two on the upper floor, now partly blocked.

The entrance is at ground floor level, through a forebuilding; the inner passage being defended by a portcullis and a two-leaved door. Both storeys are pierced all round by arrow-loops, so placed that the loops of the upper storey are in vertical line midway between those of the ground storey. The floor of the upper storey and the roof over the keep were supported centrally by a pier, the stone foundations of which were found about fifty years ago. The partition walls have all disappeared but it is probable that each storey was divided into four rooms corresponding with the four lobes. The north and west rooms on the ground floor have each a fireplace and a latrine and there is a well in the west room. Two spiral stairways rise from ground level to the upper floor and the battlements. At upper floor level three small turrets project out on corbels at three of the re-entering angles of the lobes, the fourth angle being occupied by the forebuilding. The north-west turret is for latrine service; the other two contain additional stairways to the battlements. The forebuilding is of three storeys, the first being the entrance porch, the second the chapel, which has richly moulded arcades, and the third a small chamber from which the portcullis was operated.

Dunstaffnage, Argyll, and Yester and Hailes, East Lothian, were all three built in the third quarter of the thirteenth century.

Dunstaffnage castle stands on a rocky peninsula guarding the entrance to Loch Etive, near Oban; its lofty walls rising sheer up from the edge of the rock, following its quadrangular contour. The gateway is at one corner of the castle, 15 ft. above the level of the ground outside, and was approached by a flight of steps up to a drawbridge crossing a gap at the head. The keep is one of the round corner towers and stands facing the gateway diagonally across the bailey.

Yester castle occupies the point of a high promontory at the junction of Hopes Water and a small burn and is defended on the far side of the point by a deep ditch running from one stream to the other. The gateway and large portions of the curtain on the south have been destroyed; but the north curtain, which is built straight across the promontory cutting off the extreme point, with its return walls east and west, still stands to a great height. There is a postern opening on to the point in the north curtain.

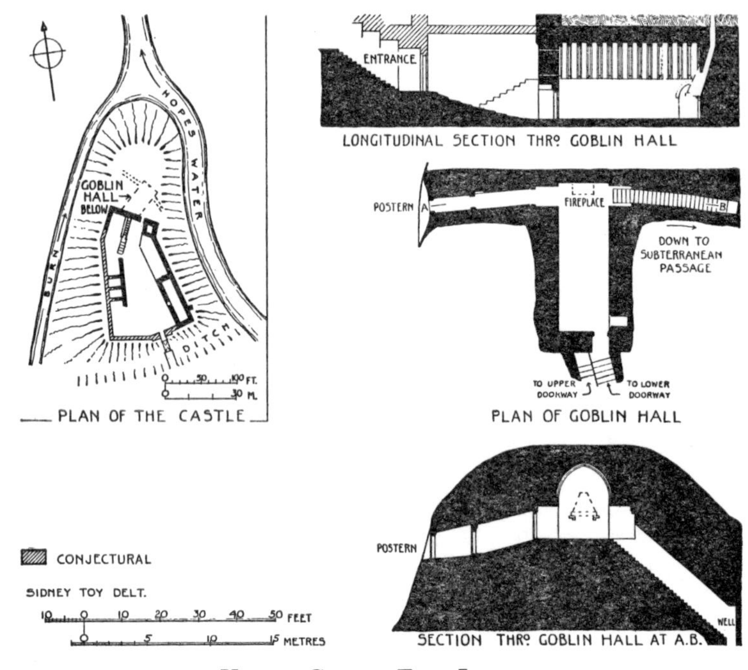

YESTER CASTLE, EAST LOTHIAN

A notable feature of Yester is the subterranean room called Goblin Hall, which lies beneath the soil outside the north curtain. It is a fine chamber, 37 ft. long by 13 ft. 2 in. wide, built of ashlar and covered by an acutely pointed vault; the vault being strengthened by numerous transverse ribs, closely spaced. The hall was divided into two storeys by a timber floor, now destroyed, at the level of the springing of the vault. Both storeys were entered by doorways at the south end of the hall which were reached by a flight of steps down from the bailey; the upper door from a level midway in the descent and the lower one from the foot of the

York. Clifford's Tower from the North-East.

Kiessimul Castle from the Sea.

Warkworth Castle. The Grey Mare's Tail Tower.

Coity Castle. The Ovoid Tower.

flight. There is a large fireplace at the north end of the hall and a spacious cupboard in the west wall. There are no windows, so that the lighting must have been entirely artificial.

At the north end of the hall are two pointed doorways, one on either side and both defended by strong timber bars. That on the west, which, in addition to the bar appears to have been protected by a portcullis, opens to a vaulted tunnel, cut through the rock. The tunnel after passing a second door midway in its length issues at a postern on the precipitous face of the bank of the stream. The doorway on the east side of the hall opens to a vaulted stairway which descends rapidly to end in a sheer rock face. Infilling at the foot of the steps indicates a well which has been filled up with stones.

The purpose of this remarkable and elaborate "dug-out" is clearly military. It forms a well provisioned and secure headquarters, of which there is no indication above ground, for use in times of stress. From it a hard-pressed garrison could carry out a surprise sortie or make an effective escape.

Hailes castle stands on a promontory on the right bank of the river Tyne, near East Linton. It follows a plan, very prevalent in Scotland, of a rectangular enclosure, defended by a strong curtain often without wall towers, and a bold square keep projecting out from the curtain at a strategic point. Here the castle is oblong and runs east to west on the river bank, with the keep projecting out at the head of the promontory on the west. The south wall, towards the field, is 8 ft. 6 in. thick; the main gateway is in this wall and there is a postern to the river in the north wall. The postern, or water gate, is reached by way of a steep stairway, with a vaulted and ribbed roof, which passes down through the wall to a landing stage. The landing is divided by a gap, formerly spanned by a drawbridge, into two parts of which the outer part, standing high out of the water, must have been reached from the river by a flight of steps up.

Dunollie, Argyll, and Kiessimul, Outer Hebrides, also probably date from the latter half of the thirteenth century though hitherto both of them have been assigned to a later period. In each case the castle consists of a single ward, enclosed by a strong wall, and there is a large square keep set diagonally at one corner of the courtyard.

Dunollie castle stands on a precipitous high rock on the east shore of the Firth of Lorne, near Oban. The south and west walls of the square courtyard have fallen down the face of the cliffs on which they stood but the north and east walls still stand to a considerable height, the first being 11 ft. and the second 9 ft. thick. The main entrance gateway is on the east side of the castle and there is a postern in the thick wall on the north; the postern taking two right-angle turns in its passage through the curtain. The keep is of three storeys, the first being covered by a barrel vault and the others divided by timber floors. Straight mural stairways ascend from the basement to the third storey and from there a spiral stairway rises to the battlements. Each of the second and third storeys is well lighted, has a fireplace and a latrine; the windows of the third storey, obviously the great chamber, have stone seats.

Kiessimul castle stands on the sea shore at the south point of the Isle of Barra. Though relatively small its high walls, strong keep, and secure position, made it one of the most formidable strongholds in the north of Britain. Since there is no note of its existence before the early part of the fifteenth century it has been assumed that it belongs to that period, despite its obviously more ancient character. But if all buildings were dated on that principle their history would become meaningless. Actually there is no account whatever of its construction and there is every reason to believe that its builder, far from being atavistic, was well acquainted with the principles of military architecture prevalent in his day. From the evidence of its structure it belongs to the thirteenth century, probably the latter part of that period, and it is one of the most interesting castles in the country. Additions were made in the fifteenth century, as for example the machicolations high above the entrance gateway and above the doorway into the keep; and the buildings of the courtyard, or barmkin, now very ruinous, were built or rebuilt in the seventeenth and eighteenth centuries.

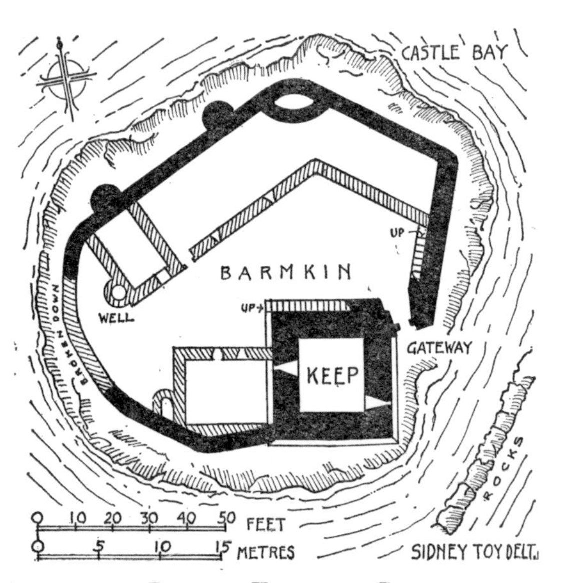

PLAN OF KIESSIMUL CASTLE

But the curtain wall and the keep both relate to the thirteenth century (pp. 128a, 130).

The castle has an irregular shape, following the contour of the rock on which it stands. The keep is on the south, built half without and half within the curtain and looking directly seaward. There is a tower at a re-entering angle of the curtain on the north and two small round towers project out from the curtain on the north-west. The gateway, now blocked, is on the south side of the castle, near the keep, and was reached by way of a narrow channel of the sea between the keep and a reef of rocks. It was defended by a machicolation, built out from the parapet of the curtain. The curtain walls are crowned by a parapet which rises to so great a height that the sills of the few embrasures it contains are themselves about 6 ft. above the wall walk, suggesting a raised timber walk which could be removed in the event of the walls being scaled by the enemy. At a convenient level below the embrasures are square holes in the parapet for the reception of the beams which supported the temporary staging.[5] The parapet of the shell keep at Tamworth castle, probably a thirteenth-century reconstruction, is of somewhat similar character.

When the earlier editions of this book were published the internal buildings were ruinous and there was a wide gap in the curtain wall on the west. At present in the ownership and occupation of Mr. Robert L. Macneil, the Macneil of Barra, the castle is in process of restoration under careful supervision and, while preserving its historical features, of adaptation to the requirements of modern residential amenities. The keep possesses many interesting features. Its walls, unpierced but by rare loopholes, rise severely up from a tall battered plinth, presenting a most formidable aspect towards the line of approach. The keep is of three storeys surmounted by a tall parapet similar to that on the curtain. The entrance is at the second storey, on the north side facing the courtyard, and is now approached by a ladder. The original approach appears to have been by flights of steps rising from the north side of the keep to the wall walk on the curtain at the east then, turning back, by another flight rising to the level of the entrance doorway, with a gap, spanned by a drawbridge, between the head of the stairs and the doorway. The steps have been broken down, but the foundation of the lower flight still remains against the keep.

In the entrance passages a stairway on the right descends in the thickness of the wall to the basement, which is now filled up with debris. Another mural stair rises to the third storey, and from there a stairway, opening from a jamb of the north window, leads to the battlements. Here, at a later period, advantage was taken of the great height of the parapet for the addition of a fourth storey and

[5] Vide Toy, *Castles,* p. 21.

the raising of the wall walk to parapet level. The machicolation projected out from the parapet over the entrance doorway to the tower formed part of these later works.

In the design of castles during the third quarter of the thirteenth century there is already a tendency to discard the keep as a special building and to incorporate its functions in the gates and towers of the curtain, which are now built on more powerful and scientific lines. Inverlochy castle, near Fort William, and Barnwell castle, Northants, both built at this period, the latter about 1266, are early examples of this movement. Both are rectangular fortresses with straight sides and round towers at the corners.

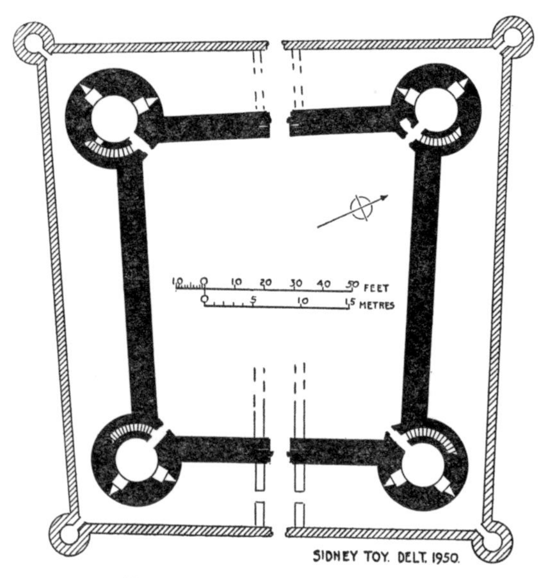

Plan of Inverlochy Castle

Inverlochy castle stands on the south bank of the river Lochy on ground which has a gentle slope north-west to the river. It is a rectangular structure with double walls and has circular towers at the corners of both curtains; there were gateways in the east and west walls but both outer gateways have been destroyed. The outer curtain was added in the fifteenth century; it is 3 ft. thick and is now in a very fragmentary condition, as are walls which flanked the passage between the outer and inner gateways.

The inner wall, which is 9 ft. thick, with its towers and gateways, dates from about 1270; it was originally surrounded by a moat and the gateways, now in a very ruinous condition, were approached by drawbridges; a portion of the check for the reception of the bridge when raised is still to be seen in the gateway on the east, which was the side of approach. Each of the gateways was defended by a portcullis and a strong door secured by heavy timber bars. The four towers are of similar design, all are of great projection and circular both internally and externally. They are of three storeys, pierced with arrow-loops with triangular feet, and are entered directly from the courtyard at ground level; on one side of the entrance passage a mural stair rises concentrically with the wall to doorways on the second and third storeys. On the side facing the courtyard three of the towers have straight splayed faces but the splay of the north-east tower projects out in the middle as an obtuse prow. The south-west tower, the largest of the four, was probably the residence of the chief in the time of the siege; it has a latrine and there is a wide fireplace on the third storey.

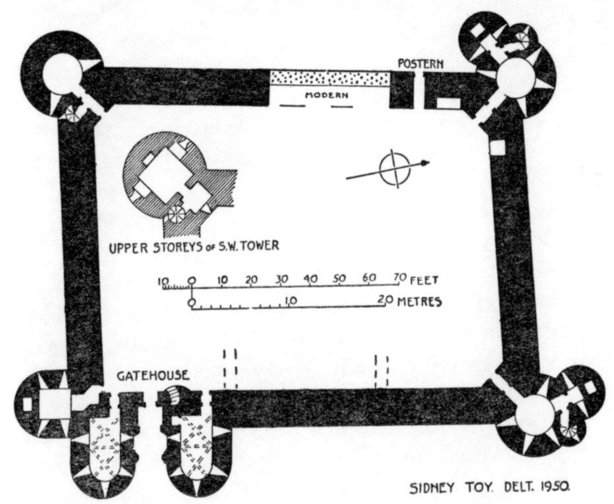

PLAN OF BARNWELL CASTLE

The whole castle is very ruinous and all internal buildings, which surrounded a small courtyard, have disappeared.

Barnwell is a rectangular castle with the long sides running north and south; its walls are 12 ft. thick and 30 ft. high. There is a tower of bold projection at each corner and a powerful gatehouse at the south end of the east wall, associated with the corner tower at that point. There is evidence that the castle was originally surrounded by a ditch. All the internal buildings have been destroyed (pp. 133, 142a).

The gatehouse with its flanking towers projects far out from the face of the curtain and has a long vaulted entrance passage, which was defended by a portcullis and two lines of double doors. Vaulted guardrooms with doors opening from the courtyard flank the passage on either side. The upper storeys of the gatehouse, as of those of the adjoining tower are reached by a flight of steps up from the courtyard near the inner entrance of the gateway passage. The towers at the other three corners of the castle are all entered from a doorway in the courtyard and, like those at Inverlochy, their upper storeys are reached by a stairway at this level; here, however, the stairs are spiral. The tower at the south-west corner, like that in the corresponding position at Inverlochy, was clearly used for residential purposes. Internally, the first storey only is circular; the two upper storeys (there are three storeys) are relatively large square rooms with two wide and deep recesses running the full height of the room, one on either side, and a small entrance lobby. There is a latrine, formed in the adjoining portion of the curtain, and there is a fireplace in each of the two storeys.

Each of the other two towers is a trefoil structure, composed of the main body, which is circular, and two lobes of different sizes protruding from it. The smaller lobe, placed between the other and the main body, contained the spiral stairway to the upper floors. The other lobe contained the latrines; the shaft of the upper latrine falling down behind the lower one and both discharging into a pit open to the outside face of the wall and to the ditch. In each of these towers there is a fireplace in the second storey. There is a postern in the north curtain. The arrow-loops in the lower storeys of the castle are distinguished for having two horizontal slots but no enlargement at the foot (p. 154).

Two eighteenth-century reports of this castle provide further evidence of the reserve with which some statements of total destruction must be taken. In 1704 the castle is said to have been "late demolished" and, writing in 1748, Stukeley says that the Duke of Montague (who died in 1709) "had pulled the castle down". Actually, though all the buildings of the courtyard have been destroyed, the walls, gatehouse and towers are fairly complete.

Meanwhile many castles already in existence were greatly enlarged and strengthened during this period. Warkworth, Kenilworth, Chepstow, The Tower of London, Saltwood, and Corfe are good examples.

Warkworth stands on an expanded loop of the river Coquet, pointing northward, with the town on the actual point of the loop and the castle on the narrow neck between the town and the open country on the south. The castle consists of a keep, standing on a mound, and a bailey stretching southward from the keep. The mound is most probably a natural hillock, round the base of which the river formed its course, gradually eating more and more into the left bank and receding farther and farther from the right. The town is mentioned in eighth- and ninth-century records, but the castle was first laid out in its present form by Robert de Mowbray, Earl of Northumberland, in the latter part of the eleventh century.

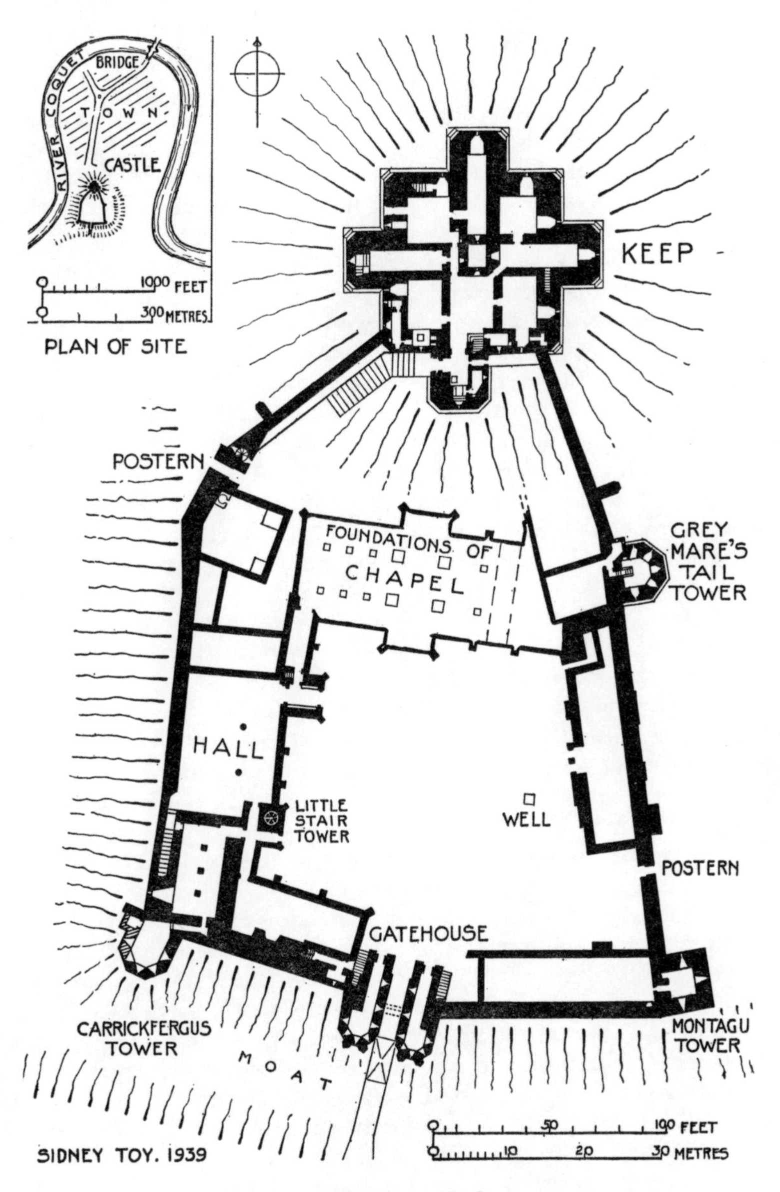

PLAN OF WARKWORTH CASTLE

Some lower parts of the east wall of the bailey are of this period. But between 1191 and 1214 the fortifications were rebuilt on a more powerful scale; the gatehouse, Carrickfergus tower, the great chamber, and the north-west postern were all built at that time. The Grey Mare's Tail and the turret between it and Montagu tower were added about 1260 when parts of the curtain, including long stretches, with the buttresses, on either side of the keep were rebuilt. The keep, described in Chapter Eleven, was rebuilt on its present imposing scale about 1390, incorporating in its west wall a postern of a much earlier period (pp. 128b, 135, 142b, 147, 222a).

The castle has a shovel-shaped plan with the gatehouse in the middle of the outer side and a tower at either end of it. There are two posterns, one at the north-west and the other at the south-east of the bailey. The great hall and residential quarters are ranged against the west wall, occupying the site of those of the twelfth century, fragments of which still remain. The range was again largely rebuilt in the fourteenth century, but the great chamber with its undercroft, at the south of the hall, dates from the early years of the thirteenth century and is connected by passages with Carrickfergus tower. The chapel was built in the fourteenth century. The whole range is now in a very ruinous condition, but the Lion tower, the lower part of which is the porch to the great hall, and the Little Stair tower at the south-east corner of the hall, both stand to practically their full height. Montagu tower, at the south-east corner of the bailey, was rebuilt about 1465. The gatehouse is described in Chapter Seven.

The Grey Mare's Tail is a remarkably fine tower, built of ashlar and still complete from its battered plinth to the parapet; it projects in semi-octagonal form entirely on the outside of the curtain. Each of the five outer faces is pierced by a crossed arrow-loop, so long that it extends through two storeys of the interior. There are three cross slots in each loop, two at the head and one near the middle. At the foot the loop is spread out horizontally to give lateral range for attacks on sappers (p.128b). There are holes at parapet level for temporary hoarding. Two powerful and well designed buttresses on the north side of the bailey, of the same period as this tower, are of unusually great projection and have splayed edges and weathering. Stretching from east to west right across the north side of the bailey are the foundations of a cruciform church, of about 1400, founded, after a mode then prevalent, for a college of priests within the precincts of the castle.

Kenilworth castle came into the hands of the crown about 1200 and during the reigns of John and Henry the Third was so strengthened that at the time of the Barons' War, in which it played a most conspicuous part, it was one of the strongest castles in the kingdom. Held by that redoubtable warrior Simon de Montfort and afterwards by his son, it proved impregnable to all attacks from without. In the memorable siege of 1266, which lasted for six months, it successfully repelled all assaults by the royal forces and surrendered only when the garrison was ravaged by disease and had run out of supplies (pp. 137, 139, 153).

Situated in the heart of England and surrounded by dense forests, the additional fortifications consisted largely of powerful and extensive outworks. The inner bailey (Chapter Five) stands on a natural knoll at the foot of a valley. Early in the thirteenth century a large outer bailey was built which, encircling the older work on

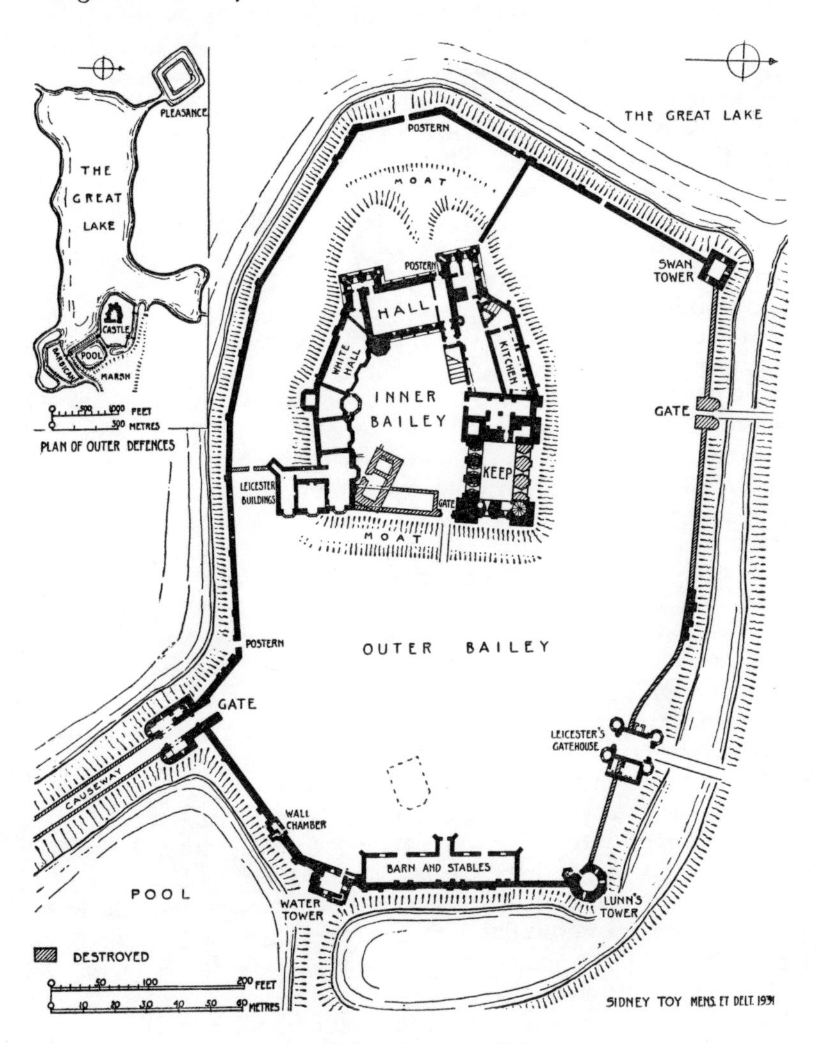

PLAN OF KENILWORTH CASTLE

the west, extended far from its walls on the east, partly blocking the mouth of the valley. Then from the outer bailey a long causeway, afterwards called the Tilt Yard, was thrown across the remaining portion of the mouth, damming up the stream which flows through the valley. By this means the long sheet of water, called the Great Lake, was formed which, from the west wall of the castle, stretched three-quarters of a mile up the valley. Further protection was provided by two lines of moats on the north and by a barbican and an outwork at the main entrance on the south-east.

The outer bailey was enclosed by a strong curtain wall, buttressed at frequent intervals and having strong towers at the north-west, north-east and south-east. The main gatehouse, called Mortimer's gate, is at the inner end of the dam and there was a second gatehouse at the outer end and a third on the barbican. Mortimer's gate has been destroyed down to the base and only fragments remain of the other two. There was a gateway in the north wall of the bailey, which has been totally demolished, and a postern to the lake on the west. All these works were built between 1200 and 1260. Lunn's tower, at the north-east corner of the bailey, is one of the earliest of them; it is a cylindrical tower of three storeys, has a wide spreading plinth and pilaster buttresses. The entrance is at the ground floor and the upper levels are reached by a turret stairway which projects out into the courtyard. A modern stairs, built beside the old one, now rises from the second storey to the summit. Each of the second and third storeys has a fireplace and a latrine. Swan tower, at the north-west of the bailey, now in ruins, has a square base and an octagonal superstructure.

Water tower, at the south-east, is a well designed structure of about 1240, still complete except for its battlements. It is of two storeys, is semi-octagonal towards the field, rising from a square base, and is entered at ground floor level. The first storey has a window, with seats, to the courtyard, a latrine, and a water gate, now mutilated, which opened on to the Pool at the east. A drain, or sluice, which ran across from the Great Lake to the Pool, passes beneath the floor. The upper floor, reached by a spiral stairway, was a very agreeable room, having three windows, a fireplace, and a latrine; a small sleeping chamber opens out from the main room.

A short distance along the curtain south of the Water tower there is a most interesting wall chamber formed within the curtain itself. It is entered directly from the courtyard and consists of a vaulted room and a latrine approached by a passage from the room. The room is a comfortable little apartment with a large fireplace, a cupboard of two tiers, and a lancet window to the courtyard. On the east side of the bailey there is a fine Elizabethan gatehouse, built of brickwork about 1570; the curtain wall was adjusted to it as can be seen by the toothing now exposed on both sides.

Chepstow castle was greatly strengthened during the first part of the thirteenth century by the addition of powerful works at both ends of the narrow tongue of land on which it stands. At the higher end on the west a barbican was formed, which was defended by its own ditch and a strong wall with a gatehouse at one end and a tower at the other. On the lower ground at the east end of the castle a large outer bailey was projected forward with walls of great bulk on the more vulnerable sides facing east and south, that on the south being about 18 ft. thick for the greater part of its length. Along the north wall, which is backed against the cliffs, a sumptuous range of residential buildings, including a spacious great hall, was built, all now very ruinous.

The south wall is flanked by the outer gatehouse at one end and a powerful tower, called Marten's tower, at the other. The gatehouse is an imposing structure, still standing to its full height less the battlements. It has a round tower on either side, that on the edge of the cliff being smaller than the other which more directly faces towards the field. The outer part of the gateway passage was defended by two lines of machicolations, a door, and two portcullises. The second line of machicolations consists of two large circular holes which pass down through the wall from the fourth storey of the gatehouse, thus providing a long drop for the missiles cast down through them. The inner part of the passage has been destroyed.

Marten's tower projects well out at the south-east corner of the

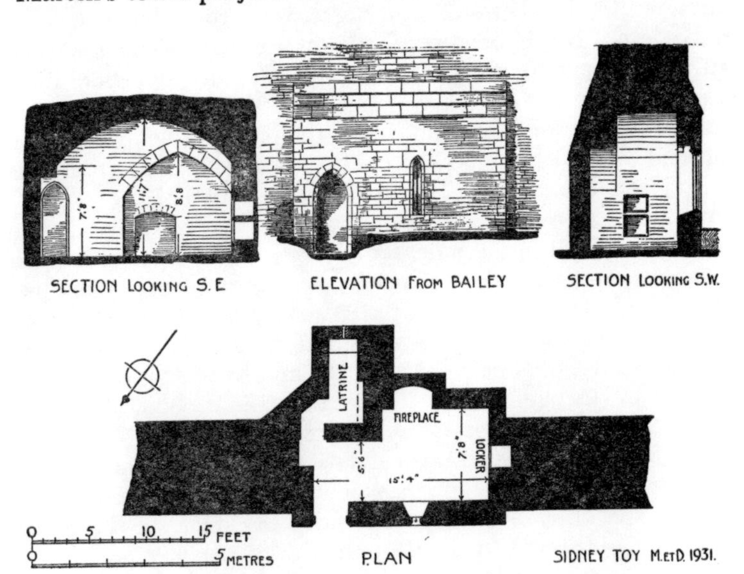

KENILWORTH CASTLE. WALL CHAMBER NEAR WATER TOWER

bailey, commanding the outer faces of both the south and east walls. It has a round outer face, rising from tall pyramidal spurs, is of four storeys including a low basement, and is still complete to the crest of its battlements. This tower was clearly the residence of the officer commanding the garrison; it is a complete dwelling, is strongly defended, and is in full command of the walls. The entrance is at the second storey, level with the courtyard, the basement being below that level; it is defended by a portcullis and a door. From here the upper levels are reached by a spiral stairway. The entrance floor has two fireplaces and was probably the kitchen. The two upper storeys are lofty rooms with arrow-loops to the field, and windows, which were enlarged in the sixteenth century, to the courtyard. The third storey room has a passage leading to the wall walk on the south curtain, the outer door being protected by a portcullis, and on the north side of the room there is a small chamber, formed in a square turret attached to the tower. Above the chamber and opening out from the top room is another small chamber, which has a lavabo basin, a small fireplace and is lighted by three windows. On account of its lavabo, said to be a piscina, this small apartment has been called an oratory, but it was probably a well lighted and comfortable retiring chamber with windows for observation in three directions.

Those merlons of the parapet on Marten's tower facing towards the field have each in the centre of the coping a stone figure of a soldier of the period, all now very much weatherworn. Such figures occur elsewhere, as at Caernarvon; their purpose, if not purely decorative, is obscure, for if it was to mislead the enemy then the deception must have been of short duration on all occasions.

At the Tower of London, Henry the Third built or rebuilt the walls and towers of the middle bailey about 1250, and at Saltwood castle, Kent, the outer bailey was added about 1240.

At Corfe castle a splendid hall, a chapel, and extensive domestic offices were raised in the inner bailey early in the thirteenth century and at the same time the defences were improved by a deep moat, called John's Ditch, which was dug across the hill on the side of approach. The middle bailey was built about 1240 and the outer bailey about 1280. The curtain of the middle bailey follows round the crest of the hill with a sharp salient at the west; the salient terminating in a large octagonal tower, now in ruins, called Butavant. The middle bailey has a strong gatehouse on the south, the line of approach, and a postern on the north. The most striking point of the outer bailey is the relative thickness on the flanking walls, east and west. At the west the fall of the ground is gradual and there is a flat open space at the foot of the hill. Here the wall is 10 ft. 6 in. thick and is defended by four strong towers.

At the east the fall is precipitous and there is no vantage ground beyond. The wall on this side is only 7 ft. thick and has but two towers, spaced widely apart (pp. 86a, 86b, 87, 151).

A prominent and interesting feature of Coity castle, Glamorgan, is a wall tower which projects boldly out into the moat from the south side of the inner bailey. Coity castle consists of a circular inner bailey, dating from the twelfth century, with a square keep on the west side, and an outer bailey added in the fourteenth century. The gateways and the domestic quarters of the inner bailey were rebuilt in the fourteenth century; the latter, which included a great hall and a chapel, are now very ruinous (pp. 128b, 141, 142).

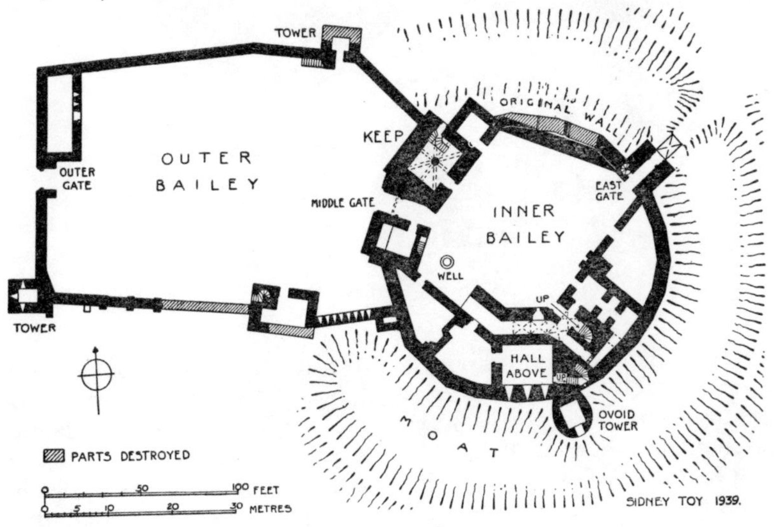

PLAN OF COITY CASTLE

The wall tower mentioned above was built in the early part of the thirteenth century; it is ovoid in plan and was originally of four storeys but the fourth storey has been destroyed. The three upper storeys were tiers of latrines and the basement the latrine pit. The storey above the pit was an open room containing three latrine seats, side by side. In the next storey two latrine seats, side by side, are screened off from the room by partition walls; one window serving both the cubicle and the room, the partition passing up its centre. The top storey had one seat which was probably in a separate cubicle like those below but the partitions have been destroyed. A stairway with passages to all three upper storeys rises from the domestic buildings within the curtain.

Criccieth castle was built about the middle of the thirteenth century. The design both of the gatehouse and the curtain points

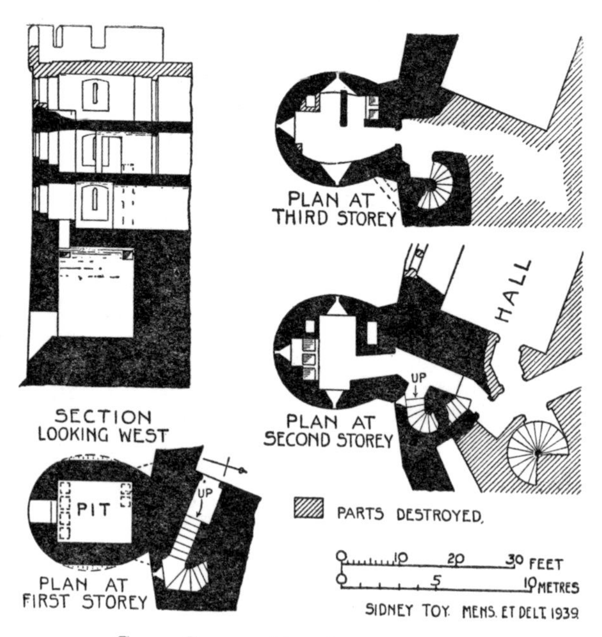

Coity Castle. The Ovoid Tower

to that period, and although Edward the First repaired and strengthened its fortifications no large sums, such as would be requisite for an entirely new castle, occur in the very careful accounts of that king's building activities. The castle stands on a promontory jutting out into the sea from the north coast of Cardigan Bay and consists of two baileys, one within the other. Only fragments remain of the outer bailey. The inner bailey has a lozenge shaped plan and is defended by a polygonal curtain which has no wall towers. There is a strong gatehouse at the north of the bailey and a postern on the south. A large rectangular structure at the south-east, looking seaward, of which only the lower parts of the walls remain, was possibly a keep (p. 142a).

Ewloe castle, Flint, built by Llewelyn ap Griffith about 1257, is a good example of a Welsh fortress of this period. It stands between two deep ravines at the converging point of the streams running through them. It consists of two baileys in line, east and west; the inner bailey with a strong keep in its centre being on the east. The keep has a U-shaped plan with the apsidal end looking east towards the field. At the extreme west point of the outer bailey, towards which the north and south curtains diverge, there is a large circular tower but there are no towers elsewhere on the curtain.

Barnwell Castle from the South-East.

Criccieth Castle from the North-West.

Warkworth Castle. The Gatehouse from the South.

Richmond Castle. Scolland's Hall, Interior.

CHAPTER SEVEN

CURTAIN WALLS, GATEWAYS, AND BUILDINGS OF THE BAILEY, 1050 TO 1270

CURTAIN WALLS

THE curtains of the eleventh- and twelfth-century castles were often plain walls, without towers or other defences than their battlements, as at Totnes, Devon, Trematon in Cornwall and Eynsford in Kent. When the castle stands on high ground the curtain follows the irregular contours of the site, as at Richmond and Ludlow. But when upon level ground the walls are built with long straight sides, as at Sherborne and Skenfrith.

On level sites the curtain was surrounded by a moat, as at Sherborne, or defended partly by a river and partly by a moat, as at Skenfrith. But when standing on a hill with steep cliffs or precipitous rocks on one or more sides the moat is restricted to that side where the approach is more gradual, as at Corfe and Beeston. The gateway is usually at the foot of the side of approach.

From the early part of the twelfth century curtains are strengthened at strategic points by wall towers which in the earlier works are square, project on the outside, and are spaced widely apart. Wall towers in this country, though occasionally solid up to the level of the wall walk as at Conisborough, are normally hollow from the courtyard upwards. At Framlingham they are open at the back, the side towards the bailey.

GATEWAYS

The gateway into the bailey was generally a substantial building of two or three storeys and was approached from across the moat by a drawbridge; at Dover there are two large gateways in the curtain of the inner bailey, one at the east and the other at the west end, and there was an outwork or barbican in front of each of them. Gateway passages were defended by portcullises, doors, machicolations, and arrow-loops.

Portcullises are generally made of oak, plated and shod with iron, and moved up and down in stone grooves. They are usually operated from a chamber over the gateway by means of ropes or chains and pulleys, and sometimes also by a winding drum. The device was in use long before our era and is described in a treatise on military tactics written in the fourth century B.C. "You should have ready above the centre of the gateway a gate of the stoutest possible timber overlaid with iron. Then when you wish to cut off the enemy as they rush in you should let this drop down and the gate itself, as it falls, will not only destroy some of them but will also keep the foe from entering, while at the same time the forces on the wall are shooting at the enemy at the gate."[1] The portcullis was used with great effect against Hannibal at Salapia in Italy in 208 B.C.[2] It was frequently employed by the Romans, as at Aosta and Pompeii, and by the Byzantines. It appears to have been introduced in this country in the early part of the twelfth century and examples of that period at Colchester and Arundel have been noted above.

Machicolations, sometimes misnamed meutrières, are apertures in the vaults or ceilings of gateways through which missiles were thrown down upon the heads of those endeavouring to force their way through. Sometimes they are formed over the outside face of the gate enabling the defenders, by pouring water down through them, to quench fires made by the enemy against the doors with the object of burning them down; and this appears to have been their original position and object.[3] Machicolations were also built on the crest of the walls and towers to repel the operations of sappers at the base. In this position they first took the form of hoards, or brattices, timber platforms projected out from the battlements in times of siege. Hoards are depicted on the walls of the temples of Upper Egypt and were in use in ancient and mediaeval times. By the end of the twelfth century of our era temporary hoarding began to give place to machicolations in stone; but it was not until the end of the thirteenth century that the change became general and hoarding was still in use in old castles at a much later period.

In addition to the main gateway there were usually one or more posterns placed in such positions in the curtain that a sally could be made or escape effected unobserved by the enemy. At Donolly, Argyll, the postern makes a zig-zag passage through the wall. At Ludlow and Pontefract the postern goes through one of the wall towers, that at Ludlow making a right-angle turn in its course.

In the gateways at Exeter, about 1070, Ludlow, 1090, Sherborne, 1120, and Newark, 1130, the passages were defended by doors and machicolations but there were no portcullises; at Sher-

[1] Aeneas Tacticus, XXXIX, Loeb edition, 1933.
[2] *Polybius,* X, 33, and *Livy,* XXVII, 28.
[3] *Vegetius,* IV, 4.

borne and Newark a two-leaved door stood midway in the passage. In the gateway to the inner bailey at Longtown, built about 1180, there is a portcullis, placed about two-thirds of the way through the passage from the entrance; there was probably a door near the inner end of the passage where the masonry has been broken away but there was none near the portcullis. The rooms above the gateways at Exeter and Ludlow are described in Chapter Five.

At Exeter the gateway projects entirely outside the curtain and has on the outer side a short but lofty barbican. The gateway passage is spanned at either end by a round arch of two orders, 10 ft. 3 in. wide. The outer arch is now blocked and its details are concealed, but it was probably closed by a two-leaved door and secured by a timber bolt. Within the doorway on the right there is a postern, which was constructed about 1250 and overlooked the ditch. In the north jamb of the postern there is an opening terminating in a small round hole on the outer face of the wall. The short lateral walls of the barbican extend out into the ditch, which passes in front of the gatehouse, and the drawbridge worked between them. The outer end of the barbican is quite open up to a level sufficiently high to admit light to the windows of the upper rooms of the gatehouse. At this height the lateral walls are spanned by a round arch, supporting the end wall of the barbican, and a floor, now destroyed, was formed on the level of the top storey of the gatehouse. This elevated barbican was a formidable fighting post, commanding from its battlements not only the approaches to the castle but from apertures, or machicolations, in its floor also the drawbridge and ditch below (p. 80a).

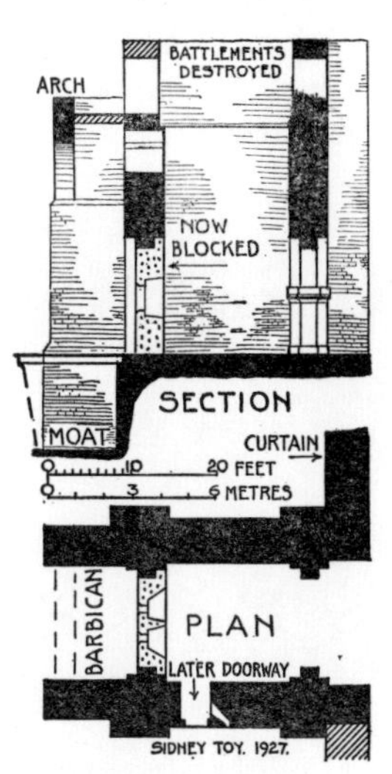

EXETER CASTLE. THE GATEWAY

The gateway at Ludlow, in contrast with that at Exeter, projects almost entirely within the bailey, but it also had a short barbican, or porch, 8 ft. 6 in. long. The gateway passage within was 29 ft. 6 in. long, enriched by wall arcades on either side. In addition to the main doorway, now destroyed, between the barbican and the passage there is an unusual form of wicket or sally port. A small doorway on one side of the barbican opens to a short mural passage which leads round that side of the main door and opens out beyond it into the gateway passage.[4] It is probable that the barbican was commanded from an aperture in the floor above but

[4] Vide *The Castle of Ludlow,* Archaeologia, 1908, 257–328.

later alterations have removed all evidence of the original disposition (pp. 76, 80a).

The gatehouse at Sherborne projects mainly outside the curtain. It was originally of three storeys, the two storeys over the gateway containing rooms for the guard and one of them having doors to the wall walk of the curtain; the present fourth storey was added at a later period. The gateway had only one barrier, a two-leaved door placed about a third of the way through the passage from the entrance; there was no portcullis. The flanking walls are solid except at the end towards the bailey, where there is a mural chamber, forming a porter's lodge, on one side and a spiral stairway to the upper levels on the other.

The south gatehouse of Launceston castle, now very ruinous and its inner portion entirely destroyed, was built about 1160; it was of three storeys and the outer portion, including the flanking

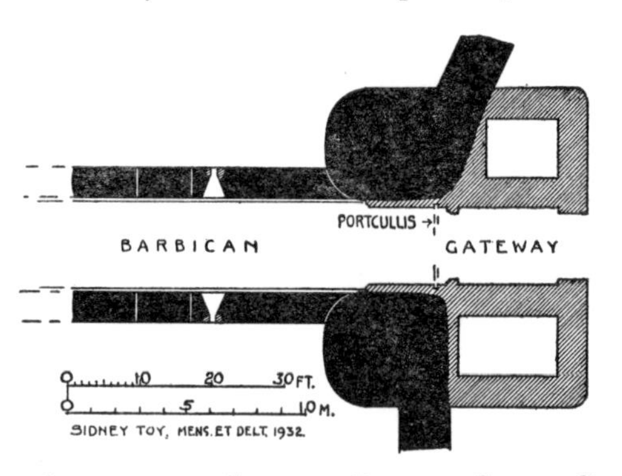

LAUNCESTON CASTLE. PLAN OF SOUTH GATEWAY

towers, still stands to the height of the base of the third storey. The passage was defended midway in its length by a portcullis and a door. The towers are drum-shaped with flattened outer faces, like those of the gateway at Penrice, but these towers are solid up to the full height they now stand, as are those flanking the gateway at Longtown. In front of the gateway are the remains of a long and narrow barbican which crossed the moat on low arches and was defended by arrow-loops on either side.

During the first part of the thirteenth century great advances were made in the design of gatehouses and the elaboration and scientific disposition of their defences.

The gatehouse of Warkworth castle, built in the first years of the thirteenth century and still standing up to and including its parapet, presents a severe aspect to the field; the only openings on the outer face are arrow-loops. It projects half without and half within the curtain and has semi-octagonal towers, buttressed at the angles. Defence against sapping was obtained by hoarding at parapet level, the holes for the beams of which are still to be seen, and there is a stone machicolation between the towers, the latter added about 1300. The moat in front of the gate was spanned by a long drawbridge which, when raised, fell back into a recess over the entrance. The gateway passage with its pointed barrel vault is still complete though the rooms above the vault have been destroyed. It was defended by a portcullis, a machicolation, a two-leaved door near the inner end, and arrow-loops in the side walls (p. 142b).

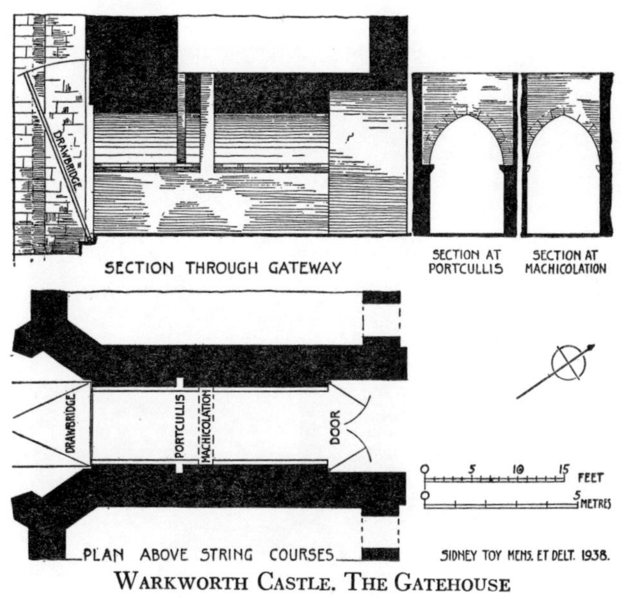

WARKWORTH CASTLE. THE GATEHOUSE

The portcullis is of unusual construction. Chamfered string courses run through the passage at the springing line of the vault and the grooves for the portcullis, usually carried down to within a few inches of the ground, stop on the flat upper faces of the string courses, 7 ft. above the ground. The portcullis must have been of special construction. It probably had a horizontal beam, stretching from side to side, which in its descent came to rest on the string courses while its main portion, between the strings, descended to the ground, perhaps fitting into a groove there. The string courses are not carried across the space where the machicolation in the vault occurs lest missiles cast down should fall upon them and not upon the enemy. The north-west postern of the bailey had a portcullis of the same kind and date, but the design must have proved unsatisfactory for it does not appear to have been followed elsewhere.

Constable's Gate, the principal entrance into the outer bailey of Dover castle and one of the most imposing gatehouses in the country, was built in the early years of the thirteenth century. Having been in continuous use as a residence from the time of its construction to the present day it has been subjected to much alteration and addition; but the original building is so far complete that it is possible to disentangle it from its post-military accretions and supply its missing parts (pp. 148, 150a).

This gate is of most unusual design; it consists of a main body, a porch set at right angles to the axis of the gateway, and a wing

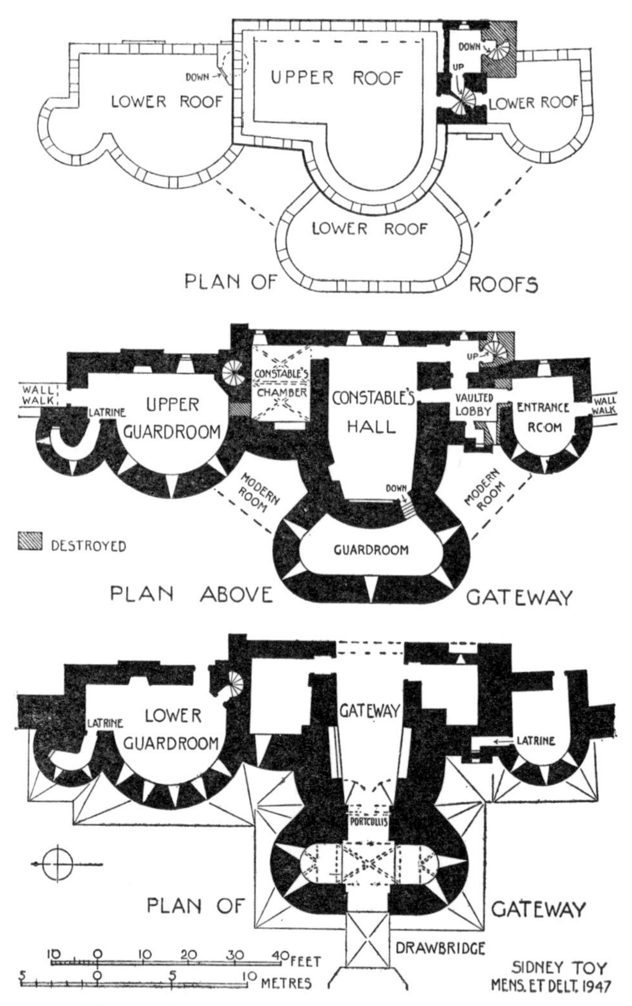

Dover Castle. Plans of Constable's Gate

on either side. It is of two storeys and preserves its original height to the present day; the round towers of which it is composed rising from square bases with tall pyramidal spurs. The central body of the structure, having the gateway and guardrooms in the first storey and the lofty Constable's residence above, has always been higher than the flanking towers. In modern times, probably early in the eighteenth century, the porch was heightened for an upper room, and bridges with rooms upon them thrown across on either side from the porch to the lateral towers. Other alterations include a room formed in the roof space over the Constable's Hall and a wooden stairway from the hall up to this room; the stairway rises in a circular shaft which has been hacked out in the core of the wall at the south-west. A large modern block has been added at the south-east and a short original stairway near the junction of this block with the old gatehouse has been removed.

A wide and deep ditch, spanned by a drawbridge, passes in front of the gatehouse while the ditch itself was reached through a long barbican of later date now in ruins (p. 150a). The first part of the gateway passage is a long and narrow porch, set crosswise with the gateway and having arrow-loops in its apsidal ends, commanding the lateral approaches; the porch is still covered by its original roughly ribbed vault. The entrance doorway to the porch has been altered and its early defences obscured. The gateway passage was defended by a portcullis and a two-leaved door; beyond the door it widens out from 9 ft. to 15 ft., seats for the guard being provided in long recesses on either side. The floor rises 6 ft. from the outer to the inner ends of the passage.

The Constable's residence consisted of a large and lofty hall over the gateway, an entrance room on the south, a sleeping chamber vaulted in two bays on the north, and a guardroom over the porch. There was a fireplace in the hall, and doubtless a latrine originally opened out of the vaulted lobby on the south over one still to be seen at ground floor level. The entrance to the residence was from the wall walk on the curtain on the south side of the gatehouse. The battlements of the residence, which included the main body of the building and the flanking tower on the south but not the flanking tower on the north, was reached by a stairway in two sections. The lowest section, which was relatively short, has been taken away. It must have been entered from the passage at the south-east corner of the hall and rose to the level of the foot of the turret stair on the south, which is still intact. The turret rises above the vaulted lobby and has one doorway to the battlements of the south flanking tower and another at the top to the battlements of the main central body. A third doorway has been cut through at a later period to the room formed in the roof space.

Originally there was no connection between the Constable's quarters and the flanking tower on the north; the existing passage between was driven through the wall at a later period. This tower with its latrine turret was distinctly for the accommodation of the military guarding this point. Further there was no direct connection between the upper and lower rooms of the tower itself. The lower room was entered from the courtyard and from it a spiral stairway rises to the battlements of the tower without any intervening doorway; the label over the head of the doorway at the foot of this stairway has a well designed curled stop. The upper room of the tower was entered from the wall walk on the curtain running northward, the entry being defended by a small porch of which only vestiges now remain. There was no stairway from this room to the battlements of the tower, which are on a lower level than those of the Constable's residence, and no other exit from the room than the entrance doorway. Therefore all three doorways of the tower, which is sufficiently spacious to accommodate a large body of men, were under the direct surveillance of the guard on the battlements of the residence; and the men were divided into two distinct groups. The Constable, from his post, could not only direct operations against a common enemy but also defend himself against the possible treachery of his own troops.

Blackgate, the main entrance into the bailey at Newcastle, is another gateway of unusual design. It was built about 1247 and consists of two gatehouses, one behind the other, connected by lateral walls and thrust so far out beyond the bailey as to command the outer face of the west curtain wall. The inner gatehouse has been largely destroyed but the outer one still stands to the full height of four storeys; the two upper storeys were rebuilt in 1619.

The outer gate is flanked by half-moon towers and was defended by a drawbridge, a portcullis, and a two-leaved door; guardrooms on either side are entered by doorways at the inner end of the passage. The walls of the passage are enriched by wall arcades. The second storey is, and probably was, when first built, one large room without partitions; it was entered from the walk on the south wall connecting the two gatehouses (p. 97).

The inner gate is defended in front by a deep pit, stretching across from wall to wall, and there is a postern through the wall at the south end of the pit, from which a sally could be made on those attacking the outer gate. The inner gateway passage is so ruinous that, with the exception of the drawbridge, the traces of its defences are lost. The drawbridge was of unusual design. Three long grooves, into which the beams supporting the inner part of the bridge fell when the bridge was open, project inward from the pit; the bridge being pivoted on the inner edge of the pit. This device, which occurs also at Goodrich and in the Tower

Dover Castle. Constable's Gate.

COLCHESTER CASTLE.
FIREPLACE IN KEEP.

CAERNARVON CASTLE. THE EAGLE TOWER.

CAERPHILLY CASTLE. THE SCREEN WALL.

of London, was probably introduced in this country about 1300 and is referred to in Chapter Twelve under drawbridges.

The gateway into the middle bailey at Corfe, built about 1240, was defended by two portcullises, one at either end of the passage, a two-leaved door, and a machicolation in front of the door; the machicolation spans the passage from side to side in four sections, divided by ribs. Here the portcullises and the machicolation were all operated from the third storey of the gatehouse.

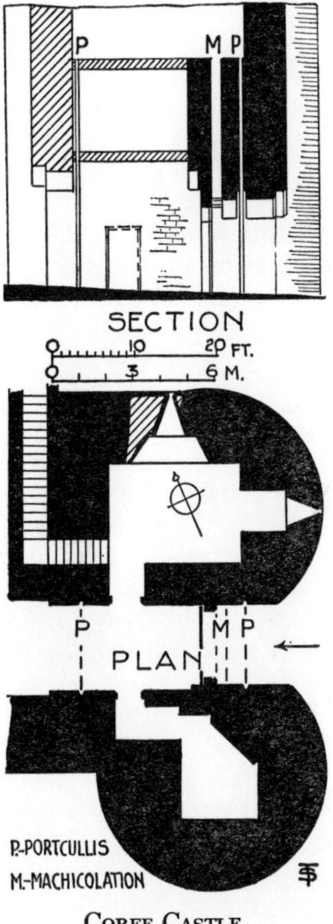

Corfe Castle.
The Middle Gateway

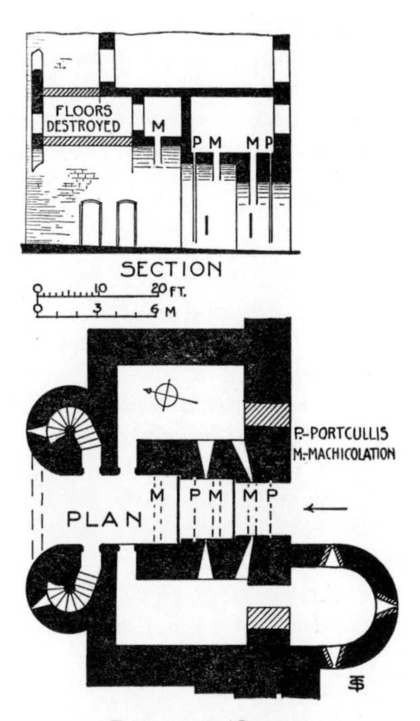

Pembroke Castle.
The Gatehouse

The gatehouse at Trematon was built about 1250 and is one of the most beautiful and complete examples of the period; it projects entirely outside the curtain (p. 50). The passage was defended by a two-leaved door, placed in the middle, and two portcullises, one at either end. Two arrow-loops command the approach to and entry into the passage and there is a guardroom on either side farther in. The footway rises 5 ft. from the outer to the inner end of the gateway. There are two storeys above the passage, reached by a spiral stairway opening from the courtyard. Both rooms have fine stone fireplaces; the lower room has a mural chamber on either side and a passage from the upper room leads to a latrine.

The defences of the gateway now become more numerous and more scientifically disposed. At Pembroke castle the gatehouse to the outer bailey was covered by a barbican, now destroyed. In the gateway passage are two systems of barriers in succession, each system consisting of a portcullis, a machicolation, and a two-leaved door, while beyond the inner door there is a third machicolation. All the machicolations are wide openings spanning the passage from side to side. There are arrow-loops in the walls on either side. Projecting from the inner face of the gatehouse, immediately above the passage there was a fighting gallery, built on a bridge thrown across between two stair turrets. The gallery was entered by a doorway in the inner wall of the gatehouse and had battlements towards the bailey. It provides for the event of the gateway being carried by assault, as from this commanding post an enemy rushing into the bailey could be attacked vigorously from the rear.

ARROW-LOOPS

The defence of all fortifications in ancient and mediaeval times was principally from the battlements of the walls, gateways and towers. But arrow-loops made in the curtain below the level of the battlements were introduced at Syracuse as early as 215 B.C. They were described by Philo of Byzantium about 120 B.C. and were introduced in the fortifications of Rome in the fourth and in those of Dara in the sixth century of our era. But they do not appear to have been in general use in Western Europe until the twelfth century.

Arrow-loops enabled the defenders to fire at the enemy outside the fortress while they themselves were hidden and safe behind its walls. When built in the walls below the battlements each of them consists of a narrow vertical slot which widens laterally from outside to inside to an internal wall recess; the recess being for the accommodation of the archer. The splayed jambs of the slot enabled the bowman to direct his fire on both sides as well as in front, and since the sill was deflected steeply downwards from inside to outside he commanded the ground below him also. The recess was often provided with one or two seats.

In the ancient form the outer hole was a simple vertical slot, those at Syracuse being 4 in. wide and 6 ft. long, and this simple form was maintained in the earliest examples of the Middle Ages, though the width was reduced. Even after more developed forms were in general use, and side by side with them, the simple slot was still employed, as at Corfe where many arrow-loops of about 1280 are plain slots 1½ in. wide and 12 ft. long. One of the earliest arrow-loops in this country is that guarding the steps of approach to the original entrance of the keep at Colchester, dating about 1080.

The arrow-loops of the battlements of the keep at Kenilworth, dating about 1130, open off a gallery at the level of the roof gutter. These battlements were originally of two tiers but the upper tier at parapet level has been destroyed. The recesses for the archers, opening off the gallery, are from 5 ft. to 5 ft. 3 in. wide by 7 ft. high to the crowns of their heads and have seats at the inner angles. In their original condition the loopholes were plain vertical slots from ½ in. to 1 in. wide and from 5 ft. 6 in. to 6 ft. 7 in. long. At present the lower third of the slot is cut away on the outside to the form of a triangular foot, 2 ft. 6 in. wide at the base. This alteration was probably made during the barons' war of the thirteenth century in order to give the crossbows, then in use, greater lateral play. The cutting is roughly made in the three loopholes on the south but more skilfully done in the two on the west, where a cross slot was also added.

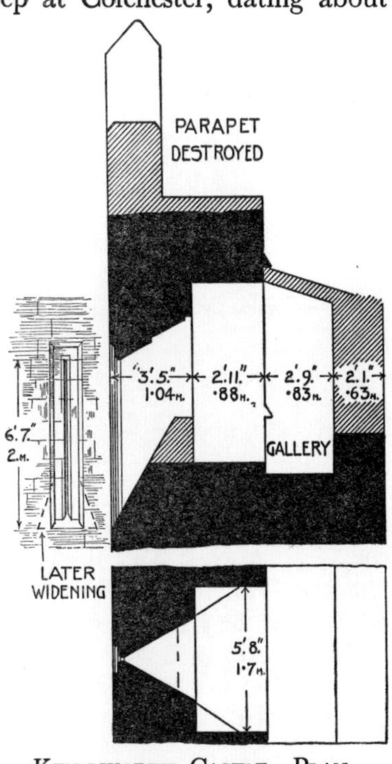

KENILWORTH CASTLE. PLAN, SECTIONAL ELEVATION OF BATTLEMENTS OF KEEP, AND ARROW-LOOP

Towards the end of the twelfth century the loopholes were generally built with triangular feet, as at Skenfrith, and sometimes with a horizontal slot, giving the form of a cross, as at Trematon; both dating about 1190, that at Trematon inserted in older work. The horizontal slots, which are widely splayed inwards, gave the archer a wide lateral sweep for his arrows and bolts and were introduced especially for the use of the crossbow. The arrow-loops in the battlements of the north curtain of Manorbier castle, of about 1200, have square-cut cross slots, while those in the battlements of the keep at Pembroke have no cross slots but are square-cut at the base. The enlargement at the base gave the archer greater range when shooting low.

During the thirteenth century arrow-loops were usually terminated both at the head and foot by circular holes and if there was a cross slot that also had a circular hole at either end, as in the Water tower at Kenilworth. Sometimes the cross slot is formed of two contiguous circular holes, as in the wall towers of Ewenny

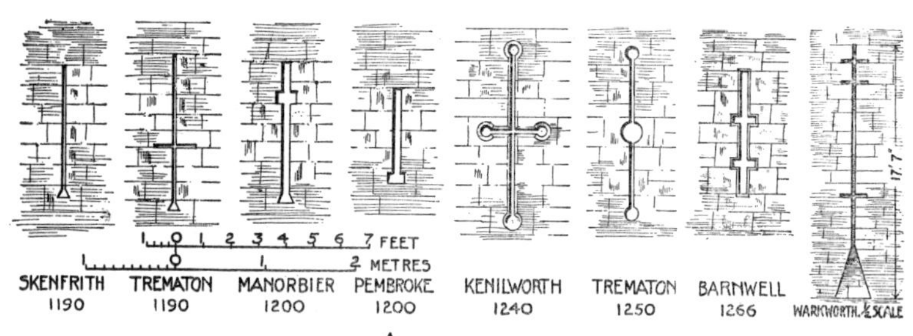

ARROW-LOOPS

Priory, Glamorgan, or again takes the form of a large circular hole, as in Marten's tower, Chepstow, and the gateway at Trematon. At Barnwell there are two square-cut cross slots but no enlargement at the head or base. The remarkable arrow-loops in the Grey Mare's Tail tower, Warkworth, were noted in the last chapter. They are 2½ in. wide by 17 ft. 7 in. long, the triangular opening at the foot is 2 ft. 7 in. wide at the base by 3 ft. 8 in. high, and the horizontal slots are 1 ft. 11 in. across. No further development in the design of arrow-loops occured until the introduction and effective use of firearms in the fifteenth century.

BUILDINGS OF THE BAILEY

Normally the buildings within the bailey included a large hall, called the Great Hall, for the general use of the garrison. Sometimes the hall with its offices stood away from the curtain but was more often built against it, the curtain forming one of its sides. The kitchen was near the hall if not adjacent to it and there was often a well near the kitchen. In some of the earlier castles, as at Chepstow, Richmond, Eynsford, and Grosmont, the hall was virtually the keep.

Scolland's hall, Richmond, built about 1080, stands at the south-east corner of the bailey, overlooking the river Swale, the curtain at the corner forming two of its walls. It is of two storeys; the lower storey entered at ground level and the upper, the hall proper, reached by an outside stone stairway rising from the courtyard to a doorway in the north wall (p.142b). The lower storey has seven small square-headed windows on the side towards the river and a round arched opening in that towards the bailey. In the hall above there are four windows on the side to the bailey, five on that overlooking the river and one in the west end, all originally two-light windows divided by a mullion with attached shafts. The windows are now ruinous on the outside and one in each of the lateral walls has been replaced by later work. The entrance doorway is contemporary with the hall; it is of two orders with jamb shafts. At the north-west corner of the hall there was a stairway to the battlements.

Eynsford castle, Kent, stands on the right bank of the Darent and commanded an ancient ford which crossed the river a short distance to the north. It has a single egg-shaped bailey with a rectangular hall standing away from the curtain near the north

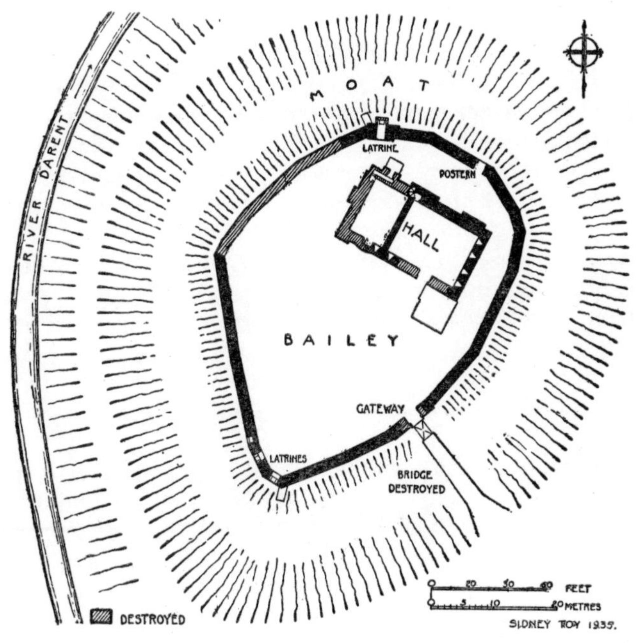

PLAN OF EYNSFORD CASTLE, KENT

end. The castle is surrounded by a wide and deep moat which, in rainy seasons, is still filled with water from the river. It was built in the early part of the twelfth century and is a most valuable example of its period in that there are no discernible additions to the original structure. It is built of flint in excellent lime mortar, tiles being used as bonders here and there.

The curtain wall is polygonal in plan with the longest straight side towards the river; it has a battered plinth 8 ft. high, is 5 ft. 4 in. thick above the plinth, and rises to the height of 30 ft. to the wall walk. It is faced with flint on both sides. The curtain is so thin in relation to its height that, having regard to the materials of which it is built, some form of shuttering must have been employed in its construction. And the work was well done for the greatest portion of it, including short pieces of the narrow wall walk and of the base of the parapet, stands to this day. There are no wall towers and originally there were no buttresses, the existing buttresses being modern. The gateway, now destroyed, was at the south-east of the bailey and a ragged hole in the wall at the north-east is probably the site of a postern. There are three latrines at the south of the bailey and one near the hall at the north; the last probably had a connecting passage from the hall.

The hall is in a very ruinous condition. It was a rectangular structure divided by a cross wall into two unequal sections and was apparently of two storeys; the western and smaller section has been destroyed to the ground and only fragments of the lower storey remain of the larger section. From a survey made in 1835 some of the missing details can be supplied, though only the ground floor existed when the survey was made. In the east end wall of the larger section are four loopholes, there is a doorway from the bailey on the south and what appears to be the base of a spiral stairway at the north-east. In the other section there were apparently a fireplace and a loophole in the south wall and a passage to the latrine, mentioned above, at the north-west corner. This building must be regarded rather as a dwelling-house than a keep; its walls are but 5 ft. thick and it is otherwise not designed for serious defence; its builders obviously relied on the strength of their curtain and outworks.

At Grosmont, Mon., dating about 1150, the hall projects eastward outside the bailey and is built on stronger lines than that at Eynsford. It is a rectangular building with its long sides running north and south and is divided into two unequal sections by a cross wall; its outer corners are reinforced by clasping buttresses. The present curtain wall of the bailey, which lies to the west of the hall, with its gateway and wall towers was built in the first part of the thirteenth century. But a portion of the original curtain, incorrectly dated in the " official guide ", still remains running out from the hall on the north side of the bailey. The inner bailey was surrounded by a deep moat and there was an outer bailey on the south-west.

One of the finest halls of the early period is that of the palace of Westminster, built in the last years of the eleventh century, which, though not part of a fortress, claims notice on grounds of size and structural importance. As first built the hall was of the same width and length as at present and still retains its original walls with portions of their early arcades. It was lighted on either side by tall clerestory windows and had a mural passage on either side at clerestory level, open to the interior by a continuous row of arches. In 1394–1402 the side walls were raised, the windows reconstructed, two towers built at the north end, and the hall covered in a single span by what is the most beautiful open timber roof in existence.

At Sherborne castle, about 1120, the hall forms part of a group of buildings standing in the middle of the bailey and constructed round a courtyard. The group forms a complete quadrangular fortress within the castle, with the hall, now very ruinous, on the north side of the courtyard, the domestic and service quarters on the other three sides and the keep projecting well out at the south-west corner. The hall of Devizes castle, of the same period, has been destroyed to the foundations, but these show that it was a large building standing within the bailey, clear of the walls and near the keep. It was divided by arcades into a nave and two aisles. The great hall of Farnham castle, built about 1140 and remodelled in the seventeenth century, is described in Chapter Four.

The hall of Leicester castle, built about 1150, retains many of the oak pillars and struts, by which it was divided into nave and two aisles, in their original positions. A scalloped capital belonging to one of the pillars is preserved on the modern stairway. The hall stands within the bailey with its axis running north and south. The kitchens, destroyed in 1715, were at the south end of the hall and beyond the kitchen there still remains a vaulted undercroft,

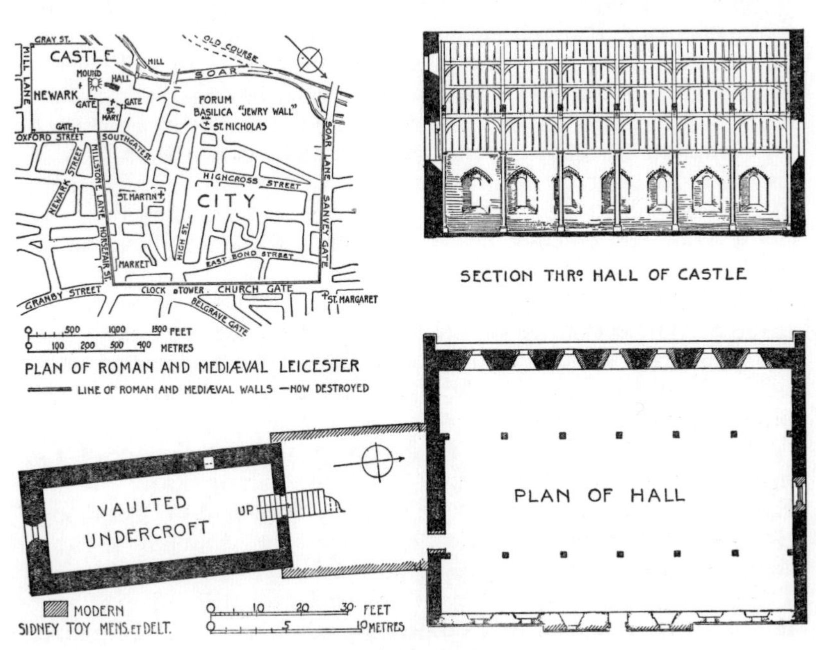

Leicester Castle

18 ft. wide by 50 ft. long. The living quarters, now destroyed, were doubtless at the north end of the hall on the site of what was known as Castle House. A mound, rising at the south-east of the hall, is probably the site of the original keep, but since the mound was lowered 15 ft. in the early part of the last century all traces of its buildings are lost.

Constable's hall, built against the north wall of Durham castle about 1170, is, despite later alterations, a well-preserved and elegant structure of its period, of great length and height; it is of two tall storeys, connected by wide spiral stairways. The entrance is at the lower storey through a large and richly decorated doorway, which owes its almost perfect preservation to the fact that it was blocked for many years. It has a round head of five orders, alternately wide and narrow, and jamb shafts with cushion capitals. The old Constable's hall, now called the Norman Gallery, occupies the upper floor of the building. It is a lengthy apartment with arcades on both sides and appears to have been open originally from one end to the other. The arcades have alternately large and small arches, the former opening to windows and the latter to recesses. The arches of the arcades have chevron mouldings and spring from detached shafts with long scalloped abaci. The windows, now altered, were originally of two round-headed lights divided by a shaft.

Another well-preserved hall of the twelfth century is that of Oakham castle, Rutland; it was built, with adjoining living rooms and kitchen, long since destroyed, about 1180. This hall consists of a nave and two aisles, one on either side, having round-arched arcades with richly sculptured capitals and arches. As can be seen on examination of the exterior and interior faces of the south wall, the entrance doorway has been removed from its original position at the east end to the middle of the wall. Oakham, however, was not a castle but a manor house, defended by a curtain wall and a ditch.

The hall of Corfe castle, built about 1210, and that of the King's castle at Winchester, about 1222, are good examples of early thirteenth-century halls. The former, which had well-designed twin-light windows with simple head tracery, is very ruinous, but the latter is well preserved.

Winchester Hall, built on the site and incorporating some of the masonry of an earlier hall, is a remarkably fine structure; the first English parliament was held here in 1254. It consists of a nave and two aisles separated by an arcade of five pointed arches on either side; the whole measuring internally 56 ft. 3 in. in width and 110 ft. in length. The arcades are well proportioned and have tall clustered pillars with moulded capitals and bases. Originally the hall was covered by a high pitched roof which embraced both nave and aisles, and was lighted by dormer windows; traces of the windows are still to be seen in the aisle walls. Later the walls between the dormers were built up to a general level, the upper parts of the dormers taken down, and the large circular lights in the heads of the windows rebuilt in the new intervening masonry. The whole building was thoroughly restored and re-roofed in 1874.

WINDOWS

In the earlier castle windows of the eleventh century the design follows the Saxon tradition, as in the gatehouse at Exeter. Here in a room over the gateway is a window, of about 1070, of two triangular headed lights separated by a wide mullion. Neither the jambs nor head are splayed but, like their mullion, are carried straight through the wall. It is similar to the window between the tower and nave of Deerhurst church, built some twenty years previously.

But generally the windows of the upper or living rooms of the eleventh century were from 12 to 18 in. wide and about 4 ft. high. They had round or flat external heads, flush with the outer face of the wall, and their internal jambs and rear arches were either splayed or opened out in orders; they were normally set at the outer end of a tall and wide recess. Among the best preserved examples are those of the keeps of Colchester and Canterbury, both of about 1080, Conisborough, about 1180, and Pembroke, about 1200. In the earlier windows light was considered of much less importance than safety. The light admitted through the small windows of the thick walls at Colchester must

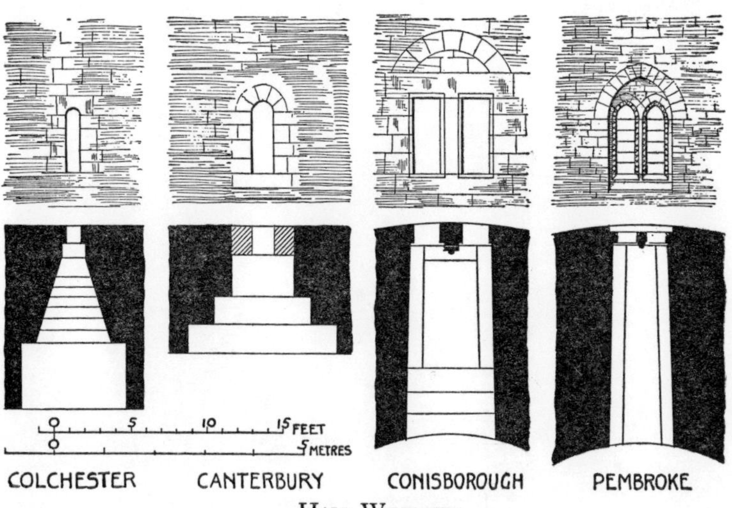

Hall Windows

have given but poor illumination to the great halls within. But such windows could be quickly closed by shutters and even when open the danger from enemy missiles was relatively small. At Canterbury the outer openings of the upper windows have been destroyed and their original dimensions can only be conjectured. The internal jambs and heads, in lieu of being splayed, open out in three plain orders.

By the latter part of the twelfth century it was considered desirable that more light should be admitted to the living apartments and the first step in this direction, apart from increasing the width of the openings, was the making of two openings in one internal recess, or a two-light window. The windows of the keep at Longtown are early examples under one decorated relieving arch, though here the mullions have been destroyed. At Conisborough the twin lights of the windows of the keep are much larger and are brought closer together than those at Longtown. Each of the lights is 1 ft. 10 in. wide by 4 ft. 8 in. high, has a square head, and is recessed inside for a wood shutter. The mullion has an internal projection in the middle of its height with a hole in it for the bar which secured the shutter when closed. The internal recesses are deep and high and are provided with stone seats at the breasts of the windows as well as on either side.

In the windows of the keep at Pembroke the development has advanced another step; the lights are lancets, are divided only by a narrow mullion, and are under a single pointed head. The windows are enriched externally with dog-tooth ornament and sculpture and internally have the same provision for shutters as at Conisborough; there are long seats on either side of the internal jambs. Later when windows became wider and had head tracery they were defended by the stanchions and saddle bars

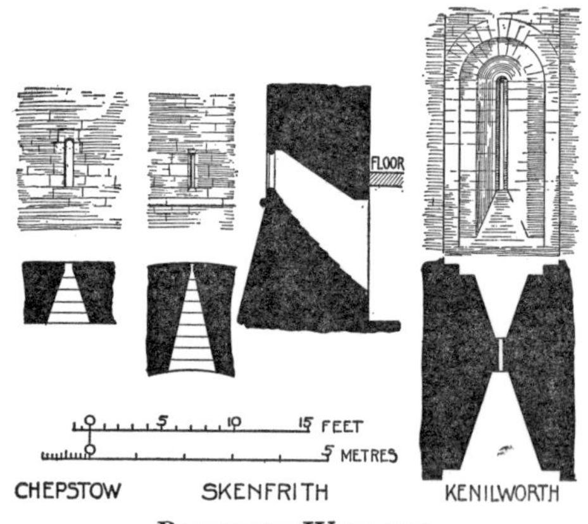

Basement Windows

which supported the leaded lights, or by iron grilles. Saddle bars were introduced in the windows of the keep at Pembroke.

On ground floors and basements the windows were narrow single lights often mere loopholes intended rather to ventilate than give light to the storerooms on which they opened. In the early examples they were flush with the outside face of the wall, their inner jambs and rear arches widely splayed, and their sills often stepped rapidly down from outside to inside. The lower windows of the keep at Chepstow, about 1070, are early examples. In order to raise these loopholes beyond the reach of sappers they were often placed so high in the wall as to be above the level of the next floor; their inner heads and sills being deflected rapidly downwards to the level of the rooms they ventilated, as at Canterbury and Skenfrith. The openings are sometimes splayed on the outside as well as within, as at Lydford and in the fine example at Kenilworth (p. 160).

FIREPLACES

Fireplaces of the latter part of the eleventh century were plain arched openings with semi-circular heads and backs. Their flues after rising a short distance within the wall passed through to the outside face and terminated in one or two loopholes; the loopholes being concealed in the inner angles of buttresses, as in the Tower of London and in the keeps of Colchester and Canterbury. The lower courses of the backs of the fireplaces, where combustion occurred, were built of selected stones, often in herringbone courses.

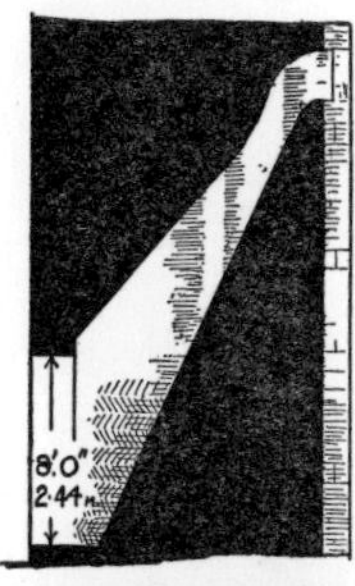

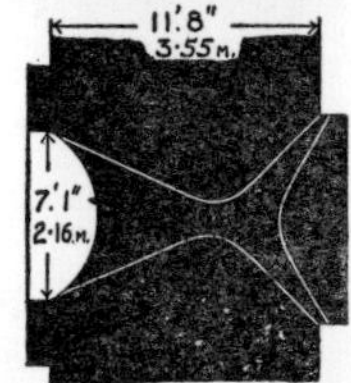

Colchester Castle. Plan and Section of Fireplace in Keep

Conisborough Castle. Fireplace in Keep

From the early part of the twelfth century the jambs were enriched with small shafts and the arches with chevron mouldings, as at Castle Hedingham and Rochester. The fireplace sometimes projects out slightly from the wall and has a straight moulding at the head, as at Rochester, but there is no real hood. The circular kitchen fireplaces at Canterbury, Castle Rising, and Portchester have been noted in the descriptions of the keeps of these castles. Very little alteration was made in the form of the ordinary fireplace before the last quarter of the twelfth century. In the keep at Newcastle, 1172–77, the flues are still carried through the wall to loopholes on the outer face, but here the semi-circular back gives place to the straight back with splayed sides (pp. 150b, 161).

In the keep at Conisborough, about 1180, there is a marked development. The flues pass up within the wall to the top where they terminate in a chimney, and a tall hood is built above the fireplace. The head of the fireplace is a flat lintel, built of voussoirs with joggled joints, which supports the hood. Here the hood was a necessity of construction, since the fireplace forms a chord across a circular chamber and any head built above its lintel to direct the flue into the wall must fall back against the sides of the chamber as it rises. From this period the fireplace normally had a straight back and hood; the hood projecting well out from the face of the wall and supported on either side by a corbel, or a shaft with carved capital and base.

CHAPELS

The chapel held an important position in the life of the castle. When not in the keep as described in previous chapters it generally stood in the bailey, either associated with the domestic buildings, as at Durham and Farnham, or isolated from them, as at Ludlow and Castle Rising. At Richmond it was formed in one of the wall towers.

St. Mary in Castro in the old bailey of Dover castle is probably the earliest as it is certainly one of the most imposing and well preserved of our military chapels. It is a large cruciform church, built about A.D. 1000, and is still complete, including the original central tower and the tall east and west arches of the crossing. The north and south arches of the crossing were rebuilt in the twelfth century and the whole church has been restored in modern times (p. 98).

The old chapel of Durham castle, built in 1072 against the north wall of the bailey, is a particularly beautiful little structure. It consists of a nave, with an arcade of four arches on either side, and two aisles. The round arches of the arcades are supported on tall circular pillars with sculptured capitals and moulded bases; the capitals having varied carvings of grotesque figures. The chapel measures internally 23 ft. 9 in. across by 32 ft. 3 in. long, is vaulted, and retains its original stone paving. The paving is laid in herring-bone pattern except for a path along the axial line where the stones are set square. The chapel of St. John in the White tower of the Tower of London of about 1080, was described in Chapter Five.

St. Nicolas, Richmond castle, is formed in the ground storey of Robin Hood tower on the east side of the bailey and dates about 1080. It is a small oratory, measuring internally 9 ft. 6 in. by 12 ft. 9 in., and covered by a barrel vault. There is a wall arcade of five arches on either side. At the east end is a recess for the altar with a small central window, and high up on either side of the recess is a small circular opening splayed both outwards and towards the inside face of the wall. The round chapel at Ludlow has already been described (pp. 57, 76, 95).

At Farnham the original chapel, built about 1140, still stands adjoining the residential buildings at the south-west of the court-yard. Raised on a crypt its floor is on a higher level than that of the hall and is reached by a flight of steps up. It has a rectangular nave, covered by a slightly pointed barrel vault, and a small chancel. A north aisle with an arcade of pointed arches on circular pillars was added about 1180, but at a later date the aisle was destroyed and the arcade blocked.

CHAPTER EIGHT

PERIOD OF EDWARD THE FIRST

EXTENSIVE experience in siege operations at home and abroad had clearly pointed out to that sagacious monarch Edward the First and his barons the defects in their fortifications, and in the new castles they built at home these defects were rectified. The reign of Edward the First was a most brilliant period of military architecture, during which some of the most powerful castles of any age or country were built in Great Britain. Considerable attention was still paid to outworks, but the general tendency was to concentrate the general defence on a four-square castle, enclosed by one or two lines of walls and having a strong round tower at each corner of the inner line. Powerful gateways now take the place of keeps and there is a more liberal provision of gateways and posterns.

A serious defect in the earlier castles lay in the fact that there was generally only one gateway and one postern. The last word in siege operations must always be starvation. A king might be secure behind the walls of a powerful stronghold but, in the event of a siege by a stronger force than his own, unless he had adequate means of bringing in supplies, of making sorties, or of effecting escape, he was doomed sooner or later to defeat. In the new castles more gateways were provided and in many cases the difficulties of investment were increased by extensive outworks. The design of the inner bailey also secured greater mobility to the defence forces and better supervision to the commanding officer.

One of the earliest of these castles is Caerphilly, Glamorgan, built 1267–77. Caerphilly castle stands on what was an island in a lake; the lake being fed by a stream and held in by a great screen wall, or dam, which was a most formidable barbican protecting the approach from the east. A large outwork defended the approach from the west. The castle is rectangular and is surrounded by two lines of curtain walls; the inner wall having a tower at each corner and two large gatehouses, one in the centre of each of the east and west walls. The towers project so far out beyond the corners that they commanded the outside faces of the walls from end to end. The outer wall is thinner and lower than the inner wall; it has gateways on the east and west but no corner towers. The east gateways look towards the barbican, from which they were approached by a drawbridge; the west gateways were reached by a drawbridge from the outwork (pp. 150b, 165, 238, 239).

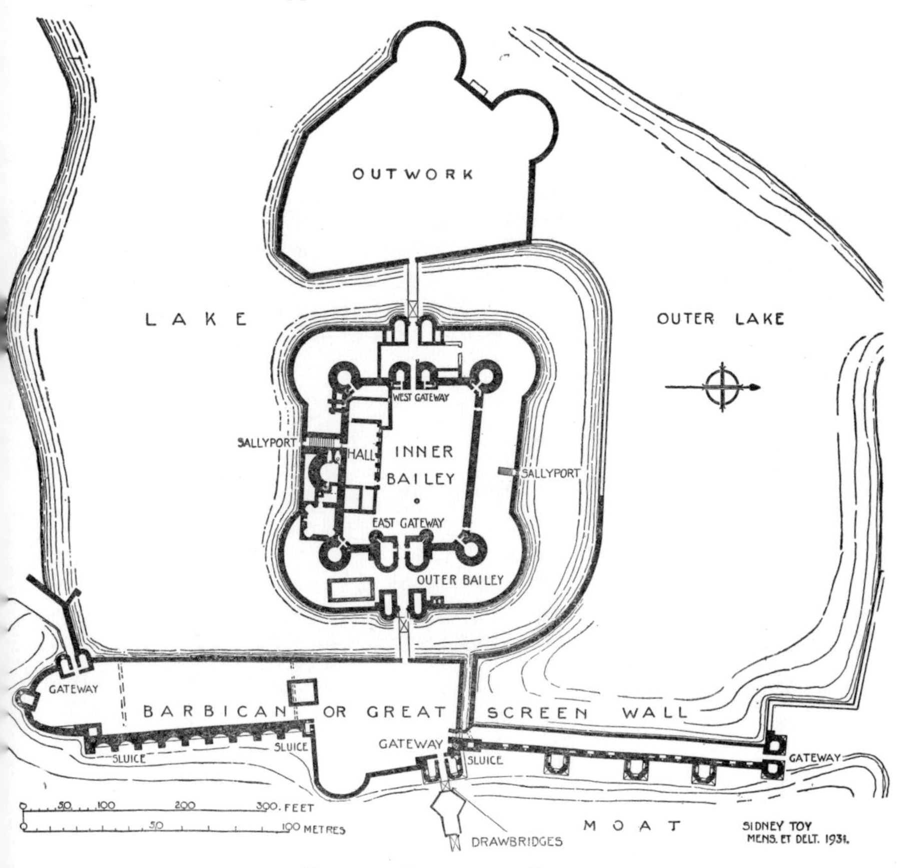

Plan of Caerphilly Castle

In addition to the gateways there were three posterns in the inner wall, two on the north and one on the south, and there were two in the outer wall. The hall and living rooms are built against the inner face of the inner wall on the south, and the kitchen, bakehouse, and other domestic offices in the space between the two walls behind the hall. The south postern in the inner wall opens directly out of the hall to a vaulted stairway down to the postern in the outer wall, the door at either end being defended by a portcullis.

The outer door opened on to the lake, from which supplies could be brought in, sorties made, or escape effected, by boat.

The stronghold and venue of last resistance of Caerphilly was the east gatehouse of the inner wall, the outer part of which is now destroyed. There were sumptuous living rooms and a small oratory in the upper storeys and the gateway passage was strongly guarded at both ends, the defences at the west end being reversed so that the gatehouse could be held against an enemy who had penetrated into the bailey. The circulation of the bailey was greatly facilitated by a mural passage which is carried all round the inner wall, at a height 15 ft. above the ground, and opens on to the large halls of the east and west gatehouses. The passage was defended by four portcullises, one on either side of each gatehouse.

The massive screen wall of the barbican is supported in the southern portion of its length by a series of huge buttresses, spaced closely together; the thrust of the wall being directed on to the buttresses by concave interspaces. The northern portion of the wall is supported by three strong towers with tall pyramidal spurs, the spurs rising to the height of the wall walk. The whole screen from

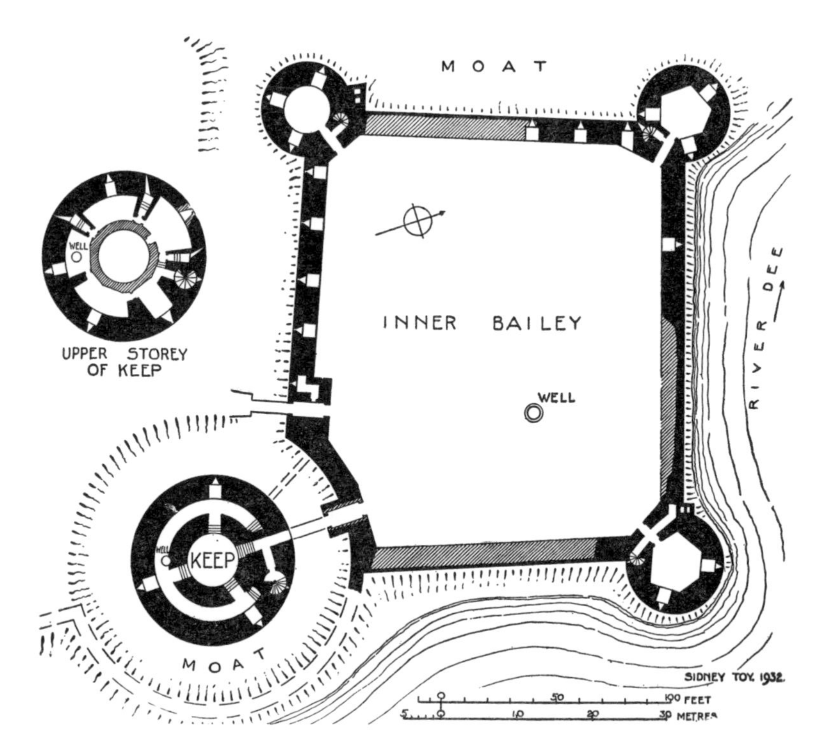

PLAN OF FLINT CASTLE

end to end is a powerful and imposing work of military architecture. Three sluices, by which the level of the water in the lake was regulated, run through the wall; one of them worked the water wheel of a mill on the barbican.

While the underlying principles of development are maintained, the design of a fortress must always depend largely on the character of the site it occupies and the special purpose it has to fulfil. Again surprise and secrecy, as invaluable factors in defence, themselves demand endless varieties of plan and disposition of buildings. Flint castle, built 1277–80, Conway, 1283–87, and Caernarvon, 1285–1322, each formed part of an establishment which included a fortified town.

At Flint the ultimate stronghold was a large cylindrical keep, which stands isolated, at one corner of the castle, like the donjon at Lillebonne in France, and is surrounded by its own moat. This keep, now destroyed down to the lower parts of the walls of the second storey, was a powerful structure with an external diameter of 71 ft. and was probably three storeys in height. In design it has no parallel in this country, though it bears considerable resemblance in plan to the huge round towers at Old Cairo.[1] It is built of two concentric shells which in the basement are separated by a circular vaulted passage but in the upper storeys were connected by thick radial ribs, dividing the interspace into halls and chambers. The circular space in the centre of the keep formed one large hall in each storey (p. 166).

The keep was reached from the inner bailey by a drawbridge over the moat and entered at a level midway between the basement and the floor above. From the entrance passage steps descend to the basement and a wide spiral stairway, opening out from the passage, leads to the upper parts. In the circular passage of the basement there is a well, the pipe of which was carried up to the floor above. The second storey has a large central hall surrounded by five rooms of varying size, one of which, containing the well shaft, was probably the kitchen. The ribs, or partition walls, radiating towards the centre, diminish in thickness as they pass from the outer to the inner shell, and latrines are formed in the wide outer ends of three of them.

Conway castle stands on a high rock on the shore of the estuary and, following the contour of the rock, is long and relatively narrow. It is defended by eight towers and has a gateway at either end, each gateway being flanked by two of the towers and covered by a barbican. A cross wall divides the castle into two baileys of unequal size. The outer bailey, the larger section, contains the great hall and the domestic and service offices of the garrison; the inner bailey the royal apartments and private offices. The gateways are

[1] Vide "Babylon of Egypt", *Brit. Archaeol. Journal,* 1937.

constructed through the curtain wall and are defended only by the adjoining wall towers; there are no gatehouses. The security of the castle depended largely on the difficulty of access to it. On the west, the town side, entrance into the castle by an enemy could only be effected after climbing a steep stairway, crossing a drawbridge, and breaking through three gateways in succession—all in the face of direct fire by the defenders from the towers and walls on every side. The approach from the estuary to the east gate was commanded for the whole of its course by the east barbican, which towered high above it, and by the tower which stood out into the estuary. The inner gateway at each of the east and west entrances was defended by a machicolated parapet, which stretched across from one flanking tower to the other, by heavy timber beams, drawn out across the passage from holes on both sides, and by two-leaved doors. In addition the passage in the western gateway was guarded by a portcullis and a wide machicolation in its vault (pp. 169, 170a).

In the inner bailey there are two posterns. One of them is in the south wall, standing high above the rocks on the edge of the river. While being useful for hauling in supplies brought by boat it would also be of service in an emergency for escape by means of a rope ladder. The other postern is in the north-east tower and opens on to the stairway leading down to the estuary. The north-east tower probably contained the royal private chambers; it has a beautiful little chapel and, in addition to the postern, has means of exit by passages and stairways radiating from it in all directions.

The circulation of the wall walk is uninterrupted all round the curtain, thus enabling the defence forces to rush speedily to any desired point in the battlements. All the eight towers have beam holes for hoarding and four of them have high turrets from which the approach, or the distant operations, of an enemy could be observed.

Caernarvon castle stands on relatively level ground, though there is a slight fall from the east, where there was a mound, to the west. The plan resembles an hour glass, narrow in the middle and bulbous at both ends. It is a very powerful structure, surrounded by strong and lofty walls and defended by two gatehouses and nine wall towers, many of the towers having turrets projecting high above the battlements. All the towers stand astride of the wall walk and so interrupt its circulation. The north side of the castle faces towards the town and the south side towards the river. One gatehouse, called the King's Gate, stands in the middle of the north wall and provides direct entrance from the town to the inner bailey, occupying the west half of the castle. As originally designed this gatehouse was to extend from north to south across the castle at its narrowest point, dividing the inner from the outer bailey; but at

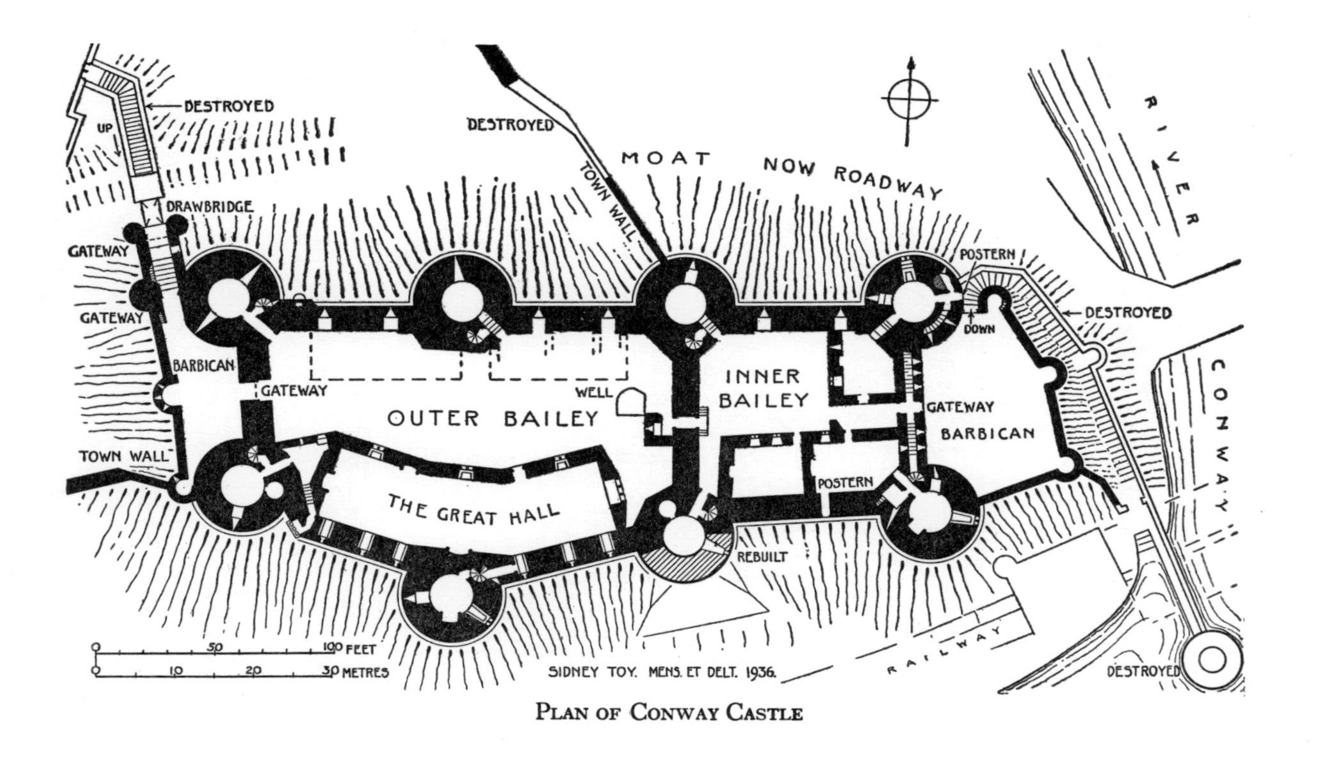

PLAN OF CONWAY CASTLE

present it extends only half-way across and it is probable that the scheme was never completed. The outer bailey is entered by Queen's Gate, an imposing structure placed beyond the town walls at the east end of the castle (pp. 150b, 170b, 171, 245).

There are three posterns, all from the inner bailey. One postern, called the Water Gate, opens on to the river from the Eagle tower at the west end of the castle; another, penetrating the south curtain, and reached by flights of steps down from the great hall, gives access to the river on the south. The third is in the wall tower on the north side of the bailey and opens on to the moat between the castle and the town.

Eagle tower is a particularly strong and well-defended building, and preserves in its design the essentials of a keep. From it the whole fortress could be commanded; it contains a private chapel, and through its water gate supplies could be brought in and entry or escape effected. Attached to the north side of the tower are the remains of a wall, 13 ft. 6 in. thick, which jutted out into the river. This fragment contains one jamb of a low gateway with the groove for the portcullis by which the gate was closed; and, at a higher level, a passage to the chamber, now destroyed, from which the portcullis was operated. It is suggested in the "official guide" that the space between this wall and the west wall of the town was occupied by a gatehouse. But since the gateway is at water level and is clearly a water gate it is much more probable that the space was occupied by a dock and that the fragment containing the gate into the dock is the remains of a screen wall similar to the Gunner's Walk at Beaumaris. The town wall is not diminished in thickness on approaching the castle here as it is on the east side, and as it was on both sides at Conway.

The curtain wall and towers on the south front of the castle, facing the river, have two tiers of mural passages with arrow-loops to the field. On the north front, towards the town, some of the arrow-loops are so constructed that from one recess archers could be firing in two or even three different directions; in others, openings from three recesses converge towards one loophole. When put in a state of defence the castle was bristling with archers, standing at different levels in the mural passages and behind the battlements. On the south side there would be three tiers of armed men.

Though the internal buildings of Caernarvon are now represented mainly by foundations its magnificent curtain walls and towers are practically intact. Caernarvon castle, with its powerful fortifications almost complete, is a priceless heritage and one of the finest examples of military architecture of the Middle Ages in existence.

Harlech castle, Merioneth, built 1285–90 on a hill, and Beaumaris castle, built 1295–1320 on the sea shore, both show the

Conway Castle from the South-West.

Harlech Castle from the North.

Caerlaverock Castle from the North.

CAERNARVON CASTLE FROM THE RIVER.

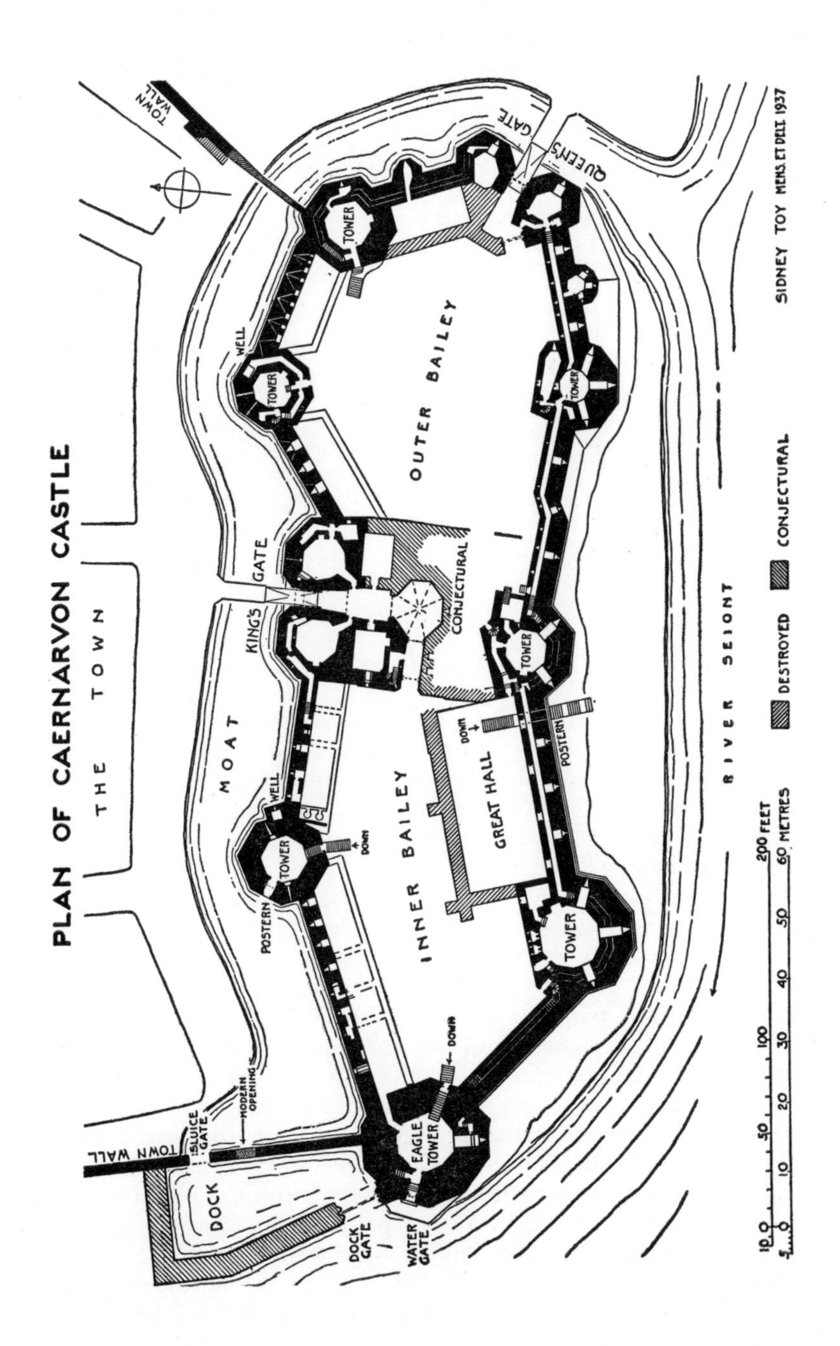
PLAN OF CAERNARVON CASTLE
THE TOWN
TOWN WALL
MOAT
KING'S GATE
QUEEN'S GATE
OUTER BAILEY
INNER BAILEY
GREAT HALL
TOWER
TOWER
TOWER
TOWER
TOWER
TOWER
EAGLE TOWER
WELL
WELL
POSTERN
POSTERN
DOWN
DOWN
DOWN
CONJECTURAL
CONJECTURAL
TOWN WALL
SLUICE GATE
MODERN OPENING
DOCK
DOCK GATE
WATER GATE
RIVER SEIONT
DESTROYED
CONJECTURAL
SIDNEY TOY MENS. ET DELT 1937
200 FEET
60 METRES

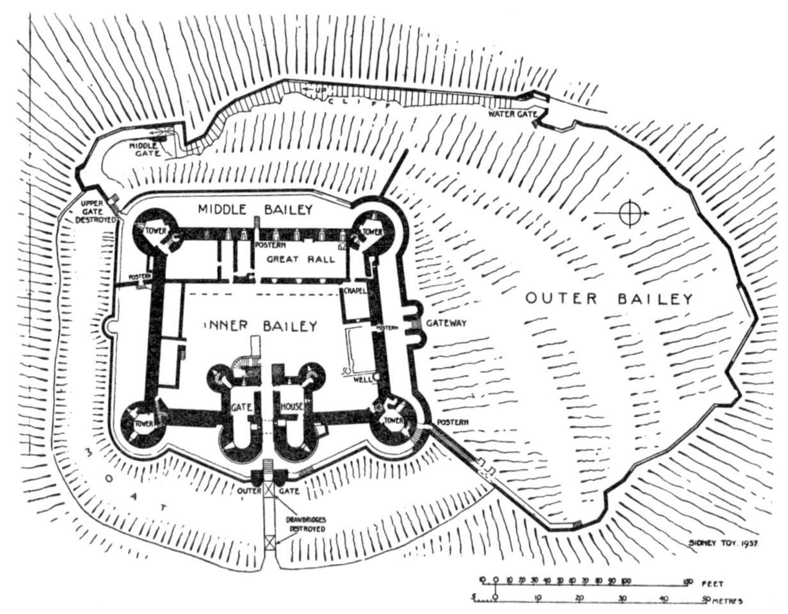

Plan of Harlech Castle

development of the principles of defence suitable to the sites they occupy.

Harlech castle is a rectangular fortress enclosed by two lines of walls, forming the inner and middle baileys, and defended by an outer bailey which extends down the precipitous slopes of the hill and covers its north and west sides. The east and south sides are defended by a wide moat. The inner bailey has a tower at each corner and a large gatehouse in the middle of the east front; the corner towers having the same bold projection as those at Caerphilly. There is a postern in the north wall and one in the west wall, the latter leading directly out of the great hall. The middle bailey, actually a narrow terrace between the two walls, is obstructed at one point by a cross wall with a postern. It has two gateways and two posterns in the curtain, one of the gateways being in line with the gatehouse and the other opening on to the outer bailey; both posterns, one at the north-east and the other at the south-west corner, descend by flights of steps to the outer bailey.

The outer bailey rises up in a series of precipitous rocks, tier upon tier, and the approach to the upper fortress from the Water gate at the foot of the hill was by a steep path cut into the rock against the west curtain. Any other line of approach through the bailey would involve a perilous climb over rocks to the north gateway. The path was defended at a point about two-thirds of its course by a gate with a ditch and a drawbridge and terminated at the top in a postern under the command of the south-west corner tower. A wing wall, jutting out from the upper fortress, intercepted the circulation from one part of the outer bailey to the other. From the north and south, therefore, the approaches were strongly defended both by nature and military art (pp. 170a, 172, 242).

But the vulnerable side of the castle is that facing towards the higher ground on the east, and it is here that the military strength of the fortress is particularly concentrated. The east front of the inner bailey is powerfully built. There is a strong gatehouse in the middle and a tower at either end; the curtain on the north side of the gatehouse is 9 ft. 8 in. thick and that on the south side 12 ft. 4 in. thick. As originally designed the other three walls of the curtain were to be only 6 ft. thick, but after being built up to about one-third of their present height it was decided to make them stronger, and as finished they are about 9 ft. thick. The approach from the east was defended by two drawbridges, one at either end of the bridge crossing the moat, and two gateways; all under fire not only from the walls and towers in front but from the wide wall walk of the outer bailey on the right flank. The outer gate was defended by a two-leaved door, and the long passage of the gatehouse by a stout timber bar, three portcullises, two doors, and eight machicolations.

At Harlech the gatehouse was the stronghold of the castle. It stands astride of the wall walk, which is otherwise continuous all round but is here checked by a door on either side, and its strongly fortified gateway passage could be held as well against a force which had penetrated into the bailey as one outside the walls. The existing stairway on the west side is of much later date.

Beaumaris castle, standing on level ground by the sea, is defended regularly all round. It consists of two lines of fortifications, forming the inner and outer baileys, and, except at one point where the sea enters to form a small dock, is surrounded by a moat. The inner bailey is almost square; its walls are about 15 ft. 6 in. thick and are defended by six towers and two large gatehouses; the gatehouses being opposite to each other like those at Caerphilly. Each of the gateways was defended by three portcullises and two doors and as far as is indicated, for the vaults have fallen, also by machicolations. As at Harlech, the defences of both these gateways were so disposed that they could be held as well against the inner as the outer bailey. The south gatehouse was further protected by a small barbican. Both gatehouses were substantial structures containing large halls and rooms. In the central wall tower on the east side of the bailey there is a beautiful vaulted chapel, practically intact.

The wall walk is continuous except at the gatehouses, where it is barred by doors on both sides. In the north gatehouse, which was the stronghold of the castle, the doorway to the wall walk on either side stands slightly clear of the inner face of the wall, leaving an open space across the angle between the walk and the doorway. This space was spanned by a bridge which was probably of timber and could be taken away when it was desired to isolate the gatehouse from the walk. Vestiges of the stone supports of the bridges are still to be seen. Circulation of this castle was greatly facilitated by a mural gallery which runs round within the curtain at a height about midway between the courtyard and the wall walk, with doorways into the gatehouses. In its course the gallery opens on to four groups of latrines, one group near each corner of the castle.

As finished about 1290 the inner bailey constituted the whole castle; the outer wall was not added until about 1316–20. This wall is built in nine panels and is defended by numerous towers placed at short intervals apart. The gateways are built considerably out of line with those of the inner wall, thus involving the exposure

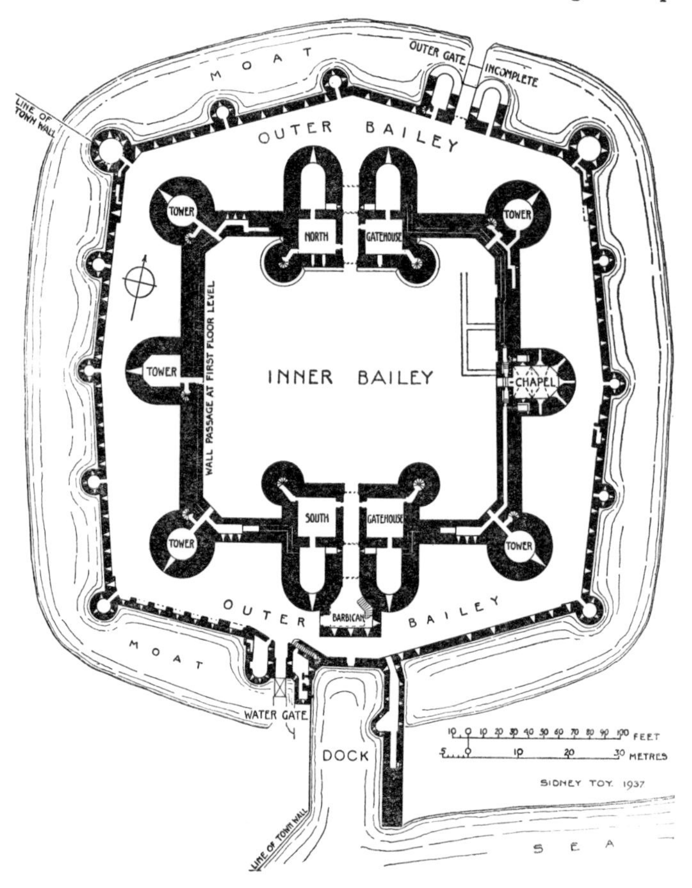

PLAN OF BEAUMARIS CASTLE

of the flank of any enemy advancing from the outer to the inner gate. The north gateway is in a fragmentary condition and was probably never completed; but the water gate on the south, guarding the dock and the entrance to the town, is in fairly good condition except at the back.

On the south side of the castle there is a small dock, which runs in from the sea between the walls of the town and a fortified jetty called the Gunner's Walk. The Gunner's Walk defended the dock in all directions, as well from a mural gallery and chamber within it, with arrow-loops on both sides, as from its battlements on the top. At the head on the dock there is a doorway in the curtain for landing stores.

At Kidwelly, Carms., the inner bailey, built about 1280, preceded the outer bailey by some thirty years. The castle stands at the mouth of a small river in a creek of Carmarthen Bay, on the site of a Norman fortress. The inner bailey is square; it has a round tower of bold projection at each corner, a gateway in the middle of the south wall, and a postern in the north wall. The gateway, though defended by the corner towers on the south side, was in itself of such simple and relatively weak design that one must assume the maintenance of the outer defences of the earlier castle pending the rebuilding of the outer bailey. A tower, with a chapel occupying a most exposed position in its upper storey, projects out from the east wall.

The outer bailey was built in the early part of the fourteenth century. Its east wall, on a high bank above the river, is in a straight line with the east wall of the inner bailey, which joins it at both ends; but the west wall sweeps round in crescent form from one end of the river wall to the other, enclosing the inner bailey and having a gateway at the north point and a large gatehouse at the south. The gatehouse is a powerful structure, capable of being held independently of the rest of the castle, and it has a particularly formidable appearance. Its flanking towers are conical and the whole structure, diminishing in width as it rises, assumes the awesome form of the pylon of an Egyptian temple.

Goodrich castle shows some interesting developments of the square plan. It was built about 1300 on the site of an earlier castle, enclosing the keep, described in Chapter Five. The castle stands on high ground overlooking the Wye and is defended on the north and west by steep falls down to the river and on the south and east by a wide moat, cut out of the rock. It consists of a square inner bailey, an outer bailey covering the north and west sides, and a semi-lune barbican (pp. 176, 177, 216a).

Here the gatehouse stands at the corner of the inner bailey, taking the place of one of the round towers, and the passage through it is not central but on one side of the building itself, thus

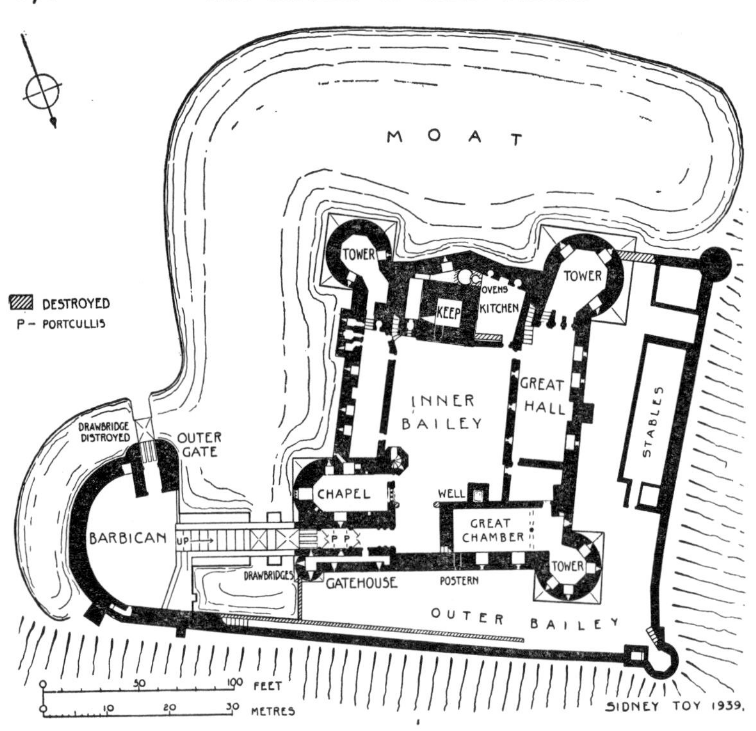

Plan of Goodrich Castle

bringing the gateway more under the command of the defenders on the north wall. This disposition of the passage also allowed greater space for the chapel on its south side. The south curtain is composed of two straight portions forming an obtuse angle in the centre, pointing outwards; a design which not only gives greater strength to the wall, forming a kind of spur, but brings the two portions more under the command of the adjoining towers. The corner towers on this side have very tall pyramidal spurs, those of the south-east tower rising up to a level near its battlements.

The gatehouse is very strongly defended. A barbican, projecting well out into the moat, has its entrance at right angles to that of the gatehouse. An enemy, having carried the barbican, must turn left and cross the bridge, which is interrupted by two gaps with drawbridges, in face of close fire on his flank from the battlements on the north wall of the outer bailey. The gateway into the barbican, as well as that through the gatehouse, was defended by a drawbridge which worked on a pivot in the middle and dipped down into a pit at the outer end. The defences through the gatehouse, consisting of a double system of door, machicolation, and portcullis, are all placed in the outer half of the passage.

About 1280 Edward the First surrounded the Tower of London with its existing outer wall and wide moat and rebuilt the Water Gate to the Thames. The gateway at the south-west corner of Edward's wall is defended by a second gate, built at the far end of a long bridge running westward from the first, and by a barbican with a third gate, called Lion Gate, beyond the second; the gateway to the barbican being set at right angles to the bridge. All three gateways were defended by drawbridges (p.237). That before the Lion Gate, as revealed by excavations made in 1936, rotated on a central pivot; when raised the outer end dipped down over the moat, and when lowered back in position its three heavy beams fell into corresponding grooves at the inner end. Except for the additional gate the whole design of this entrance, including the semilune plan of the barbican, bears close resemblance to that at Goodrich (p. 69).

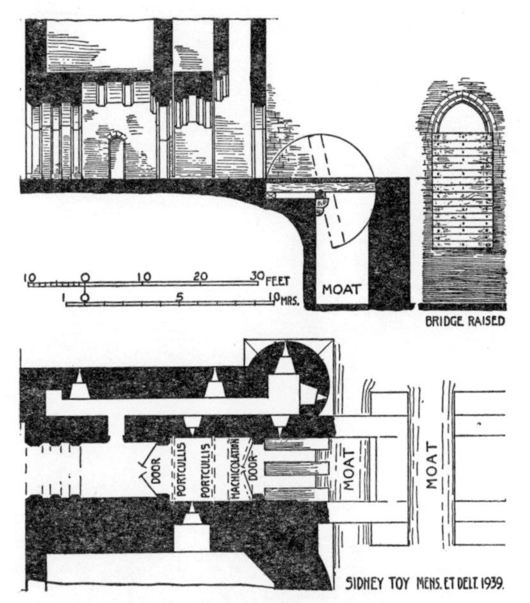

GOODRICH CASTLE. THE GATEHOUSE AND DRAWBRIDGE

The castles at Rhuddlan and Aberystwyth, both built by Edward the First about 1280, have each a diamond-shaped plan. At Rhuddlan there are two powerful gatehouses, facing each other across the minor axis of the inner bailey, and a round tower of bold projection at each of the acute angles. The curtain walls have a tall, battered plinth, are 9 ft. thick, and rise to a great height. The gatehouses are placed slightly out of line with each other. An outer bailey, the defences of which have been largely destroyed, surrounded this curtain. Of the castle at Aberystwyth there are now only a few scattered remains; it was defended by two lines of walls, both diamond-shaped in plan, and a moat. The inner curtain had a large gatehouse at the east angle of its minor axis, a round tower at each of the other angles, and a postern in the middle of the north-west wall. The outer curtain had gateways in line with the gateway and the postern of the inner wall.

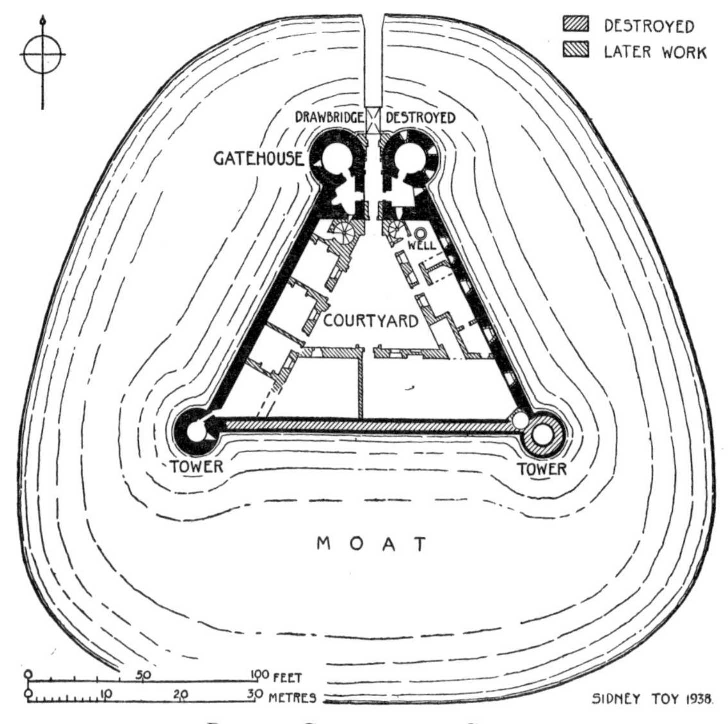

PLAN OF CAERLAVEROCK CASTLE

Caerlaverock castle, Dumfriesshire, following the contour of the rock on which it stands, is constructed on a triangular plan, with a powerful gatehouse at one corner and a round tower at each of the others. The castle was first built about 1280, suffered the memorable siege and capture by Edward the First in 1300, was dismantled in 1313 and, after repair, again overthrown in 1356, to be again rebuilt about 1400. It is now ruinous. Through all these vicissitudes the castle as seen to-day agrees exactly with the description of it given in a poem of about 1300. "In shape it was like a shield, for it had but three sides round it, with a tower at each corner, but one of them was a double one, so high, so deep and so wide, that the gate was underneath it, well made and strong, with a drawbridge and a sufficiency of other defences. And it had good walls, and good ditches filled right up to the brim with water "[2] (pp. 170a, 178).

That statements of utter destruction made by contemporary and later writers are often inaccurate has been shown above. There can be no doubt that the walls of this castle embody much original masonry. This is clearly the castle to which the poem refers and not the diamond-shaped building the foundations of which lie a short distance to the south of it. The gatehouse was rebuilt about 1390, the corner towers were restored about 1400, and of the buildings round the courtyard, now ruinous, the west range was built in the fifteenth and the east and south ranges in the seventeenth century.

Often the owner of an existing house, on application to the king, received licence to " crenelate ", or fortify, it, and such was the case with Stokesay castle, Shropshire. The house, consisting of a fine hall with residential quarters at one end and a kitchen at the other, was built mainly about 1240. In 1291 a licence to crenelate having been granted to the owner, Laurence de Ludlow, he built a curtain wall enclosing a bailey on the east side of the house, with a gateway, later rebuilt, on the east side of the bailey and a fortified tower on the south side; surrounding the whole fortress by a moat.

Leeds castle, Kent, situated on level ground, stands within an extensive sheet of water, formed by damming up the river Len and enclosing three islets which, as they project in succession out into the lake from the south-west corner, constitute the barbican, the bailey, and the keep. The islets are connected with each other, and the barbican to the bank, by narrow viaducts with gaps spanned by drawbridges; the keep, but for its bridge to the bailey, standing free in the middle of the lake.

The site was fortified by the Normans and the cellars at the north-east end of the bailey are of their period; but the earliest existing work above the base dates from about 1280, when the castle fell into the hands of the crown. Henry the Eighth added the upper storey to the keep and built the Maiden tower in the bailey. Owing to drastic modern works of reconstruction and building the castle has lost much of its historic value; it does retain, however, many features of great interest.

The bailey, occupying the largest of the islets, is surrounded by two lines of walls, the outer wall being defended at intervals by bastions. In the viaduct between the bailey and the keep there are two drawbridges. The keep, called the Gloriette, rises sheer out of the water, it has a tall plinth and there is a postern near the edge of the water. The hall, chapel, and other internal buildings of the keep are ranged round a small courtyard. An interesting feature of

[2] *The Siege of Caerlaverock*, Ed. Nicholas, 61–63.

the chapel is that its " low side window " overlooks the lake, thereby negating many theories as to the purpose of these openings.

A remarkable building of the castle is the bath at the water's edge on the south-east side of the bailey. It is a vaulted chamber, about 23 ft. long by 17 ft. wide, lined at the bottom and sides with slabs of Reigate stone, 2 ft. square, to contain water 4 ft. deep; the water entering from the lake through an inlet, defended by a portcullis. On one side of the chamber, above water level, there is a ledge and recess for the bather and there is a dressing-room above. The bath was built about 1291 by Edward the First and is referred to in the account of the exchequer of Eleanor of Castile.

In sharp contrast to castles like Leeds, situated on level ground in well-ruled districts, are those built in isolated outposts such as Carreg Cennen, Carms., in the mountainous country of South Wales, and Dolbadarn, Caerns., at the foot of Snowdon.

Carreg Cennen is said to have been first built by a Welsh chieftain in the last decade of the twelfth century, but the structure was clearly remodelled in the latter part of the thirteenth century. The castle stands perched up like an eagle's eyrie on the top of a high peak with precipices on three sides and a steep rise on the fourth. From a mediaeval standpoint, and with skilled defence, it was practically impregnable and only to be taken after the exhaustion of the supplies of its garrison. It was reduced to its present state of ruin in the latter part of the fifteenth century, when, having become a holt for a band of robbers, serious steps were necessary to root out the band and render their stronghold indefensible. But the curtain and towers still stand almost to their full height, less the battlements, and the fortress has lost little of its formidable aspect.

The castle consists of a single square bailey with a round tower at each of the north-east and north-west corners, a square tower at the south-east corner and a buttress-like turret at the south-west corner. A square tower projecting out from the middle of the south wall was the keep; it was connected with the residential quarters within the bailey and could be defended independently. The gatehouse is in the middle of the east wall. The well lies part way down the precipice beyond the south-west corner of the curtain and is reached from a postern in the south wall, the postern taking a right-angled turn through a buttress. Outside the postern a steep stairway, cut down through the rock and lighted by loopholes opening out to the cliff face, leads to the drawing place.

Dolbadarn is an isolated round tower, which guarded the pass of Llanberis; it appears to have stood at the south end of a small elliptical bailey, now outlined only by scattered pieces of rock. The tower has a battered plinth and is of three storeys; the first storey being a storeroom without light or ventilation and entered through a trap-door in the floor above. The second storey was the entrance floor; the doorway, now broken away, being reached originally by a movable stair. The present stairway up to the door, rising concentrically with the tower, is of much later date. The second storey was lighted by two windows and had a large fireplace and a latrine. The third storey, reached by a spiral stairway, had also a fireplace and a latrine and was lighted by three windows. A second stairway, only a few feet distant from the first and connected with it by a short passage, rises to the battlements.

CHAPTER NINE

WEAPONS AND SIEGE OPERATIONS OF THE MIDDLE AGES

Among the hand weapons in use during the Middle Ages the ordinary bow and arrow still held a strong position, and that long after the introduction of the crossbow. The crossbow came into prominence in European warfare early in the twelfth century. It consisted of a wood stock, similar in form to the butt of a musket, and a bow fixed to one end of the stock. In the earlier forms the bow was made of wood or a composite of wood, horn, sinew and glue, but after about 1370 it was made of steel. The bowstring was stretched by means of a lever or small windlass and the bolt, or quarrel, was released by a trigger. The wounds inflicted by this weapon were considered to be so barbarous and cruel that its use was proscribed by the Lateran council of 1139. But despite this prohibition the crossbow was in general use by the end of the twelfth century and, except among the English, was the favourite weapon from that time to the end of the fifteenth century. In open warfare the English preferred the longbow, which was about 6 ft. long. The longbow was light while the crossbow was heavy and cumbersome. With the longbow the archer could shoot about five arrows while the crossbowman was discharging one bolt, and he could keep his eye on the foe during the adjustment of a new missile while the crossbowman's whole attention was required for this purpose.

For general use in fortified places, however, where the crossbowman would have support for his bow and be himself secure from attack, the crossbow with its heavier missile, greater force, and larger range was by far the superior weapon. The effective range of the longbow was about 220 yards, that of a fifteenth-century crossbow was from 370 to 380 yards, and with some bows even greater. In 1901 Sir Ralph Payne-Gallwey, using a crossbow of the fifteenth century with a steel bow, shot several bolts across the

Menai Straits at a point where the distance was from 440 to 450 yards.[1] Much longer ranges have been claimed.

Scaling ladders were used at all periods, some of them being made of thongs and thrown over the walls.[2] Battering rams were built within strong timber houses, which were mounted on wheels and as a protection from incendiary missiles were covered with raw hides or iron plates. They were brought up to the walls by teams of men working from the inside and propelling them along by means of poles. When in position the wheels were removed and the machine fixed by wooden pegs. The ram had an iron head and was swung to and fro by picked men working on either side. Rams were cumbersome machines and working under constant exposure were often destroyed, their heads were sometimes caught and held by chains let down from the walls. In the latter part of the twelfth century they were being gradually superseded by powerful trebuchets and other projectile engines.

Siege towers were built of timber, covered with raw hides and mounted on wheels. Their great height enabled the besiegers to fight on a level with the defenders on the walls, or even the towers, of the besieged fortress. When brought up close to the walls a bridge was thrown across from the tower to the battlements of the castle and those within the tower rushed across the bridge to the wall walk, while others swarmed up the tower and over the bridge in a continuous stream. A penthouse was a covered passage, built of timber and covered with raw hides, which gave protection to the men employed in constructing a causeway across the ditch and undermining the wall beyond. A cat was a long movable structure, made of the same materials and used for the same purposes as a penthouse. It was brought up in position either by means of rollers and levers or of pulleys and windlasses, and when the ditch was filled in the cat was moved across the causeway and formed a secure shelter for those sapping the wall. Mantlets were wood screens placed in suitable positions before the besieged fortress for the protection of small bodies of archers.

Projectile engines, worked by means of springs, thongs, twisted ropes, or counterpoised weights, have been given various names, sometimes interchangeable; they may be grouped under three heads. The *petriaria,* an engine for casting huge rocks of stone; the *ballista* or the *mangonal,* for throwing stones of about half cwt.; and the catapult or the scorpion, for casting smaller stones, darts, and firebrands. The Charter rolls contain numerous references to such engines. By the end of the twelfth century projectile engines had become almost as powerful as early cannon. At the siege of Acre in 1189–91 the King of France had a petriaria, called "Mal-

[1] Sir Ralph Payne-Gallwey, *The Crossbow,* 1903, 14.
[2] *Acts of Stephen,* Bk. I.

voisine", or bad neighbour, which by its continuous blows broke down part of the main wall of the city; and during the same siege an engine of King Richard of England killed twelve men at one shot. This latter incident so greatly impressed and astonished the Saracens that they brought the stone ball to Saladin for his inspection.[3]

As far as is known none of these powerful engines has survived. Drawings from contemporary data have been made by M. Viollet-le-Duc and others. But with the exception of a sketch of one part of a trebuchet in the *Album* by Villard de Honnecourt, an architect of the thirteenth century, there are no reliable contemporary illustrations. A trebuchet was a powerful projectile engine, worked by springs and counterpoised weights, and the sketch illustrates its framed soleplate. Probably there were also sketches of other parts of the engine, but if so they are among the missing drawings of the collection.

The missiles included stones, darts, poles with sharpened ends, and firebrands. In the hasty collection of ammunition on a surprise attack any suitable objects that could be seized, such as millstones, were put into the engines and hurled at the enemy. Paving stones from the street were brought to the walls and thrown from the engines mounted there; pots of quicklime and bars of forged iron were also used.[4] In 1339 during their attack on the castle of Thin, in the Low Countries, held for Edward the Third of England, the French hurled dead horses and other carrion into the castle in order to spread disease among the inhabitants.[5] Fire was always one of the chief weapons. Flaming torches, burning pitch, and boiling oil were thrown from the walls on the besiegers, and burning and highly inflammable missiles were cast from the engines on both sides.

When direct assault on a castle had failed, attempt was made to bring down the walls either by sapping at their bases under the protection of a penthouse, or by mining below their foundations. The procedure in sapping operations was to excavate a large cavity at the base of the wall, propping and strutting with timbers as the digging progressed. When the cavity was large enough the timber was fired, the men withdrew and, if the work had been well done, on the consumption of the wood the wall above collapsed. In mines the tunnels were begun, under concealment, some distance from the walls and the object of the operations was either to overthrow the walls by destroying the foundations, as in sapping, or to dig below the foundations and issue within the fortress.

Mining was often effective in taking a fortress but occasionally it miscarried. At St. Malo, Brittany, in 1377, the besieged made a sally from the town and broke into a mine which was being driven

[3] Geoffrey de Vinsauf, III, 7. [4] Froissart. [5] Ibid.

towards its walls, burying the men, who were never seen afterwards, in the tunnels.[6] Countermining was the most usual defence against these operations. During the siege of St. Andrews castle, Fife, in 1546–47, the besiegers drove an underground tunnel towards the castle from a point about 130 ft. from the walls. Countermining was then undertaken by the garrison, and after some tentative efforts to locate the advancing mine they eventually broke into it at a spot about midway between the walls and the point from which it started. The countermining was so exact that, although the mine had deviated considerably from a straight course, the countermine broke into it at its near end, and at the convenient level immediately above the heads of the enemy. Both mine and countermine are still preserved.

Siege operations are best understood and the whole purpose of military defences appreciated by a perusal of the very vivid descriptions of sieges given by contemporary chroniclers. One of the most detailed and instructive of these accounts is that by Guillaume-le-Breton of the siege of Château Gaillard, a powerful castle on the Seine built by Richard the First of England in 1196–98 and lost under King John in 1204.

SIEGE OF CHÂTEAU GAILLARD, 1203–1204

Château Gaillard stands on a precipitous hill 300 ft. above the Seine and consists of three baileys, arranged in line. The inner bailey stands on the edge of the cliff and the triangular outer bailey, with a strong tower at the far corner, points inland towards the only line of approach. There are deep moats between the baileys and surrounding the whole castle except along the face of the cliff. At the time of the siege the castle was held for King John by Roger de Lacy.

In 1203 Philip of France advanced towards the castle and after desperate struggles on both sides took the town of Les Petits Andeleys, which King Richard had built on the Seine at the foot of the hill. Having regard to the strength of the castle Philip decided to starve the garrison into submission; and with this end in view he dug two lines of trenches, running from the water inlet on one side up to the top of the hill on which the castle stands and from there down to the river on the other side. At intervals in the space between the trenches he built timber towers and placed guards not only in the towers but also all along the intervals between them. The area thus isolated included the castle and the little valleys surrounding it. Philip's troops then entered upon a period of three months vigilance; and thereupon ensued one of the most terrible events in the history of the Middle Ages.

When Les Petits Andeleys was taken a large number of its in-

[6] Ibid.

habitants, occupying a thickly populated street on the hillside, flocked up to the castle, begged permission to enter, and were received within its walls. But as the siege was prolonged one thousand of them were sent out and were allowed to pass through the French lines. Later, as the reserve of supplies became less and less, de Lacy, selecting those most useful to him, sent forth the others who, including women, children and infirm men, numbered four hundred persons. Conditions inside the castle having become severe they went out with joy, but when the gate was closed behind them they were met with a volley of missiles from the French, who had been ordered to allow no one to pass through the lines. Then, repulsed on both sides and under continuous attack, they found themselves confined to the valleys between the castle and the French trenches. There they remained during a severe winter suffering intensely from want, hunger and exposure, endeavouring to sustain their existence on such winter herbs as they could find. Dogs which had been driven out of the castle were seized and eaten, the skins as well as the flesh. A new-born infant was immediately devoured. Their condition was so deplorable that at length, after three months of intense suffering, those of them who survived were allowed to pass through the French lines; but nearly all of this remnant died on taking food.

In the spring of 1204, following these events, Philip set up his siege engines on the high ground at the south-east and began his assault of the castle. His engines included petriaria, mangonals, mantlets and a very high siege tower. He also built a long penthouse for the protection of those employed in building causeways across the ditches. The garrison on its side replied vigorously to the attack and, casting showers of stones from their engines, caused such great loss to the enemy that he decided on other tactics. The French, under the protection of their shields, then began sapping operations against the round tower at the salient point of the outer bailey, and were successful in excavating a cavity, firing their timberwork, and bringing down the tower. The outer bailey was then taken and operations were begun on the middle bailey.

Against the curtain on the south side of the middle bailey there was a building which had latrines in its lower storey and a chapel in the upper storey; the latter having a window in the outer wall. A French soldier, observing this window, made endeavours to reach the foot of the wall below it. Knowing that there must be a drain from the latrine he, with some others, set out to look for the issue of the drain along the river bank.[7] They found the outlet, crawled up through the drain and reached a point just below the chapel window. Here, mounting on the shoulders of one of his com-

[7] Probably rather a case of actual knowledge than of casual observation.

panions, the soldier sprang up to the window and by means of a cord helped up the others. Having got within the building they began to make a great noise, and the garrison thinking that a large number of the enemy had entered set fire to the building and retired into the inner bailey. Seeing the structure they had entered on fire the French soldiers sought and secured safety in the vaults and before the fire had died down they rushed out, lowered the drawbridge between the outer and middle baileys so that the other forces could enter, and the middle bailey was taken.

Then the French, under the protection of their machines, proceeded to undermine the curtain of the inner bailey. By countermining on the other side the garrison broke into the enemy's tunnel and drove them out. But the wall, weakened by excavations on both sides and battered by a powerful petriaria throwing huge blocks of stone, was fissured and breached and the French rushed through the breach into the inner bailey. Even then none of the garrison surrendered but all fought as long as it was possible to do so.[8]

SIEGE OF ROCHESTER CASTLE, 1215

Rochester castle, having fallen into the hands of the disaffected barons, was besieged by King John in 1215. John brought up his siege engines against the castle and pounded relentlessly at its walls, his troops working in relays. But the garrison replied with such effect and caused such execution in the ranks of the royal forces that other methods of attack had to be adopted. The king then employed miners to break through the curtain, and when a breach was made and the troops had entered within the bailey, the garrison, after a valiant fight, retired within the keep. The miners then attacked the keep and broke into that also. Even then those within fought desperately, and John's forces were compelled to retreat again and again with great loss. At length, having sustained a continuous siege for nearly three months, and themselves brought to the verge of starvation, the garrison surrendered.[9] The turret at the south-east angle of the keep of Rochester castle was rebuilt about this period and there can be little doubt it was here the breach was made.

SIEGE OF DOVER CASTLE, 1216

In the following year Louis, Dauphin of France, in the course of his operations in England in support of the insurgent barons, laid siege to Dover castle. Louis had received from his father, the King of France, an exceptionally powerful petriaria and with this and other siege engines he made a violent and incessant attack on the walls. The garrison under the leadership of the constable, Hugh de

[8] Guillaume-le-Breton, descriptions in prose and verse.
[9] Roger of Wendover.

Burgh, replied with such devastating effect that the French, feeling their loss, moved both their engines and their camp farther back. Meanwhile King John died and Louis and the barons who were with him, thinking that England was now in their power, called upon the constable to surrender, offering him great honours and high position. But the constable refused to give up the castle and Louis had perforce to call off his troops and leave Hugh in full possession.[10]

SIEGE OF BERKHAMSTED CASTLE, 1216

Occasionally a garrison in great straits after a long siege, was ordered to surrender by a king or leader on humanitarian grounds, though the fortress was held for him. Shortly after leaving Dover the Dauphin appeared before Berkhamsted castle. While the investing army were pitching their tents the garrison made a sally, seized much of the enemy's baggage and equipment and retired back safely with the booty. Next day, having set up his petriaria and other siege engines all round the walls, Louis began to pour a destructive shower of stones into the castle. The garrison replied with such devastating effect as to cause great slaughter among the enemy. But after a protracted siege Henry the Third himself ordered the constable to surrender.[11]

SIEGE OF BEDFORD CASTLE, 1224

In 1224 some disaffected knights, having seized one of the king's justiciaries and imprisoned him in Bedford castle, the king, who was then holding a council at Northampton, marched to Bedford and invested the castle. Before the attack the Archbishop of Canterbury and other prelates who were with the king's forces solemnly, with lighted tapers, excommunicated the garrison. Henry had set up his petriariae and mangonals all round the walls and began a furious and constant attack; to this assault the garrison replied with no less deadly effect on the king's forces. Then the king brought up a siege tower, of special design and construction, which was strong enough to support ballistae and was so high that the men within it commanded the whole interior of the castle; any defender exposing himself became an immediate target. Eventually with their engines, and working under the protection of two penthouses which they had brought up to the walls, the king's forces broke into the bailey and began to destroy the curtain and attack the keep. After a siege of two months the garrison surrendered and sued for the king's mercy.[12]

[10] Ibid.
[11] Ibid.
[12] Ibid.

The great strength of mediaeval fortresses is amply demonstrated by the effective resistance they offered to attack during long sieges and against almost overwhelming odds. In 1265 Kenilworth castle held out for a whole year against all the royal forces and siege engines which could be brought up to its attack. And even at the end of that time, when their provisions had become depleted, the defenders surrendered only on conditions favourable to themselves. The long and effective stand made by Pontefract castle against the forces and artillery of Cromwell in 1648 was referred to in the description of that castle. Corfe castle successfully repelled for nearly three years, May 1643 to March 1646, the sustained attack of the Parliamentary forces equipped with all the latest weapons of the day, and it was not by force of arms but through the treachery of one of its men that it was eventually taken.

When a fortress could not be reduced by direct attack efforts were often made to secure the treacherous assistance of a disaffected or mercenary member of the garrison, or, failing this line of approach, to attain the desired end by trickery. Edinburgh castle is said to have been captured in 1341 by the latter means. While a large party of besiegers lay in ambush outside the castle, another party carrying sacks and disguised as merchants bringing supplies to the garrison went up openly to the gate. When the gate was opened to them by the unsuspecting porter the pseudo-merchants deposited their loads on the ground in positions where they prevented the gate from being closed. Then these men, throwing off all disguise, were joined by those in ambush and together, taking the garrison completely by surprise, they captured the castle.[13]

[13] Froissart.

CHAPTER TEN

CASTLES OF THE FOURTEENTH AND FIFTEENTH CENTURIES

After the brilliant Edwardian period of military architecture there followed, in the design of new castles and additions to old ones, an obvious and ever growing tendency to concentrate on the development of the amenities rather than of the defences. That the latter were by no means neglected is proved by such powerful structures as the gatehouses at Alnwick, built in 1314, and Warwick, built about 1370. But the desire for improved domestic comfort is clearly shown in those castles with ranges of residential and service quarters, built round a rectangular courtyard, as at Bolton, Yorks., and Bodiam, Sussex.

FORTIFIED TOWERS

Meanwhile large numbers of fortified towers with no other outer defences than the wall of the courtyard in which they stood were being built throughout northern Britain, and particularly in the border counties of the north of England and south of Scotland where raids were of frequent occurrence. Though there are earlier examples, as Pendragon, Westmorland, built in the twelfth century, the towers date mainly from the fourteenth century and later periods. These towers though varying in size and internal arrangements according to the status and means of their builders are generally of rectangular plan, are of three or four storeys, and have thick walls crowned by embattled parapets. The upper storeys are reached by spiral stairways, formed in the corners of the towers and terminating in turrets. Normally the first or the second storey is covered by a barrel vault and often additional storeys are formed by the construction of timber floors at the level of the springing line of the vaults. In many towers the upper storeys are vaulted and when there is a vault at the summit the roof is formed by laying flat stones upon its upper surface.

The entrance is either at the first or the second storey; when at the second it is reached by a movable stairs or ladder. In towers where the basement was used principally for stores the basement often had an outer door and no connection with the storeys above. Sometimes, as at Threave, where the entrance is at the second storey, a small prison is formed in the basement. The upper storeys contained the hall, the great chamber and other living rooms. Mural chambers were formed in the corners of the tower and in some cases, as at Craigmillar and Chipchase, additional space was secured by a small projecting wing which was carried up the full height of the tower. Clearly the enjoyment of privacy and the ordinary social amenities in such confined quarters were considerably restricted, and additional rooms were often formed by the subdivision of the halls of one or more of the storeys. Well preserved towers of this kind are the Vicar's Pele, Belsay, and Chipchase, all three in Northumberland; Dacre, Cumberland; Craigmillar, Midlothian, and Threave, Kirkcudbrightshire.

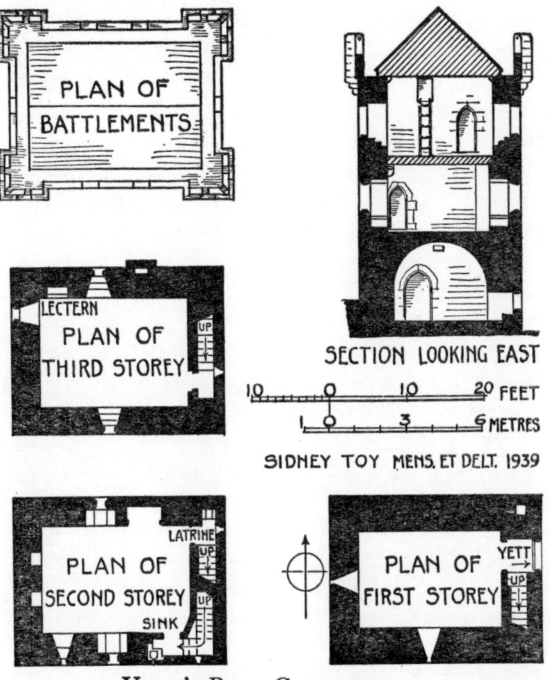

VICAR'S PELE, CORBRIDGE

Vicar's Pele stands in the churchyard of Corbridge and, as its name implies, was doubtless the fortified residence of the priest in charge of the parish and responsible for the services in the church. It is a strongly constructed tower of three storeys, faced with ashlar and surmounted by an embattled parapet. It was built in the early years of the fourteenth century. The entrance, defended by an iron armoured door, or yett, is at ground floor level and gives admittance to the first storey and to a straight mural stairway rising to the second storey. The first storey, or basement, is covered by a barrel vault and lighted only by two narrow loopholes; it was the storeroom. The second storey was the living room; it is lighted by two windows with seats, has a large fireplace, two lockers, a lavabo basin, and a latrine, also a loophole for observation purposes. Another straight mural stairs leads to the third storey, which was the bedroom and had a timber floor, now destroyed. This chamber had no fireplace; it has three small windows which, like those in the room below, were closed by wood shutters. In one corner is a recess containing a stone book-rest, or lectern; the room probably served the priest as an oratory as well as sleeping chamber.

The battlements were reached from the upper room by a ladder and a doorway in the roof gable; they were strongly defended. The embrasures were closed by wood shutters and in the sides of the merlons are sockets for the pivots on which the shutters were hung. At each corner of the tower the parapet is projected out on corbels to form machicolations. Vicar's Pele is a most valuable and well preserved example of a priest's house, built at this period in a disturbed border country. In case of sudden raid it was capable of offering strong resistance to the enemy when manned, as it doubtless was, by a body of men prepared for such an emergency (pp. 191, 192a).

Belsay is a strong rectangular tower of three storeys, the lower storey only being vaulted; it was built about 1340. On the west side two wide wings, one at either end, project forward to provide space for additional chambers, opening from the hall at each storey, and for a wide spiral stairway which rises from ground level to the battlements. The entrance is at the first storey and opens on to a small lobby with doors to the main room on this floor, to the chambers in the wings, and to the stairway. The main room was the kitchen, it is vaulted and has a fireplace and a well. In the second storey the main room was the great hall; it was lighted by three windows and has a fireplace. Opening from it are two sleeping chambers, one of which has a fireplace and a latrine. The third storey contained the great chamber and rooms similar to those immediately below. The spiral stairway terminates at wall walk level. At the top of the tower four round turrets, springing from corbel courses at the corners, rise above the battlements, their summits being reached from the wall walk by stone stairways; the tower and the turrets have machicolated parapets.

Chipchase castle, on the North Tyne, is a well preserved and large fortress tower of about 1340; it is faced with ashlar, is of four storeys, and a turret, springing from corbel courses, rises from battlement level at each corner. In this tower additional space is

Corbridge. The Vicar's Pele.

Chipchase Tower.

Elphinstone Tower from the South-East.

Pickering Castle. Diate Hill Tower.

Threave Castle from the South-East.

Craigmillar Castle from the South-East.

secured by a single wing, which projects out at the south end of the east side and rises to the full height of the building. The entrance is through the wing at the first storey; it is defended by a stout oak portcullis and a door secured by two timber bars; the portcullis, still in position, was operated from a small chamber above the doorway. The first storey was the storeroom and has neither windows nor ventilating shaft. At one end there is a well, the water from which was drawn up to the room above through a trap-door in the vault covering this storey. The second storey was but dimly lighted by two loopholes; it has a fireplace and a double locker (pp. 192a, 193).

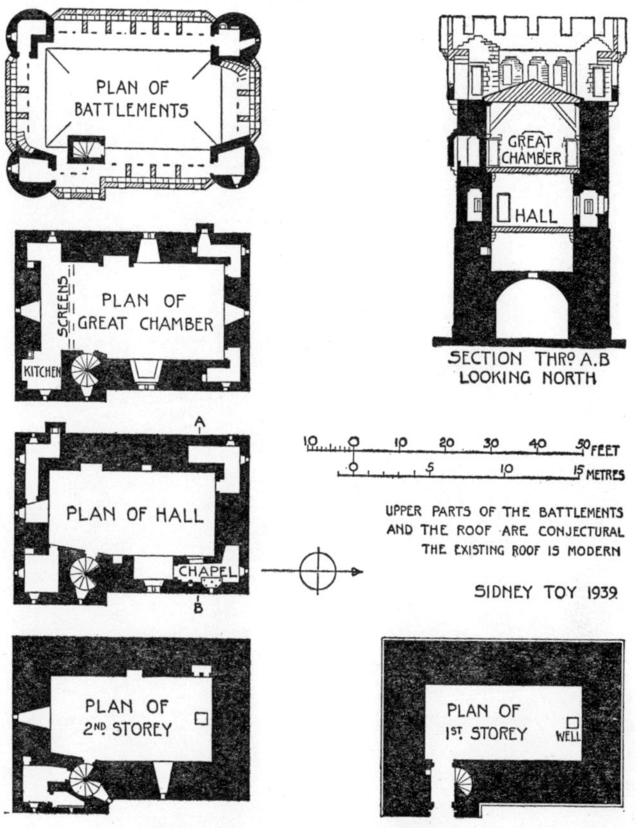

CHIPCHASE CASTLE. THE TOWER

The third and fourth storeys have well lighted halls with fireplaces and latrines, and doorways lead from them to mural chambers. At the north-east corner of the third storey there is an oratory, formed in the wall; it retains its piscina and stone altar table. The doorway into it is in a jamb of one of the windows and there is an opening directly into the hall through which the ministrations at the altar could be followed. At the south-east corner of the hall there is a small chamber with a fireplace. The fourth storey was the great hall; it has a large fireplace and one of its two-light windows is provided with stone seats. A portion at the south end was screened off from the main hall and at the south-east corner, beyond the screen, now destroyed, there is a small kitchen with fireplace and sink.

The battlements are broken down to a level just above the machicolations but enough remains to indicate their character. They were of two tiers. The lower tier, at the level of the wall walk, has a machicolated parapet. The upper tier was at the level of the battlements of the turrets, received intermediate support between the turrets on cross walls and was reached by steps up from the wall walk.

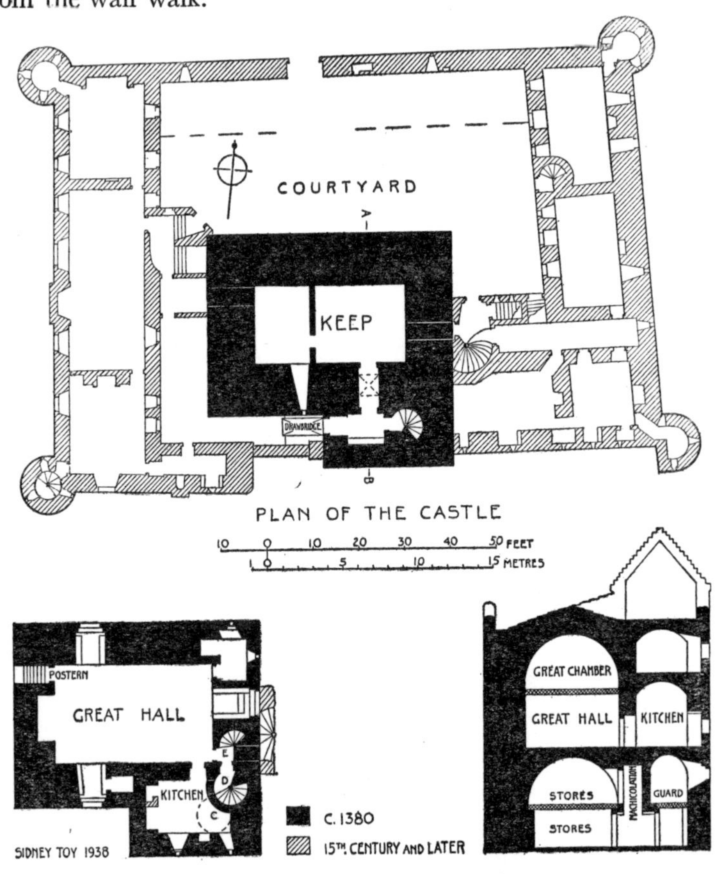

CRAIGMILLAR CASTLE WITH PLAN OF THIRD STOREY AND SECTION THROUGH KEEP

Dacre castle, built in the early years of the fourteenth century, is a compact rectangular tower of three storeys with square turrets at the corners. The turrets rise from ground level; those at the east and west corners being of considerable size, of great projection, and set squarely while the others are smaller and are set diagonally with the corner. The entrance is at the first storey, through the square west turret, and opens to the cellars and to the foot of a spiral stairway rising to the upper levels. The first storey is divided into two barrel-vaulted cellars; the north cellar having a separate stairway to the hall above. The second storey was the hall. It has a large fireplace with an oven opening out of it, a lavabo, and a latrine, and opening from the hall are three chambers and a wide recess. The third storey was the great chamber. It has windows with moulded rear arches, a fireplace and a latrine and also opens to chambers in the turrets; one turret having a tier of three chambers.

A noteworthy feature of this tower is the lavabo in the hall. Although for purely domestic purposes it is designed in all respects like the piscina in a church. It is formed in a niche with moulded jambs and trefoiled head and has a multifoil basin with a shelf above.

Craigmillar castle is built on an eminence and its tower, which is among the finest and best preserved of its type, stands on the edge of a low cliff. The tower was built about 1374 and at first stood alone without other defences; the bailey was not built until about 1427. An outer court was added and the buildings of the bailey were altered at later periods (pp. 192b, 194).

The tower is rectangular with a turret projecting out on the side towards the cliff. The main body is of four storeys, the second and fourth being covered with barrel vaults and having timber floors dividing them from the storeys below. The turret was also originally of four storeys, all vaulted except the lowest, but a fifth storey, now largely destroyed, was added at the summit in the sixteenth century.

The entrance is at the first storey and was most skilfully defended. It is placed at the re-entering angle of the wing and was gained only after passing round two sides of the tower and along the face of the cliff. Immediately in front of the doorway there was a deep chasm, spanned by a drawbridge. The entrance has its floor 3 ft. below the sill of the doorway and was commanded from above by a small guardroom; so that an enemy who had broken through the door would stumble or have his attention diverted by the sudden drop and be at the mercy of those in the guardroom. The chasm is now filled in and the floor of the lobby has been raised. From the lobby a doorway on the left leads by a lofty passage to two doors, one above the other, opening to the storerooms of the first and second storeys. The upper door, which must have been reached by a ladder, opens on to a kind of machicolation over the passage.

To gain the rooms of the third and fourth storeys it was necessary to ascend three spiral stairways in succession. The first, marked C on the plan, rising from the lobby to the guardroom; the second, D, from that level to the level of the great hall in the third storey; and the third, E, from the great hall to the fourth storey and the battlements. Each of the short passages between the stairways was closed by a door. The great hall is well lighted by three windows with window seats, and has a large fireplace at the west end. On the north side of the fireplace a passage and flight of steps led down to a doorway on the outside face of the tower. This opening was adjusted to additions made here later, and since removed, but it was originally a postern by which escape could be effected. The passage goes straight through the wall and is not likely to have led to a latrine as has been suggested. A doorway at the south-east corner of the hall leads to the kitchen, formed in the turret. The low pitched roof of the tower is of stone slabs, laid down on the crown of the vault. At the battlements the parapet rises flush with the wall faces, without either string course or corbels.

Threave castle stands on the edge of an island on the river Dee and was defended on those sides not washed by the river by a ditch and an outwork. It consists of a great rectangular tower, built about 1380 by Archibald, Earl of Douglas, known as Archibald the Grim, and outer defences which were probably added in the following century and are now in fragments (pp. 192b, 197).

The tower measures 45 ft. 6 in. by 24 ft. internally at the base, where the walls are 8 ft. thick, and is of five storeys, the second only being vaulted. The entrance, reached originally by a movable stair, is at the second storey and opens to a large kitchen with a wide fireplace at one end, three lockers in the walls, and a latrine at one corner. The approach to the basement must have been through a trap-door in the floor of the kitchen for there is no other means of access. The basement has a large square well in one corner and, near the well, a stone sink with a drain through the wall. At another corner there is a small vaulted prison, or " pit ", screened off from the rest of the apartment by walls 4 ft. thick; it has a latrine and a ventilating shaft but no window and was also entered by a trap-door in the room above. From the kitchen a spiral stairway in one corner of the tower leads to the upper levels.

The third and fourth storeys are well lighted living rooms with fireplaces, lockers, and latrines; there are no mural chambers. In the east wall of the third storey, directly above the entrance to the tower, there is a postern which appears to have led out on to a timber bridge spanning the gap between the tower and the exist-

THREAVE CASTLE. THE TOWER

ing outer gateway. Two corbels which may have supported such a bridge at the tower end have been cut flush with the wall face. A corbel projecting out from the battlements high above this point is all that remains of a machicolated parapet defending both the entrance to the tower and the postern. The fourth storey was divided by a screen into two compartments and there is a fireplace in each of them. At the level of the fifth storey, which was originally the roof space, a large beam-hole passes round through the middle of the walls on all sides of the tower. This continuous hole, large enough for a boy to crawl through, has been the occasion of much conjecture, but there can be little doubt that it indicates the position of strong bonding timbers, buried in the walls and long since decayed or destroyed. The clear span across the narrow part of the tower at this level is 27 ft., and without such powerful ties the lateral thrusts of the roof and upper floors would be too great for the resistance of the side walls.

On the faces of three sides of the tower, just below the battlements, are triple rows of small holes. It has been suggested that these holes were made for hoarding. But apart from the fact that they do not occur on the entrance side of the tower where such defences would be mostly needed, any platform projected out from them would be so insecure a post as to be as dangerous to the defenders as to the enemy. The holes are not deep and are arranged alternately in the same manner as those in a dovecote and were doubtless made for a colony of pigeons, like those at the summit of the keep at Conisborough.

The tower at Cawdor castle most probably dates from the latter part of the fourteenth century. It has been assumed too readily that because a licence to fortify the castle was issued in 1454 the earliest part of the existing structure, the tower, was built at that time. But a licence to crenellate, particularly in Scotland, by no means determines the date of a fortified building on the site indicated. Largo castle, for example, was already in existence when a licence to build a fortalice there was granted in 1491 and, having regard to the relatively few licences which have been preserved of the great number of towers built, it is unsafe to date a fortified tower on the evidence of the licence alone (pp. 199, 200a).

That a castle existed at Cawdor in the fourteenth century is proved by two entries in the Exchequer Rolls of expenses *pro Castro de Caldor*, one in 1396 and the other in 1398.[1] Cawdor was a royal castle and was given to the Thane of Cawdor by James the Second of Scotland who, in a licence to fortify granted in 1454, made the stipulation that he and his heirs should have right of entry into the castle when they so desired; a proviso similar to that made at the present time when a donor wishes to reserve a part of his house for his private use. In addition to the evidence of the Rolls the tower, apart from later alterations, is similar in design to those described above.

Cawdor castle is a rectangular structure standing on the steep bank of a small stream, with a square tower, or keep, in the centre and ranges of buildings surrounding three small courts. The castle is defended on the west by the stream and on the north and east by

[1] *Rotuli Saccarii Regum Scotorum*, ed. Burnett, 1880, 404, 455.

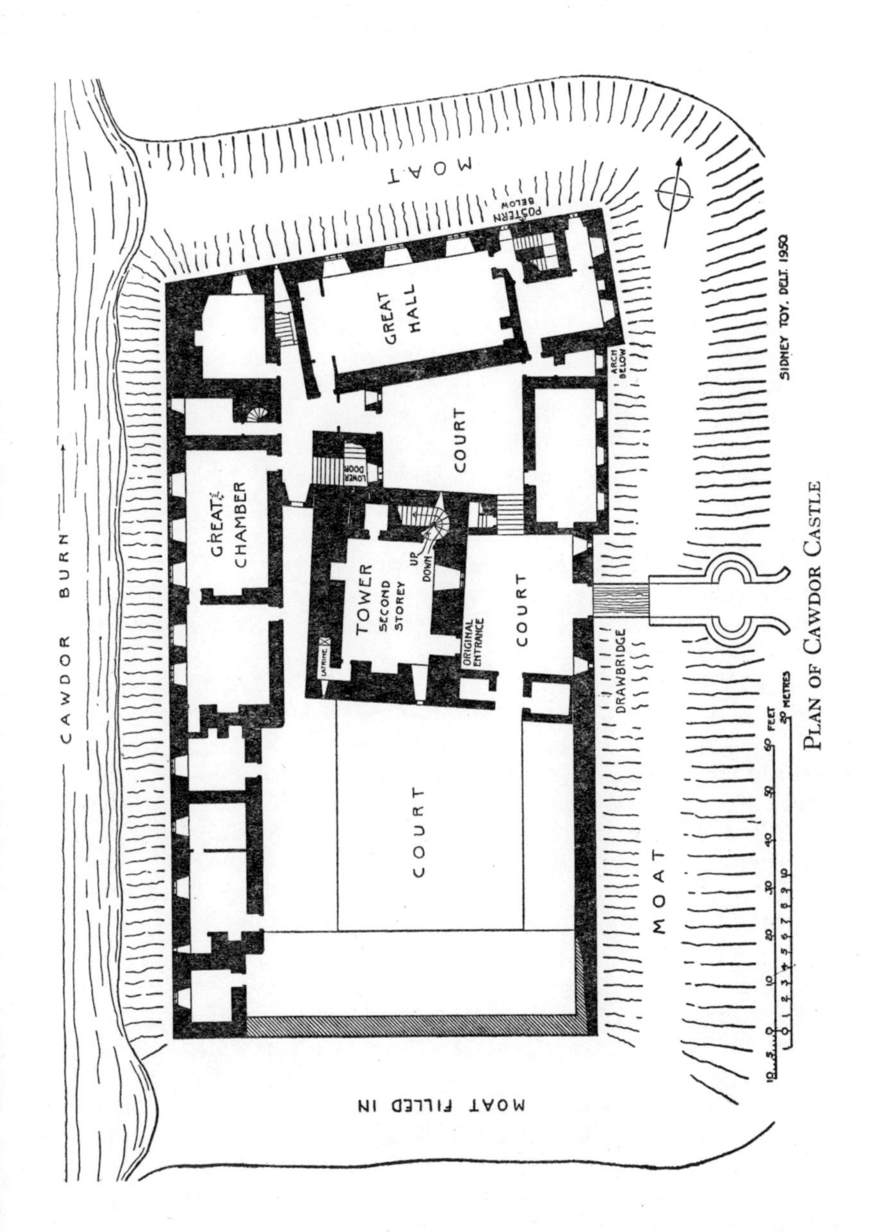

PLAN OF CAWDOR CASTLE

a deep dry ditch, which formerly extended along the south side also; but that portion has been filled in. The entrance is in the middle of the east curtain wall; it is approached by a drawbridge over the ditch and opens on to a small court opposite the keep.

The keep as originally built was of four storeys, each of the first and fourth being covered with a barrel vault. The original entrance, probably reached by a movable stair, was at second storey level, near the south end of the east wall; it is blocked but its outline is to be seen clearly on the wall face. This storey was lighted by windows on the east and south, it has a mural chamber in the north wall and a latrine in the south-west corner. Access down to the basement from here was by a straight flight of steps in the north wall and to the upper floors by a spiral stairway at the head of the straight flight, in the north-east corner of the tower. The parapet surmounting the tower, like that of the keep at Craigmillar, rises straight up from the wall face without either string course or corbelling, and it is very probable also that the original roof was composed of stone slabs laid directly on the external surface of the vault. The present roof chamber was formed in the seventeenth century. Rising from the floor and reaching to the vault of the basement there is the trunk of an old thorn tree which is held by tradition to have existed on the site before the erection of the tower, and to have been built round and allowed to remain untouched ever since.

The alterations effected by the Thane of Cawdor following his acquisition of the tower in 1454 included the blocking of the old entrance and the opening out of a new one at the foot of the straight stairway to the basement, still some few feet above ground level. He defended his new doorway by an iron yett, said to have been brought from Lochindorb, a castle which, under orders from the king, he himself dismantled, and by a machicolation which projects out from the parapet high above the doorway. He also built the bartizans at the corners of the parapet.

The fact that these features are of fifteenth-century character, and that they are no less obviously the result of alterations, is in itself clear evidence of the existence of the tower at the time of the grant. It is most probable also that the Thane's plans included the ranges of buildings to the north and west of the tower, if, indeed, the lower parts of their walls are not his work; for otherwise there would be little point in making the new entrance which forms such a convenient access to the tower from them.

These buildings include the great hall, now the drawing-room, in the north range, and the great chamber, now the dining-room, in the west range; they were completed or greatly altered in the sixteenth century and again drastically remodelled in the seventeenth century. At the junction of the north and east ranges of the castle

[Country Life

CAWDOR CASTLE. THE TOWER FROM THE EAST.

WARWICK CASTLE. CAESAR'S TOWER FROM THE RIVER.

BOLTON CASTLE FROM THE SOUTH-EAST.

are two tiers of small chambers which were formerly latrines, discharging into a pit with an open arch to the east ditch; the arch is now blocked. At the east end of the north wall of the castle there is a postern at basement level. The great hall, the great chamber, and a room above the great hall each contains a fine stone fireplace. The last two are elaborately carved and date from the latter part of the seventeenth century; that in the great hall, which has a deep plain frieze with a sculptured hart's head in the centre, was inserted in the early part of the seventeenth century but widened and reset in the latter part.

While on the subject of border towers it will be convenient to note briefly here some of later date than that covered by this chapter; great numbers of them, called Pele towers,[2] were built during the fifteenth and sixteenth centuries. The constant raids for cattle and movable goods among the inhabitants of the border country made the provision of places of refuge for person and property a dire necessity. These little fortresses consist of a stone tower and a small courtyard, called a barmkin. Cocklaw, Northumberland; Newark, Selkirkshire; Elphinstone, East Lothian; and Orchardton, Kirkcudbrightshire, are typical examples, all built in the first part of the fifteenth century.

Cocklaw is a rectangular tower having its main rooms occupying the body of the building and its tiers of mural chambers formed in a very thick wall at one end. The entrance is through the thick wall at ground floor level and opens to a lobby with a small prison on the left and a stairway to the upper floors on the right. The doorway was defended by machicolations which projected out from the parapet high above it. There is a postern opening out from the main room of the second storey, 17 ft. above the ground, from which escape could be made by a rope or ladder.

Newark tower is of six storeys, the second storey only being vaulted. Here the original entrance was at the third storey and gave direct access, through a lobby, to the great hall; entrance through the lobby being defended by a mural guardroom which opens out into it. A spiral stairway at one corner of the tower descends to the second storey and another stairway at the opposite corner descends to the ground floor; the present outer doorway at ground floor level is of later date. Both stairways rise to the battlements where each terminates in a gabled turret, or caphouse. The kitchen is at one end of the great hall, from which it was doubtless separated by a screen, now destroyed; it has a very large fireplace. Each of the upper storeys appears to have been divided into two rooms by wood partitions.

Elphinstone castle is one of the most complete and interesting of these towers, well preserved and protected by a modern roof.

[2] For Pele vide *Trans. Glasgow Archaeol. Soc.*, 1891, Pt. II.

When all the floors for which provision is made were in position it was of five storeys, the second and third being covered by barrel vaults. Within the walls there is a most complicated and elaborate system of stairways and mural chambers. The first and second storeys were low cellars separated by a timber floor, now destroyed. The third storey contains a lofty vaulted great hall and the fourth and fifth storeys formed the main retiring and sleeping rooms.

ELPHINSTONE TOWER

The entrance is on the north side of the tower, slightly above ground level, and opens on to the two tiers of cellars. On the right of the entrance lobby is the guardroom, while on the left a flight of steps rises within the thickness of the north wall to the great hall. An enemy ascending this stair would not only be under attack from the rear by the defenders in the guardroom but also from above through an opening in the wall between the hall and the stairway. The great hall is well lighted and amply provided with mural chambers at the corners and sides; there is a large fireplace at the west end and at the east end a portion of the room has been screened off to form a kitchen. Two spiral stairways ascend from this level to the summit of the tower (p. 192a).

At the north-west corner of the great hall there are two mural chambers, one above the other, for the private use of the owner of the tower. There is a separate stair connecting the chambers, and in the upper chamber there is a small fireplace and also an opening overlooking the hall. A doorway at the foot of the private stairs opening into a window recess of the hall, and a hole in the upper chamber broken through into the flue of the hall fireplace, are both works of later periods.

Orchardton tower, differing from the normal form, is circular; it is of four storeys, the lowest only being vaulted. There is a direct entrance to the basement from the courtyard, but the entrance to the other rooms of the tower is at the second storey; the basement is rectangular internally while the upper rooms are circular. The second storey is the great hall and from it a spiral stairway rises to the upper levels. There is a lavabo in the hall of somewhat similar design to that at Dacre; it has a trefoiled head under a sculptured triangular label and a multifoil basin.

TOWERS ADDED TO EXISTING CASTLES

Additions made in the fourteenth century to existing castles often included a strong tower containing one or more private chambers and sometimes, as at Ludlow and Warwick, many tiers of chambers. Each chamber is well lighted and has a fireplace and a latrine, the latter reached from the chamber through passages with right-angled turns. The upper part of Gold Hole tower, Richmond castle, was rebuilt in the early years of the fourteenth century to contain a complete private chamber, entered from the wall walk of the curtain. Rosamund's tower, Pickering castle, Yorks., built about 1330 some one hundred and fifty years after Rosamund's time, is a good example of a complete tower of this kind. Pickering castle consists of two baileys with a large shell keep, now very fragmentary, standing on a high mound between them; the inner bailey and the keep date from the twelfth century and the outer bailey with its towers, of which Rosamund's is one, was added in the first part of the fourteenth century (p. 192a).

Rosamund's tower is a square building of three storeys, projecting outside the wall. The first storey, isolated from the upper part of the tower, is entered directly from the courtyard; the upper storeys are entered from the wall walk and together form a complete and agreeable private residence. Two mural passages, one at each storey and connected by a spiral stairway, run through the north wall of the tower in line with the curtain and the rooms open from these passages. The stairway, which rises to the battlements, is at the west end of the passages; the lower passage terminates at the east end in a latrine, but the east end of the upper passage opens on to the wall walk of the curtain, which is on a higher level on the east than on the west side of the tower. The lower room, perhaps for an attendant, has two tall windows but no fireplace. The upper room is a comfortable and pleasant chamber with a large two-light window on the south, a small window in each of the east and west walls, a wide fireplace, and two wall cupboards. A doorway in the east wall opens on to a latrine. Steps built against the north wall of the tower and a doorway opened out in the lower mural passage belong to a later period (p. 192a).

At Ludlow when the great chamber was constructed, about 1330, a tall rectangular tower, projecting outside the curtain and containing four tiers of private rooms, was built at the same time. The three lower storeys of the tower open out from the large rooms of the great chamber building and of the adjoining building on the east; while the top storey is reached by a spiral stairway, rising up from the great hall, and a mural passage from the head of the stairs. The two lowest storeys are each divided by a partition wall into two chambers, but each of the two upper storeys consists of one large room (p. 76).

All the chambers have windows with window-seats and each is provided with a latrine, approached through passages with right-angled turns. There is a fireplace in each of the two large upper rooms. The best room is that on the top floor, approached directly up from the dais of the great hall. It is a pleasant and spacious chamber with a fireplace and lighted by four tall transomed windows, two in the wide wall on the north and one in each of the east and west walls. On the south side of the room there is a spacious cupboard.

Warwick castle had not recovered from the great damage it received during the wars of the Barons until the latter part of the fourteenth century, when extensive works then carried out converted it into what was at once a powerful fortress and an agreeable residence. A new curtain was built along the north side of the

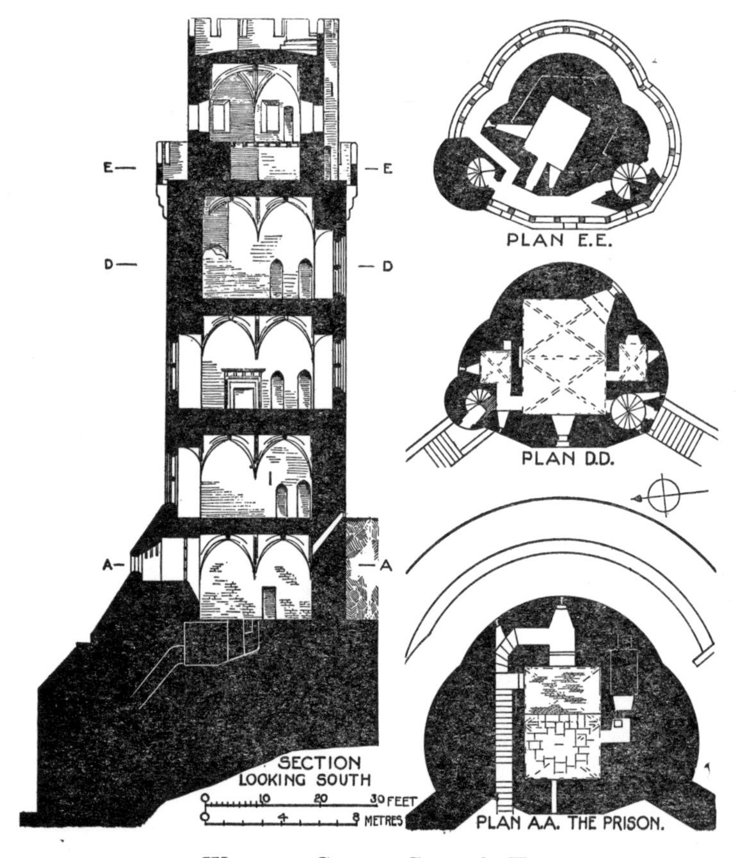

WARWICK CASTLE. CAESAR'S TOWER

bailey, towards the town, with a strong gatehouse and barbican in the middle and a powerful tower at either end; the tower at the east end called Caesar's, and the other, Guy's tower. The great hall and the domestic quarters on the south-east side of the bailey, facing the river, were also rebuilt on spacious lines at the same time. Both Caesar's and Guy's towers contain many tiers of private rooms; each room is well lighted, has a fireplace, and opening from it on one side is a mural bedroom and on the other a latrine. In the design of both towers considerations of defence and comfort are skilfully adjusted, and both are capable of being held independently.

Caesar's tower occupies a strategic position at the north-east corner of the castle; it is a tri-lobed structure 133 ft. high from the foot of its massive plinth, outside the castle, to the top of the upper parapet. It is of six storeys, all except the rectangular chamber forming the fifth storey covered with thick stone vaulting. The lowest storey was a prison; it is below the level of the bailey, which is 49 ft. above the base of the plinth outside, and is reached from a doorway in the courtyard and a flight of steps down. The entrance to the storeys above the basement is from the wall walk on the curtain on the south side, a spiral stairway inside the door leading down to the lower and up to the upper floors. The second, third and fourth storeys are alike; in each there is a large rectangular room with a fireplace, a mural chamber and a latrine. The fifth storey is a rectangular ammunition stores, at the level of the lower battlements, and the top storey is a large hexagonal guardroom. There are two tiers of battlements and the two highest storeys of the tower, restricted in size, rise above the gallery of the first tier. The lower parapets are machicolated and the merlons of both parapets have cross-shaped arrow-loops (pp. 55, 200b, 204).

Guy's tower is multangular externally and of five storeys, all vaulted; the top storey being an octagonal guardroom covered with a very thick and strong vault. The four storeys below the guardroom have each a large room with mural chambers disposed in much the same manner as in Caesar's tower; there is no prison. The battlements have a machicolated parapet and are of one tier only.

Both towers are built astride the curtain and interrupt the circulation of its wall walk. The entrance in each case is from the wall walk on the lofty curtain at third storey level and on that side of the tower nearest the residential quarters. At the entrance one spiral stairway descends to the lower and rises to the upper floors, with doorways at each floor, and to the battlements. From the battlements another stairway descends directly to the wall walk on the other side of the tower without any intervening doorway. The existing opening into the tower at the foot of this stair in Caesar's tower was roughly driven through at a later date. So in order to pass from the wall walk on one side of the tower to that on the other an enemy must ascend one stairway to the top of the tower, cross the battlements, and descend the second stairs on the other side, exposed to attack from the defence forces all the way.

CASTLES REBUILT OR OF NEW FOUNDATION

The new castles built during the first half of the fourteenth century followed closely on traditional lines. In some of them, as at Dunstanburgh, the gatehouse is the strong point. But in many others a rectangular or square keep occupies the highest or most important point in the curtain, while the gateway, often commanded by the keep, is a separate structure.

Dunstanburgh castle stands on a high promontory on the coast of Northumberland and is protected on two sides by sheer cliffs. It was built between 1313 and 1316 and was defended by a curtain with wall towers and a gatehouse, the latter occupying the most vulnerable point on the south. Liburn tower, a wall tower projecting out at the west of the bailey with its inner wall in line with the curtain, though it stands astride of the wall walk does not obstruct it; the walk is carried through from side to side by a mural passage. The gatehouse, always the strong point of the castle, was remodelled later in the century.

Etal castle, Northumberland, built 1341–45, has a rectangular keep at the north-west corner of the bailey while the gatehouse is at the south-east corner. The keep is of four storeys and is designed on the lines of a border tower, each storey having a large central hall and mural chambers at the sides opening out of the hall. At Gleaston, Lancashire, built about 1330, the keep occupies the highest point at a corner of the bailey. It projects entirely outside the curtain and thus commands not only the approach to the gateway, which passes through the wall immediately to the south of it, but also the outer faces of the walls on either side of the corner.

Naworth castle, Cumberland, built in 1335, has a square keep, called Dacre Tower, which projects out at the south-west corner of a trapezoidal bailey. The gateway to the bailey pierces the curtain immediately to the north of the keep which, from its battlements, commands the approaches to the gate from all directions. Residential and service quarters, rebuilt in the sixteenth century and much modernised in later times, are ranged against the curtain round a a central courtyard. A turret rising above the battlements at one corner of the keep, and reached from the battlements by a stone stairs, served the purpose both of a watch tower and of a beacon.

Knaresborough castle, Yorks., was rebuilt in the first half of the fourteenth century on the site of an older castle; it stands on high ground overlooking the river Nidd and was defended by the river on the west, a ditch on the east, and a deep ravine on either flank. There are two baileys in line running east and west; the inner bailey on the west nearest the river and the outer bailey nearest the town. The outer and inner gateways have been destroyed, but the keep, which stands at one corner of the junction of the two baileys, still remains, though in ruinous condition.

The keep, an exceptionally interesting structure, is of four storeys, the first being below the level of the courtyard; both the first and second storeys are vaulted. The north end of the keep, which protrudes outside the curtain, is semi-hexagonal but the portion inside the wall is square. Owing to the destruction of some parts and the alteration of others the reason for some of the features of this building is now obscure. The entrance is on the east side at the third storey and the approach to it was probably by a stairway at the south-east corner of the keep, subsequently altered and now much broken away; it was defended by doors and a portcullis. On the west side of the entrance hall, opposite the doorway, there is a wide recess, extending across practically the full width of the room; it has a projecting ledge 1 ft. 9 in. above the floor.

On the south side of the entrance hall, facing the bailey, there is a large window which has been called a doorway and may possibly have been used as a door at a later date. But the opening was designed and used during the military period as a window. Its rear arch is that of a window and not a doorway; it has no defences, for the exterior grooves, said to indicate a drawbridge, correspond to no known method of operating that device. The facing stones below the sill have been torn away and there has been a low barrel-vaulted chamber or archway in the courtyard below the window. Apart from small loopholes this appears to have been the only window in the entrance hall. *See Appendix D:* KNARESBOROUGH CASTLE *and Appendix E*: MAXSTOKE CASTLE.

Edlingham castle, Northumberland, built about 1350, has a square keep of three storeys with diagonal buttresses at the corners. Here the keep was clearly the normal residential quarters and was approached through a fore-building. The first storey was the kitchen; it had a wide fireplace, a well, a latrine, and apparently a sink, for there is a drain through the wall. The second storey was the living-room, a lofty vaulted hall with clerestory windows and fine fireplace, the latter having pilaster jambs with carved heads and a flat, joggled lintel, now broken down.

Queenborough castle, Sheppey, Kent, built 1361–77 and destroyed in the seventeenth century, was designed on a circular plan. The outer bailey, defended by a moat and a powerful wall, surrounded and was concentric with the keep. There was a gateway on the west and a postern on the east side of the curtain and the radial passage across the bailey between each of them and the keep was defended by screen walls on either side. Thus in the event of the outer bailey being carried by assault these vital passages could still be held. The keep, rising high above the outer wall, was defended by six round towers, two of them placed closely together in order to defend the gateway between them. The entrance to the keep faced towards the postern and not the main outer gate; an enemy, therefore, having rushed through the gate, must circulate half round the bailey before reaching the entrance to the keep. Within the keep the buildings were ranged round a circular courtyard.

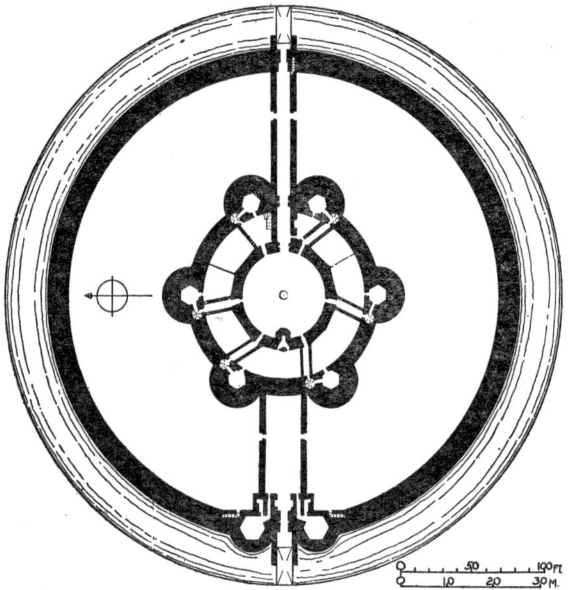

PLAN OF QUEENBOROUGH CASTLE

The castles of Edinburgh and Stirling though on ancient sites were considerably altered in the fourteenth century and later periods. Each is perched on the summit of a high hill with precipitous faces on all sides but one. As castles of the kings of Scotland they have both been kept so closely in touch with the domestic improvements of the day, receiving inspiration largely from continental sources, and have suffered so much from attack and destruction that little now remains of the mediaeval defences but the curtain walls.

Edinburgh castle stands on the top of a hill 270 ft. high, with precipitous falls from the summit all round. On the east the sheer face ends about halfway down the hill and from that point the fall eastward to the city is gradual. The approach is by the sloping causeway leading up from the city to the foot of the steep face, where a moat, formerly spanned by a drawbridge, cuts through the causeway. From this point the summit is reached by a steep path which winds up, east to west, halfway round the castle, under fire from the walls above and barred by three gateways in succession. St. Margaret's chapel, a tall vaulted building standing on the highest point of the castle, dates from about 1100, but the oldest portions of the existing defences are the east curtain wall and the basement of a building called David's tower, both dating from the fourteenth century; the wall has been considerably rebuilt. The palace, occupying the southern portion of the upper bailey, is an unfortified royal residence, the earliest portion, the east wing, dating from the fifteenth century.

Stirling castle, the focus of contention for many centuries, stands on a precipitous hill and the only approach is by a wide causeway on the south, crossed at the head by two ditches. There are two baileys in line, north and south; the castle buildings occupying the southern bailey, which is on the highest point of the hill and next the causeway. The lower parts of the curtain wall are probably of early mediaeval date but the earliest buildings now within the castle relate to the fifteenth and sixteenth centuries, and even they have been subjected to drastic internal alterations in the process of conversion into military barracks; they enclose two open spaces called the upper and lower courts.

The great, or Parliament, hall on the east side of the upper court, was built in the latter part of the fifteenth century and before its mutilation was a magnificent structure with an exceptionally fine open timber roof, now destroyed. The royal palace, on the west side of the lower court, was begun in 1496 but built principally during the first half of the sixteenth century. It is an elegant structure in the French Renaissance style with elaborate external decorations and is built round a court, called the Lion's Den. Although it is surmounted by a battlemented parapet and its large windows are covered on the outside by stout iron grilles the palace has little or no military value.

Dunnottar castle, near Stonehaven, stands on the flat summit of a high rock which juts out into the North Sea, has precipitous sides all round and is joined to the mainland only by a narrow causeway; the causeway itself being commanded from high above by a narrow promontory of the rock called the fiddlehead. The natural defences, therefore, are formidable. Though the site has been occupied from remote times the earliest existing defences were built in the latter part of the fourteenth century. The fortifications built at this period were concentrated on the line of approach. A strong and lofty curtain, pierced by the gateway, was thrown across the gap at the head of the causeway, the fiddlehead was fortified, and the keep was built on the summit at this end of the rock (pp. 210, 216b, 248).

The gateway was defended by a strong door and a portcullis and from it steep flights of steps lead sinuously up the rock to the fiddlehead and from thence to the keep.[3] Between the fiddlehead and the keep there is a postern which now opens on the cliff face from the bottom of a pit but was probably reached by a flight of steps down from the path. From here supplies could be hauled up in baskets or escape effected by a rope ladder.

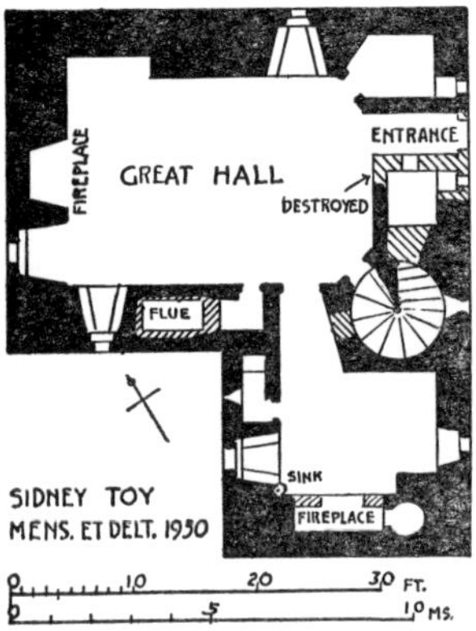

DUNNOTTAR CASTLE. PLAN OF THE SECOND STOREY OF THE KEEP

The keep is especially interesting both in respect to its original plan and the alterations effected about the latter part of the fifteenth century. It is of L-shaped plan and of four storeys, of which the first only is vaulted. The first storey contained the storerooms and a small "pit", or prison; the second storey formed the hall with the kitchen in the wing, and the upper storeys were the private rooms and chambers. The original entrance was at the second storey at the east end of the hall, and was probably approached from without by a movable stair; it was defended on either side by a mural guardroom, one of which is broken away. From this level a straight flight of steps in the west wall, leading off from a spiral stairway, descended to the basement and the spiral stairway ascended to the upper rooms. The hall is lighted by windows with stone seats, has a fireplace in the west wall, a wide and deep recess near it in the north wall and a small chamber in the south wall. The kitchen has a fireplace with an oven on one side, a sink with a drain from it, and a latrine; extra floor space is obtained by a wide recess on one side.

In the alterations referred to, a kitchen, having a wide fireplace and a sink, was formed in the basement, the timber loft of which, built on the axial line of the vault, was removed, and a doorway opened out from the small lobby at the foot of the basement stairs. The old entrance, directly above, was then converted into a window. It is significant that both doorways were formed on the east side of the keep, opposite to that facing the line of approach; the doorway in the basement opened out from a loophole in the north wall is of much later date. When the alterations were made the mural chamber on the south side of the hall was curtailed by the insertion of the large flue for the new kitchen fireplace. The small guard-

[3] Cf. Dunnottar Castle, Dr. W. D. Simpson, 1942.

room on the south side of the old entrance was probably opened laterally at a subsequent date.

The palace now occupying a large portion of the flat surface of the rock west of these defences consists of ranges of unfortified buildings dating from the sixteenth and seventeenth centuries. When it was built a new approach up to it from the outer gateway was constructed. The new path, branching off to the left of the old stairway, consists principally of a rising ramp which goes practically straight up towards the palace, passing through two tunnels, now

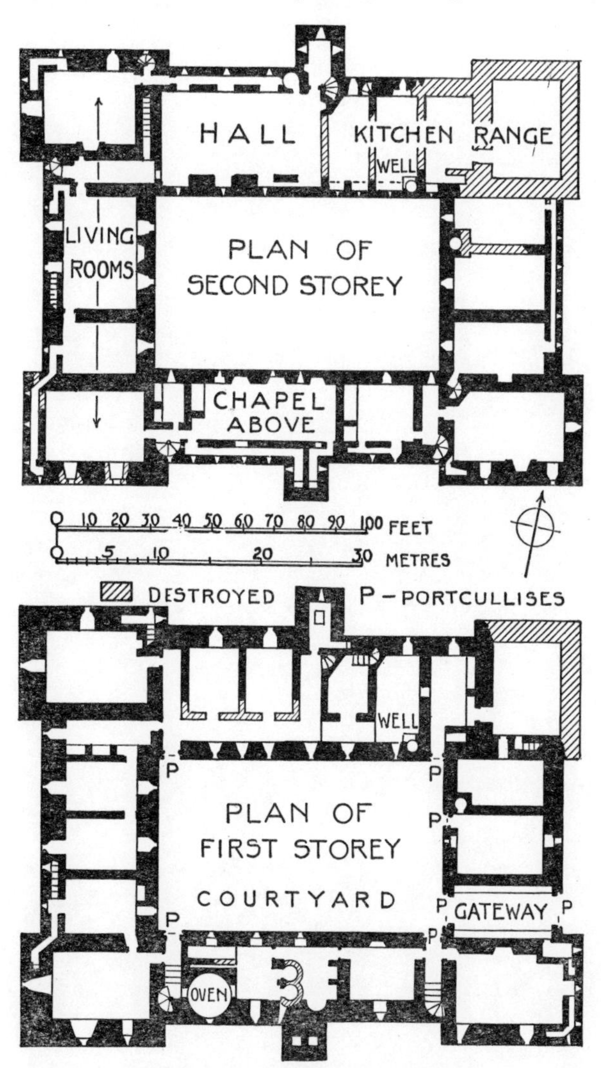

Plans of Bolton Castle, Yorks

broken through, in its course. At the same time the defences of the gateway were strengthened.

Development on the lines of improved domestic convenience and social amenity is clearly seen in those rectangular castles raised in the latter part of the fourteenth century, as Bolton, Sheriff Hutton, and Wressle, all three in Yorkshire; Shirburn, Oxon.; and Bodiam, Sussex. Sheriff Hutton is in a very ruinous condition and only the south side remains of Wressle castle. Shirburn, built about 1378, though its openings have been modernised and the red brickwork of which it is constructed covered with a thick coat of plaster, is complete. These castles have a rectangular plan, a tower at each corner and often one in the middle of two or more of its sides, and ranges of domestic, service, and military quarters, built against the curtain and surrounding a courtyard. The corner towers of Shirburn are circular, but those of the other castles referred to are rectangular.

Bolton castle, one of the most perfect and well-preserved structures of this design, is a large building with lofty curtain walls, a rectangular tower of five storeys at each corner, and a turret in the middle of each of the long sides, north and south. Domestic and service quarters, built against the inside face of the curtain and of three storeys, are ranged on all sides round a spacious courtyard. Originally the windows opened mainly on to the court, the narrow windows in the outer walls being few and confined to the upper storeys. The mullioned windows now in the outer faces of the towers are of much later date (pp. 200b, 211).

The entrance is by a vaulted gateway which is carried through the east range of buildings and defended by two portcullises, one at either end of the passage. The guardroom and quarters for the defence forces are in the east range above and to the north of the gateway. The first storey of the ranges on all sides includes vaulted cellars, storerooms, stables, bakehouses, and brewhouses. All the windows to the basements are narrow and every doorway in the courtyard, including that to the guardroom and those to the stairways leading to the upper floors, is defended by a portcullis. An enemy who had gained the courtyard must still break through these defences, under fire from the ranges of buildings all round, ere he could take the castle.

Residential and service quarters are conveniently disposed in the second and third storeys of the ranges. The great hall is at the second storey on the north with the kitchen and its offices, now largely destroyed, to the east of it; one room between the hall and the kitchen contains a well. West of the hall, and carried all along the west range of buildings, are two tiers of large comfortable rooms, well lighted and provided with fireplaces and latrines. At the third storey in the south range there is a chapel, lighted by tall pointed windows on both sides and approached not only from this floor but, by a spiral stairway at the west end, directly from the two floors below.

Bodiam castle, 1386 to about 1390, has a circular tower at each corner, a gatehouse in the middle of the north side and a square tower in the middle of each of the other sides; the square tower on the south having a postern at ground floor level. The castle stands in a rectangular moat, fed from the river Rother, and is defended by a barbican and an outwork, both within the moat. Approach to

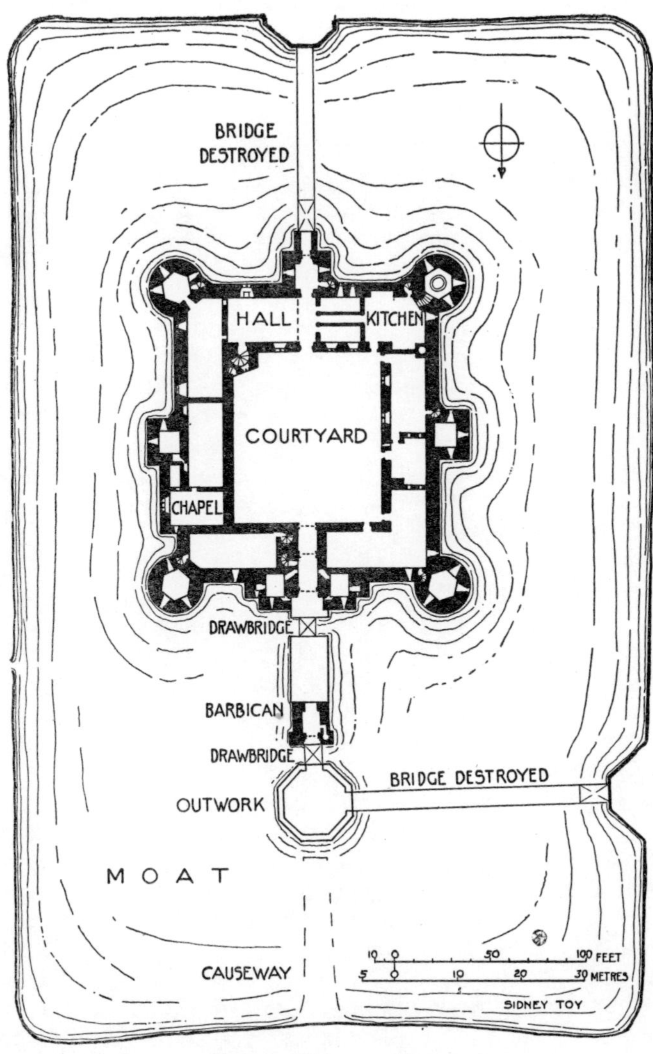

PLAN OF BODIAM CASTLE

the castle was by way of a timber bridge which spanned the moat between the abutment on the west bank and the octagonal outwork. So placed the bridge was at right angles to the gateway and stood exposed to flank fire from the walls of the castle; it was entered from the bank by a drawbridge. To reach the barbican it was necessary to turn right on the outwork and cross a second drawbridge, and from the barbican a third drawbridge led to the main gateway of the castle. From the postern on the other side another long timber bridge, having probably a drawbridge at either end, led across the moat to the south bank, near the river. Both the bridges to the outwork and from the postern have been destroyed and the castle is now reached by a causeway, built probably in the sixteenth century, between the north bank of the moat and the outwork (pp. 213, 216a).

The gateway is defended by machicolations at parapet level and by loopholes with oillets. Within the passage there are three sets of barriers, one at either end and one in the middle, each set consisting of a portcullis and a door, the set of the inner end being arranged against attack from the bailey. One of the mediaeval portcullises, made of oak plated and shod with iron, still remains. Both the passages of the main gateway and of the postern are covered with ribbed vaulting, the bosses of which are pierced with round holes about 6 in. diameter. The under-surfaces of the bosses are about 2 ft. 6 in. below the floor level of the rooms above. The use of them as arrow-slits must have been very limited, but they are numerous, are widely dispersed over the vaults and, camouflaged by the bosses, were doubtless designed for surprise attack, by missiles, on an enemy below. Both the gatehouse and the tower over the postern have machicolated parapets.

The buildings within the castle, two storeys in height, are ranged round a rectangular courtyard. On the south are the great hall, the buttery, pantry, and kitchen; on the east, opening from the great hall, the private and guest rooms and the chapel; on the west, adjoining the kitchen, the servants' rooms and other domestic offices; and on the north the military quarters. The passage to the postern opened off from the "screens" at the west end of the great hall. Maxstoke Castle (Appendix E, p. 285) is of this period.

In castles built in the fifteenth century on the four-square plan, as at Caister, Norfolk, 1432–50 (Appendix F, p. 287); Compton, Devon, c. 1420; Herstmonceux, Sussex, 1441, and Kirby Muxloe, 1480–84; the domestic amenities were still further developed.

Compton is rather a fortified manor house than a castle and is defended on all sides by a high wall in lieu of a moat. Here the great hall, now destroyed, was built across the middle of the castle, cutting the courtyard into two sections, north and south. The south court was enclosed by ranges of buildings on all sides, but the north court had buildings on three sides only, the fourth side being the lofty outer wall of the castle containing the entrance gateway. On the east, west, and south sides the curtain wall stands so far out as to leave spacious open courts between it and the ranges of buildings on these sides; but on the north the rooms flanking the north court abut directly against the curtain. This side, being the most vulnerable, is defended by many machicolations, which jut out at intervals along the wall at parapet level; a large one built out on corbels overhanging the entrance gateway.

The residential quarters occupied the west and south-west sides of the castle, while the domestic offices were on the east side; they were connected by the great hall which crossed between the two courts. On the west side of the north or entrance court there is a chapel with one traceried window towards the court and another in the outer wall on the north.

The central position now occupied by the great hall of a castle is a marked development in plan. Away from the curtain, the great hall could have large windows on both sides and the fireplace and the oriel could be on either side; further, this plan made a great improvement in the disposition of the living rooms. The plan had been adopted at an earlier period, as at Haddon Hall, Derbys. (Appendix G, p. 290), where a great hall was built across the courtyard in the early part of the fourteenth century; the same plan was also followed about 1380 at Farleigh Castle, Somerset (Appendix H, p. 291).

Herstmonceux is a large rectangular castle, measuring externally 219 ft. by 208 ft.; it is built of red brick with stone dressings, the latter of a tint blending well with the brickwork, and is defended by a moat. The walls have a tall battered plinth, they rise to a considerable height and are defended by octagonal towers of great projection at the corners and semi-octagonal towers at intervals along the sides. The gatehouse is in the middle of the south front. It was defended by a drawbridge which worked on the counterbalance principle; within the tall arch over the doorway are the long grooves for the reception of the beams of the bridge when raised. The towers flanking the gateway are octagonal up to the height of the parapet of the curtain and circular above that level. They are pierced by three rows of cross-shaped arrow-loops, oiletts for firearms being inserted below the first row. The gatehouse is surmounted by two tiers of battlements, the lower tier being machicolated. On the north side of the castle there is a postern through the middle tower (p. 216a).

After having been neglected for some forty years, the interior of this castle was gutted in 1777 and the materials used for building purposes elsewhere; the existing reconstruction carried out in recent years is on entirely new designs. Fortunately, detailed plans of the buildings as they were before 1777 were made before the demolition took place and are still available. There were ranges of two-storey buildings on all sides, while another block containing the great hall stood across the spacious courtyard. The residential quarters, with a chapel in the middle of the east wall, were on the east side of the castle, the kitchen and domestic offices on the west, and the guard-room and military quarters near the gatehouse on the south. Buildings shown extending north and south from the great hall range and dividing the central space into four courts were most probably built in the sixteenth century and later periods.

At Kirby Muxloe a rectangular castle was built round an old manor house, the great hall range of which, crossing the middle of the courtyard, was retained as part of the new works. Apart from foundations and low fragments of walling, all that remains of this castle are the gatehouse and the north-west corner tower; the latter complete, including the battlements, and the gatehouse complete in respect to the first and part of the second storey only. The castle is built of brick with stone dressings, and is surrounded by a moat which is fed from a nearby stream; there was a square tower at each corner and the gatehouse stands in the middle of the north front.

The gateway was defended at the outer end by a drawbridge, a portcullis, and a two-leaved door and by a two-leaved door at the inner end. The gatehouse is flanked by octagonal turrets on both the outer and inner faces, each of those towards the courtyard enclosing a spiral stairway, constructed entirely of brickwork. The intricate curves and sweeps of the underside of the spiral vaults on which the treads are built are formed with remarkable skill and address; the treads are of specially selected bricks, laid on edge. There is a similar stairway in the north-west corner tower. Directly above the plinth of the outer faces, both of the gatehouse and the north-west tower, are rows of gun-loops with circular openings at the base; the circular holes, 6 in. diameter, were for small cannon and the slits above them for sighting. There are no arrow-loops in the remaining walls. *See Appendix F:* CAISTER CASTLE; *Appendix G*: HADDON HALL *and Appendix H*: FARLEIGH CASTLE.

Bodiam Castle from the North.

Herstmonceux Castle from the South-West.

Goodrich Castle from the South-West, showing tall spurs.

Bywell Castle. South-West Turret.

Dunnottar Castle from the West.

Tantallon Castle from the South-East.

CHAPTER ELEVEN

DEVELOPMENT OF THE TOWER HOUSE

It has been noted above that in the latter part of the thirteenth century powerful gatehouses began to take the place of keeps as the ultimate posts of resistance. The same design was followed in many of the castles built during the fourteenth and early part of the fifteenth century. At Tantallon, East Lothian, about 1370, and St. Andrews, Fife, as rebuilt about 1390, the gatehouse, occupying the middle of a screen wall in each case, was the stronghold of the fortress. At Doune, Perths., about 1390, the gatehouse, while being adjacent and having direct access to the residential quarters, was so designed that when desired it could be completely isolated from them.

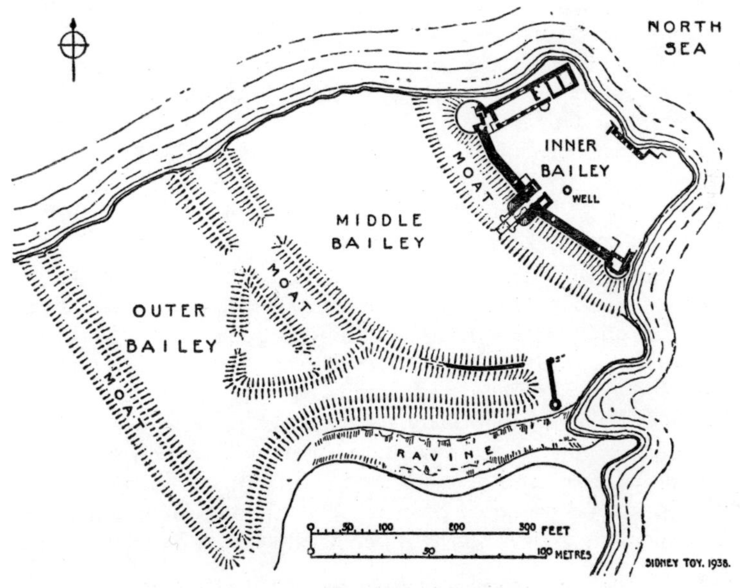

Plan of Tantallon Castle

Tantallon castle stands on a bold promontory jutting into the North Sea and is protected on three sides by precipitous cliffs. On the land side it was defended by two baileys, a ravelin, and three lines of ditches; the outer bailey and the ravelin are probably later additions. The inner bailey is at the point of the promontory, cut off from the outer works by a massive screen wall, built across from cliff to cliff; the wall having a gatehouse in the middle and a round tower at either end. Along the edge of the cliff on the other sides of the bailey were the domestic and military quarters now, except for the west range with its hall, kitchen and other offices, largely destroyed. The outer portions of the towers at either end of the screen wall and a barbican which was added later to the gatehouse have also been destroyed. But the gatehouse and the screen wall on either side, which is over 12 ft. thick, stand to their full height, including portions of the parapets (pp. 216b, 217).

The gatehouse was at once the principal residence and the stronghold of the castle; it contains tiers of large rooms, well lighted from the courtyard, and provided with hooded fireplaces and latrines, and from this point the whole of the defence operations along the front could be directed. The strength of Tantallon rested largely in its natural defences, being protected on three sides by precipitous cliffs rising sheer out of the sea, but the powerful screen wall and outworks rendered the position almost impregnable.

Doune castle is built on a high bank of the river Teith at its junction with the Ardock Water; it is roughly rectangular with the residential quarters concentrated on the north side of the bailey. Other buildings which stood against the south and east walls have been destroyed, but those on the north are roofed over and, thanks to careful modern restoration, are in a remarkably good state of preservation. The gatehouse, the strong point of the castle, is at the north-east corner of the bailey, towering high above the lofty curtain. At ground level in the west wall there is a postern which is reached by a flight of steps down from the kitchen and there is a well in the courtyard, near the kitchen (pp. 219, 222a).

The lower storey of the gatehouse is occupied by the gateway with a guardroom and small prison on one side and a storeroom and a well chamber on the other. The well chamber is in the basement of a round tower which projects out at the north-east corner of the gatehouse and commands the entrance. The long gateway, which runs obliquely through the building, was defended at the outer end by a machicolation, opening from a window recess in the hall above[1] and a two-leaved iron yett, still in position; and at the inner end probably by a wood door long since destroyed.

The dwelling rooms above are completely isolated from the gate-

[1] Clearly a narrow machicolation across the middle of the passage and not a portcullis slot.

way and are approached by a flight of steps up from the courtyard. They are of three storeys, the first containing a large room called the Baron's hall, the second containing mainly a spacious great chamber, and the third the more private rooms. The second and third of these storeys are reached by a stairway at the north-east corner of the Baron's hall. Between these tiers of rooms and the great hall, to the west of the gatehouse, there is a very thick wall. Formerly there was no way through this wall from the Baron's hall, the existing opening being made at a much later period, but there was a way down, by a spiral stairway, from the great chamber; the door at the foot of the stairs opening on to the dais of the great hall. Normally the lord of the castle and his people would use the great hall, or their services otherwise would be considerably

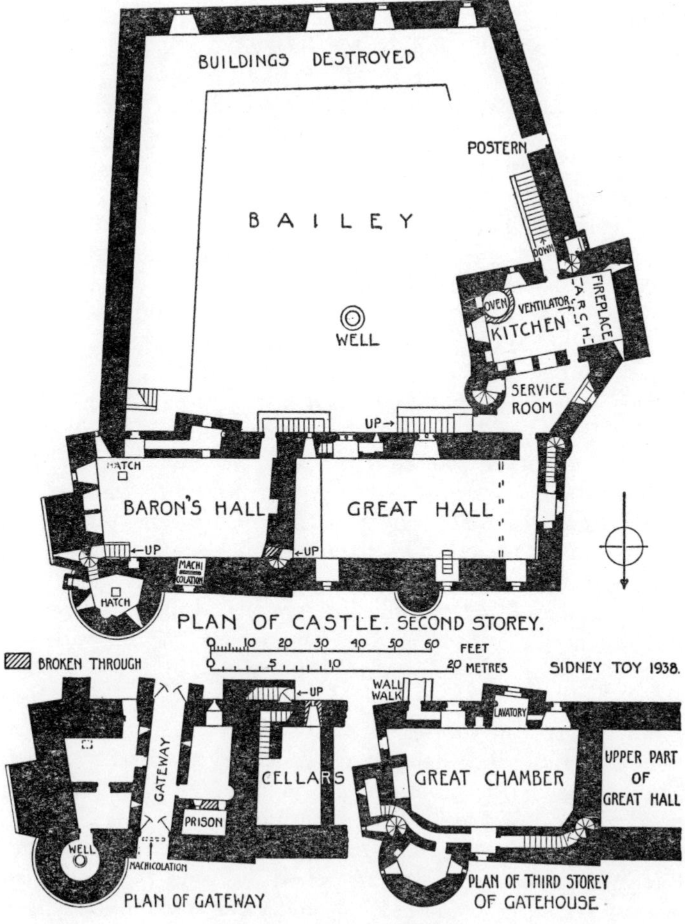

PLANS OF DOUNE CASTLE

restricted, but at the top of the stairs there was a strong door which closed and was barred against the great hall, and when closed and secured cut off all entry into the lord's preserves from that direction.

The great hall, extending from the gatehouse to the north-west corner of the castle, is of one storey only, above its cellars, and was covered by an open timber roof; it is approached by a separate stairway up from the courtyard and a service room and kitchen opens from it at the west. The gatehouse at Doune marks a great advance on that at Tantallon in respect to independence and isolation. Every necessity of life is provided for, including water from the well and provisions from the store room, both drawn up through trap-doors. Further, the building could be isolated and held as well against an enemy within as without the castle.

Bywell castle, Northumberland, consists solely of the gatehouse, built about 1430. That a bailey formed a part of the original scheme there can be no doubt, but since the building stands with its inner face close to the river Tyne it is difficult to envisage the kind of bailey it was proposed to enclose; a fragment of curtain wall projects from the north-east corner of the gatehouse. The gatehouse is of three storeys, has an embattled parapet and a turret at each corner. The first storey contains the gateway with the guardroom on one side and stores on the other; the gateway being defended at the entrance by a portcullis and a two-leaved door. Access to the residential rooms in the upper floors was strongly defended. The approach is by a straight mural stairway opening off the inner end of the gateway; the foot of the stairs being defended by an English form of yett—an iron gate with oak panels—and by a machicolation from a window recess above.

The battlements are noteworthy. On the north and south sides, high above the gateway, the parapet is projected forward on corbels to form a series of four machicolations, defending the passage at both ends. The turrets also have machicolations; but there the construction is unusual. The turrets are square but their parapets are octagonal and the machicolations are formed by long single stones which are placed across the corners of the turrets and support the diagonal sides of the parapets (p. 216a). A similar design was adopted in the turrets of Lumley castle, County Durham.

While progress in the design of the gatehouse continued a still stronger and more independent residence for the lord of the castle was in course of development. The freedom hitherto exercised in the disposition of the domestic buildings within the castle became a source of danger. At Bodiam none of these buildings could be held against an enemy who had penetrated into the courtyard, or against mercenaries who had become disaffected or treacherous. Mercenaries were now generally employed by those leaders who could afford to pay them; they were lodged within the castle and their loyalty could be relied upon only to the extent of their interests. The independent gatehouse was one attempt to meet dangers from this source.

But the gateway is a vulnerable point which had to be defended by a drawbridge and elaborate systems of doors, portcullises, machicolations and arrow-loops, all greatly restricting the design of the house above, and it became obvious that the independent residence should be distinct from the gateway; a tower-like residence, strongly fortified and placed at a point in the curtain away from the gateway, was evolved as the result of these considerations. The tower house developed on lines of elegance and dignity as well as of strength; for considerations of beauty and pomp were never absent from the mind of the mediaeval builder. No doubt such tower houses as those at Tattershall and Buckden were influenced by examples abroad, but the early date of some and the great variety of our tower houses indicates an independent establishment and growth in this country.

Among the earliest of these structures is the Eagle tower at Caernarvon, built about 1290 (Chapter Eight). Far removed from the gatehouse, the Eagle tower is a complete fortress in itself and has its own postern to the river. There is no connection, either by wall walk or mural passage, between the tower and the exposed curtain running south-east from it, but there is a doorway to the wall walk of the curtain on the north-east, enclosed within the town. The latter leads to a well and another postern. The Eagle Tower is a powerful strong point; it occupies a commanding position in respect to the castle and the town, is capable of independent resistance, and is provided with ample means of making a sally, bringing in supplies, or effecting escape (pp. 150b, 171).

Later outstanding examples of tower houses in Britain are at Dudley, Worcs., built about 1320; Nunney, Somerset, 1373; Warkworth, Northumberland, about 1390; Borthwick, Midlothian, 1430–40; Tattershall, Lincs., 1433–43; and Ashby-de-la-Zouch, Leicester, 1474–76.

Dudley castle was founded in the twelfth but rebuilt in the early years of the fourteenth century, and as remodelled at the latter period a tower house was erected on the old mound. The tower house at Dudley is a powerful oblong structure of two storeys with a round tower at each corner; it stands at the south-west angle of the bailey, projecting partly inside but mainly outside the curtain. By order of Parliament the outer half of the building was blown down in 1647, but the inner half with its flanking towers remains to the full height. It was a complete dwelling with stores and domestic offices on the ground floor and living and service rooms on the upper floor. The entrance was from the bailey at ground floor level; it was defended by a portcullis and a two-leaved door. From this level one stairway leads out of the entrance passage up to the great hall and another, formed in one of the towers, rises up to the "screens". Private chambers opening from the great hall, and service rooms from the "screens" were formed in the corner towers. Later in the century an embattled terrace was built in front of the entrance.

The builder of Dudley castle was doubtless Sir John de Somery, its owner from 1300 to 1321. Taking advantage of the disturbed state of the country in Edward the Second's time Sir John's conduct became so outrageous that an official report was drawn up against him. The report stated "that he has obtained such mastery in the county of Stafford that no one can obtain law or justice therein; that he has made himself more than a king there; that no one can dwell there unless he buys protection from him either by money or by assisting him in building his castles, and that he attacks people in their own houses with the intention of killing them unless they make fine for his protection."[2]

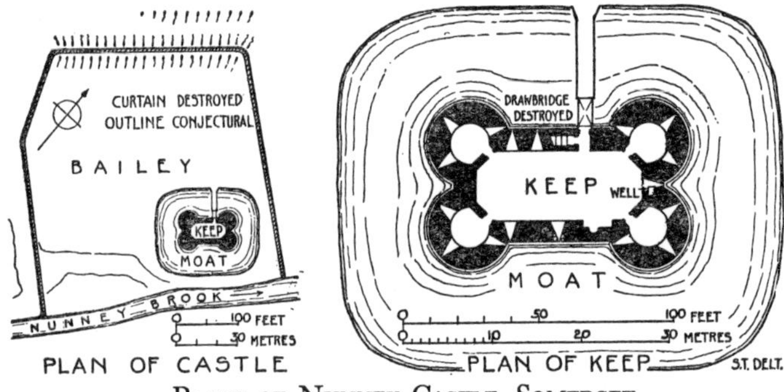

PLANS OF NUNNEY CASTLE, SOMERSET

The tower house at Nunney now stands isolated, but there are traces of a bailey to the north and west of it. It is of similar form to that at Dudley, though much longer in comparison with its width, much higher—it is of four storeys—and of much less sturdy construction. The north wall of the tower at Nunney fell down in 1910; the tower is surrounded by a moat. The entrance is from the bailey on the north at ground floor level and admits through a vaulted passage to the first storey, which contains a wide fireplace and a well and was probably the kitchen. A straight mural stairway from the entrance leads to the second storey and from there a spiral stairway in one corner of the tower rises to the upper levels. The great hall is at the third storey and chambers are formed in the corner turrets. In the top floor of the south-west turret there is a small oratory with a piscina and original altar.

[2] Call. Pat. Roll., 1307–1313, 369.

Warkworth Castle. The Keep from the Bailey.

Doune Castle from the North-East.

Glamis Castle from the South. [*Country Life*

Tonbridge Castle. The Gatehouse from without the Bailey.

Warkworth keep, built on the mound and occupying the site of an earlier structure of which it incorporates a postern, is one of the most complete as it is one of the finest tower houses in this or any other country. In plan it resembles a Greek cross, consisting of a large square body with a square turret projecting from the middle of each side; all the angles both of the main body and the turrets being splayed. The keep is of three tall storeys with a central square turret rising high above the battlements. The entrance is at ground floor level, at the head of a flight of steps ascending the mound; it is defended by a portcullis, a door, and by a pitfall with a movable cover inside the door. Opposite the entrance there is a postern leading out on to the wall walk of the curtain on the east side of the castle, and at the north-west of the tower, outside the castle walls, is the postern retained from the previous building (pp. 135, 222a)

The interior is designed on advanced principles. There is a liberal provision of halls and chambers, and the desired seclusion of the lord's quarters from the domestic offices and rooms is attained without severing communication between them. The ample provision of stairways and passages here would do credit to a large modern mansion. On the first storey are stores, cellars, guardrooms, and a prison with a cell below; on the second storey are the great hall, the great chamber, a chapel, and the kitchen and its offices; and on the third storey are the private chambers and bedrooms. In the domestic quarters near the kitchen there is a double lavabo, similar in form to a piscina. There are four stairways, rising from various points in the building and leading from the first to the second storey, and four others rising from this level to the third storey. The great hall, the apse of the chapel, and the kitchen all rise through both the second and third storeys. The rain water falling on the roof was collected and brought by pipe down a small central court, called the lantern, to a large stone tank at the bottom.

At Dunstanburgh, John of Gaunt, then owner, made himself a tower house, about 1380, by blocking the gateway at both ends and remodelling the gatehouse. He then made a strongly defended ward within the bailey adjoining his tower house and opened out a new gateway in the curtain just beyond the ward. The new ward while being a strong defence for the tower on the bailey side also provided secure accommodation for domestic offices of more ample character than could be formed within the tower house. At Llanstephan, Carms., the gatehouse of the outer bailey was remodelled in much the same manner, though there the new gateway adjoins the old gatehouse and there is no separate ward within the bailey. At St. Andrews, Fife, the change was not made until the sixteenth century.

St. Andrews castle occupies a site very similar to that of Tantallon, though the promontory is much lower and the natural defences much less formidable; it has also a similar plan to Tantallon and is designed on much the same defensive principles. It was rebuilt in its present form about 1390 with the gatehouse in the middle of its screen wall. About 1570 the gateway was blocked, the whole building remodelled, and a new gateway opened through the wall to the west of it.

In Scotland where the traditional castle frequently consisted of a strong tower and fortified courtyard the development at this period often took the form of a tower house, at once spacious, convenient, and strong. Glamis is an example.

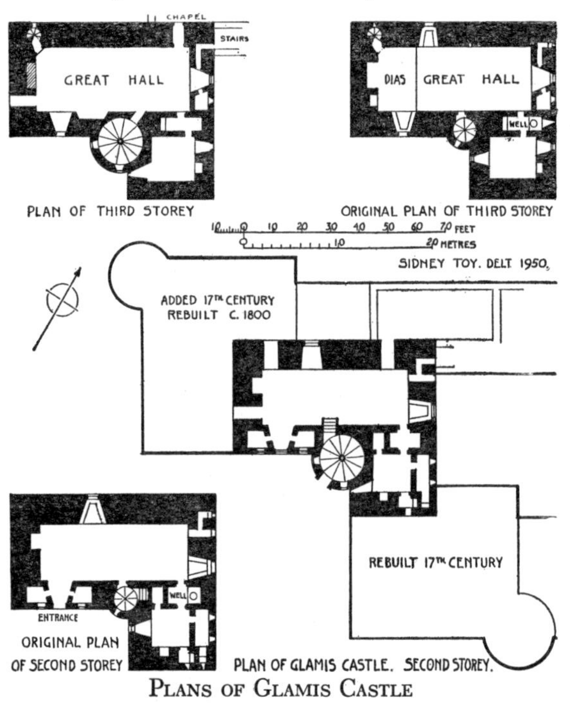

Plans of Glamis Castle

Glamis castle stands on an old site and although it is not possible now to associate even the site with any event prior to the fourteenth century, there is no doubt that the existing buildings occupy ground which was fortified and held by the kings of Scotland from a very early period. The castle as it existed in 1376 was given in that year by Robert the First to John Lyon, Lord Glamis, on the occasion of his marriage with the king's daughter, and whatever may have been the character of the building he received it is clear that John Lyon at once began its complete reconstruction. The earliest part of the present castle, the rectangular tower with the short wing attached to it at the south-east corner, dates from his period; it occupies the central position round which the later buildings are grouped. Of the mediaeval outer defences all but two wall towers have disappeared (pp. 222b, 224).

Considerable alterations were made in the seventeenth century. The central stairway, rising from ground floor to roof, is of that period, as are the upper parts of the tower above the first four storeys, its bartizans and its roofs. The main entrance door at the foot of the stairway is defended by an iron yett. The stairway is wide and of easy gradient, winding round a large hollow stone newel, down the centre of which pass unseen the long cords and weights of the large clock seen outside at the head of the stair turret. The rumbling of the weights in their confined space especially at the striking of the clock in the dead of night, may account for some of the "ghostly" manifestations associated with the castle. On the roofs are fine wrought iron ridges of foliated design with finials shaped as thistles, roses, and fleur-de-lys. Of two wings, set at diagonally opposite corners of the main building, that at the west was added in the seventeenth century and rebuilt about 1800. The east wing, while dating principally from the seventeenth century, incorporates in its lower part walls of a much earlier period including a wide stone fireplace. Residential quarters extending eastward from the tower date principally from the last decade of the nineteenth century.

The tower was originally of four storeys only; it was surmounted by an embattled parapet some of the corbels of which still remain projecting from the face of the wall. Each of the three lower storeys is covered with a barrel vault. The rooms were considerably remodelled in the seventeenth century, the windows enlarged and passages to the new wings opened out; but the preservation of mural chambers and other original features and the traces of blocked openings in the walls render the early disposition of the rooms perfectly clear.

The first storey contained the kitchen and the storerooms; it has a circular well the pipe of which was formerly carried up through two storeys with a drawing place at each level. The second storey contained, as at present, a large rectangular room unobstructed by partitions and having windows with stone seats; there was a latrine, altered by later work, at the north-east corner. As may be seen by close inspection of the outside face of the masonry and by the disposition of the original stairways within, the original entrance to the castle was on this floor. It was by a doorway near the west end of the south wall, now converted into a window, and was flanked, as the window still is, by a small mural guardroom on either side; the doorway must have been reached by a flight of steps, movable or fixed.

From this level access to the basement was by a straight flight of steps passing down through the south wall, and to the upper floors by a spiral stairway ascending from the head of the straight flight. The flight down to the basement is intact and there are still vestiges of the lower part of the spiral stairway, which was in the same position at the inner angle of the building as that occupied by the present stair turret. The plan of this floor was much the same as that of the original entrance floor of the keep at Cawdor, the basement reached by a straight flight of steps down and the upper floors by a spiral stairway at the head of that flight.

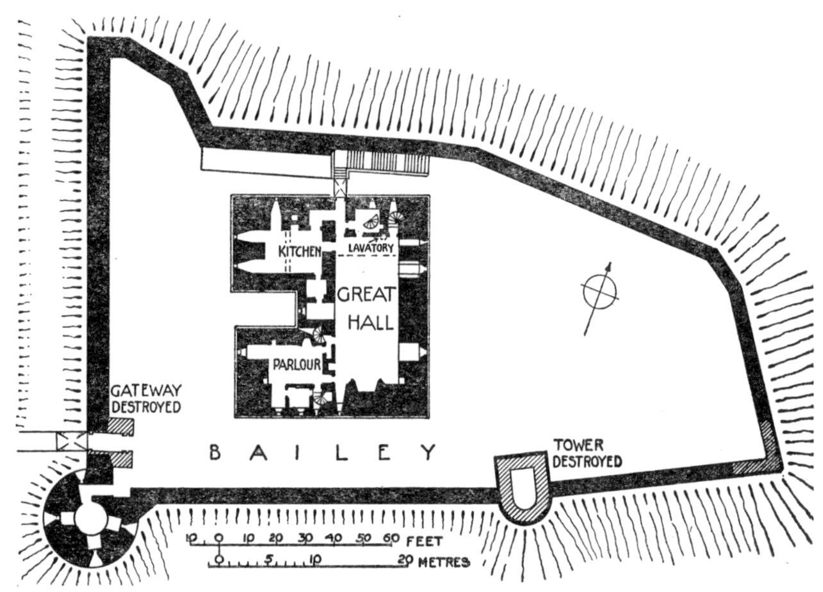

PLAN OF BORTHWICK CASTLE

The third storey contains the great hall in the main body of the tower and a retiring chamber in the small wing. The great hall is a lofty and spacious room, 54 ft. long by 21 ft. 6 in. wide internally; it was considerably altered and embellished in the seventeenth century. Originally the dais was at the west end of the hall and there was a large fireplace in the west wall. A private spiral stairway at the north-west corner led up from the dais to the rooms and chambers of the fourth storey. In the east wall there were a mural chamber and a latrine opening off, one on either side, from the jambs of the window at that end; the chamber still exists but the latrine, like that below it on the second storey, has been converted into a passage.

In the alterations carried out in the seventeenth century

the entrance to the private stair, though now reopened, was blocked; the old fireplace at the west end was also blocked and a large new fireplace with a wide flat joggled arch and elaborate overmantel opened out near the middle of the south wall. At the same time a plastered ribbed ceiling with ornamental pendants was formed on the under surface of the barrel vault. A chapel with decorations of this period opens off from the north-east corner of the hall.

By the fifteenth century the tower house design had taken deep root and many such structures were built during that period, either as a normal part of a new castle or a desirable addition to an old one. Borthwick is an example of a new castle with its tower house standing free within the bailey. At Tattershall and Ashby-de-la-Zouch the tower was added to an existing castle; in each case it stands astride the curtain, and protrudes beyond it.

Borthwick castle stands on a promontory at the junction of two streams; it has a wedge shaped plan with the long sides running west to east and meeting at the point of the promontory. The gateway is at the south end of the west wall, which forms the base of the wedge, and is defended on the flank by a strong circular tower. The tower house while designed as a convenient residence is also a powerfully built structure, vaulted at several storeys and at the summit. It consists of a main rectangular body and two wings, both wings projecting from the west side and rising to the full height of the tower. There are two entrances, one above the other in the middle of the north front. The lower doorway opens from the courtyard to a flight of steps leading down to the vaulted cellars of the first storey, or basement. The upper doorway is at the second storey and is now reached by a stone bridge thrown across from the wall walk of the curtain; the wall walk being gained by flights of steps up from the courtyard. Originally the gap between the walk and the tower would be spanned by a draw-bridge (pp. 226, 228).

The second storey contains the great hall, the parlour, the kitchen, and mural chambers leading out of each of them; the parlour opening from the dais end of the hall and the kitchen from the "screens" at the other end. At the dais end of the great hall there is a fine fireplace with a tall pointed hood, which rises up to within a few feet of the lofty vault, and in the wall on the right of the dais there is a wide recess which must have served as a sideboard. The recess is enriched by moulded edges, a cinquefoiled head, and a label with foliated finial; and halfway in its height is grooved at the sides and back for an oak shelf. In the screens at the other end of the hall there is a beautiful lavabo, partly broken away at the basin. It has a traceried canopy, a shaft with capital and base supporting the basin, and is in all respects similar to a church piscina of the period. It was used by the host and his guests for washing their hands preparatory to dining in the hall.

From the second storey, spiral stairways descend to the basement and rise to the upper floors and battlements; the kitchen wing having a special service stairs. The roof covering is laid directly upon the external surfaces of the uppermost vaults. The battlements are considerably mutilated and on the east side they were destroyed entirely during the Civil war of the seventeenth century, when the facing stones of the upper portion of this wall were also broken down. There was a round bartizan at each corner and a continuous machicolated parapet all round the tower.

BORTHWICK CASTLE. THE TOWER FROM THE NORTH-WEST

The tower house at Tattershall was built on the west side of the inner bailey of a thirteenth-century castle. The old curtain wall was taken down at this point and the tower, constructed of brick with stone dressings, built in its place; the inner wall of the tower lining with the curtain and the main portion projecting out into the moat. Apart from foundations of wall towers and fragments of masonry in line with the curtain the older defences of the castle have been destroyed. The great hall which ran parallel to the tower on its east side has also disappeared and little now remains of the kitchen which projected outward from the curtain at the south of the tower.

This tower is unquestionably the most imposing and elegant building of its kind and period in the kingdom. It is a rectangular structure with an octagonal turret at each corner, is of five storeys, including the vaulted basement, and rises to the height of 100 ft.

to the top of the parapet and 120 ft. to the top of the turrets. There are three entrance doorways, all at ground floor level and all opening from a forebuilding which formerly stood between the tower and the great hall. One of the doorways opens to a flight of steps leading down to the basement, where there are storerooms and a well. Another doorway leads straight into the second storey, containing a large central hall with a wide fireplace and side chambers, formed in the turrets, opening off the hall. There is no stair from this floor either to the basement or to the third storey above; communication must have been through the forebuilding.

The third entrance doorway leads up to a wide spiral stair in the south-east turret, which rises to the upper levels, passing a doorway to the upper storey of the forebuilding and another to the wall walk on the curtain. The three upper storeys were the private residential quarters; in each there is a large hall with chambers at the sides. The halls are well lighted with traceried windows, have each a wide fireplace, and are approached from the stairway through vaulted lobbies and corridors. The vaults of these passages as well as those of the window recesses in the halls are decorated with sculptured armorial bearings.

There are four fireplaces, including that in the second storey. They are of stone and have wide openings with moulded arches and high panelled heads of varied design, carved with foliated and heraldic ornament. The heraldry represent the shields and armorial devices of Lord Cromwell, Lord Treasurer of England 1433–43, who built the tower. The fireplaces are all well preserved despite the abuse to which they have been subjected. In 1911 the tower was bought by an American syndicate, the fireplaces were sold separately and brought to London with the object of their despatch to and sale in America. But through the public-spirited and timely action of the late Lord Curzon of Kedleston, who had meanwhile acquired possession of the tower, they were purchased in 1912, brought back and replaced in their original positions.

There is only one stairway in the tower but that is a spacious spiral structure with stone steps, each of one piece with the newel, and a stone handrail hollowed out in the wall. The battlements are in two tiers; the lower tier having machicolations and openings in the parapet for wood shutters. The tower was therefore strongly defended at the summit. But its windows are large, all the floors above the basement are of timber, and the defences of the entrance must always have been remarkably weak. It is clear that personal comfort and convenience combined with architectural dignity were the governing factors in the design of this up-to-date and palatial residence.

At Ashby-de-la-Zouch the tower was added to a large manor

house, dating from the twelfth but practically rebuilt in the fourteenth century. The house has an aisled hall with domestic offices and a spacious kitchen at one end, and residential quarters, including a particularly fine chapel at the other. In 1474 William, first Lord Hastings, was granted a licence to crenellate, and during the following two years he restored the existing structures, raised a curtain round the courtyard on the south side of the house and built a magnificent tower house in the middle of the south wall of the curtain.

The tower house consisted of a main rectangular body of four tall storeys and a small wing on the east divided into seven storeys of lesser height. The entrance, protected by a portcullis, is from the courtyard at ground floor level, and from this level a spiral stairway at the north-east corner of the tower rises to the battlements, with doorways to each floor of the main body and of the wing. Both the first and second storeys of the main building are vaulted; the first storey containing the storerooms and the second a spacious and lofty kitchen. On the third storey were the great hall and a small oratory and on the fourth storey the great chamber.

That this tower was a powerful as well as a handsome structure is evident from a report on the castle sent to Parliament in 1648 and the subsequent action taken by that body to prevent it giving them further trouble. In the report, dated May 6th, 1648, the commissioners say " We are likewise informed that the Great Tower of Ashby-de-la-Zouch" is "a place of considerable strength". On orders for the "slighting" of the castle being issued, the south wall of the tower was undermined and the whole outer half of the building blown down by gunpowder, leaving the inner portion in the exposed and stark condition it is in at present.

Later tower houses in Scotland were generally built on strong lines though the defences were for the most part confined to the battlements and bartizans, to strong grilles in front of the windows, and to gunloops round the base of the walls.

Elcho castle on the Tay, three miles below Perth, is among the most perfect and well preserved of these later tower houses. It was built in the sixteenth century and consists of a long rectangular body with two square wings and two round turrets projecting from it. The castle is of four storeys with bartizans at the top storey.

The entrance is through the south-west wing at ground floor level and opens on to the first storey, containing the kitchen and storerooms, and to a wide stairway rising to the second storey. On the second storey are the great hall, the great chamber with a sleeping room opening from it, and another room. One stairway at the north-east corner of the hall leads down to the first storey and up to the higher levels. Two chambers in the north-west wing formed a private suite, the stairway connecting them by-passing adjoining rooms.

Along the base of the building on all sides is a line of gunloops for small ordnance; the gunloops are widely splayed horizontally towards the outer face in order to provide the greatest lateral sweep for the piece, they are spaced widely apart, and are about 3 ft. above ground level. The other defences are strong iron grilles protecting the windows and an embattled parapet over the entrance wing at the south-west of the building. The parapet is limited to the entrance wing, except that at the re-entering angle beween the east wall of the wing and the main structure it is carried diagonally across the angle to form a machicolation defending the entrance door below.

The tower house built at Buckden Palace, Hunts., about 1480, and that at Holyrood Palace, Edinburgh, about 1520, are both rectangular structures with a turret at each corner somewhat resembling in appearance the tower at Tattershall. But the residential factor is completely dominant in both of them and neither could offer effective resistance to serious attack.

CHAPTER TWELVE

CURTAIN WALLS, GATEHOUSES, AND BUILDINGS OF THE BAILEY, 1270 TO 1500

CURTAIN WALLS AND WALL TOWERS

CURTAIN walls and wall towers were now usually built with deep battered plinths, for greater stability and additional protection against sapping operations. Curtains were normally from 6 ft. to 9 ft. thick above the plinth, and from 20 ft. to 30 ft. high to the level of the wall walks, though some of them are much thicker and higher. The walls of Conway castle are 10 ft. 9 in. thick all round, those of Beaumaris 15 ft. thick all round. Often the walls on the more vulnerable side of a castle are thicker than elsewhere, as already noted at Harlech; at Caernarvon the sides of the castle exposed outside the town are 15 ft. thick, while those enclosed within the town are only 9 ft. thick and are much lower.

Wall towers are of various shapes, round, octagonal, multangular and square; the last being in frequent use during the fourteenth century. Often the tower was built square at the base and round or semi-octagonal above; thus having the dual advantage of a widespread solid base, difficult to sap, and an upper surface with no sharp corners to hide the sappers. The corners of the base were adjusted to the upper surfaces by pyramidal spurs, which in the earlier towers were relatively low, as those of Marten's tower, Chepstow. But later in the period spurs were built higher and higher up the tower until they reached to the parapet, as those at Goodrich and of the screen wall at Caerphilly. Prows, projections like the cutwater of a bridge, rising through the full height of the tower are rare in this country. The only real example known to the author in Great Britain is that of the keep at Kiessimul, though the solid turret of the keep at Caldicot was probably designed for the same purpose (pp. 128a, 130). As shown above, the pyramidal projections of the keeps of Barnard and Bothwell castles are of totally different character.

Watch towers, or bartizans, commanding the field in many direc-

of the merlon was finished with a roll, to prevent arrows which had struck the splayed surface of the coping from glancing over the parapet. At the Eagle tower, Caernarvon castle, the projecting water drip at the bottom of the coping stones is carried down the sides of the embrasures as a protection of the openings from arrows glancing along the sides of the merlons.

Circulation of the wall walk behind a crenellated parapet in times of siege must always have been attended with considerable danger and from the thirteenth century the embrasures were often covered by wooden shutters placed on the outside. The shutters were hung on the top, worked in sockets on either side, and opened out from the bottom. Even when open sufficiently to permit attack on the enemy operating below they still formed adequate protection for the defenders. The sockets were so made that the shutters could be taken out when temporary hoarding was built outside the

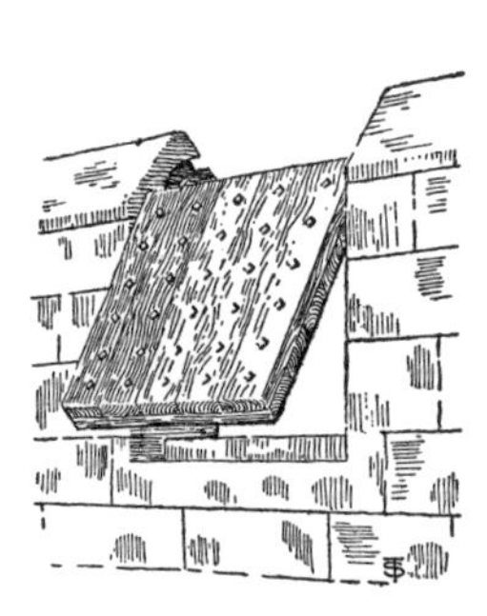

SINGLE SHUTTER

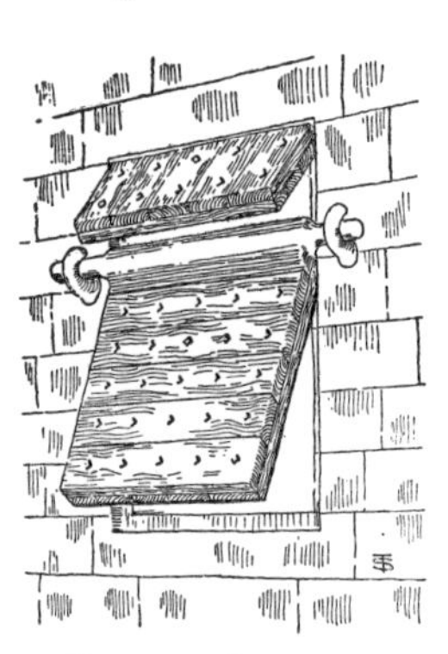

DOUBLE SHUTTER

parapet and the embrasures used for access to it. In many cases where the original parapets remain, as in the Vicar's Pele, noted above, and the barbican, Alnwick castle, sockets are cut in the stonework on either side of the embrasure showing that the trunnion of the shutter fitted into a hole on one side and into a slot on the other. At the east gate in the town walls of Conway two embrasures of the parapet, facing each other over the entrance to the gateway, are each shielded by a large, thin, stone slab projecting out at right angles to the face of the parapet. When the wall walk was roofed the wood shutters were sometimes made in two parts, the upper part being left slightly open for light and ventilation and the lower part, which was the largest, opened out when required.

HOARDING AND MACHICOLATED PARAPETS

Hoards, or brattices, were temporary wooden galleries built on the outside of parapets in time of siege to protect the bases of walls and towers against sapping operations. The galleries were built in rows of beams about 10 in. square and long enough to pierce through the parapet, to which they were wedged, and extend about 4 ft. 6 in. beyond the outer face, where they were supported on brackets. Floor boards were laid on the projecting ends of the beams, a wide aperture being left for machicolation, and the gallery was protected by a screen on the outside and covered with a pent roof. Extensive structures of timberwork built out from the castle walls were vulnerable targets for the enemy's burning missiles and timber gradually gave place to stonework; the first step in this direction was a row of stone corbels on which the brackets for the hoarding were built when required.

Towards the end of the thirteenth century machicolated parapets of stone were built at points particularly exposed to attack, such as gateways, while hoarding was still employed at other parts of the castle. At Conway the east and west gateways of the castle were defended by stone machicolated parapets, stretching from one flanking tower to the other, while the towers all round the castle have beam holes for timber hoarding. It was not until the fourteenth century that machicolated parapets were in general use. Sometimes, as at Chipchase, Borthwick, and Tattershall, the machicolations are continuous all round, but they are often restricted to the corner turrets and the portion of the parapet above the gateway, as at Bywell.

SKETCH OF HOARDING

Machicolations continuous along the curtain wall like those at the south side of the bailey at Craigmillar are rare in Great Britain. In some castles, as Caernarvon and Harlech, the parapets are not machicolated nor are there holes for hoarding, reliance being placed on the ability of the towers to sweep the outer faces of the walls between them. In some foreign castles the curtain wall was defended on the outside by a vaulted passage, or casemate, which ran along from tower to tower above the inner edge of the moat and had arrow-loops to the field, but such defences do not appear to have been in use in this country before the introduction of artillery.

DRAWBRIDGES AND DEFENCES OF THE GATE

Drawbridges were operated by many different methods. Some of them, as the outer bridge at Caerphilly, appear to have been simply drawn back across the opening. A large number of them, as at Conway, were hinged on the inner side and, by means of chains attached to the outer side and by pulleys, were raised up until they stood vertically against the face of the gate and formed an additional barrier to the passage. This was a very common method and appears among the earliest forms. At Dunscaith on the Isle of Skye, the drawbridge worked between two stone arches thrown across the ditch; but this is an unusual and insecure form, since the isolation is imperfect. Dunscaith castle stands out into the sea on a precipitous rock and is approached across a deep ditch strewn with sharp stones.

In another method, as at Caernarvon and the barbican gate at Caerphilly, the bridge was pivoted about a third of the way in its length and counterbalanced by a weight at the short end. When the bridge was raised the short end, which was nearest the gate, descended into the pit and the long end over the moat rose up to block the passage. Here the pit formed an additional obstacle to a forced entry (pp. 238, 245).

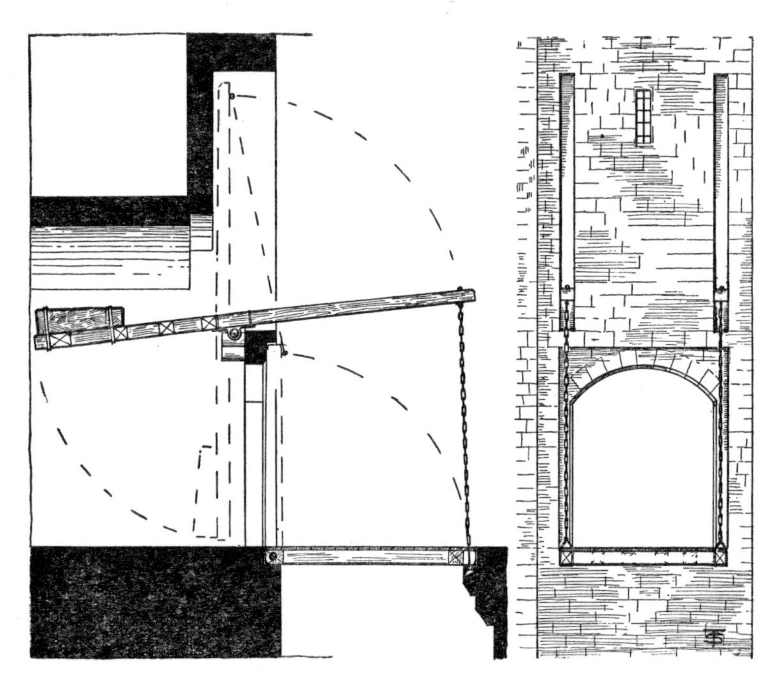

METHOD OF RAISING DRAWBRIDGE WITH COUNTERBALANCED BEAMS

The drawbridges at the Lion Gate of the Tower of London, the Black Gate, Newcastle, and the two gates at Goodrich all worked on a system in which the pivot was placed near the middle of the bridge and, when raised, the outer end of the bridge dipped down into the moat and the inner end swung up to block the passage. Since there was no moat or pit at the inner end three long horizontal grooves, into which the stout beams of the bridge fitted when down, were formed in the gateway passage (pp. 97, 177).

A further method, introduced about 1300, made use of long beams mounted over the entrance arch at the base of tall, vertical recesses, one on either side. The beams worked on a pivot at their centres and projected half outside and half inside the gateway. Chains connected their outer ends with the outer side of the bridge and the bridge, being hinged on the inner side, was raised by means of counterbalances on the inner ends of the beams; no pit was required. When the bridge was raised to a vertical position it fitted into a square-headed recess and the outer ends of the beams fell back into the vertical recesses. Examples of this last method are at Herstmonceux, Bothwell, and Dalhousie. When there was a small doorway for foot passengers on one side of the main archway the side door was provided with a separate bridge and beam (p. 236).

Portcullises and machicolations were now used in many series in the gateway, the latter normally opening across the full width of the passage and both often operated from different storeys of the gatehouse. There were also two or more two-leaved doors. The order in which these defences were arranged varied slightly, but the portcullis was placed in front of the door, which it defended, and there was generally a machicolation in front of the first portcullis. Often there were machicolations between the portcullis and the door, as at Caerphilly, or again a continuous series of them along the passage, as at Harlech. The passages were also defended on either side by arrow-loops. In some castles the gateways were further guarded at the outer end by stout timber bars, which were drawn across the openings from out of long sockets in the walls where they normally rested. At the gate of the outer bailey of Conway castle there were two such bars, drawn out from opposite sides and one 2 ft. above the other.

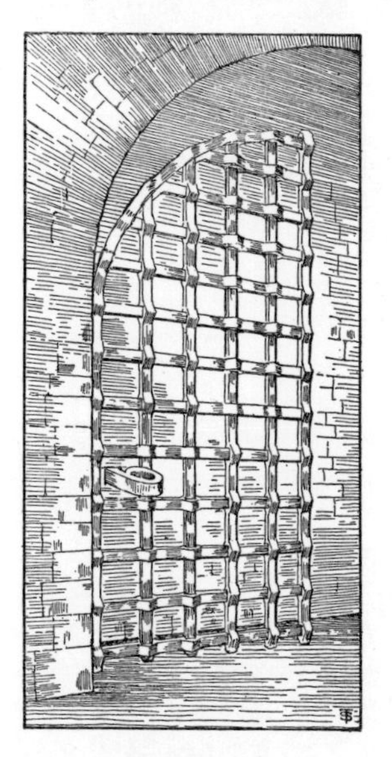

DOUNE CASTLE.
LEAF OF IRON YETT

In the north of England and in Scotland the gateways are often closed by iron gates called yetts, in lieu of or in addition to wood doors. Yetts are powerful iron grilles, hung on hinges and secured when closed either by bars drawn across the opening from out of a socket in the wall or by iron bolts attached to the yett. There are two methods of construction. In Scotland the bars of which the gate is composed were so forged that the vertical and horizontal pieces penetrated or formed sockets for the others in alternate panels. In England all the vertical bars pass in front of the horizontal bars and the joints are riveted or clasped alternately; the intervals between the bars being filled in with oak panels. The former are the strongest forgings but not lending themselves to infilling they are open grilles. The yett at Doune is of two leaves, hung on hinges. It is made of $1\frac{3}{4}$ in. by 1 in. bars and the meshes are $7\frac{3}{4}$ in. square. When closed it was secured by a heavy iron bar, $2\frac{1}{4}$ in. square, which was drawn across the gateway by a handle from out of a socket in the wall. One of the leaves contains a wicket gate (p. 237).

GATEHOUSES

Gatehouses reached their fullest and highest development in the second half of the thirteenth century; they were of three or four storeys and were normally flanked by towers. The approaches were commanded from the battlements and from arrow-loops in the walls. The main gateway was often defended by an outwork or

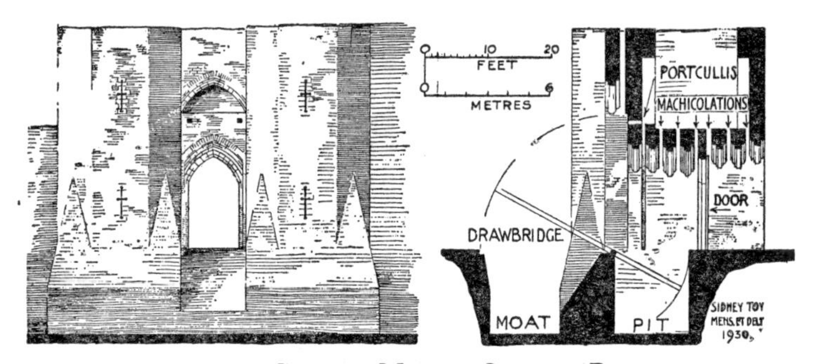

CAERPHILLY CASTLE. MIDDLE GATE OF BARBICAN

barbican. One of the finest and most powerful barbicans is that formed by the great screen wall at Caerphilly; it has three gateways, one in the middle and one at either end. The middle gate is further protected by a causeway with two drawbridges. When the castle was put in a state of defence the outer bridge was probably drawn back over the causeway, but the bridge near the gate worked on a pivot, the inner end descending into a pit as described above. The passage through the gate was barred by a portcullis and a heavy door and defended from above by many machicolations, all the full width of the passage.

As noted above the east gatehouse of the inner bailey of Caerphilly was the strong point of the castle; unfortunately the outer part of this exceptionally fine structure has been destroyed but the inner part remains. The defences at the inner end of the passage were clearly designed to operate against attack from within the bailey; the door closed against the bailey and the portcullis was on the bailey side of the door. In the vault are six square holes, three in front of the portcullis and three between the portcullis and the

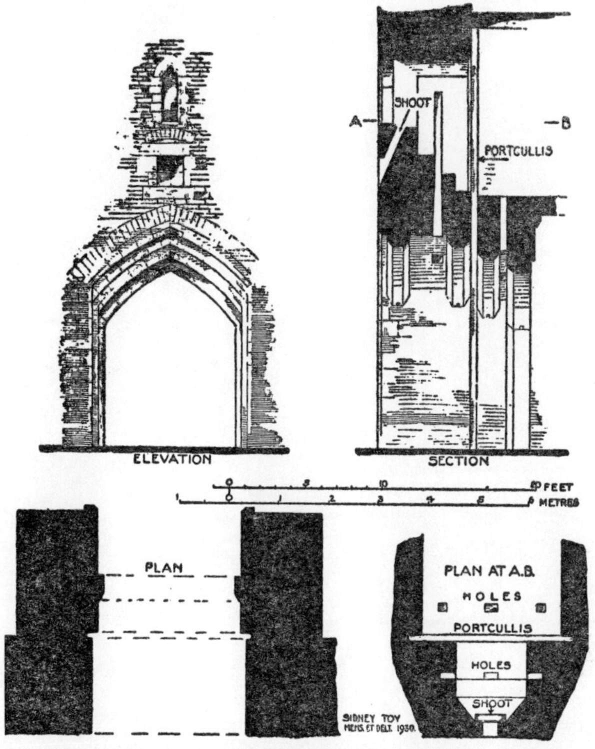

CAERPHILLY CASTLE. INNER GATEWAY OF THE EAST GATEHOUSE

door. These holes must have been either additional water shoots or for throwing down lethal matter upon assailants; there is not sufficient height in the recesses above them to allow for the use of vertical obstructive poles.

A common method of attack on a gate was to pile up faggots or other combustible material against it and set fire to the heap, with the object of burning down the doors. In this gateway there is provision for quenching such a fire by pouring water on it from a shoot immediately above the entrance. At Caerphilly the outside dressings of the shoot have been mutilated but the gateway of Leybourne castle, Kent, of about 1300, has a similar shoot the stonework of which is intact. At Leybourne the slot, resembling that of a letter box, measures 1 ft. 7½ in. by 2 in. On the inside it opens out funnel shaped in the sill of the window above the slot. There are indications that it was lined with lead (pp. 239, 240).

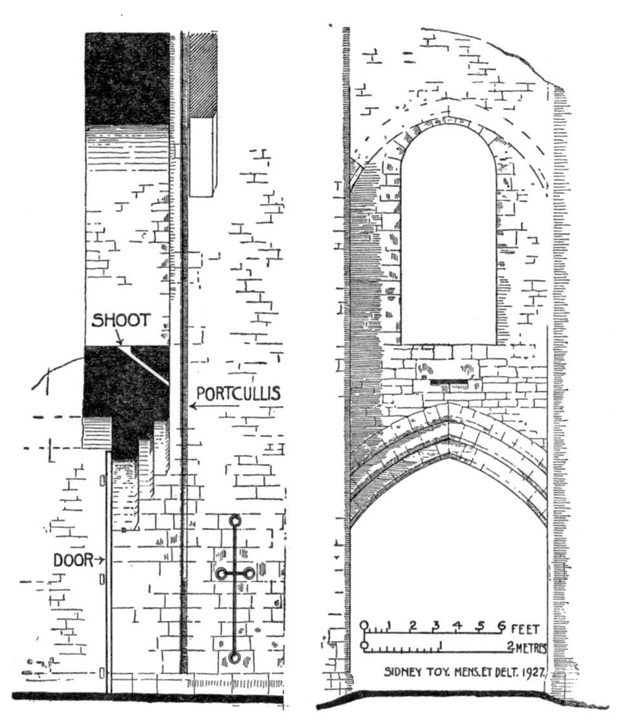

Leybourne Castle, Kent. Gateway

The gatehouse of Denbigh castle, built about 1280 and now in ruins, was a powerful structure. It consists of three towers ranged in triangular form round a central hall; two of the towers flanking the gateway and the third standing within the bailey. The moat in front of the gatehouse was crossed by a drawbridge which worked on a pivot and had a balance pit like that at Caerphilly. The gateway is in two sections; the outer sections leading into an octagonal vaulted hall, and the inner section, after a right-angled turn within the hall, opening out into the bailey.

The outer section was defended by two portcullises and two doors and the inner section, now largely destroyed, probably had similar defences; there were doubtless also machicolations in the destroyed vaults. Here assailants who had negotiated the barriers and survived the assaults of the first section of the gateway and had penetrated into the hall found themselves under attack from five arrow-loops in the side walls, one facing directly towards the entrance, and probably from machicolations in the vaulting. Further they must turn right and run the gauntlet of the inner section before reaching the bailey.

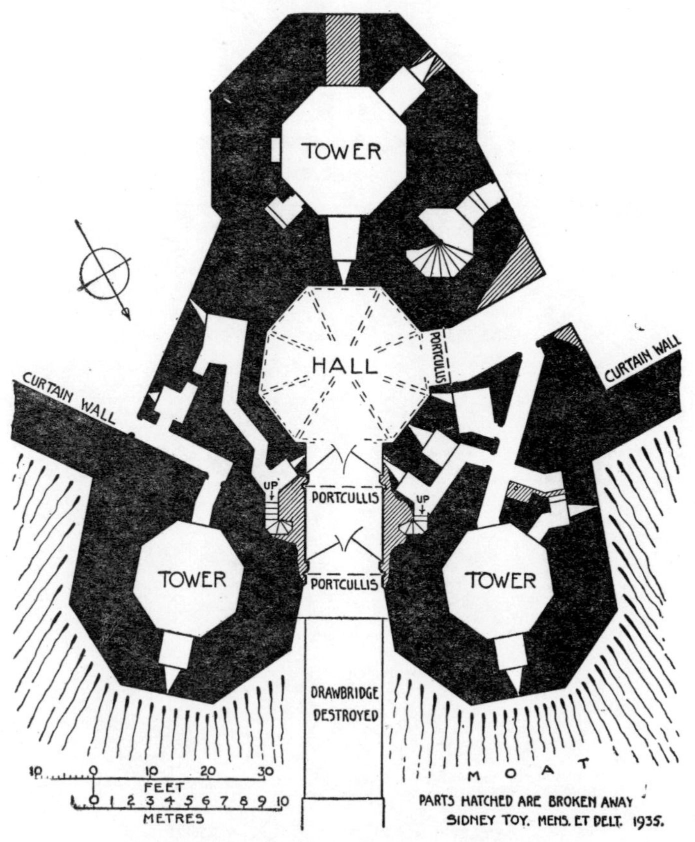

DENBIGH CASTLE. PLAN OF THE GATEHOUSE

At Harlech the passage through the gatehouse was defended first by a stout timber bar, drawn across the opening from out of the wall on one side, and then in succession by a portcullis, a portcullis and door, and another portcullis and door; the last set being at the inner end and defending the passage against the bailey. In addition there are arrow-loops in the side walls and seven machicolations in the vault. The machicolations are spaced at short

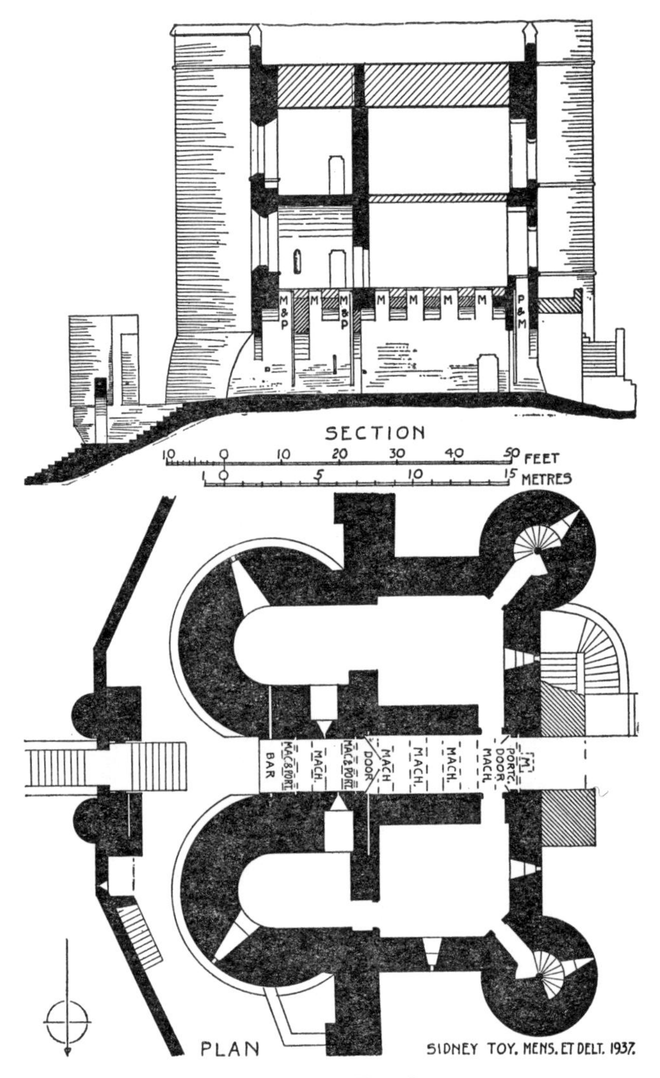

HARLECH CASTLE. THE GATEHOUSE

intervals throughout the passage, those at either end defending the outer and inner portcullis respectively.

Immediately above the outer part of the passage there is a small chapel with a vestry on either side. It has been stated frequently that when the portcullises were raised they must have blocked the chapel and the only door into it. But on close examination by the author of the springers of the arch behind each of the two portcullises concerned (the crowns of these arches being broken down) it was obvious that the arch was carried down at least 6 ft. below the vault of the passage, and also that the wood floor of the chapel was about 1 ft. 6 in. above the upper surface of the vault. When raised (incidentally the normal position) the portcullises did not protrude above the chapel floor. Indeed that this was the case is proved by the portcullis at the inner end of the passage which obviously could not have been raised above that level.

The gatehouse at Goodrich was defended by a drawbridge which swung on a central pivot and dipped down at the outer end when raised. Here the corbels which supported the bearings of the pivot remain, and the three long grooves in the floor for the beams of the bridge when lowered are intact (p. 177).

One of our finest gatehouses is that of Tonbridge castle, Kent, built about 1300. It is a formidable and imposing structure of five storeys, one below ground level, and is flanked by round towers which rise from octagonal bases with pyramidal spurs. The arrow-loops are vertical slots with circular feet and trefoiled heads; the latter a purely decorative feature (pp. 59, 222b, 243).

The gateway was defended in front by a drawbridge and

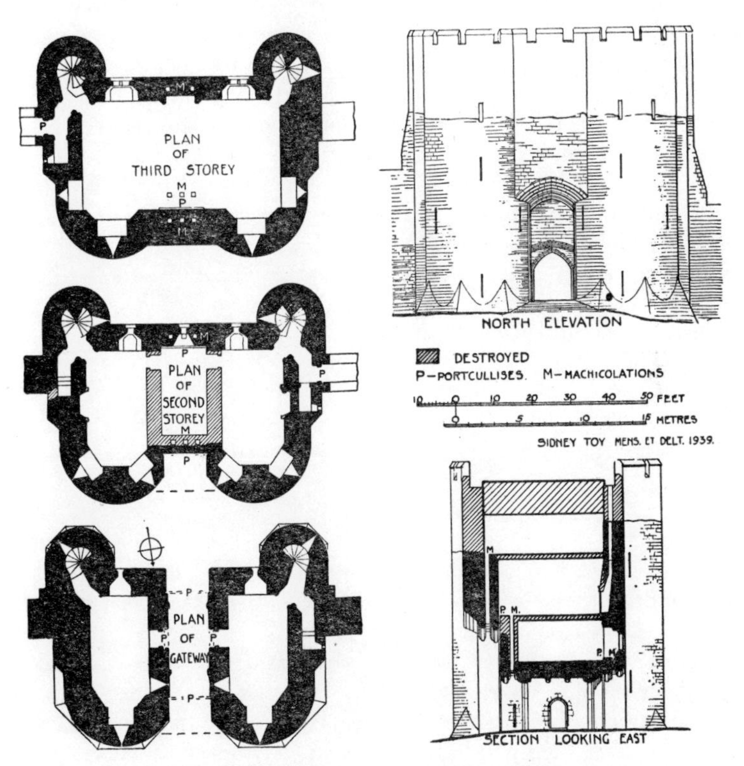

TONBRIDGE CASTLE. THE GATEHOUSE

throughout the passage by two portcullises, one at either end, two double doors, and three rows of machicolations, each row consisting of three holes, 1 ft. square. These defences are so skilfully disposed that some of them could be operated or used from each of the three storeys above the gateway. The central portion of the passage was the porch to the gatehouse; doors on either side, each defended by a portcullis, gave admission to the guardrooms on either side of the passage, to the storerooms of the basement below, and to the stairways rising to the upper levels. The outer portion of the passage was defended in succession, beginning at the outer end, by a row of machicolations, a portcullis, a second row of machicolations, and a two-leaved door.

The first set of these machicolations were carried up through the wall to open out in the floor of the top, or fourth storey above ground level, while the portcullis and the second row of machicolations extended up to the third storey, where was the great hall. The defences at the inner end of the passage are reversed to operate against attacks from the bailey. In succession, beginning at the bailey end, there is a row of machicolations, a portcullis, and a two-leaved door. Here the portcullis and the middle hole of the row of machicolations rise to a room immediately over the gateway while the two end machicolation holes rise to the top storey. In this gatehouse, therefore, the passage was commanded by arrow-loops from the guardrooms on either side and defended from every storey above it.

The great hall, occupying the whole floor space of its storey, is a handsome apartment lighted by traceried windows from the courtyard; it has a wide fireplace, the hood of which was supported on shafted jambs with grotesque heads. The building is flanked on either side of the face towards the bailey with a stair turret, rising from ground floor to the battlements, with doorways at each storey. There is a doorway opening from the gatehouse to the wall walk on the curtain on either side, each of them defended by a portcullis.

Undoubtedly the defensive principles of mediaeval gateways reached their highest point in the King's Gate at Caernarvon, built 1316–20, in part destroyed or more probably never finished as first designed. The plan bears some resemblance to the gatehouse at Denbigh, with two passages at right angles to each other and a large hall at their junction, but the passages here are longer and their defences much more numerous and elaborate than those at Denbigh. The approach was by a drawbridge which worked on a pivot between the moat and a pit.

The outer passage was defended by four portcullises and two doors and was commanded from above by seven lines of machicolations. The first machicolation covers the head of the first

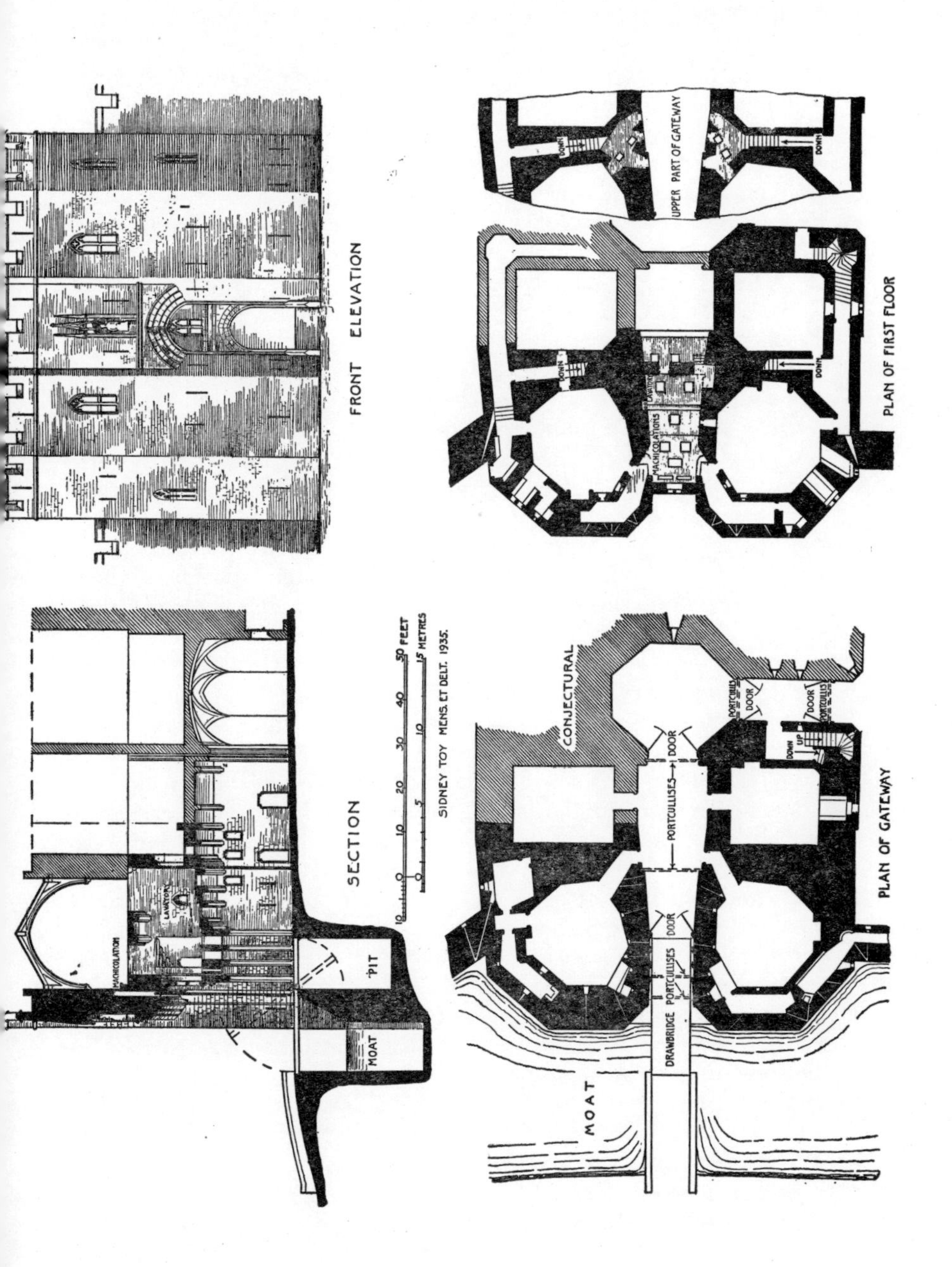
FRONT ELEVATION
SECTION
MACHICOLATION
LAVATORY
PIT
MOAT
10 0 10 20 30 40 50 FEET
0 5 10 15 METRES
SIDNEY TOY MENS. ET DELT. 1935.
UPPER PART OF GATEWAY
DOWN
DOWN
MACHICOLATIONS
DOWN
DOWN
PLAN OF FIRST FLOOR
CONJECTURAL
DOOR
PORTCULLISES
DOOR
PORTCULLISES
DRAWBRIDGE
MOAT
PORTCULLIS
DOOR
DOOR
PORTCULLIS
DOWN
UP
PLAN OF GATEWAY

portcullis, so that when attacked by fire the portcullis could be drenched with water; both were operated from the third, or uppermost, storey of the gatehouse. Beyond the first two-leaved door, about a third of the way through, the passage gradually widens and increases in height to another point about two-thirds of the way through when it becomes parallel again. In addition to the other defences the passage was under attack from numerous arrow-loops on either side and its middle portion, from a height 12 ft. above the ground, was commanded by six doorways, three on either side, through which heavy missiles and obstructive material could be cast down upon the enemy. These high doorways and the small chambers from which they open are reached by flights of steps down from the second storey of the building; machicolations in the floors of the chambers command the entrances to the guard-rooms on either side of the gateway.

Only one side of what appears to have been an octagonal hall and only one side of the passage from the hall to the bailey now remain. But these fragments clearly indicate that the inner passage was designed to have a portcullis and a two-leaved door at either end, the set farthest from the hall being reversed against the bailey. So that in addition to the overhead and lateral defences there were throughout this gateway six portcullises and four two-leaved doors.

The room of the gatehouse immediately above the forepart of the entrance passage has on one side a lavabo with a trefoiled head and two basins and on the opposite side a small window. The lavabo has been called a piscina and the room in which it occurs a chapel. Now apart from the fact that there was no lack of chapels elsewhere in the castle, the use of this room for such a purpose is in the highest degree improbable. Two portcullises were operated from it, there are five lines of large machicolations in its floor, and two latrines open out of it. The similarity of construction and ornament between lavabos and piscinae has been noted above. The lavabo was no doubt for the ablutions of those engaged in the many activities, and necessities, of the defence; and the window opposite the lavabo was not made to enable persons in the adjoining room to look in this direction but, obviously by its construction, to augment the light of that room, which is a very sombre apartment with two other " borrowed lights " opening into the passage to one of the latrines.

The west, or outer, gateway at Alnwick, Northumberland, has a barbican which forms an extension of the gatehouse. Alnwick castle, begun in 1096, dates mainly from the first half of the twelfth century and consisted originally of a large shell keep and two baileys extending east and west from the keep, much on the plan of Arundel. In continuous occupation, it has from time to time been subjected to drastic alteration, particularly in 1764 and 1854; but it preserves its original contour and retains many features of considerable interest. The outer gateway and barbican, which are connected by high walls flanking the passage between them, were built in 1310–14. There were two drawbridges, one defending the barbican and the other the gatehouse. The wood shutters in the parapet of the barbican have been referred to above. An unusual feature of this building is an elaboration of those half figures on the parapet at Chepstow and Caernarvon. Here are full length figures of men, perched perilously on the coping of the parapet both of the gatehouse and the barbican; they were put up during the restoration of 1764 and probably bear no relation to those, if any, they replaced (p. 256a).

At Warwick castle the gatehouse, built about 1370, also has a barbican to which it is connected by the walls of the passage

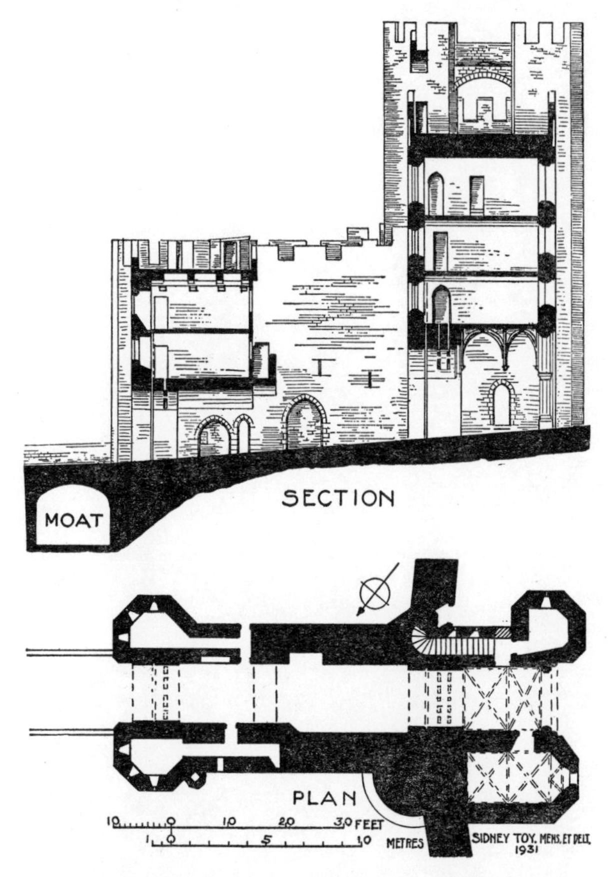

WARWICK CASTLE. THE GATEHOUSE AND BARBICAN

between them. The drawbridge in front of the barbican has been replaced by a permanent bridge of stone and there are now no exposed traces of a second drawbridge before the main building, though there probably was one. The approach to the barbican, which is of three storeys, was commanded from its turrets and battlements. Should the outer gate be carried, an enemy rushing through the passage between the barbican and the gatehouse would be exposed to attack from the battlements all round the open passage, and in the rear from a gallery on the inner face of the barbican. The upper floors of the barbican, its battlements, and the battlements on the walls flanking the open passage, are all reached by a mural rising ramp in the east wall of the passage, opening from a doorway in the courtyard (pp. 247, 256a).

The footway rises rapidly from the outer face of the barbican to the inner face of the gatehouse and the passage is further

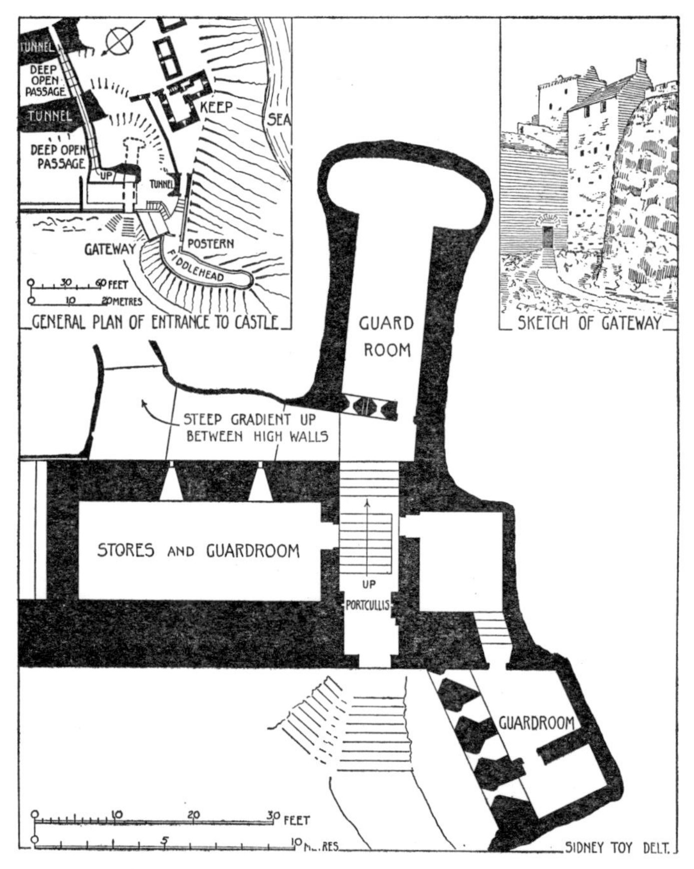

DUNNOTTAR CASTLE. PLAN OF THE GATEWAY

defended throughout its length by a portcullis and a row of machicolations at the barbican, and by a portcullis, a two-leaved door, and two lines of machicolations at the gatehouse.

The gatehouse rises three storeys above the gateway and has a turret at each of its four corners. The turrets are carried high above the roof and are connected to each other over the roof by embattled bridges. There are therefore three tiers of battlements; those on the barbican and the lateral walls of the open passage, secondly those on the roof of the gatehouse, and thirdly, dominating the whole, those on the turrets and the bridges between them; and all three are in direct connection by spiral stairways. There is a doorway to the wall walk of the curtain on either side of the gatehouse, but there was no straight way through. To cross from the wall walk on one side of the gatehouse to that on the other it was necessary to ascend one stair to the roof, cross the roof, and descend by a stair on the other side.

The gateway into Dunnottar castle, as remodelled in the sixteenth century, was exceptionally formidable. The approach to the gate is defended on the right by a tall five-storeyed building, which is backed against the cliff and commands the path by tiers of gunloops. The entrance gateway, as noted above, was defended by a portcullis and a guardroom on either side of the passage. Within the passage a flight of steps rises up directly in face of another guardroom. This last guardroom is actually a cave hewn out of the rock and is blocked at the entrance by a stone screen pierced with four gunloops. The gunloops are arranged four-square with a slight hole in the centre and point towards the entrance. Arrived at this point in face of artillery fire it is necessary to turn sharply to the left, ascend a narrow defile, open to flank fire, turn right and continue the ascent to the summit of the rock, passing through two tunnels en route (pp. 216b, 248).

When a castle stands on the sea shore or beside a river there is often a water gate in the outer curtain, through which supplies could be brought in by boat, sorties made, or escape effected. The water gate at Caernarvon, which was defended by a portcullis, and those at Beaumaris and Hailes have already been noted. The finest and best preserved water gates in Great Britain are those of the Tower of London and of the castle at Newport, Monmouth. At the Tower of London there are actually two water gates, one called the Cradle Tower and the other St. Thomas's Tower, or Traitors' Gate. The Cradle Tower was a private entrance to the royal lodgings; it was built about 1350 and was a vaulted gateway, defended by a portcullis at both the outer and inner ends.

Traitors' Gate was first built in the middle of the thirteenth century but was largely reconstructed about 1300. Here the water entered to form a pool within the gateway passage. Thus while a friendly boat could enter and landings be effected under the protection of the building itself, an enemy endeavouring to enter and force the gate would find himself exposed to both overhead and flank attack, which in such restricted space he would have little opportunity to counter. The pool was entered through a wide archway, defended by a portcullis, and was defended within on three sides from arrow-loops opening from mural galleries. A flight of steps rises up from the pool to the level of the bailey.

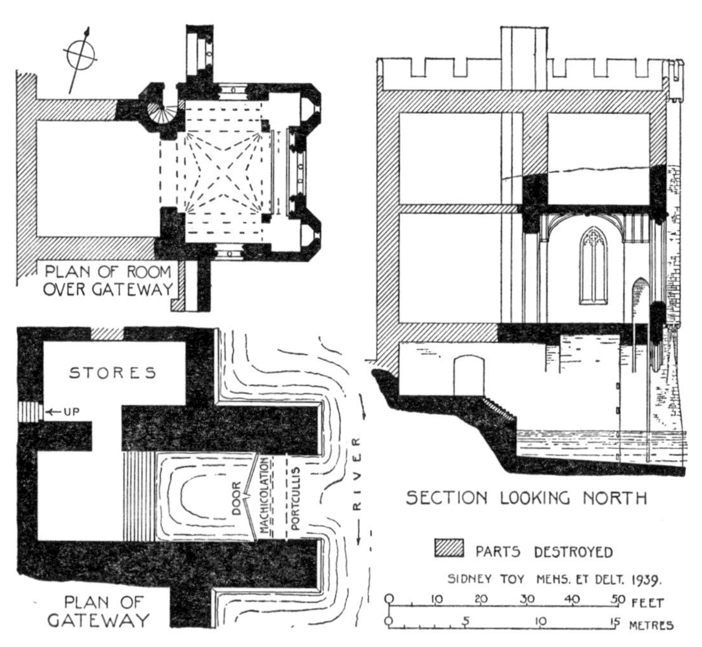

NEWPORT CASTLE. THE WATER GATE

Newport castle now consists only of what was the east front of a rectangular bailey; except for foundations all other parts of the fortress have been destroyed. The east front, facing the river Usk, has a fine water gate in the middle and a tower at either end. Internally the towers are square but externally they are octagonal and rise from square bases with tall pyramidal spurs; the turrets flanking the water gate also have pyramidal spurs. The lower part of the water gate, the curtain on either side, and the two end towers were all built about 1300; but the upper part of the water gate with its fine vaulted hall, miscalled a chapel, was rebuilt in the fifteenth century, and what remains of the parapet on the curtain is of this later period. The whole has been considerably restored in recent years and much of the window dressing is modern.

The water gate at Newport juts out into the river, which is tidal at this point, so that at high water the lower storey enclosed a pool into which boats could enter and unload at the far end. The entrance was defended in succession by a portcullis, a narrow machicolation which has been misnamed a portcullis, and a powerful two-leaved door; the hinges for the door still remain. At the head of the steps there is a landing quay and on the right of the quay a large vaulted storeroom. From the storeroom steps rise to a door which opens on to the courtyard (pp. 250, 256a).

BUILDINGS OF THE BAILEY

The arrangement of the internal buildings of the bailey, with slight variations, followed a plan common throughout the whole mediaeval period. The great hall with the residential quarters at one end and the domestic offices at the other stood away from the main entrance, either facing it from the opposite side of the courtyard, as at Harlech and Bodiam, or in one of the lateral ranges, as at Caerphilly and Bolton. The chapel was adjacent to the residential rooms, and the military quarters and the stables were near the gateway.

Generally the great hall is a lofty apartment lighted by large windows and having an open timber roof; it often stands on a vaulted undercroft. Fireplaces were normally in the side walls. Fireplaces in the middle of the hall never could have been satisfactory; where they occurred in the later periods the hearth was provided with a reredos and hood, the smoke escaping through a louvre in the roof. At one end of the hall there was a raised platform, or dais, for the high table. At the other end a passage called the screens ran across from side to side between the end wall and a partition; the partition supported a minstrels' gallery above the screens. The main doorway of the hall, usually entered through a porch, was at one end of the screens and a postern at the other. There were normally two doors in the partition to the hall and three in the end wall; of the latter the middle one led through a passage to the kitchen while one of the lateral doors opened to the pantry and the other to the buttery.

The ranges of buildings at either end of the hall were of two or three storeys; the solar and private rooms of the principal residents, and the chapel, being at the dais end of the hall and often reached by a stairway at that end. Extending from the kitchen on the other side were ranges containing the brewery, bakery and other domestic offices. Within or near the kitchen there was a well and there were often one or more large ovens. An oven at Ludlow castle is 12 ft. 6 in. diameter and one at Bolton castle 14 ft. 6 in. diameter.

Many great halls are built on a magnificent scale with large traceried windows, wide richly moulded fireplaces, and fine open timber roofs; some of them have been described above. One of the finest halls of this period is that on the west side of Durham castle, built by Antony Bek about 1290; it is a lofty and well proportioned structure with an open timber roof and lighted by tall windows. Another handsome hall was that built by John of Gaunt at Kenilworth in 1392.

The halls built by Bishop Gower, 1328–47, at the episcopal palaces of St. David's, Lamphey, and Swansea, have all a structural feature which calls for special attention. That at St. David's, now in a ruinous condition, is a typical example. Immediately below the parapet of the great hall of St. David's palace there is an unbroken arcade of pointed arches, which are placed closely together with small attached shafts between. The sills of the arches rise steeply up from a string course on the outer face of the wall to a ledge which supported the wall plate of the roof on the inner face. The upper portion of this continuous ledge is now much broken away. That the arcades are not machicolations is clear from the position they occupy in relation to the roof, and from the fact that any missile thrown down their steep slopes would ricochet far beyond the base of the walls and well away from any sappers operating there.

The practical value of the arcades is that they are outlets for the rainwater and snow falling on the roof, which was probably of fairly high pitch. There are similar rows of large openings at the base of the parapet of the chapel of St. Catherine at Abbotsbury, Dorset. There, the covering of the steep roof comes down directly to the openings and there are no other outlets for rainwater. The palaces were designed rather as stately dwellings than fortified retreats. At St. David's there is a beautiful rose window at the east end of the great hall and rows of tall windows on either side, as well towards the field as to the courtyard. That embellishment was a strong factor in the design is obvious from the fact that the arches are continued as blind arcades across the gables of the hall, where they could have had no possible practical value.

Linlithgow Palace, West Lothian, has a spacious and lofty great hall, dating from the fifteenth century, which was lighted by clerestory windows. There is a continuous stone seat on either side of the hall and a high plain wall, formerly covered with tapestry, between the seat and the window sills; statues were placed at intervals along the side walls. Two mural galleries, one at floor level and the other at the level of the clerestory, run along on one side the whole length of the hall. At the dais end there is a large window on one side and a spiral stairway to the upper rooms on the other, while in the end wall there is a magnificent fireplace. The fireplace is so wide between the extreme jambs (it measures 21 ft.) that it is divided into three bays by intermediate pillars. The dais end of the hall is covered by a stone vault but the main portion had a fine hammer-beam roof, now destroyed. (Appendix I, p. 292.)

The large windows of the great halls, and elsewhere where they occurred in a castle, were protected by strong iron grilles; and when this defence is taken into consideration the rooms on which the windows opened were not so vulnerable as they now appear when the ironwork has been removed, as in the great hall at Kenilworth. In Scotland the grilles were of small mesh and projected slightly from the outer face of the wall, as still existing at Elcho and Stirling; they were generally forged in the same manner as yetts. Grilles may be a menace to those within as well as a deterrent to those without. At the castle of Frendraught, Aberdeenshire, a fire having broken out during one night of 1630, Lord Aboyne and other occupants of the building were burnt alive because they could not escape through the grilled windows.

The kitchen was an important building in a castle, often rising through two storeys and having wide fireplaces with ovens opening out of them. Among the finest mediaeval kitchens in this country are those at Durham cathedral and Glastonbury abbey, both monastic establishments; but the great kitchens of the castles of Raby, Farnham, Cockermouth, and Ashby-de-la-Zouch were almost equally imposing buildings. The kitchen of Raby castle, Durham, built about 1380 and still complete, measures internally 30 ft. by 29 ft. and rises through two storeys. The lower storey is square; the upper storey is octagonal and has a stone vault with a louvred lantern in the centre. A mural gallery runs round the walls at the level of the high windows, with flights of steps at intervals leading down to the kitchen floor. There are wide fireplaces in three of the walls. The kitchen at Ashby-de-la-Zouch, now partly destroyed, was a spacious vaulted building of about 1360 with wide fireplaces, ovens, and a well.

Chapels, sometimes small oratories, were often separate buildings of considerable size and elegance, such as the chapel with large traceried windows built in the fifteenth century at Ashby-de-la-Zouch. In the fourteenth and fifteenth centuries it became the custom for the owners of important castles to found a college of priests either adjacent to or actually within his fortress. At Tattershall, about 1450, Lord Cromwell rebuilt, on a handsome scale, the old parish church, which stood immediately to the east of his castle, assigning the nave to parochial uses and reserving the choir for the use of a college of priests he established there. St. George's chapel, Windsor, was built within the castle walls, as was the collegiate chapel at Warkworth noted above.

PRISONS

Though the name prison is often applied to ill-lighted rooms which were in fact storerooms or latrines there was usually one, and in large castles two or more, prisons. The basement of the south-east tower of Skenfrith castle was a prison, entered through a trap-door in the room above, and having no other outlet than a ventilating shaft, which passed up through the wall to a small opening on the outer face. There are similar cells at two of the towers of Conway castle; though there the openings are larger and pass more directly to the outside, admitting a dim light as well as air.

The basement of Caesar's tower, Warwick, was a prison. It has no connection with the upper storeys of the tower but is reached by a flight of steps down from the courtyard to the prison door. From this point another flight of steps leads up to a gallery between a small window and an opening, formerly closed by a grille, looking into the prison, so that the warder could overlook the prisoners from the gallery without entering the cell. The cell is paved partly with stone and partly with bricks; it has a ventilating shaft to the courtyard and a door on one side opens to a latrine (p. 204). A prison in the basement of the keep at Warkworth is lighted by a small window and has a fireplace, two cupboards, and a latrine.

At Dalhousie castle, Midlothian, the prison is approached by a mural stairway down from the first floor of the keep and is entered by a small doorway, 1 ft. 10½ in. wide by 3 ft. 4½ in. high. The cell has a latrine and a ventilating shaft but no window. The doorway of the small prison of Crichton castle, Midlothian, stands 6 ft. above the floor of the cell and is only 2 ft. 5 in. high. The cell at Warwick measures 19 ft. 3 in. by 13 ft. 4 in.; that at Dalhousie 10 ft. 10 in. by 10 ft. 3 in.; and that at Crichton 7 ft. 2 in. by 6 ft. 8 in.; all three have stone vaults.

STAIRWAYS

Stairways either ascended in straight flights through the walls or rose up at one point in spiral form. Spiral stairways were first built on vaults which ascended round a central newel. The vaults were constructed on timber centering which was probably moved upwards as the work proceeded; and the stonework forming the steps laid on the upper surface of the vaulting. By this method relatively small stones could be used for the steps and the width of the stairway was unrestricted. But the process absorbed a considerable amount of time and the necessity for speed in military work demanded a more expeditious method of construction.

From about the end of the twelfth century spiral stairways were, with few exceptions, composed entirely of a series of steps, each step being cut out of one stone and sufficiently long to form a section of the newel at one end and to tail into the wall at the other. The first steps are built upon solid masonry; the others as they rise require no other support for the portion free of the wall than the newel and the edge of the step below. At Caerphilly and in the stairways of the towers flanking the east wall of Newport castle the steps are laid on thin vaulting composed of courses of flat stones. The stones of each succeeding course passing diagonally across those below give a curious network effect to the spiral vaulting. Later, in brick-built castles vaulting again became general, both the vaults and the treads being of brickwork, as at Nether Hall, Essex, about 1470, and Kirby Muxloe, 1480–84. In the north of England, as at Alnwick, Warkworth, and Belsay, the head of the spiral stairway is sometimes finished in fourteenth-century work with an "umbrella" vault. In this form the circular newel is carried up high above the top step as a central pillar for a ribbed vault, the ribs springing from the pillar and radiating to the wall all round.

By far the greatest number of these spiral stairways in castles turn to the right as they ascend; so that while those defending them from above have the greatest space in which to use their sword arms, enemies mounting would be at a disadvantage in this respect. But since in a close fight there must be many occasions when the positions are reversed, there are generally some stairways which turn left as they rise. In the inner bailey at Caerphilly seven stairways turn right and two left. At Conway castle seven turn right and one left. At Beaumaris out of ten stairways four turn left, and at Caernarvon seven turn right and four left.

GARRISONS

The number of fighting men quartered in a castle varied greatly from time to time and depended on the conditions of peace or war, on the status and means of the commander, and on the faithful performance of military obligations. The permanent garrisons provided for the royal castles of Caernarvon and Conway in 1284 were as follows. For Caernarvon, in addition to the constable, there were to be two serjeant horsemen, who had charge of the castle in the absence of the constable, ten serjeant crossbowmen, a smith, a carpenter, an artificer, and twenty-five footmen-at-arms; in all forty men.[1] For Conway, in addition to the constable and his household, there were to be thirty fencible men in all, consisting of fifteen crossbowmen, a chaplain, a smith, a carpenter, a mason, an artificer, and ten others—janitors, watchmen, and other ministers of the castle.[2] In 1401 to 1404 the garrison provided for

[1] Cal. Rot. Wall., 1284, 288.
[2] Ibid. 292.

Caernarvon castle in addition to the constable was a hundred men, consisting of twenty men-at-arms and eighty archers; for Conway castle seventy-five men, consisting of fifteen men-at-arms and sixty archers; for Harlech castle ten men-at-arms and thirty archers; and for Beaumaris castle fifteen men-at-arms and one hundred and forty archers.[3]

[3] Acts of Privy Council, Vol. II, Hen. IV, 64-66.

[*Country Life*

ALNWICK CASTLE. THE BARBICAN.

WARWICK CASTLE. THE GATEHOUSE FROM THE BAILEY.

NEWPORT CASTLE. THE WATER GATE AT LOW TIDE.

Monmouth. The Bridge from the South.

[*Daily Graphic*

Deal Castle from the Air.

Fincastle from the Air.

CHAPTER THIRTEEN

TOWNS, FORTIFIED BRIDGES AND CHURCHES

TOWNS

FROM the earliest times cities grew up below or near a citadel, which occupied a dominating position over their fortifications. A Norman town frequently extended from the foot of the castle of the lord under whose patronage it developed; the mound with its keep often having the bailey on one side and the town on the other. The castle stood in a commanding position from which the garrison could either protect the town or defend themselves against it in the event of its fall or of the disaffection of its inhabitants. Totnes, Launceston, and Pleshey are examples of this plan.

During the latter part of the thirteenth century many new towns were built in this country, a large number of them founded by Edward the First; Kingston-upon-Hull, Conway, Caernarvon, and Winchelsea are all of this period. Where the site permitted the towns are rectangular, as at Flint, but many of them are of irregular plan, as Conway and Winchelsea. Parallel streets intersecting at right angles divide the town into rectangular sections, two or more being open spaces and the rest occupied by houses. One of the open spaces was the market place, having streets passing along on all four sides but none crossing the centre. Another open space, generally near the market place, was occupied by the church.

In laying out the plan of the defences of a town some special conditions had to be considered. Unlike a castle the space within the walls was occupied by blocks of houses which, if not properly planned, would greatly impede the circulation of the troops. The open market place, forming a rallying point in time of siege, was generally near the centre of the town and the streets opening from it led directly to the gateways and walls. As in Roman camps and towns there was a road passing all round the fortification immediately inside the walls. This road, called the *pomerium*, gave direct access to the curtain and wall towers at all points and allowed the rapid movement of troops and siege engines from one point in the defences to another. The wall walks are reached from ground level at intervals along the curtain by flights of steps built against the inside face of the wall. The gateways of a town were more numerous than those of a castle and the points they occupied in the walls were governed largely by the positions of the highways on which they opened. Generally the defences of the gateway passages were directed entirely against attack from without.

York, Chester, Southampton, and Tenby are among many other towns in Great Britain which still preserve fortifications of various mediaeval periods. At York in addition to its Roman and mediaeval walls there are four mediaeval gateways, called Bars. But the best preserved and most complete fortified towns of the Middle Ages in this country are those of Conway and Caernarvon, built by Edward the First in the latter part of the thirteenth century. Each of them is directly associated with a castle and both retain their walls and wall towers in fairly good condition.

Conway has a triangular plan with its base running along beside the river at the east and its apex terminating in a round tower on high ground at the west. The castle stands on a rock at the south end of the base. A wing wall, terminating by a tower, ran into the river from each end of the base, together forming a safe harbour, protected on either flank. The average thickness of the town walls is 5 ft. 7 in. but they are corbelled out near the top on the inside to allow greater width for the wall walk; the average height from the ground to the wall walk is 24 ft. The wing wall running into the river on the north side of the harbour is 10 ft. 7 in. thick. A ditch ran round outside the walls from one point of the river to the other. Wall towers, generally open at the back, occur at frequent intervals, and numerous flights of steps ascend to the wall walk near the towers.

The towers of town walls were often built with no wall at the back and show an open gorge towards the town; the gorge usually being left quite open from the base upward save for a stone or movable wood bridge at the wall walk. They stand astride of the walk with their lateral walls ending abruptly either flush with the inside face of the curtain or slightly beyond it. Often the tower was entered by a door on one side, and to pass from the walk on one side to that on the other it was necessary to ascend to the top of the tower. So that if one section of the curtain was carried that section could be isolated by removing the wood stairways in the towers. This arrangement can be seen clearly in the town walls of Conway, though the work is in places broken away. On one side of the tower there was a doorway from the wall walk to the timber floor of the interior; but there was no doorway on the other side. To reach the walk on that side it was necessary to ascend to

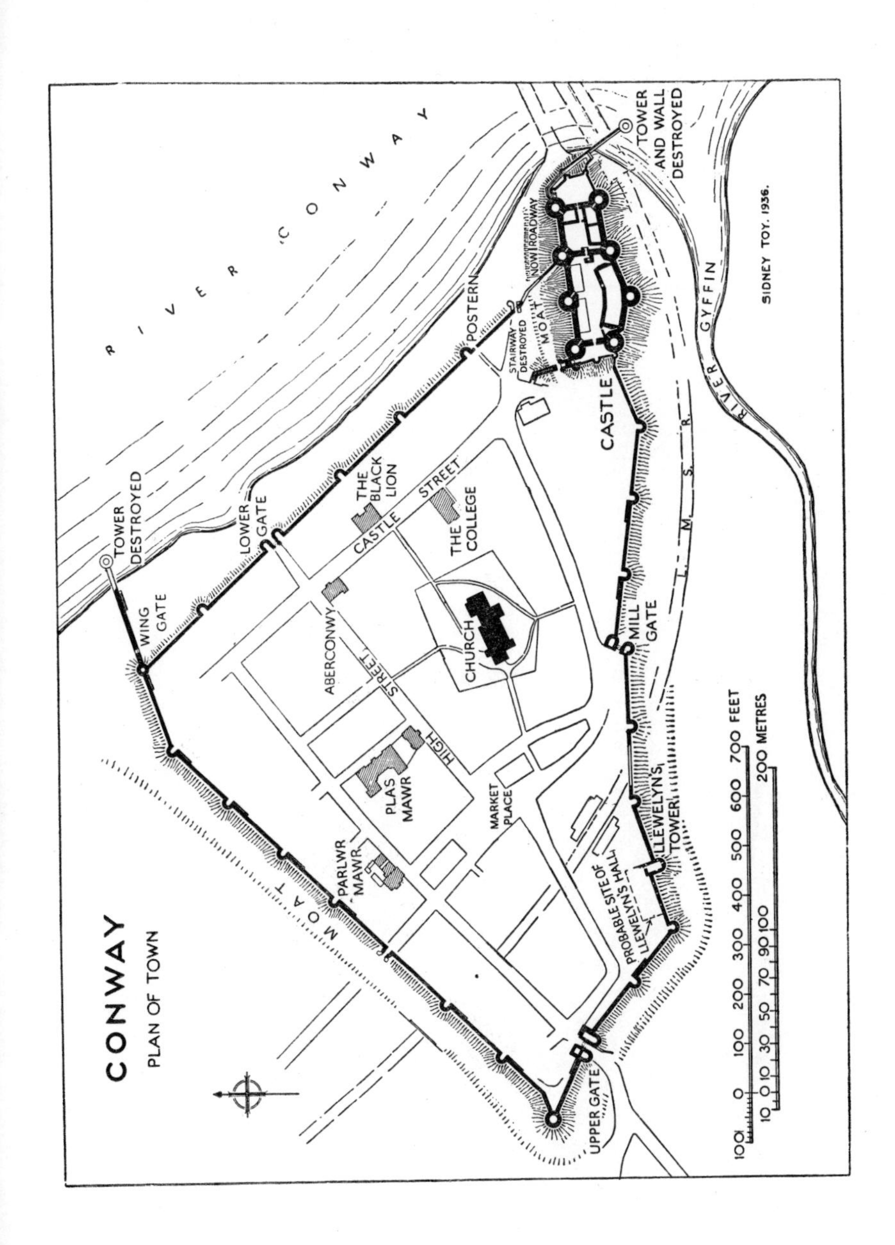
CONWAY
PLAN OF TOWN
RIVER CONWAY
TOWER DESTROYED
WING GATE
LOWER GATE
THE BLACK LION
POSTERN
STAIRWAY DESTROYED
NOW ROADWAY
MOAT
TOWER AND WALL DESTROYED
CASTLE
CASTLE STREET
THE COLLEGE
ABERCONWY
CHURCH
HIGH STREET
PLAS MAWR
PARLWR MAWR
MARKET PLACE
MILL GATE
L. M. S. R.
RIVER GYFFIN
LLEWELYN'S TOWER
PROBABLE SITE OF LLEWELYN'S HALL
UPPER GATE
MOAT
SIDNEY TOY. 1936.
100 0 100 200 300 400 500 600 700 FEET
10 0 10 30 50 70 90 100 200 METRES

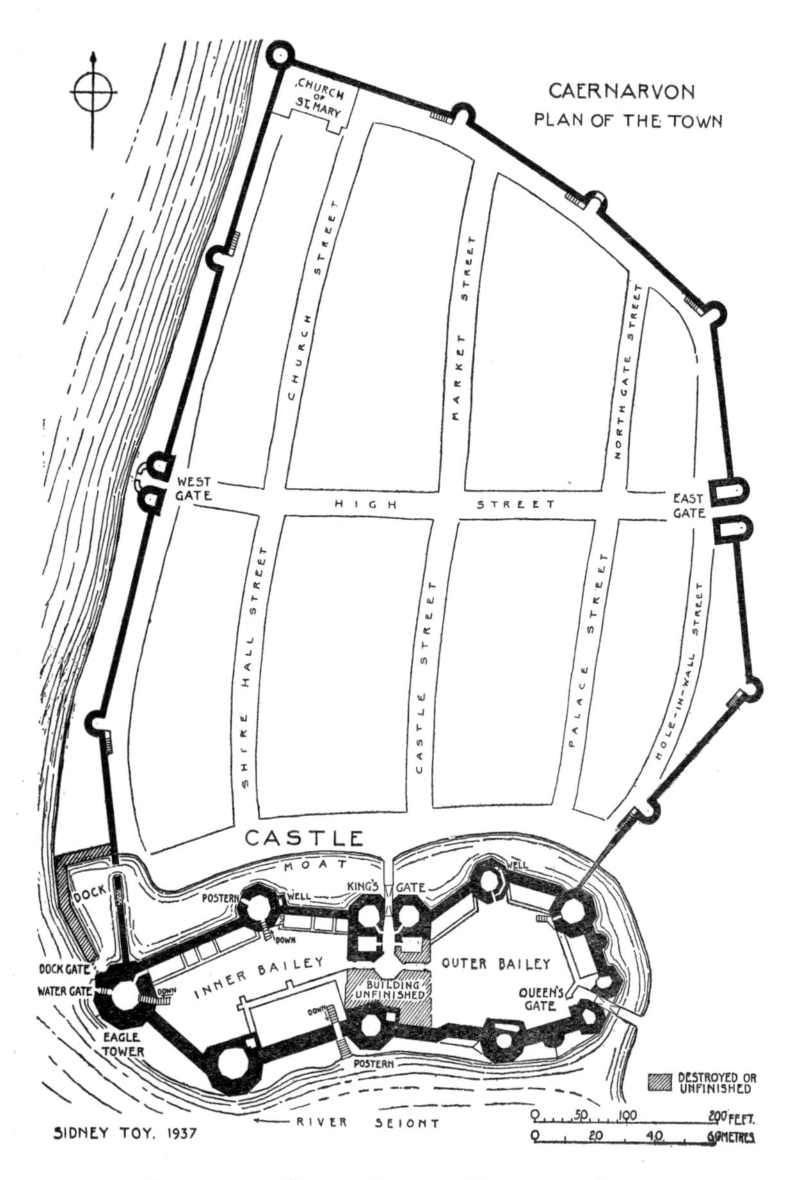

Caernarvon Castle. Plan of Town and Castle

the top of the tower by a wood stairway within and descend by a flight of stone steps built against the outer face of the tower on the other side.

But these open-backed towers, used also in some castles as at Framlingham and Corfe, are relatively weak and the chief reason for the design was probably a saving of material and labour in construction. Once an enemy had penetrated within the town or castle they could no longer be held, and not all of them could be used as a check to the circulation of the wall walk like those at Conway. At strategic points in the curtain, such as sharp angles and places particularly liable to attack, stronger towers were built. At Conway the tower at the salient angle on the west side of the town is complete all round to the height of the wall walk though it has a gorge above that level, while the tower at the land end of the wing wall on the north is complete from base to summit. The wall walk was carried all round on the town walls except where these walls joined the castle. Here, within a short distance of the castle on both sides the walk ends abruptly and the wall, taking a slight bend, is reduced to about half its thickness before being carried up the steep rock to the castle. The thin portion of the town wall is still retained on the west side of the castle, where it joins the west barbican, but through a misconception, apparently, of its purpose, and its date, the portion at the other end, running up the mound to join one of the north towers, was destroyed only a few years ago. The same defensive measure of isolation was adopted in the town walls of Caernarvon.

Conway has three main gateways, all flanked by round towers and all designed on similar defensive principles. A portcullis and a two-leaved door are placed so far within the gateway as to leave a long unintercepted space in front—the enemy is invited to enter. But this space is commanded from above by a machicolation the full width of the passage. The Upper gate, on the west, where attack was likely to occur is more strongly defended than the others. It had an embattled gallery built out in front over the entrance to the gateway and entered from one of the towers. The ditch was spanned by a drawbridge and there was a barbican in advance of the ditch. In addition to the three main gates there is a gate, now mutilated, in the wing wall on the north and a postern in the east wall near the castle (pp. 259, 260).

FORTIFIED BRIDGES

When one of the approaches to a town was by a bridge crossing a river it was important that the bridge should be fortified and protected on the far side by a barbican, or *tête-du-pont*. Though there are many fortified bridges of the Middle Ages abroad there are but two in this country which retain their original gateways, one at Warkworth and the other at Monmouth.

At Warkworth the town stands within a sharp loop of the river Coquet; it is defended on the south by the castle, which is built across the neck of the loop, and is enclosed all round elsewhere by the river. The only approach to the town otherwise than through the castle is by a bridge at the north or extreme point of the loop. The bridge with a gateway thrown across the road at its town end was built about 1400. The gateway is built of stone, measures externally 27 ft. 3 in. across by 18 ft., and consists at present of the first and part of a second storey; all above has been destroyed. The passage is placed out of the centre with the building, to allow space for a guardroom on one side; on the other side is a stairs to the upper levels. There appears to have been a heavy door at the outer end of the gateway and there were probably machicolations in the parapet above; the width between the jambs of the doorway is 10 ft. 2 in.

The fortified bridge at Monmouth is an imposing and formidable structure; the bridge itself was built about 1272 and the gateway, standing at a point a third of the length of the bridge from the town, about 1290. The passage was defended by a row of machicolations, a portcullis, and a heavy two-leaved door. This bridge stood in advance of the walls of the town and a second gateway had to be carried before the town was gained (p. 256b).

FORTIFIED CHURCHES

Many churches and monasteries occupying isolated positions, or built in the border counties between England and Scotland or England and Wales and particularly subject to raids, were fortified against surprise attack.

Ewenny Priory, Glamorgan, is our most complete fortified religious house; it is situated in the debatable country between England and Wales and was open to surprise attack from which such establishments were by no means immune. The church is a cruciform structure with powerful walls dating from the twelfth century and the original precinct wall was built somewhat later in the same period.

The existing fortifications relate mainly to the first half of the fourteenth century, when the precinct wall was rebuilt, a tower added to the south gate, and the north gate rebuilt. The battlements on the church tower with their cross shaped arrow-loops were also added at this time though they have been repaired at a later period. The precinct wall and wall towers are embattled and pierced by plain and cross shaped arrow-loops. The passage through the north gateway was defended by a portcullis, a two-leaved door, and by machicolations in the vault. These defences, like those of a town gateway, are all directed against attack from without.

Many churches in the border county of Cumberland have fortified towers where the priest and others could find relative security in times of surprise raids. At Burgh-by-Sands the tower built at the west end of the church about 1330 was constructed on defensive lines; it was of three storeys but the top storey, probably the living room, has been destroyed. The walls are from 6 ft. to 7 ft. thick. The first storey is vaulted and is entered from the west end of the church, the doorway being defended by a powerful iron yett with oak panels. The entrance into the church is commanded from the tower by an arrow-loop; a small window in the second storey of the tower looks directly into the nave.

The church towers of Newton-Arlosh, a few miles to the west of Burgh, and of Great Salkeld, six miles north of Penrith, were similarly defended. At Newton-Arlosh the wall between the tower and the church has been rebuilt and the defences of the doorway removed; the upper storeys of the tower have also been rebuilt. The first storey is a barrel-vaulted cellar with a small window on the west 7 ft. above the ground; the second storey has a fireplace and what appears to have been a latrine. The tower at the west end of Great Salkeld, dating principally about 1390, is of five storeys, including the basement, and is surmounted by an embattled parapet. Both the basement and the next storey are vaulted. The entrance is from the west end of the nave; it is defended by a panelled yett and opens on to the second storey. From here a stairway descends to the basement and up to the third storey, where there is a fireplace, and to the higher levels.

Many church towers have upper rooms designed for the permanent or occasional residence of a priest, as at Llanfihangel-cwm-Du, Brecknock, and at Iden, Sussex, where, in both towers, there is a fireplace in one of the upper storeys; but these towers were in no sense fortified. Others are so sturdily built as to be accredited with a military purpose they never possessed. St. Leonard's Tower, West Malling, Kent, built about 1120 and frequently called a keep, is the unfortified west tower of a church the ruins of which still exist. The tower has no defences, the wall into the stair at ground level is only one foot thick and could be breached with a crowbar in a few minutes, there is no fireplace or any other domestic amenity, and the windows are so large that under attack the tower would be quite untenable.

The upper part of the tower of Bedale church, Yorkshire, was a fortified residence. The lofty first storey, open to the church by a wide arch, was unfortified but the spiral stairway rising to the upper floors was defended at the foot by a portcullis. In the first of these upper floors there is a fireplace, its windows have stone seats, and a latrine opens out of it; the second, the floor of which has been removed, was probably the sleeping chamber.

St. Michael's Mount is a steep, rocky hill standing a mile out from the shore in Mount's Bay; except at low tide, when a narrow causeway of rock connects it with the mainland, it is completely surrounded by the sea. The castle, a most imposing group of buildings, stands on the top of the hill. It was in ecclesiastical hands at the time of Edward the Confessor and became an appendage of the abbey of Mont St. Michel, across the channel, about 1100. In 1190 it was fortified against Richard I and in 1473, with a small garrison, withstood a siege by Edward IV with 6,000 men for six months. It passed into the possession of Syon Abbey, Middlesex, about 1421 and at the dissolution of the abbey was given into lay hands. In 1659 Col. John St. Aubyn lived on the mount and was the last to maintain a garrison there. The original entrance, defended by a portcullis, is at the west, at the head of a steep flight of steps. The central and highest point of the mount is occupied by the church with the lodgings of the friars and military on the west, the cloister and refectory, now called Chevy Chase Room, on the south and the Lady chapel, long since fitted for domestic use, at the north-east. The church was built in the fourteenth century on the site of a church of 1135. During the nineteenth century very considerable works of repair were carried out and additions made to the buildings of the castle.

CHAPTER FOURTEEN

FORTS FOR ARTILLERY

WHILE the tendency towards the development of the amenities of the living quarters was proceeding, the use of firearms was becoming more and more general and the weapons more powerful and effective. Great strides in the design of artillery were made during the fifteenth century. In 1405 Henry the Fourth used cannon against the fortifications of Berwick-on-Tweed. Artillery was employed with great effect by the French in their contests with the English during the second quarter of the fifteenth century. At the siege of Constantinople in 1453 the Turks used a gun casting stone balls weighing 600 lbs. After the introduction of iron cannon balls in place of the stone ones hitherto employed the new weapon became so powerful as to be almost irresistible by the existing defences. In 1494 when the troops of Charles the Eighth of France marched through Italy their guns reduced fortress after fortress with astonishing rapidity. Artillery was used by the forces of both England and Scotland at the battle of Flodden in 1513.

Early cannon, however, could not be mounted on the wall walks and dipped so as to attack those operating below, and it was not until towards the end of the fifteenth century that gunloops begin to appear in fortifications, and then only in the bases of curtains and towers, and not until later that forts designed entirely for defence by heavy guns were built. From about 1540 there is a complete disseverance in Great Britain of the military from the residential structure; the latter, now more compact, becomes the practically undefended mansion house, while the former is designed purely as a fort, entirely at the disposition of the king and his ministers.

The first adjustment of the walls to the use of firearms was made in the design of loopholes, and among the earliest examples of gunloops in this country are those at Kirby Muxloe, built 1480–84. Loopholes with oillets, as at Bodiam castle and the West Gate at Canterbury, sometimes described as gunloops, were built originally for the crossbow and adapted later for artillery, as an examination of their internal recesses will disclose. At Kirby Muxloe the slot, for sighting, is separated from the circular hole below it. Later gunloops assumed various forms, but most often they were widely splayed laterally, from inside to outside, in order to give the gun the greatest possible lateral sweep, as at Caerlaverock, Elcho, and Borthwick. Towards the end of the first half of the sixteenth century guns, now of considerable weight, were being mounted on curtain walls, on flat roofs of strong towers, and on platforms of forts designed especially for them.

Political events in England led to great activity and progress in military architecture. During the reign of Henry the Eighth many old castles which had been allowed to fall into disrepair were reconditioned and put in state of defence. The introduction and use of gunpowder had reduced their defensive value but the power of firearms had not sufficiently developed to render them quite obsolete. Even the artillery of the Roundheads a century later was

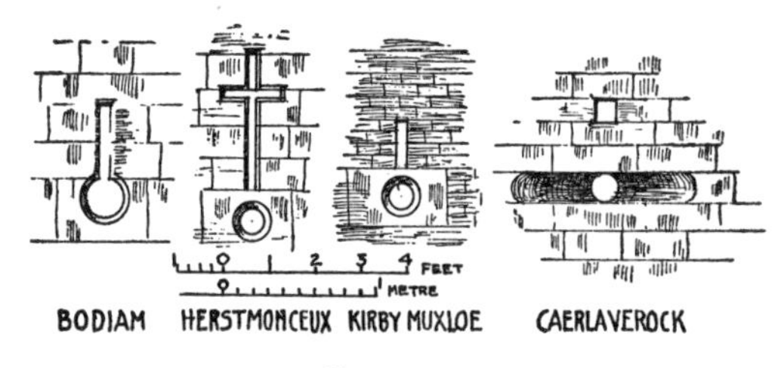

GUNLOOPS

powerless to reduce Corfe castle, though their guns battered away at its walls for nine months. But something of more modern design was necessary to meet the troubles impending on this country towards the middle of the sixteenth century. Henry had broken with the Pope and was at variance with the Emperor and might expect an invasion at any moment. He therefore decided to build at various points along the south coast of England a line of forts, designed for artillery and equipped with the latest type of guns. Well preserved examples of these forts, built about 1540, exist at various points along the south coast of England, from Deal to Falmouth.

The main principle governing the design of the new forts, or castles, was that the whole building should be concentrated in one compact block which could be defended all round by artillery; the guns being mounted on emplacements rising in tiers one behind the other. The gunloops have now wide openings, sloped rapidly down at the sills, to repel attack near the walls, and splayed outwards at the sides, as at Portland and Pendennis. When mounted

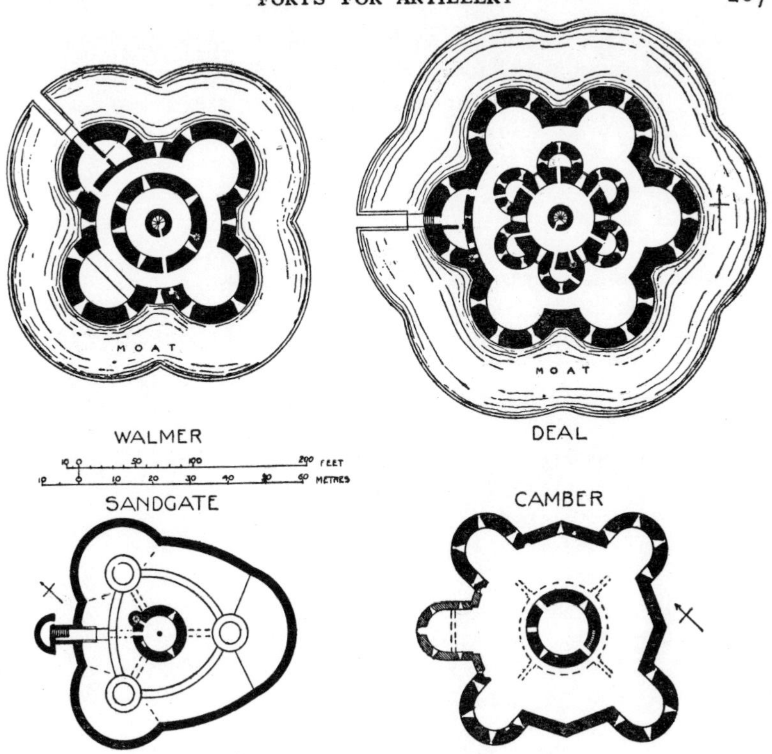

PLANS OF SOUTH-COAST CASTLES

on an upper platform the ordnance pieces fired through embrasures, splayed widely at the sides and sills to allow the greatest possible sweep in all directions. Practically complete examples still exist at Deal, Walmer, Camber, St. Mawes, and Pendennis, while others along the coast remain in part.

Deal castle is one of the largest of these forts; it has a sexfoil plan and rises in three tiers. The outer shell, or chemise, is of one storey only and rises to a flat roof, forming the first gun emplacement. Within there is a central tower with six external lobes; the lobes rising through two storeys to form the second gun emplacement. The circular nucleus of the tower rises still a storey higher to form the third tier of batteries. A spiral stairway in the centre of the tower ascends to the summit, with doorways to each emplacement. The lobes of the second tier alternate with those of the chemise, so that a concentrated fire from a large number of pieces could be directed to any point within range. The castle was surrounded by a moat, crossed by a drawbridge.

Walmer castle consists of a quatrefoil chemise of one storey and a central round tower of two storeys, the space between the chemise and the tower being roofed over for a gun emplacement. A circular stairway in the tower rises through both storeys. Another stairway leads from the vaulted space between the chemise and the tower down to a casemate, or mural gallery, which runs all round through the walls of the chemise. The gallery is pierced on the outside by numerous gunloops, fifty-six in all, from which the surface of the moat could be raked by gunfire at any point. On one side of the gallery there are recesses for ammunition and on the other side larger recesses for the accommodation of the fighting men. Ventilation and outlet for smoke are secured by circular holes in the vault of the gallery with loopholes on the outer face of the wall. The larger guns were mounted on the platform between the chemise and the tower and commanded the vicinity of the castle all round. The castle is surrounded by a moat.

Both the castles at Deal and Walmer have been altered and added to, but retain their original walls substantially intact. Sandgate castle, near Folkestone, has been partly pulled down. It consisted of a central tower and two lines of triangular shaped chemises, the inner line having towers and the outer line lunettes at the angles. The castle was entered through a D-shaped tower, placed in advance, and a connecting stairway passage. Here the lower emplacement appears to have been at the lunettes and the upper, now destroyed, at the inner chemise and towers (p. 267).

Camber castle consists of a circular tower and a multangular chemise with lobes at the cardinal points. The walls of the chemise between the north and west lobes were, at some later period, taken down and replaced by the existing semi-circular entrance porch. At Portland, a sheltered landing place where a surprise attack

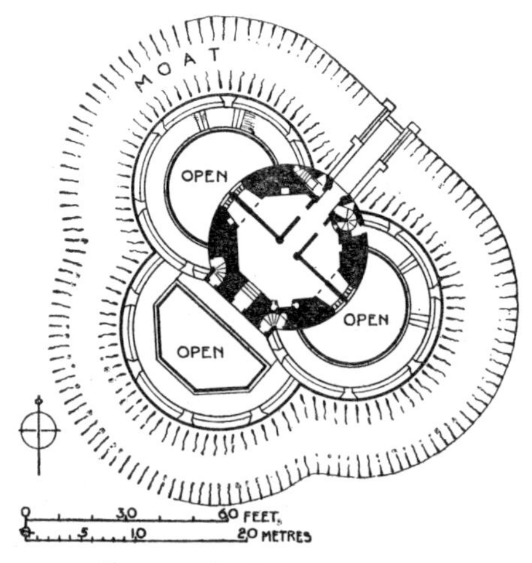

PLAN OF ST. MAWES CASTLE

might be expected, Henry built two forts, facing each other across the harbour. That on the south side, called Portland castle, is fairly complete though much repaired but the other, Sandsfoot castle, was dismantled in 1645 and is now very ruinous.

At the mouth of the Dart in south Devon there already existed two castles facing each other across the estuary. Dartmouth castle, on the west side, consists mainly of a tower, built in 1481 on the site and incorporating some of the material of an earlier structure, and a bailey. At Kingswear there are two towers, one square and the other round and both built in the fifteenth century. In time of war an iron chain was stretched across the estuary from one castle to the other to block the waterway. Henry refortified both of these castles and adapted them to artillery defences; he also built a fort defending the estuary of the river Salcombe.

Among the best preserved of Henry's forts are those at St. Mawes and Pendennis, guarding respectively the east and west shores of the entrance to that magnificent sheet of tidal water the estuary of the Fal. At St. Mawes there are three lunettes, with gun emplacements, ranged in triangular form round a circular tower. Pendennis has a round tower encircled by a low chemise with a wide gun emplacement, the tower rising two storeys above the chemise. In the latter part of the sixteenth century Pendennis fort was enclosed within an extensive bailey, defended by a curtain wall and a ditch (pp. 268, 269).

While these forts were being constructed along the south coast of England the other fortifications of the country were not neglected but it was not until the reign of Elizabeth that the whole defences of a town were replanned on the latest principles. About

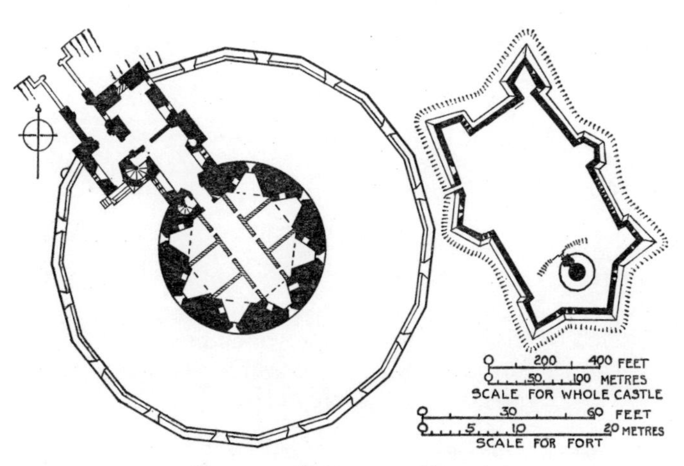

Plans of Pendennis Castle

1560 the Queen, regarding Berwick-on-Tweed as a key position of her realm, rebuilt its fortifications on the latest military plan. Washed on the south by the river Tweed and facing the sea on the east the walls of Berwick, as then reconstructed, still remain in fairly good condition except on the south where they have been largely obliterated.

The earlier defences consisted of a castle, dating probably from the twelfth century, and of town walls built in the early part of the fourteenth century. Except for fragments here and there the town walls have been destroyed and the stone used to provide material for the Elizabethan fortifications, while the castle was practically obliterated when the railway station was built in 1849. At the north-west the circular Bell tower has been rebuilt and there are remains of the large Lord's tower.

In the "Hatfield Collection" are drawings of the fortifications of Berwick made by the Elizabethan draughtsman Howland Johnson. These drawings were made between 1565 and 1575 and therefore represent the works as designed if not completed by Elizabeth; my plan is founded on these drawings (p. 271). The walls and bastions are of ashlar masonry, filled in and backed by earthern embankments; there were six bastions, an internal bulwark on the side facing the sea and four gateways; the whole surrounded by a deep moat. The bastions are brought to a point on the outer faces, like the prow of a ship, and on either side of each of them, between the bastion and the curtain wall, there is a deep recess, called a flanker, which is closed on the outer end by a cross wall pierced by two gunloops. The flankers are reached from the town side through a tunnel and steps down to a doorway on the curtain side, and their function is to command by their guns the whole outer surface of the curtain between two adjacent bastions. The bastions were surmounted by cavaliers (gun emplacements) with embrasured parapets. It is interesting to note that bastions of this kind, with flankers, were introduced into the fortifications of Verona, Italy, in 1520 and in those of Famagusta, Cyprus, in 1560.[1]

The same system of fortification was followed on a smaller scale in many of the forts raised during the seventeenth century, as at Earith, Hunts., and Languard, Suffolk, but isolated towers were still being built. At Tresco, Scilly Isles, there is a fort, called Cromwell's tower, which was built during the Commonwealth and consists of a round tower, 60 ft. high, and a battery at its base. The tower stands on the sea shore, a secure and level foundation being formed by means of arches thrown across from rock to rock. The wall of the tower is 12 ft. thick and at the summit there is a solid flat roof for a gun emplacement.

[1] Vide Toy, *A History of Fortification*, pp. 242–3.

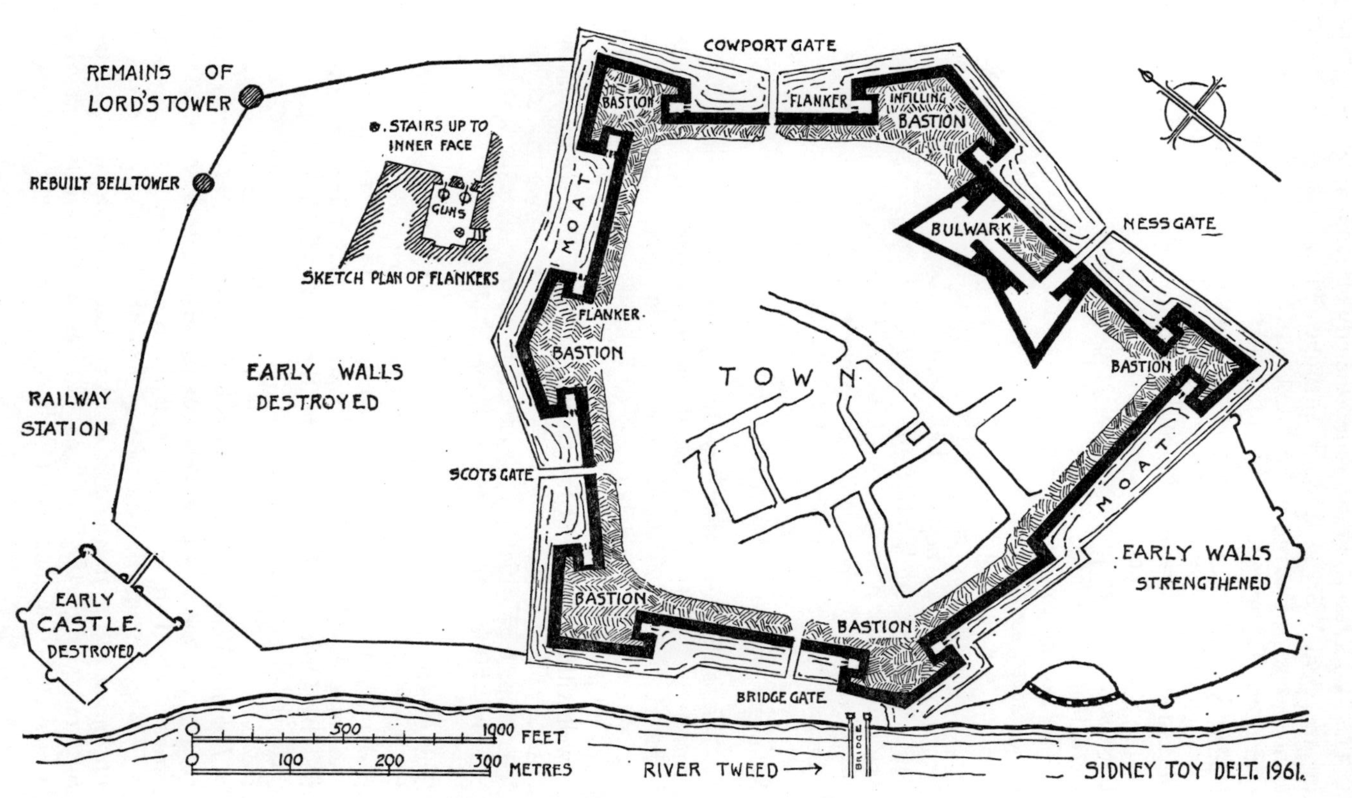

BERWICK UPON TWEED. PLAN OF THE FORTIFICATIONS

The fortifications thrown round the city of London in 1643 during the Civil War, in view of an impending attack by the royal armies, were carried out in haste and were obviously of a temporary character. Though the design of the defences was prepared by experts the bulk of the spade work must have fallen on teams of men normally employed in various trades of the city and quite unused to heavy manual labour; the teams operating at various points along the line. Although these defences were never put to the test they were probably well adapted to the emergency they were designed to meet.

The Roman fortifications of the city have been noted in chapter two. Except for the extension westward between Ludgate and the Thames to include the buildings of Blackfriars Monastery in 1276 these defences remained and were kept in repair until the continual growth of the city beyond their borders greatly diminished their defensive value and, after the seventeenth century, they were gradually either destroyed or incorporated in the buildings of the city. From the early part of the seventeenth century London was practically an open city and in 1643 Parliament, then in control of the city and anticipating an attack from the Royalists, issued the following Order on March 7th that year.

> "It is this day ordered by the Lords and Commons in Parliament, that the Lord Mayor and Citizens of London, for the better securing of and safety of the said city, Suburbs, Parliament, City of Westminster, and Borough of Southwarke shall have power to trench and stop all high-waies leading into the said city, as well within as without the Liberties, as they shall see cause. And shall also have full power and authority according to their descretion, to fortifie and intrench the places aforesaid with such outworks, and in such places as they shall think meet."[2]

The Order further calls upon all authorities concerned to ensure the carrying into effect of this Order "at their perill".

A plan of the fortifications following this Order, drawn to scale and subscribed "A plan of the city and suburbs of London as fortified by Order of Parliament in the years 1642 & 1643" was engraved by George Vertue in 1738, was reproduced in the *Gentleman's Magazine* in June 1749, in William Maitland's *History of London*, 1775 ed. and in books by later writers. In order to show clearly the line of these defences in relation to London of the present day I have prepared the accompanying plan showing Vertue's plan superimposed on a plan of the city as at present. Beginning at the north bank of the Thames about three-quarters of a mile east of the Tower of London the line ran northward to a point near the junction of Whitechapel Road with Commercial

[2] *Acts of the Interregnum*, Vol. I, p. 103.

Road; north-west to Shoreditch; then, following a curved line north of Old Street and Clerkenwell Road, crossing Oxford Street east of Oxford Circus; south-west through Mount Street to Hyde Park Corner (Mount Street probably received its name from a bulwark, called Oliver's Mount, which stood at this point). From Hyde Park Corner the line ran south-east to a point near Victoria Station; then, running parallel with Vauxhall Bridge Road to its connection across the river to Nine Elms, it turned north-east to a point south of St. George's Circus; south-east to a point near the junction of Old Kent Road with Tower Bridge Road and north-east to the south bank of the river, opposite to our starting point.

These fortifications consisted of long lines of ditches with strong points at intervals; the strong points being of varied kinds—forts, bulwarks, breastworks, hornworks, redoubts, redans and flankers, each so placed as to be within range of the one adjacent on either side. The strong points were constructed of turfs and sand, bound together by wattles and timber; they were palisaded, had portholes for guns and some of them had tile roofs. Special attention was paid to the approaches from the north; as at Shoreditch; the road from Islington; the road towards St. Giles in the Fields, and that from the west at Hyde Park Corner. At Shoreditch advanced ramparts were thrown up and at the road from Islington a strong fort was built out beyond the ditch on the west side of the road and a smaller advanced redoubt on the east side of the road further north. Apart from this main defence work barricades and iron chains were thrown across some of the courts and streets at strategic points. That these extensive works must have required vast numbers of men to carry out there can be no doubt; the main line of fortification was about twelve miles long. A description of them is recorded in a pamphlet written by William Lithgow and published in 1643. Lithgow walked all round these works while they were in progress one day in April 1643, taking twelve hours "painfully performed" to complete the circuit, following an itinerary as outlined above.[3] Lithgow writes of great bands of workers proceeding out for their day's work, each according to their trade . . . "Taylors 8,000 lusty men, Watermen 7,000, Shoemakers 5,000 odd etc. etc." Great numbers of men about forty-three different trades sallying forth in various directions for what must have been, owing to its character, for the most part the work of navvies, carrying on their shoulders iron mattocks and wooden shovels "with roaring drums, flying colours and girded swords; most companies being interlarded with ladies, women and girls; two and two carrying baskets for to advance the labour, where divers wrought till they fall sick of their pains."

[3] *The present surveigh of London and of England's State,* William Lithgow London, 1643.

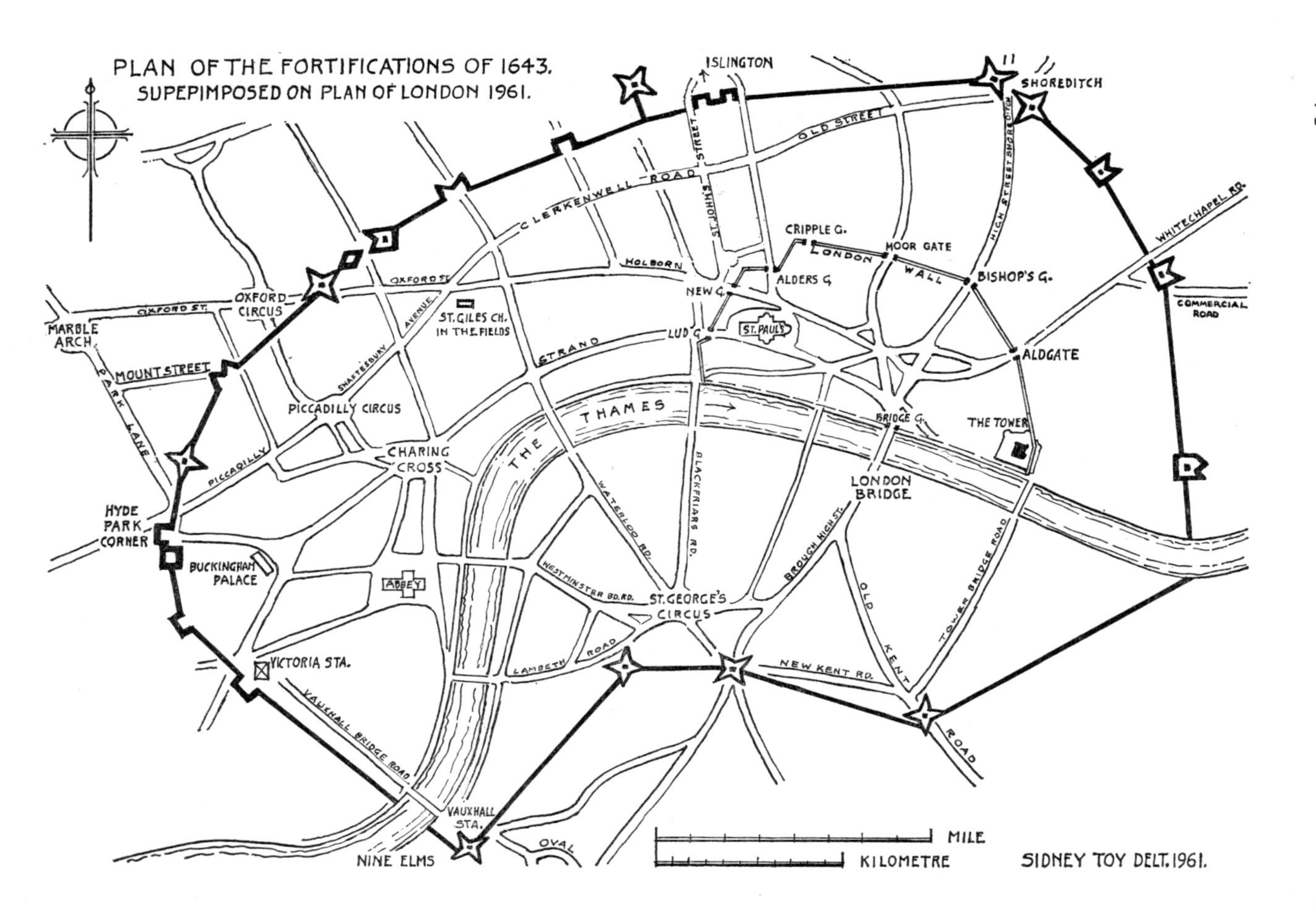

PLAN OF THE FORTIFICATIONS OF 1643.
SUPEPIMPOSED ON PLAN OF LONDON 1961.

The progress of this work is best followed from the records in the Calendar of State Papers for 1643:

13 *March.* Dreading the approach of the Royal Forces to this city (London) and unable, owing to their violent proceedings, to trust their safety to the devotion of the citizens, they have decided in Parliament to fortify this vast circuit. They have sent to Holland for engineers and already they have begun the work with great energy with a large number of navvies. But it will take a very long time and will be most difficult to defend.

20 *March.* With incredible cost and effort they are proceeding with the fortifications of the city, and they do not even cease work on Sunday, which is strictly observed by the Puritans. The plan of the work is commended by experts, but to complete and defend them must necessarily be most difficult.

27 *March.* These (fortifications) are being pushed forward with all diligence, and from the progress they are making seem likely to be of some consideration. The shape they take betrays that they are not only for defence against the royal armies, but also against tumults of the citizens, and to ensure a prompt obedience on all occasions. In consequence of this to furnish the most important positions, the city itself decided to raise 6,000 foot and 2,000 horse, whom they have already begun to enlist.

15 *May.* The forts round this city are now complete and admirably designed. They are now beginning to connect lines. As they wish to complete these speedily and the circuit is most vast, they have gone through the city with drums beating and flags flying to enlist men and women volunteers for the work. Although they only give them bare food, without any pay, there has been an enormous rush of people, even of some rank, who believe they are serving God in assisting in this pious work, as they deem it.

22 *May.* More than 20,000 persons are working voluntarily daily without pay on the fortifications of this city, which will be completed in a few weeks, and they are already beginning to furnish the principal positions with guns.

27 *May.* The people are still busy with the work of the fortifications and equally so over the destruction of crosses and figures. This very day there was a great concourse to pull to pieces the royal monuments of the church of Westminster, which was one of the first ornaments of the city, admired by all foreigners for the antiquity and perfection of the beautiful marble carving.[4]

In point of fact the royal armies never reached the city at this time and it is possible that some sections were not fully completed

[4] *Calendar of State Papers,* Vol. XXVI, 1642–43. Gerolomo Agostini, Venetian Secretary in England, to the Doge and Senate.

as designed, but that most of the work was finished, particularly on the north side of the Thames there can be no reasonable doubt.

An interesting eighteenth-century work, which though not erected in this country was built by the British for their defence, claims notice here. It is Fort Fincastle, Nassau, Bahamas, built by the Governor of the Bahamas in 1787, and now used as a signal station.

Fort Fincastle stands on an eminence dominating the city of Nassau and the approaches to the harbour east and west. It consists of a circular body, 84 ft. diameter, containing the main gun emplacement, an elevated platform for a second emplacement, and a sharply pointed prow; the whole surrounded by a wide dry ditch. It is built of local stone, a cream-coloured coral which is soft and easily worked when first quarried but hardens on long exposure to the air. The entrance is on the south side and from it a flight of steps leads up to the first emplacement, 9 ft. above the sill of the doorway. This part is surrounded by a strong parapet over which the heavy guns, working on swivels and pointing west, north-west, and south-west, fired. On the platform, which stands 12 ft. above the first emplacement and was reached by a flight of steps now rebuilt in stone, were mounted smaller guns which fired through embrasures and pointed north-east and south-east.

The function of the prow was to deflect the cannon balls fired against it and to contain within its thick masonry vaulted chambers for ammunition, stores and guardrooms. There are three chambers, all entered from the main gun emplacement and ventilated by openings which pierce the thick walls to the outer surface, where they appear as narrow loopholes imperceptible from a distance. A recess opening directly on the main emplacement was probably for ammunition required for immediate use. The stone roof of the prow slopes away on both sides from a central ridge, thus throwing off all rainwater falling upon it. Unfortunately a large tree has been allowed to grow out of and spread along the south wall of this interesting fort (pp. 256b, 271).

The progress of military architecture from this point belongs to a special field of study. Artillery was now strong enough to destroy masonry from a considerable distance. Strong and relatively low gun emplacements were constructed in place of high walls and towers. These in turn gave place to military works half above and half below the ground and finally to fortifications deep beneath the soil. In 1806 the British authorities, deeply impressed by the resistance offered to our forces from a tower at Cap Mortella, Corsica, decided, in view of the threatened French invasion, to build a series of towers of this type along the southern and eastern shores of England. The Martello towers, as they are called, are circular, are built of masonry and contain vaulted rooms for the

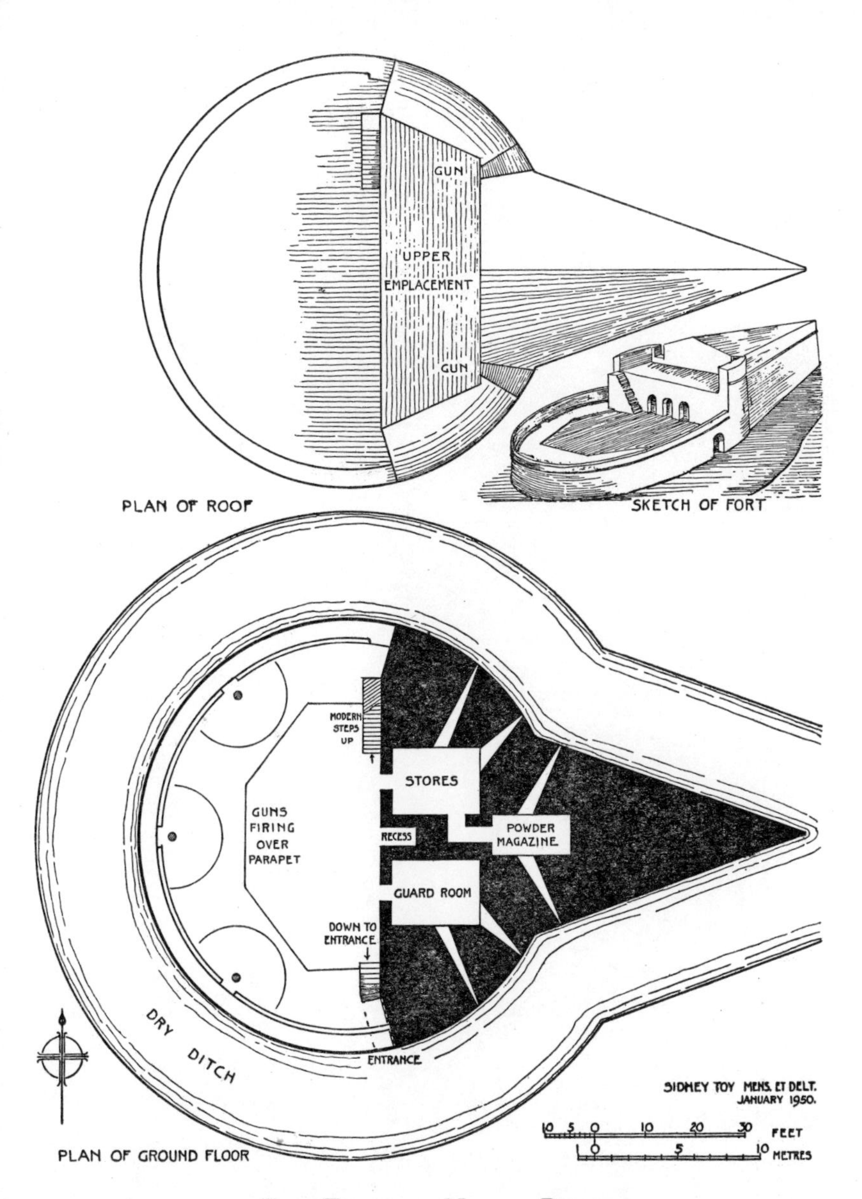

FORT FINCASTLE, NASSAU, BAHAMAS

small garrisons; they are about 45 ft. diameter, are of two storeys and have a platform for two or three guns at the summit. The entrance is about 20 ft. above ground level and was reached by a ladder, after crossing a moat by which the tower was generally surrounded. These towers afforded no protection against vertical fire and the design was soon abandoned.

APPENDIX

A. BERKELEY CASTLE, GLOUCESTER

BERKELEY Castle has an ovoid shell keep which was built about 1156 and, like that at Farnham, encased a mound instead of being built upon it. The mound here must be very much older than the present stone keep if, as is conjectured, it is of composite character, since a long period of consolidation would be necessary before it could be subjected to the extensive scarping it received. There are two wards extending east and west from the keep with a gateway between them. The inner ward is enclosed by the keep on one side and ranges of domestic buildings and offices, built mainly in the fourteenth century, on the other three sides. These latter include the great hall, a single storey structure with a fine contemporary open-timber roof; with the residential quarters and chapel on one side of the hall and the kitchen and offices on the other. During the Civil War of 1642–49 the defences of the outer ward, also built in the fourteenth century, were destroyed and a wide gap was made in the keep by blowing out a portion of its west wall, about 35 ft. wide, down to the interior ground level, p. 280.

This keep shows a development on the earlier plans and is among the latest phases of this form. Its wall rises 62 ft. above the courtyard and 40 ft. above the interior ground level; the floor of the keep being reached by a long flight of steps enclosed in a forebuilding, with doors at the foot and head of the stairs. Projecting at intervals from the side of the keep are three half-round towers, all contemporary with the shell and, as far as later alterations will permit of observation, had open gorges to the interior. Pilaster buttresses, placed at intervals round both the shell and the towers rise to the full height of the keep. There was a fourth round tower on the north side of the shell but that was replaced by the existing rectangular tower in the fourteenth century. The living rooms inside the keep in lieu of being distributed all round the interior are concentrated on the south side of the building. The north-east round tower has a vaulted well chamber at ground level and an oratory above. In the south-east tower there is a prison, said to be that in which Edward II was incarcerated when taken to Berkeley Castle.

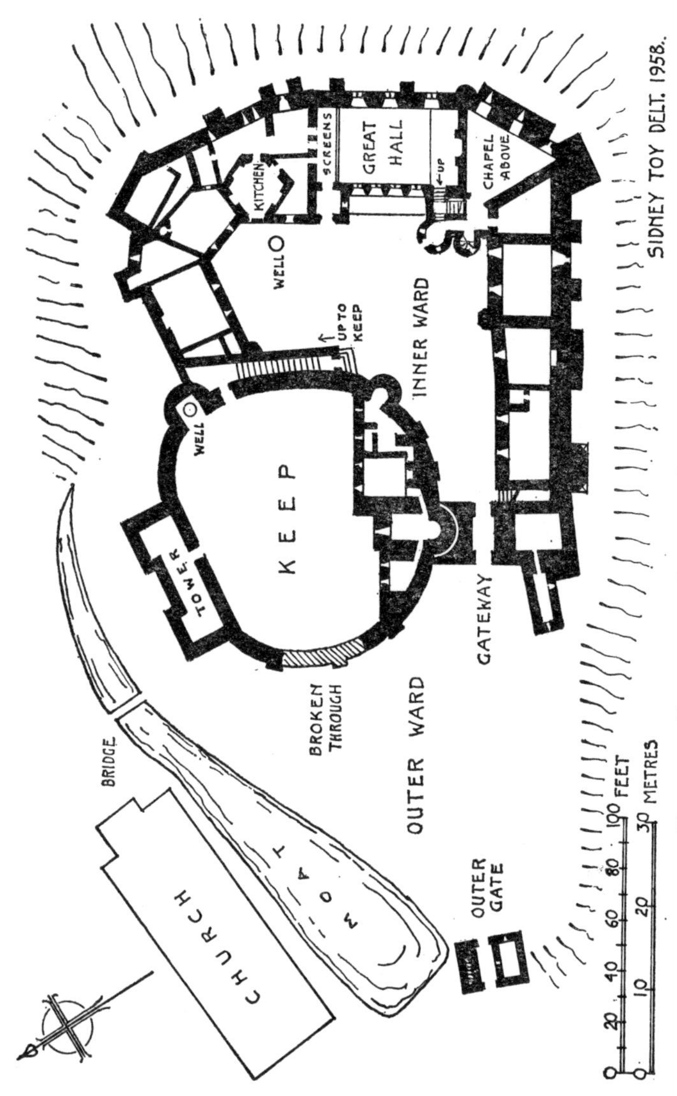

PLAN OF BERKELEY CASTLE, GLOUCESTERSHIRE

B. HEDINGHAM CASTLE

HEDINGHAM CASTLE FROM THE SOUTH-WEST

The keep, which is built of finely dressed ashlar, though it does not appear to have been subjected to siege at any time, has been twice severely damaged and twice repaired. In 1917, after being gutted by fire, in which all the timber floors and the roof were destroyed, the building was restored; the floors and the roof were reconstructed and the crown of the arch spanning the entrance hall, which had been broken down, was rebuilt. The basement of the keep was largely devoted to stores, the second storey, i.e. the storey above the basement, was the entrance hall. The flues of the fireplaces on the south side of the keep, after passing up a short distance through the wall, issue on its outside face, the outer openings being concealed by the pilaster buttress there. One of the mural chambers in the great hall, that on the north, is provided with a ventilation opening to the exterior, probably that the chamber may be used as a bedroom in addition to those in the storey above.

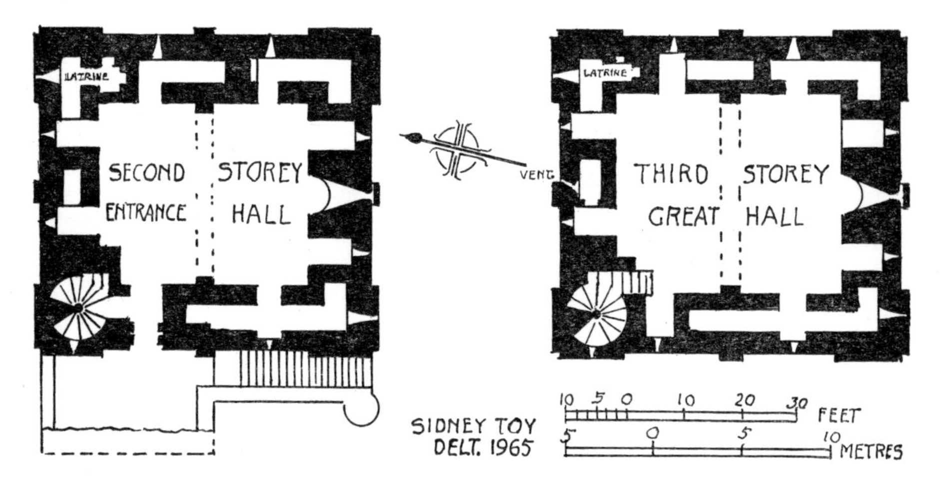

Hedingham Castle. Plans of the Second and Third Storeys

C. CASTLE RUSHEN, ISLE OF MAN

Castle Rushen, Isle of Man, is an interesting example of development from the square keep. The nucleus of this castle is a small square keep, built in the latter part of the twelfth century, to which wings were added on three sides and a strong entrance porch on the fourth during the thirteenth and fourteenth centuries. This building was attacked and very severely damaged by Robert Bruce in 1313 but was restored and refortified between 1340 and 1350. Since that period it has undergone many vicissitudes and in modern times was used successively as a prison and as a lunatic asylum, being adapted to the requirements of those institutions, but the keep, now thoroughly restored, remains much as it existed after its restoration in the fourteenth century.

The improvement secured by these wing additions was not only that they provided additional accommodation, but that from them the vulnerable corners of the square keep could be defended against the operations of the missile engines and particularly of those of the sapper. Trim Castle in Ireland has a keep of similar form to this at Castle Rushen but in that case the wings are contemporary with the body of the keep, the whole built in the early years of the thirteenth century.[1]

[1] Vide Toy, *A History of Fortification*, pp. 112–13.

The passage through the porch of the keep at Castle Rushen was defended by two portcullises and three machicolations. The curtain wall, the wall towers and the main gate were all built in the latter part of the fourteenth century, while the barbican, the round tower at the north-west and the rampart at the south-east are works of the sixteenth century. Derby House was built in 1644.

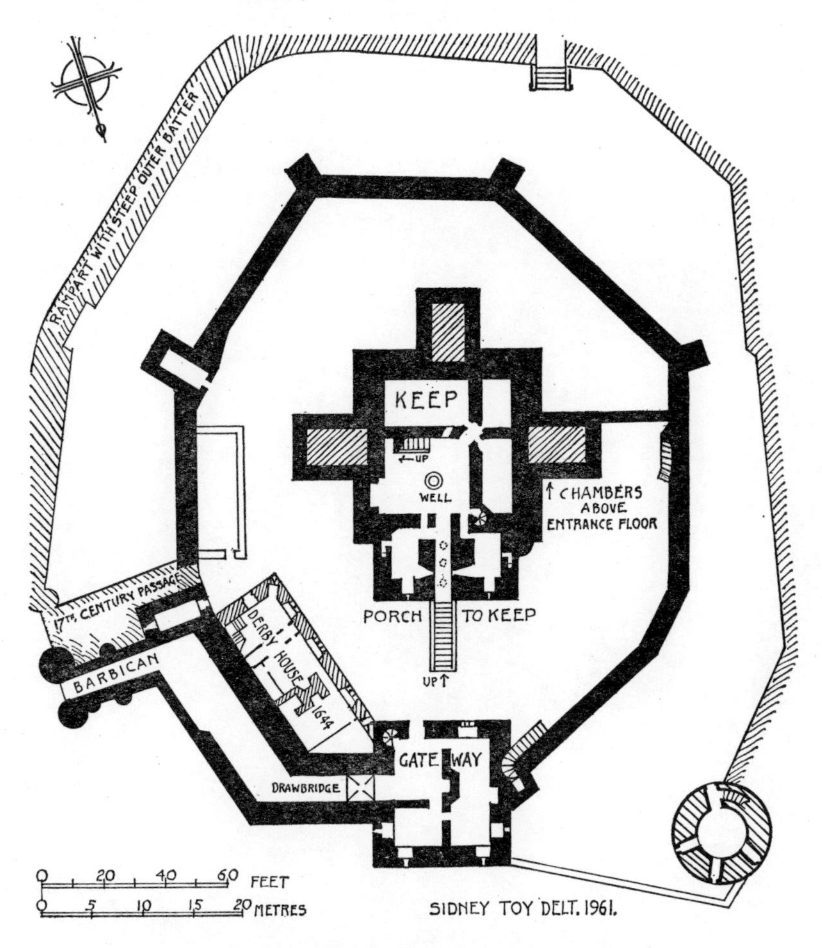

PLAN OF CASTLE RUSHEN, ISLE OF MAN

D. KNARESBOROUGH CASTLE

The wide recess on the west side of the great hall is a somewhat unusual feature. The northern half of the inner face of the wall at the back of the recess has been torn away so roughly that at one place it breaks into the flue which runs up through the wall from a fireplace in the kitchen below the hall, strongly suggesting that some fitting stood here that was removed when it had become no longer useful in this position. The southern half of the recess is occupied by a stone trough, standing 1ft. 9 in. above the floor. There can be no doubt but that this feature was a lavabo for the washing of hands before meals, and possibly for cleansing dishes afterwards. The northern half of the recess was probably occupied by a lead tank that supplied the water to the lavabo; the water coming from the well brought to light near this corner of the keep during excavations in 1926. Though lavabos were frequently built in the great halls of castles, when in that position they were generally of much smaller design, like the piscinae in churches, and not on such a lavish scale as here; often they were placed outside the hall.

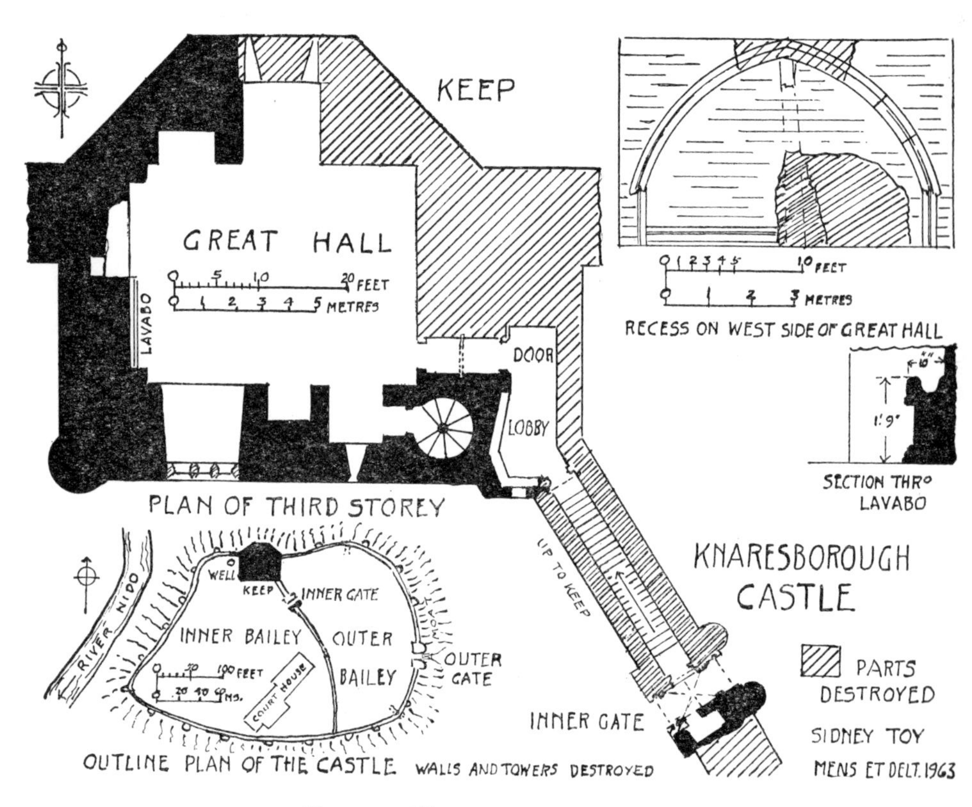

PLANS OF KNARESBOROUGH CASTLE

The walls destroyed are hatched. The stairs up to the great hall, now completely destroyed except for some traces, are conjectural; but that there was a stairway here forming the only entrance to the keep, having a portcullis at the foot and one at the head, there is no doubt.

E. MAXSTOKE CASTLE, WARWICKSHIRE

Maxstoke Castle is a four-square structure surrounded by a high embattled wall, a wide wet moat and a narrow berm between the moat and the curtain wall. Licence to crenellate his house was granted to Sir William de Clinton by Edward III in 1345 and the castle was built forthwith; it is built of red sandstone. There is a gatehouse in the middle of the east wall, flanked by semi-octagonal turrets, and an octagonal tower projecting well out from each corner of the curtain; the wall-walk is approached by stairways in the towers and communicates with the gatehouse on either side. The embrasures of the battlements are fitted for shutters for the protection of the archers firing through them, vide p. 234. The gateway passage is covered by two bays of quadripartite vaults with carved bosses at the intersection of the ribs. The wide entrance arch into the passage was strongly defended; first by a drawbridge which, when raised, fell back into a square-headed recess in the face of the gate to pre-

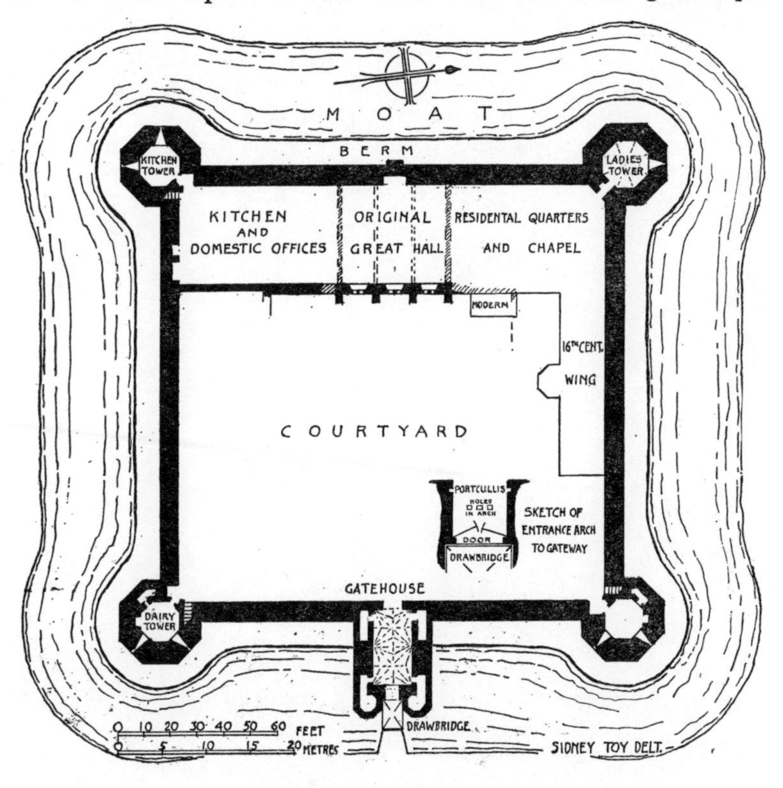

Plan of Maxstoke Castle, Warwickshire

vent an enemy from gripping it by iron grabs and pulling it down; then by a two-leaved iron-plated door; next by three stout timbers let down from three holes in the head of the arch and finally by a portcullis near the inner end of the arch.

The interior buildings, now consisting of a wide range stretching north to south along the west wall and a relatively narrow wing extending partway along the north wall were originally designed to surround the courtyard on three sites, as is clear by the corbels which still exist along the north and south walls. These buildings have been so much altered during the course of their continuous occupation from the fourteenth century up to the present day, the rooms altered and subdivided both horizontally and vertically, and large openings made in the west curtain wall which have no relation to the strong early fortification—one opening is a tall, wide window of six lights —that it is difficult now to recover all their early details. The general disposition, however, is clear for the open timber mediaeval roof of the Great hall which is still preserved in its original position in the middle of the west range. The Great hall was a single storey building of three bays having its windows in the wall towards the court and its fireplace in the curtain wall; the residential quarters were, as they still are, to the north of the Great hall and the kitchen and domestic offices to the south of it. The fact that the N.W., S.W., and S.E. towers still retain the names of Ladies, Kitchen and Dairy towers respectively points to the identity of this disposition.

[*Country Life*

CAISTER CASTLE FROM THE SOUTH-WEST

Knaresborough Castle: The Keep from the South

F. CAISTER CASTLE, NORFOLK

Caister Castle, Norfolk, was built by the renowned soldier Sir John Fastolf, who distinguished himself at Agincourt, Rouen and in other engagements in France; he was made Governor of the Bastille in 1420. For two centuries the castle was occupied by the Paston family, responsible for the "Paston Letters" of priceless historical value. The castle stands on level ground, four miles north of Great Yarmouth; it consists of a main rectangular block with ranges built round a large courtyard, an outwork on the north of the main block and another on the south. A wet moat surrounded both the main block and the north outwork, passing between the two, but not continued round the south block. Of the north outwork, the north wall, which is buttressed at intervals in its length and has a round bastion at each end, and the east wall are the only remains still standing. It was proposed to establish here in this outwork a college for priests but there is no evidence that the proposal was ever implemented. The south outwork, consisting of two wings set at right angles with a round tower at the corner, is the only portion of the castle which has been kept in repair and is still occupied; it is probable that the full design of this outwork, though never completed, was as suggested in my plan. A waterway, called the Barge Ditch, connected with the river Bure and ran through a tunnel at the base of the south wing of this building to join the moat, enabling building material and goods to be conveyed from Great Yarmouth to the castle by water—a great convenience owing to the state of the roads at that period—and discharged on what was known as the Barge Yard on the inner side of the tunnel. The walling of the castle is of brickwork with limestone dressings; the bricks are of clay dug out in the neighbourhood, are laid in English bond and are of an agreeable soft pinkish colour.

Having suffered for many centuries from neglect and more particularly from its use as a quarry for building material, what now remains of the main rectangular block, the principal part of the castle, is but a fragment of what existed or of what it was proposed

U

to build. Fortunately, however, there remains enough of the most important section of the building to enable one to recover the design of this section; while, thanks to the investigations made by Mr. C. Hamblen-Thomas, a recent owner and resident, the general disposition of the whole plan of this block has been brought to light.

The main entrance into the castle was by a drawbridge and a gate in the west wall of the north outwork and from there by a drawbridge over the cross moat and a gateway into the main block; there was also a water gate, opening on to the moat on the south and now the entrance into the castle. The plan of this main block is of a strong wall of enciente with a round tower containing a tier of private chambers at the south-west corner and ranges of buildings erected against the inner faces of the wall of enciente and enclosing an open courtyard. The Great Hall was at the south-west, the private and guest chambers on the west, the domestic and service rooms and the stores on the east and the military quarters adjacent to the gateway on the north. The round projection with adjoining chambers at the north-west corner was probably a military station commanding the entrance. In the siege to which this castle was subjected 21 August to 26 September, 1469, its relatively small garrison opposed a stout resistance to the overwhelming forces and powerful artillery brought against it by the Duke of Norfolk; and it was only through lack of supplies and disappointment of relief that it surrendered.

The castle, or at least the remaining part of it, was of three storeys; the outer walls of the third storey being projected out on continuous corbel tables (p. 284a). The Great Hall extended up through the first and second storeys and was lighted on the outside by a row of two-light, square-headed windows, which still exist though some of them are blocked; what openings there may have been on the court side is unknown. The dais was at the west end of the hall where there was a wide fireplace and, at the south-west corner, an alcove with traceried windows; the quadripartite vault of the alcove has been destroyed. On the right of the alcove a moulded doorway leads to the ground storey of the tower.

The tower rises to the height of 90 ft. is round externally and contains within a tier of five hexagonal chambers, each with a window, a fireplace and a latrine, the latter formed in a stack projecting on the north side of the tower; the tower is also pierced with gunloops at various stages. The ground storey was originally a private chamber, opening off the Great hall but having no communication with the chambers above. On the south side of this chamber there is a recess containing two gunloops at different heights, the upper one reached by a short flight of steps. This recess with the gunloops, for which there is a slight projection on the outside, belongs to the original work, but at a later period an opening

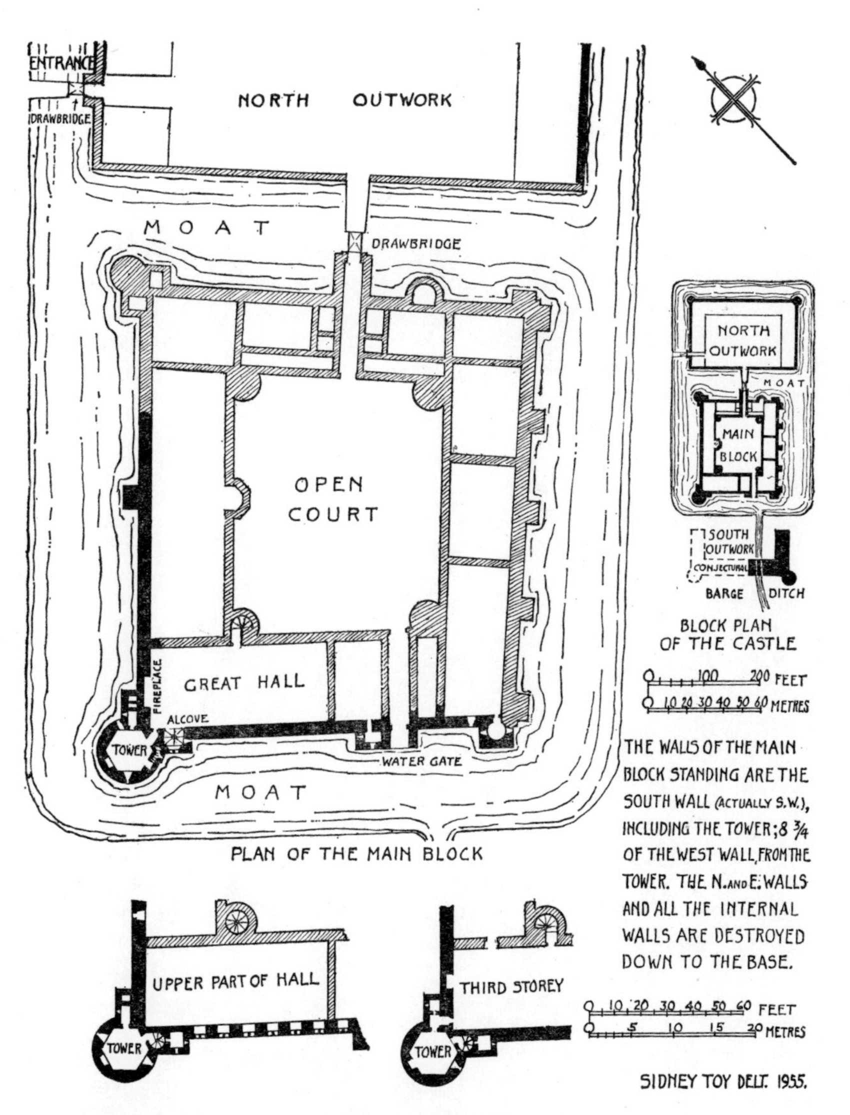

CAISTER CASTLE, NORFOLK

has been roughly driven through connecting the upper end of the recess to the base of the newel stairway above, which is at the second storey; from here the stairway ascended to the top of the tower, with openings to the upper chambers. On examination of the break through from the recess it is clear that it is roughly done and is no part of the original work; the inner jamb of the gunloop has been cut away to secure a free passage.

There must therefore have been a stairway from the Great hall and the obvious position for it was at the south-west corner of the courtyard. On investigation the round base of such a stairway was discovered. That stairway must have ascended directly to the floor level of the third storey, and from that level, through a doorway clearly to be seen, the tower chambers and newel stairway were reached, the newel stairway descending to the second storey of the tower and ascending to the battlements, communicating to each chamber en route. One gunloop opening out from the end wall of the lowest latrine must have been formed when these conveniences were no longer in use.

Although gunpowder played the most important and decisive role in the siege of Caister Castle in 1469 bows, probably crossbows, were also in use for defence. Lady Margaret Paston in a letter to the owner of the castle, then in London, writes "Your brother and his fellowship stand in great jeopardy at Caister, and lack of vituals, loss of men failed in gunpowder and arrows, and the place sore broked with guns of the other party."[2]

There is a row of arrowloops in the north wall of the north outwork.

G. HADDON HALL, DERBYSHIRE

Haddon Hall was a Manor house which, for its defence, the owner, Richard de Vernor, was granted in 1199 a licence to surround it with a wall 12 ft. high; it was obviously not to be regarded as a fortification for the licence stated specifically that the wall was not to be crenellated; much of the present surrounding wall is of this early period, as are parts of the chapel and of the north-east gateway, originally the only, or the main entrance to the space within. In the first part of the fourteenth century the interior buildings were entirely remodelled, the Great hall built across the spacious court, dividing that court into two parts, with the residential quarters opening off from the Great hall on the south and the kitchen and domestic offices on the north. By this plan the Great hall was entirely free from the curtain and could have its windows on both sides. The

[2] *Paston Letters*, 301.

tower over the north-east gateway was also built in the fourteenth century and some alterations were made at subsequent periods; the north-west range with its tower and the Long Gallery were built in the sixteenth century.

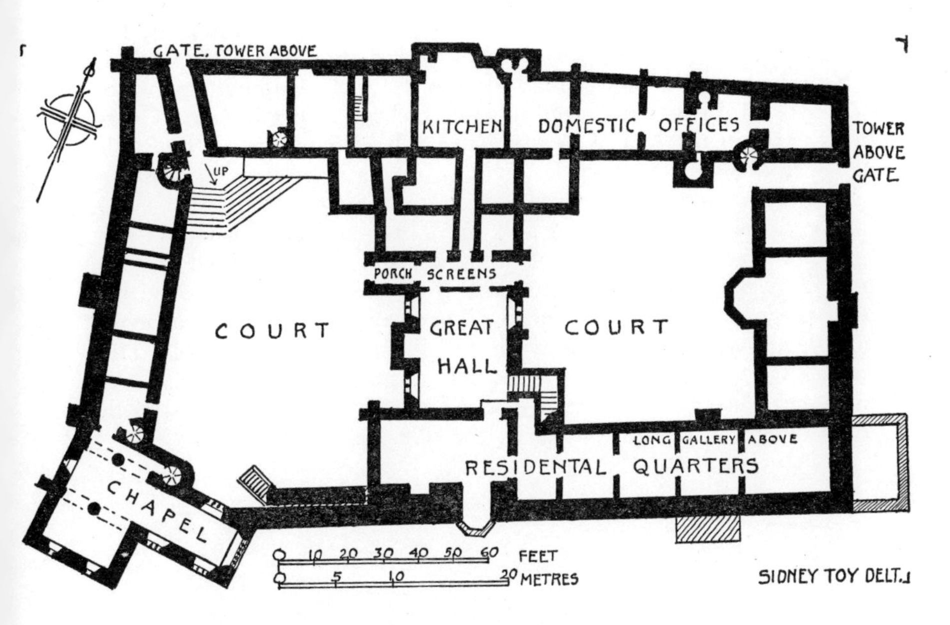

Plan of Haddon Hall, Derbyshire

H. FARLEIGH CASTLE, SOMERSET

Farleigh Castle, Somerset, in respect to the main part, was built about 1380; the bailey on the south being added some fifty years later. The main building, now reduced to its base and foundations, was a rectangular structure with a round tower at each corner and a strong gatehouse, with flanking towers, in the middle of the south side; the north-east corner tower was larger than the others and was probably the keep. The Great hall was in the middle of a range which was thrown across the courtyard, with the residential quarters on the east and the domestic offices on the west. Thus disposed, the hall had its windows open to the court on one side and to a garden on the other and was secure within its defences all round.

I. FIREPLACE IN THE GREAT HALL

The hall fireplace was normally either in an end wall or near the middle of one of the side walls. In some Manor houses, as at Penshurst Place, Kent, and Colleges, it was on a hearth in the centre of the hall; when in this position it was provided with andirons, for the support of the logs, with a reredos and probably with a hood, the smoke escaping through a louvre in the roof. Although examples of this central position existed in some colleges of Oxford and Cambridge and in the hall of Westminster School down to the first half of the nineteenth century it never could have been a satisfactory arrangement and was certainly rare.

The fireplace in the Great hall of Linlithgow Palace is one of the finest mediaeval examples in Great Britain. Its long lintel is supported by pillars with sculptured capitals, has a carved border running along its lower edge and a carved cornice, the cornice being interrupted at points in line with the pillars with head corbels. The corbels were probably for the support of statues, as in some of the mediaeval fireplaces in France, and intended to correspond with those designed for the corbels on the side walls of the hall.

FIREPLACE AT SOUTH END OF GREAT HALL, LINLITHGOW, SCOTLAND

CONCLUSION

In conclusion, there can be no security in defence unassociated with attack. There never was an impregnable castle, or fortress, from the time of the building of the powerful stronghold at Massada by Herod the Great, about 37 B.C., to the construction of the fortifications along the north coast of France by the Germans during the late war. The most powerful castles built during the Middle Ages are often those which are now the most ruinous. It is true that many of them owe their present shattered condition to deliberate and unopposed destruction after their capture; but they were captured. As we found during the late war the only effective defence lies in attack. Therefore while knowing that *Nisi Dominus costodierit civitatem: frustra vigilat qui custodit eam,* the way to deal with the aggressor is to assume the aggressive, with considerable interest; to be ready to meet your enemy at his gate, and assail him there, rather than to await his arrival at yours.

But measures of defence are scarcely less important than those of attack. Powerful defences suitable to the weapons and methods of warfare of the day have again and again saved a community, subjected to sudden and surprise attack, from being overcome; giving them opportunity to muster their forces and weapons and make other preparations for counter-attack. The main value of a new weapon or of a new method of attack is in the element of surprise it occasions. Many new weapons, from the crossbow to the atom bomb, have been regarded as portending the end of civilization. But the ingenuity of man has never failed him, and never will fail him, in the provision of adequate defence against any weapon which the human mind can devise. In this respect the study of the development of fortification in the past is not only intensely interesting but highly instructive; for though the methods adopted must be progressive, the principles involved are largely constant.

INDEX

Descriptions and principal references are in bold type

THE CASTLES OF ENGLAND AND WALES

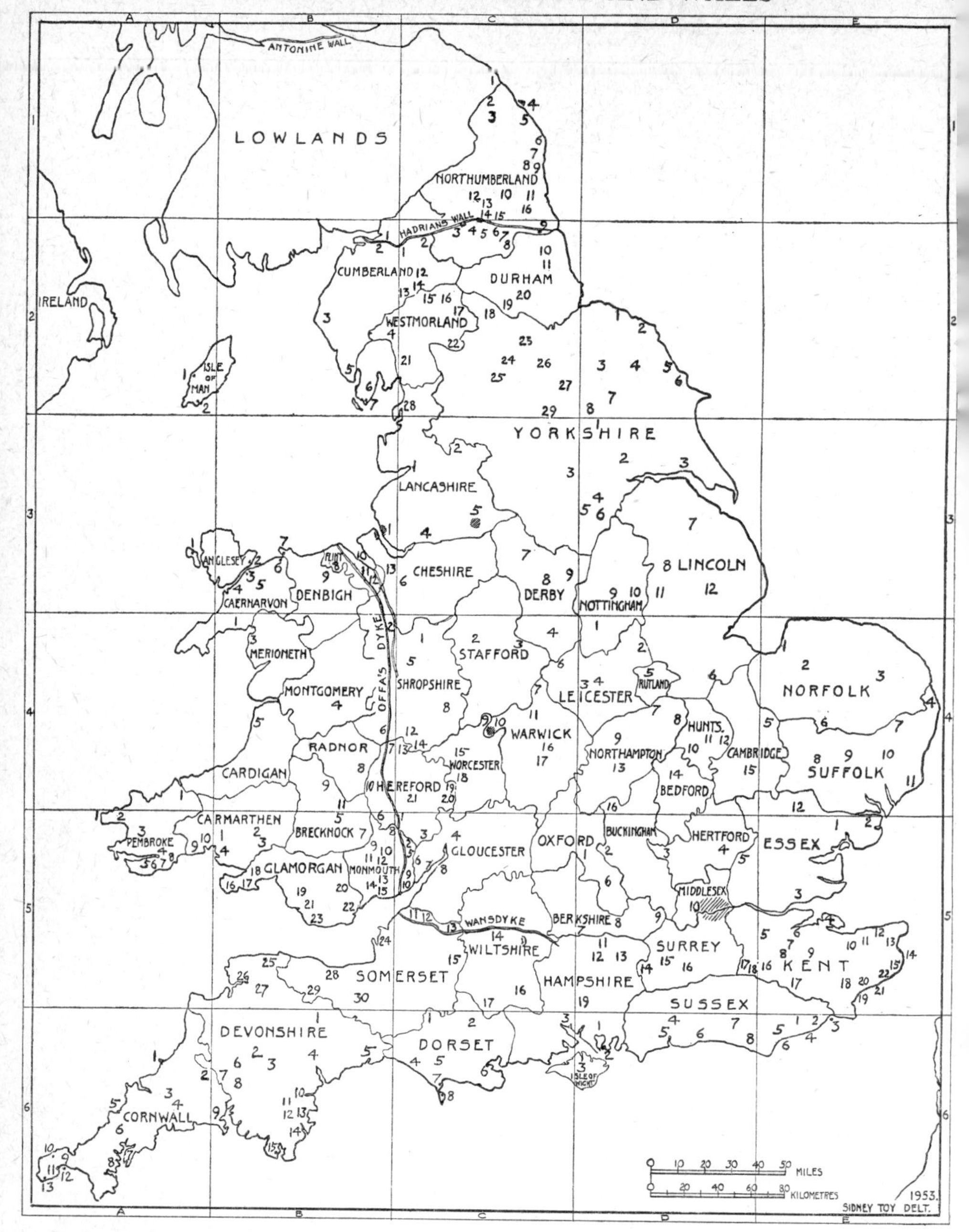

INDEX TO MAP OF ENGLAND AND WALES